Microsoft Office 2011 for Mac

STEVE SCHWARTZ

Find us on the Web at www.peachpit.com.
To report errors, please send a note to errata@peachpit.com.
Peachpit Press is a division of Pearson Education.

Copyright © 2011 by Steve Schwartz

Executive editor: Clifford Colby
Editor: Kathy Simpson
Production editor: David Van Ness
Compositor: Steve Schwartz
Indexer: Emily Glossbrenner
Interior design: Peachpit Press
Cover design: RHDG / Riezebos Holzbaur Design Group, Peachpit Press
Logo Design: MINE™ www.minesf.com

ISBN-13   978-0-321-75126-3
ISBN-10   0-321-75126-4

9 8 7 6 5 4 3 2 1

Printed and bound in the United States of America

Contents at a Glance

Table of Contents

Introduction

Welcome to *Microsoft Office 2011 for Mac: Visual QuickStart Guide*. In the pages that follow, you'll find all the information and instructions needed to quickly become productive with Office 2011.

Like other titles in the *Visual QuickStart* series, this book was written primarily as a reference. Unlike a book on a single program, however, this one covers four major applications. Rather than discuss every command and procedure in excruciating detail (as you'd expect in a one-program book), this book focuses on commands and procedures you're most likely to actually use.

About This Book

This is a book for beginning to intermediate users of Microsoft Office 2011. If you're using Office for the first time, switching from the Windows to the Mac version, or already know the basics but want to get more out of your investment in Office, this book is for you. If you learn better from step-by-step instructions and lots of graphic examples than from reference manuals that merely describe what the commands do, this book is also for you. Most of all, if you know what you want to do and want to get started in the shortest possible time, this book is definitely for you.

I've worked hard to create a book that will let you turn to the directions for any procedure, learn what it does, and do it yourself. A screen shot illustrates every significant step. The goal is to give you the information you need to make you productive as quickly as possible. Along the way, you'll find tips that offer helpful information about many of the procedures.

To make it easy for you to find the information you need at any given moment, the book is divided into sections called parts.

- Part I provides an introduction to essential Office procedures.

- Parts II through V are devoted to the core Office applications: Word, Excel, PowerPoint, and Outlook (with My Day).

- Part VI presents topics relevant to all the core Office applications: combining Office data, using Office on the Internet, and using the Office Web Apps.

Command Conventions

Office 2011's implementation of the Ribbon provides a new place where you can find and execute Office commands—in addition to menus, toolbars, floating windows, panels and panes, dialog boxes, contextual menus, and keyboard shortcuts.

Menu commands

In this book, menu components are separated by the greater than (>) symbol.

menu name > command

Example: "To forward a selected message, choose Message > Forward" **A**.

Explanation: Open the Message menu and choose the Forward command.

menu name > submenu > command

Example: "To forward the same message as an attachment, choose Message > Forward Special > As Attachment" **B**.

Explanation: Open the Message menu and choose As Attachment from the Forward Special submenu.

Ribbon commands

Ribbon components are separated by a colon (:). When choosing a command from a drop-down menu on the Ribbon, the menu-specific components are separated by the > symbol.

Ribbon tab : group : command

Example: "To format selected text as boldface, click Home : Font : Bold" **C**.

Explanation: In the Font group on the Home tab, click the Bold icon.

Ribbon tab : group : icon > menu item

Example: "To set 1" margins for the document, choose Layout : Margins : Margins > Normal" **D**.

A Choosing a command from a menu.

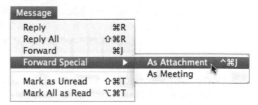

B Choosing a command from a submenu.

Home tab   Font group

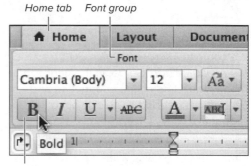

Bold command

C Clicking a Ribbon icon.

D Choosing a command from a Ribbon icon's drop-down menu.

Explanation: Switch to the Layout tab. In the tab's Margins group, click the Margins icon and choose Normal from the drop-down menu.

Note that whether a menu command or a Ribbon command is being described, the components are always presented in their proper order.

TIP Unlike Word, PowerPoint, and Excel, Outlook doesn't divide its tabs into named groups. Therefore, its commands are more compact, such as "Click Home : Delete to delete the selected message."

Toolbars, panels, floating windows, dialog boxes, and contextual menus

To prevent commands for these elements from being confused with menu or Ribbon commands, the commands are written out in plain text, such as this: "On the Indents and Spacing tab of the Paragraph dialog box, choose a paragraph alignment from the Alignment drop-down menu."

Keyboard shortcuts

A command may also have an associated keyboard shortcut that executes the command as though it had been chosen from a menu, toolbar, or the Ribbon. The convention is to show keyboard shortcuts in plain text, such as "Press Command-V to paste the most recently copied or cut item."

Too many commands, too little space

Over the years, many programs have expanded to offer users multiple ways of performing a command or procedure. With this flexibility, however, can come confusion. In previous editions of this book (as well as my other Peachpit titles), I've prided myself on detailing all the possible ways you might execute a particular command. Knowledge is power, right?

But with Office 2011's addition of the Ribbon, it occurs to me that:

- There may now be as many as half a dozen ways to execute some commands.

- Rather than helping you by allowing you to pick the most convenient method from all possible command-execution methods, I may inadvertently be adding to or creating the confusion.

- Presenting every imaginable option takes up a lot of page space and may, in fact, detract from the presentation.

Based on my new assumption that you don't want or need to know all the ways that you can choose every command, this book will try to limit the presented options to two or three. At a minimum, I'll list the menu and Ribbon commands—assuming that both exist. Keep in mind that you should still explore the available toolbars, dialog boxes, panes, and panels to see if there's a more convenient method of executing a command.

Similarly, try right-clicking selected text and objects. Microsoft provides many contextual menus that appear in response to a right-click. You may find right-clicking to be quicker than scouring Ribbon tabs, checking menus, and memorizing keyboard shortcuts.

About the Author

During his lengthy computer-industry career, Dr. Steve Schwartz has dedicated himself to educating computer users and helping them become productive with the software that's so pervasive in their business, school, and personal lives.

Steve was formerly editor-in-chief and chief methodologist for *Software Digest*, business editor for MACazine, and technical services director for Funk Software—where he provided technical support to a customer base of 750,000, trained Funk and Lotus Development personnel, directed QA, and wrote user manuals.

In addition, Steve has written hundreds of articles for computer magazines such as *Macworld*, *PCWorld*, and *Computerworld*. Since becoming a full-time author in 1990, Steve has written almost 60 books on computer and game topics. He is Peachpit Press' primary author for Microsoft Office.

Introducing Microsoft Office 2011

In this "before you get started" chapter, there's nothing you'll need to commit to memory. There will be no test.

If you're new to Office, the initial application-specific sections ("About Word," "About Excel," "About PowerPoint," and "About Outlook") will familiarize you with the tasks that the core applications were designed to help you accomplish.

If you're upgrading from Office 2008, the next section ("New in Office 2011") will point you to the important new features and changes introduced in Office 2011.

Finally, if you're still deciding whether to purchase or upgrade to Office 2011, the last section ("Office 2011 Editions") will explain the differences between the three Office 2011 editions.

In This Chapter

About Word

Word 2011 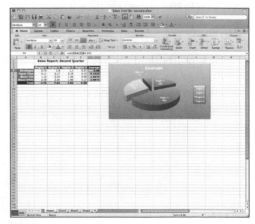, Office's word-processing application, is used to create letters, memos, invoices, proposals, reports, forms, brochures, catalogs, labels, envelopes, and just about any other type of printed or electronic document that you can imagine.

You can type text into Word and insert almost any kind of graphic, formatting the material into sophisticated documents with cover pages, tables of contents, running headers and footers, tables, footnotes, cross-references, page numbers, and indexes. If your needs aren't that expansive, you can also create simple letters and memos with Word's easy-to-use features.

Word's approach, like that of the other Office applications, is visual. As you work in a document, you see all the text, graphics, and formatting exactly as it will appear when you print. Word works in concert with the other Office applications. It can display numbers and charts from Excel worksheets, as well as slides from PowerPoint. And you can flag Word documents for follow-up in your Outlook to-do list.

About Excel

Excel 2011 **B**, the Office spreadsheet application, is used to track, calculate, and analyze data. If you want to view numeric information graphically, you can use Excel to create professional charts in dozens of colorful formats.

After typing numbers into a row-and-column cell grid in an Excel worksheet, you can enter formulas into adjacent cells that total, subtract, multiply, or divide the numbers. You can also use *functions*, special Excel formula components that help you perform complex calculations—from sums and averages to sophisticated financial computations. Excel can even calculate statistics.

You can also use Excel to create, maintain, and import lists and databases. You can accumulate text and numeric records, as well as sort, search, filter, and extract data from a database. Excel works especially well with FileMaker Pro databases.

A A Word 2011 document.

B An Excel 2011 workbook.

About PowerPoint

PowerPoint 2011 **C** is the presentation component of Office. You use PowerPoint to present *slide shows*—electronic presentations that you run on a computer screen in front of an audience. You can also create handouts and other materials you might use during a stand-up dog-and-pony show.

PowerPoint comes with dozens of professionally designed templates that take care of the presentation's look, allowing you to focus on its message. It also includes sample presentation outlines to help you get a start on the content. PowerPoint's powerful arsenal includes bulleted and numbered text slides, charts, tables, clip art, animations and movies, and drawing tools.

If you need to convey your PowerPoint presentation to an even wider audience, you can convert it to a QuickTime movie, generate a set of pictures (one per slide) that can be viewed on a computer or iPod, or broadcast the presentation on the Web.

About Outlook

As a replacement for Entourage (Office's email client), Outlook 2011 **D** helps you manage your communications and your life. Use it to send and receive email, as well as maintain your calendar, address book, to-do list, and notes.

Office includes two utilities to help you keep track of scheduled appointments and events, as well as your tasks/to-do items—even when Office isn't running. Both utilities draw from your Outlook data.

Any event, appointment, or task can have an optional *reminder* (alarm) associated with it. When a reminder is triggered, you can handle it within Office Reminders, a utility that enables you to dismiss or to temporarily "snooze" a reminder until later.

If you're primarily interested in knowing the day's scheduled items and unfinished tasks, you can use My Day to keep track of them. When you complete a task, you can check it off in My Day without having to launch Outlook. Phone numbers and other contact info are also available in My Day.

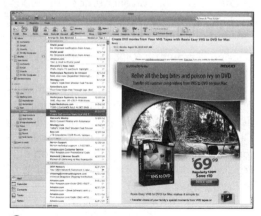

C A PowerPoint 2011 presentation.

D The Outlook 2011 Mail window.

New in Office 2011

Office 2011 has a variety of new features. Here are some of the most significant ones.

Office-wide changes

The philosophy that guided many of the changes and improvements to Office 2011 was that it should—as much as possible— match the features already in Office 2007 and 2010 for Windows. To that end, several major changes have been introduced in Office 2011.

First, to match the new, menuless interface introduced in Office 2007 and fully implemented in Office 2010, all Office 2011 applications feature the tabbed Ribbon interface. Unlike Windows users, however, Office 2011 users can choose commands from the Ribbon *or* from menus. They can continue to rely on menus, make the switch to the Ribbon, or use the Ribbon for some tasks and menus for others.

The Ribbon offers *feature discoverability*— that is, it improves the likelihood that you'll find commands and procedures that were difficult to access in menu-driven versions of Office. The Ribbon encourages users to explore Office features that they previously ignored or didn't notice.

Second, Entourage (Office's former email client) has been replaced by Outlook. For Entourage users, the switch to Outlook will be relatively seamless. Entourage email accounts and data will simply appear in Outlook on first launch. And for Outlook for Windows users, running Outlook on a Mac will be less confusing than switching to Entourage.

Third, a consistent set of image-editing tools is now available in Word, Excel, and PowerPoint. These tools enable users to crop, correct, and enhance photos on document pages—without having to resort to using other image-editing programs.

Fourth, Office 2011 marks the return of Visual Basic. Users who relied on Visual Basic macros in Excel 2004 will appreciate the restoration of VBA programmability— without needing to learn AppleScript.

Fifth, Office 2011 includes the Microsoft Document Connection application to simplify the process of accessing and sharing Office documents on a Web-based SkyDrive account or corporate SharePoint server. Office 2011 fully supports the new Office Web Apps, enabling users to create and edit Office documents from any computer with an Internet connection.

Finally, there are some smaller but still noteworthy features that are available in all or most Office 2011 applications:

- The new Reorder Object tool allows object layers to be visually manipulated.

- The Media Browser makes it easy to add photos, videos, music, clip art, shapes, and symbols to documents.

- The Project Gallery for each application has been replaced with a new Gallery with resizable thumbnails. When basing a document on a template, a new color scheme and fonts can be selected prior to creating the document.

New in Word 2011

- With the introduction of the Ribbon, Word's many toolbars and floating palettes have been eliminated, reducing onscreen clutter.

- The new full-screen view allows the entire monitor to be dedicated to reading or editing a document, eliminating normal onscreen distractions.

- The navigation pane has been enhanced to include search and reviewing functions.

- Searches performed in the navigation pane or the search box on the Standard toolbar identify matches as you type and automatically highlight every match in the document.

- When enabled, Style Guides number and color-color every applied style in a document, making it easy to spot errors and inconsistencies.

New in Excel 2011

- Conditional formatting and cell theme options are identical to those of Office 2010.

- Introduced in Office 2010, *sparklines* (in-cell charts) have been implemented.

- Filtering of tables and data arrays has been improved.

- Visual Basic macros are supported.

- PivotTables have been redesigned for ease of use and are more compatible with those of Office for Windows.

- Additional security options have been added to protect workbooks and restrict access to them.

New in PowerPoint 2011

- All users have the ability to broadcast presentations over the Web.

- Office 2008's Presenter Tools has been enhanced and renamed Presenter view.

New in Outlook 2011 and Entourage changes

- The Project Manager no longer exists.

- Identities (for multi-user Macs) are still supported but must be accessed using a separate application rather than from within Outlook.

- Received image attachments are no longer displayed in the message body, but can be viewed in a separate preview window (Snow Leopard users only).

- Contact edits can be performed in the reading pane. All changes are automatically saved.

- Entourage's gigantic, failure-prone database has been replaced with a filing system that isn't as onerous to back up or as subject to corruption.

- Filtering in Mail and Tasks lists has been enhanced and is accomplished by choosing options from a drop-down Filters menu.

- Custom Views are now known as Smart Folders.

Office 2011 Editions

Like previous versions of Office, there are multiple editions of Office 2011. Each includes Word, Excel, PowerPoint, and Messenger. Office 2011 is offered in these editions:

- **Microsoft Office for Mac Home and Student 2011.** This is the base edition. It includes Word, Excel, and PowerPoint, but omits Outlook—the email client that replaces Entourage.

- **Microsoft Office for Mac Home and Business 2011.** In addition to the other applications, this edition includes Outlook 2011.

- **Microsoft Office for Mac Academic 2011.** Available only to students and academics, this edition is identical to the Home and Business edition.

This Visual QuickStart Guide is appropriate for all editions of Office 2011. It covers the core Office applications: Word, Excel, PowerPoint, and Outlook.

Office Basics

Many basic operations in Office 2011, such as starting a new document, opening existing documents, saving your work, using common interface elements, working with text, and getting help, apply to all or most Office applications. Rather than repeat this information throughout the book, I'll cover it here. You'll want to refer back to this chapter as you delve into the application-specific chapters later in the book.

In This Chapter

Launching Office Applications

You can launch Office applications in the same manner as other OS X applications—plus some Office-specific ways.

To launch an Office application:

Do one of the following:

- Click its application icon in the Dock .

- Click the Applications folder in the Dock and choose an application from the Microsoft Office 2011 folder **B** (bottom).

- Open the Microsoft Office 2011 folder and double-click the application icon **C**.

- Double-click an alias for the Office application. (To create an alias for a program or document, select its file icon and choose File > Make Alias. Then move the alias to a convenient location, such as the Desktop.)

The application launches. Depending on your Preferences settings, the *application name* Gallery (see the next section) or a blank document appears.

A In order, these are the Dock icons for Outlook, Word, Excel, and PowerPoint.

C You can also launch an Office application by double-clicking its icon (Snow Leopard shown).

Office 2011 folder

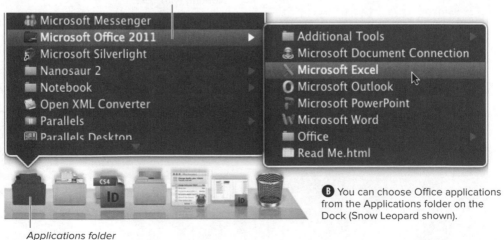

Applications folder

B You can choose Office applications from the Applications folder on the Dock (Snow Leopard shown).

Notebook.docx

D You can double-click any Office document to open it.

E You can right-click an Office or compatible document and open it by choosing Open With.

Launching Outlook from My Day or Office Reminders

If you double-click a scheduled event, to-do item, or task in My Day, Outlook will launch and open the item. Similarly, you can launch Outlook and open a selected event or task reminder in Office Reminders by:

- Double-clicking the reminder
- Selecting the reminder and choosing File > Open Item (Command-O)

To launch an Office application while opening one or more documents:

Do one of the following:

- Double-click an Office document icon or document alias. (For example, double-clicking a Word document **D** will launch Word—if it isn't already running—and open the document.)

- Choose an Office document from the Documents folder on the Dock.

- Drag the icon of a compatible document onto an Office application icon. (For example, you could drag a compatible worksheet onto the Excel icon in the Dock or in the Microsoft Office 2011 folder.)

- Select one or more document icons of the same type, right-click one of them, and choose the appropriate Office application from the Open With sub-menu **E**.

- Within Outlook or another mail application, double-click or open an Office document that's attached to an email message.

The application launches and the selected document or documents open.

TIP There is no right or preferred way to launch an Office application or open its documents. Use any method that's convenient at the moment. (Of course, the more methods you learn, the more likely you are to find one that's convenient.)

TIP Where you store your Office documents is up to you. Many users store them in folders within the Documents folder, for example. You may want to keep a few frequently used documents on the Desktop. Where the documents are stored isn't important. That you *know* where they're stored is extremely important. When saving an Office document, be sure to pay attention to its location on disk.

Using Galleries

Each Office program has a gallery that simplifies the process of creating blank documents, basing documents on templates or wizards, and opening the documents on which you've recently worked. The galleries are Document Gallery (Word), Worksheet Gallery (Excel), and Presentation Gallery (PowerPoint).

To use a Gallery:

1. Do one of the following:

   ‣ Launch an Office application. (If the application's Gallery hasn't been disabled, it will open on launch.)

   ‣ Choose File > New from Template or press Shift-Command-P. The application's Gallery appears **Ⓐ**.

2. Do one of the following:

   ‣ **Create a new document.** Select the Templates > All category (Word or Excel) or the Themes > All category (PowerPoint). Select the Word Document, Excel Workbook, or the White or Black thumbnail, respectively. Click the Choose button.

   ‣ **Create a document from a template.** Select a Templates subcategory (such as All, My Templates, or Personal Finances), select a template thumbnail, and click Choose.

   ‣ **Open a document on which you've recently worked.** Select a time period in the Recent *item* pane, select a document thumbnail, and click Choose.

> **TIP** If you'd rather not see the Gallery each time you launch a given Office application, click the Don't show this when opening *application* check box **Ⓑ**. (This must be done separately for each application.)

Categories   *Thumbnails*   *Preview*

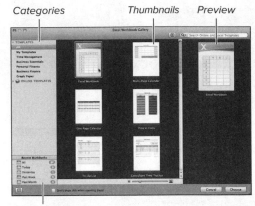

Recent documents pane

Ⓐ The Excel Worksheet Gallery.

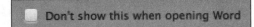

Ⓑ To prevent an application's Gallery from opening automatically on each launch, click this check box.

Supplementing the Template List

Each Gallery contains an Online Templates category. Expand it to view templates that you can download for free from Microsoft's site. If you select an online template thumbnail and click Choose, a copy of the template will download and open in Office.

For more information on working with Office templates, as well as creating your own, see "Using Templates," later in this chapter.

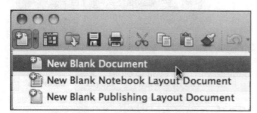

A Click the New icon on the Standard toolbar to create a new document.

B In Word, you can three types of new documents by clicking the New toolbar icon.

Creating a New Document

Unless you work exclusively with documents created by others, you'll also want to create new documents of your own. You can create a new blank document in these ways:

- **Word.** Choose File > New Blank Document.

- **PowerPoint.** Choose File > New Presentation.

- **Excel.** Choose File > New Workbook.

- **All.** Press Command-N or click the New icon on the Standard toolbar **A**. (In Word, the New icon has a drop-down menu from which you can choose different Word document types **B**.)

TIP If you don't make a choice in a Gallery (see **A** in "Using Galleries") by clicking its close (X) or Cancel button, a new blank document is automatically created.

TIP If an application's Gallery has been disabled (In the Gallery window check box or Preferences), launching the application causes a new document to automatically be created. (You can re-enable an application's Gallery In the General section of its Preferences.)

TIP As explained in the previous section, you can also create a new document in the Gallery window.

TIP If you decide that a new document isn't needed, click its red close (X) button. Don't save, if offered the option to do so.

Using Templates

Office 2011 includes a diverse collection of templates that you can use to create impressive documents without having to become a design professional.

Creating a document from a template

A *template* is a partially formed document that contains text, styles, and formatting. You can start a document with a template, and then modify its content and formatting.

To create a document from a template:

1. If the application's Gallery **A** isn't open, choose File > New from Template or press Shift-Command-P.

2. Select a Templates category or subcategory, select a template thumbnail, and click the Choose button.

    A copy of the template opens **B**.

3. Add the content, edit and format the document, and save.

> **TIP** When creating a new document from a template, you're working with a copy—not the original template. To remind you, Word names the copy Document rather than using the template name. As long as you save the copy with a new name or in a different location, changes you make won't affect the template.

> **TIP** For many templates, you can select theme colors and fonts in the preview area **C**.

Selected subcategory   *Selected thumbnail*   *Preview*

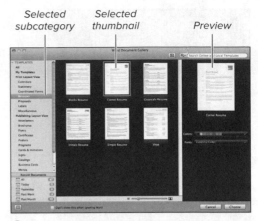

A Select a category or subcategory in the left pane to view the available templates.

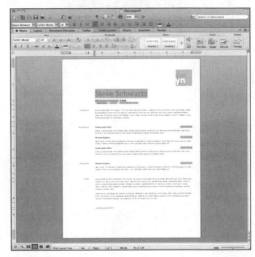

B The template includes temporary text and placeholders for items such as names and dates.

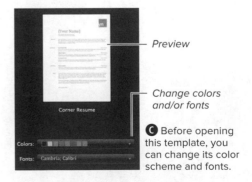

Preview

Change colors and/or fonts

C Before opening this template, you can change its color scheme and fonts.

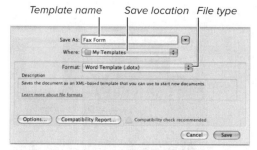

Template name   Save location   File type

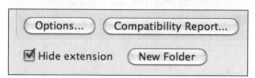

D Select *application* Template as the file type when saving a document as a template.

E The bottom-left corner of the Save As panel in Excel and PowerPoint have a check box that dictates whether the file extension is shown or hidden.

Working with Wizards

In addition to its numerous templates, Office provides a handful of wizards that help you create special-purpose documents. *Wizards* are multi-step or tabbed procedures that ask questions about the document you want to produce and then create the document based on your answers. If you like, you can edit the resulting document when the wizard is finished. Word's wizards, for example, can be used to create letters, envelopes, and labels.

In an *application* Gallery, a wizard can be identified by a magic wand in its thumbnail. Otherwise, look for Wizards in the Tools menu (primarily in Word).

Label Wizard

Saving a document as a template

You don't have to rely exclusively on the provided Office templates. You may find it useful to save your own documents as templates, allowing you to reuse them with minor changes whenever you like.

To save a document as a template:

1. Create and format an Office document. Delete text and other material that you don't want saved as part of the template, while retaining any text you'll want to use in new documents.

   For example, in a Word fax-form template, you might leave your contact information intact and add a placeholder (such as "Message text here") for the message text.

2. Choose File > Save As.

3. In the Save As panel that appears **D**, choose *application* Template from the Format drop-down menu.

4. Enter a name for the template in the Save As text box.

5. From the Where drop-down list, choose a location in which to save the template.

   Normally, you should accept the default folder (My Templates) for personal templates, but you're free to save them to other locations.

6. Click the Save button.

   The document is saved as a template.

TIP When saving any Office template or document, the appropriate file extension is added automatically. In Excel and PowerPoint, whether the file extension is *visible* depends on the state of the Hide extension check box **E**.

Modifying an existing template

You can modify the templates included with Office, as well as any files of your own that you've saved as templates. In this way, you can create templates that better serve your needs.

To modify a template:

1. Choose File > New from Template.

2. In the *application* Gallery window **Ⓐ**, select the template and click the Choose button. (If this is a personal template, select the template's thumbnail from the My Templates category **Ⓕ**.)

   A copy of the template opens.

3. Make the necessary edits and formatting changes to the template copy.

4. Do one of the following:

   ▶ To save the modified template without overwriting the original, choose File > Save As, choose *application* Template from the Format drop-down menu, change the template name, and save it in the My Templates folder **Ⓖ**.

   ▶ To replace the original template with the modified one, choose File > Save As, and choose *application* Template from the Format drop-down menu. Select the original template's filename in the list box at the top of the Save As panel and click Save. Click Replace in the confirmation dialog box that appears.

> **CAUTION** Unless you're certain that you'll never need the original template again, it's prudent to save the modified template with a new filename or in a folder other than My Templates. Doing so ensures that you can return to the original template if you ever need to do so.

My Templates

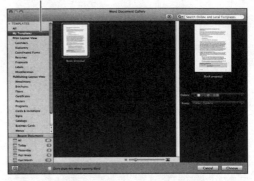

Ⓕ Personal templates are normally stored in the My Templates category, although you can optionally save them in any folder you want.

New filename   *My Templates folder*

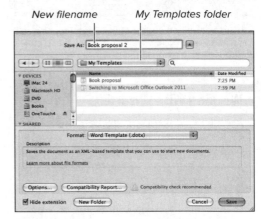

Ⓖ Changing the filename ensures that the modified template won't replace the original.

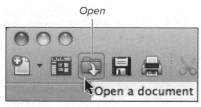

Open

A One way to call the Open dialog box is to click this icon on the Standard toolbar.

Current folder

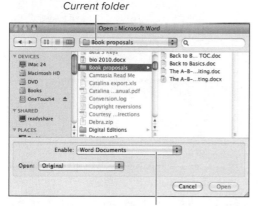

Restrict file list

B To open an existing document, choose it in the Open dialog box (Snow Leopard shown).

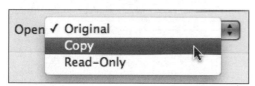

C Although you'll usually want to work with the original document, you can elect to open a copy or open the document for viewing only (*read-only*).

D The Open Recent submenu (Excel).

Opening Saved Documents

Unless you use each document you create only once (an unlikely occurrence), you'll sometimes need to open documents that you've previously saved.

To reopen a saved file:

1. Choose File > Open, click the Open icon on the Standard toolbar **A**, or press Command-O.

2. In the Open dialog box **B**, navigate to where the file is stored.

3. *Optional:* To restrict the file list, select a file type to display from the Enable drop-down menu **B**.

4. From the Open drop-down menu **C**, choose one of the following:

   ▸ **Original.** Open the original for editing.

   ▸ **Copy.** Open a copy for editing, protecting the original from changes.

   ▸ **Read-Only.** Open the document for viewing. If you edit the document, you can save the changes only if you use a different filename and/or location.

5. To open a document, select its filename and click Open or double-click its filename.

TIP If the file you want to open is one you've recently used, it may appear in the File > Open Recent submenu **D**. If so, you can open it by choosing its name.

TIP You can also open documents by choosing them from the Recent pane in the *application* Gallery (see **A** in "Using Galleries").

TIP Another way to open a document is to double-click its icon on the Desktop or in the folder in which the file is stored. See "Launching Office Applications," earlier in this chapter.

Saving Your Work

It's a good idea to save your work frequently to guard against data loss.

To save your work:

1. Choose File > Save, press Command-S, or click the Save icon on the Standard toolbar **A**.

   If the document was previously saved, the new version automatically overwrites the original file.

2. If this is the first time you've saved the document (or you've chosen File > Save As), a Save As dialog box appears **B**.

3. Enter a filename in the Save As text box.

4. Choose a file format from the Format drop-down menu.

5. Select a location in which to store the document.

6. Click Save or press Return.

7. When you're finished working on the document, choose File > Close, click the document's red close button, or press Command-W.

   Note that you don't have to close the current document to work on others. You can keep as many documents open as your Mac's memory allows.

CAUTION To save a previously saved document to a new location or with a new name (preventing the original copy from being overwritten), choose File > Save As rather than File > Save. File > Save will automatically overwrite the original document file.

TIP Word, Excel, and PowerPoint can be instructed to automatically save documents at user-defined intervals. This is known as *AutoRecover.* To enable AutoRecover and set a time interval, choose *application* > Preferences and open the Save category **C**.

A To save the current document, you can click the Save icon on the Standard toolbar.

Expand the location area

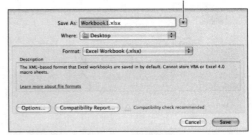

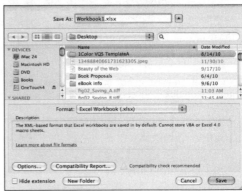

B To save a new document or to save an old one using a new name or location, enter the necessary information in the Save As dialog box. If the Where area is collapsed (top), you can expand it (bottom) by clicking where indicated.

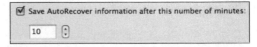

C By enabling AutoRecover, you can ensure that you never lose more than a few minutes of work.

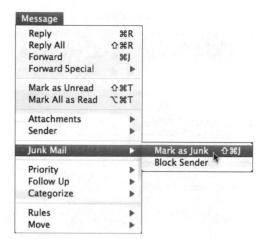

Message

Reply	⌘R
Reply All	⇧⌘R
Forward	⌘J
Forward Special	▶
Mark as Unread	⇧⌘T
Mark All as Read	⌥⌘T
Attachments	▶
Sender	▶
Junk Mail	▶
Priority	▶
Follow Up	▶
Categorize	▶
Rules	▶
Move	▶

Mark as Junk	⇧⌘J
Block Sender	

B When you move the cursor over a submenu (denoted by a right-facing triangle), a pop-out menu of additional commands is revealed.

Commands with an Ellipsis (...)

A menu command that ends with an *ellipsis* (three consecutive periods), such as Format > Cells..., means that a dialog box will be presented to you if the command is chosen.

Common Office Elements

In this section, you'll learn about many of the important Microsoft Office interface elements and program components that you'll encounter in the applications. Several of these elements, such as menus, contextual menus, and dialog boxes, are common to virtually all Macintosh programs.

Menus

Until the introduction of the Ribbon in Office 2011, choosing commands from menus was the primary way to perform most Office procedures. Whether you're working in the Finder, Excel, or some other program, a menu bar **A** (bottom) is always visible across the top of your main monitor. Menus (such as File and Edit) on the left side of the menu bar contain commands for the active program. Icon-based menus on the right side of the menu bar provide access to OS X features and utilities, such as the volume control, Spotlight, and Time Machine.

To select a menu command:

1. Click a menu (such as File) on the menu bar.

   The menu's commands and submenus are revealed.

2. Do either of the following:
   ▶ Choose a command by clicking it.
   ▶ Choose a command from a submenu by moving the cursor over the submenu and clicking the command **B**.

File menu   View menu

🍎 **Excel** File Edit View Insert Format Tools Data Window 💲 Help

A The left side of the menu bar as it appears in Excel 2011.

Ribbon

In order to move closer to achieving parity with Office 2007 and 2010 for Windows, a new interface component known as the Ribbon **C** was added to Office 2011. Unlike its Windows counterpart (which eliminated menus in Office for Windows), Office 2011 offers users a choice. Commands can be chosen from the Ribbon *or* from a menu.

Positioned beneath the toolbars at the top of each Office document, the Ribbon is divided into tabs which are further divided into groups. Each tab represents a major functional area, such as Layout or Charts. The groups within each tab subdivide the tab content into more discrete but related functions. In **C**, for example, Page Setup is merely one group in the Layout tab. To expose a command or procedure that you want to perform, the first step is to select (click) the tab that contains the command.

Ribbon controls should be readily understood. To execute many commands, you simply click the appropriate icon. Certain commands (such as the ones in **C**) present a drop-down menu. Click once to display the icon's menu and then click to choose a command from the menu **D**. Other Ribbon controls include check boxes, scrolling and drop-down galleries, drop-down palettes, and numeric controls. Most are self-explanatory.

TIP To avoid choosing a command from an icon's exposed menu, click anywhere else on the document page. This same technique can be used with menus and submenus on an application's menu bar.

TIP Some tabs are contextual and automatically appear only when you're working on a certain type of object, such as a photo, table, or chart. For example, when editing a chart in Excel, Chart Layout and Format contextual tabs appear **E**.

Selected tab

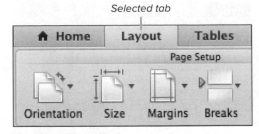

C This is a portion of the Layout tab on the Excel Ribbon. The downward-pointing triangle beside each icon indicates that a menu will be displayed when you click the icon.

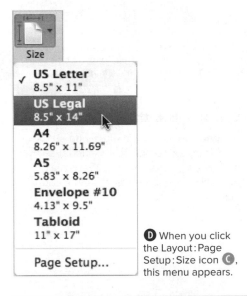

D When you click the Layout:Page Setup:Size icon **C**, this menu appears.

E With a chart or a part of it selected, the Chart Layout and Format contextual tabs appear on the Ribbon. Some contextual tabs are automatically selected for you; others must be manually selected by clicking.

F Icons on the Standard toolbar provide constant access to essential commands, such as New, Open, Save, Print, Undo, and Help.

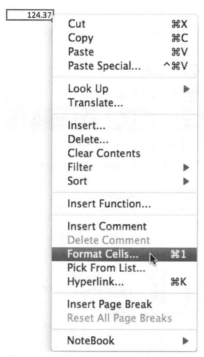

G Right-clicking a worksheet cell and choosing Format Cells may be more convenient than hunting for the equivalent menu or Ribbon command.

Toolbars

As another convenient option for choosing certain types of commands, toolbars **F** have been available in Office for many years. Because the Ribbon has made many of the toolbars redundant, each application now has only a few that you can display. To enable or disable a toolbar in an Office application, choose the toolbar's name from the View > Toolbars submenu.

TIP Office's toolbars can no longer be made to *float*—that is they are fixed in position in the document window. However, you can customize most toolbars by choosing View > Toolbars > Customize Toolbars and Menus or by right-clicking a toolbar and choosing the same command.

Contextual menus

Office, the Finder, and most other Mac applications support an additional way to conveniently execute commands. If you right-click or Control-click a selected item, such as a selected text string in a Word document, an Excel cell, or a text box on a PowerPoint slide, a contextual menu appears and presents relevant commands for you to choose **G**. Rather than search the menu bar, toolbars, or the Ribbon for the command you need, you may be able to right-click and shorten the process.

TIP It's an excellent idea to experiment with right-clicking in Office. You may find that certain commands are easier to execute this way. In addition, the contextual menu that appears can improve your understanding of the commands that are appropriate for the selected object or material.

The Toolbox

Many useful utilities can be found on the tabs of the floating Toolbox. Although the Toolbox is available in all Office applications, some of its tabs are application-specific, such as Formula Builder (Excel), Citations (Word), and Custom Animation (PowerPoint).

To introduce you to the Toolbox, this section covers the Scrapbook and Compatibility Report tabs. Other tabs are discussed throughout the book, such as Reference Tools (dictionary, encyclopedia, thesaurus) in Chapter 4 and the Formula Builder in Chapter 12.

To open or close the Toolbox:

1. To open the Toolbox, click the Toolbox icon on the Standard toolbar **H** or choose the desired Toolbox tab from the View menu **I**.

   The Toolbox opens **J** to the tab last used or to the chosen tab, respectively. To switch to another tool, click its tab.

2. To close the Toolbox, click the Toolbox icon again, click the Toolbox's red close button **J**, or choose the name of the current tab from the View menu.

TIP To move the Toolbox, drag its title bar. To collapse (roll up) or expand the Toolbox, click its green zoom button **J**.

TIP To collapse or expand sections of a Toolbox tab, click the triangle that precedes the section name.

TIP There's no Toolbox icon on Outlook's Standard toolbar. To open the Toolbox, choose a specific tab from the View menu.

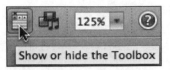

Show or hide the Toolbox

H The Toolbox icon in the Standard toolbar (Word shown).

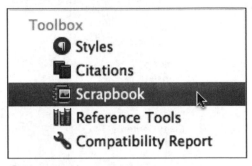

I You can open the Toolbox to a specific tab by choosing the tab from the Toolbox section of the View menu (Word shown).

J The Styles tab of the Toolbox (Word shown).

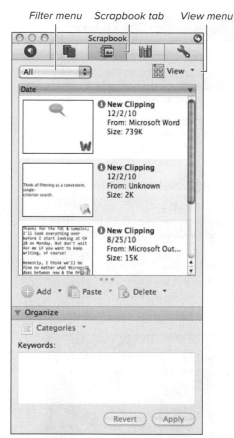

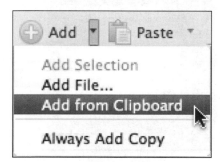

K Use the Scrapbook to store text and graphic clippings.

L Open the Add icon's menu to store information from the current selection, a file, or the contents of the Clipboard.

The Scrapbook

In Mac OS X, the Clipboard is a temporary repository for copied (Command-C) or cut (Command-X) material. The material can then be pasted (Command-V) into the same document, another document, or even a document of a different application. For instance, you can copy an image in Photoshop or Preview and paste it into a Word document.

Unlike the Clipboard, material stored in the Scrapbook isn't temporary. It remains there until deleted, and it can be pasted into any Office document. You can store material that is selected within an Office document, copied or cut material from the Clipboard, or complete files.

To add an item to the Scrapbook:

1. Open the Toolbox and click the Scrapbook tab **K**.

2. Do one of the following:

   ▸ Select an item in an open Office document, such as text, a graphic image or another object, or a cell range. Drag the item into the Scrapbook or click the Scrapbook's Add icon.

   ▸ To add the contents of the Clipboard as a Scrapbook item, click the down arrow beside the Add icon and choose Add from Clipboard **L**.

   ▸ To add a file as a Scrapbook item, click the down arrow beside the Add button and choose Add File **L**. In the Choose a File dialog box that appears, select the file that you want to add and click Choose.

   The material is added as a new Scrapbook item called a *clipping*.

To insert a clipping into a document:

1. *Optional:* Click in an active document to set the insertion mark where you want to paste the Scrapbook clipping.

2. In the Scrapbook, select a clipping to paste.

   The selected item is shaded in blue.

3. Do one of the following:

   ▸ Drag the clipping to the desired location in the document and release the mouse button.

   ▸ Click the Paste icon at the bottom of the Scrapbook window. The clipping is added to the document at the current insertion mark.

   ▸ For a text clipping, click the Paste icon's down arrow and choose Paste as Plain Text from the menu . The selected text clipping is pasted, but its formatting is ignored.

   ▸ Open the Paste menu  and choose Paste as Picture. The clipping is pasted as a graphic object.

   TIP To simultaneously paste multiple Scrapbook items into a document, Command-click to select each item and then click the Paste icon. You can also use this technique to delete multiple items.

M Additional options are available in the Paste drop-down menu.

Setting Toolbox Preferences

To view or set preferences for the Toolbox or one of its palettes, click the Toolbox Settings icon on the right side of the title bar. Set display options for the Toolbox in the top half of the window. To change preferences for a particular palette, choose its name from the drop-down Palette menu. Click OK to save your changes.

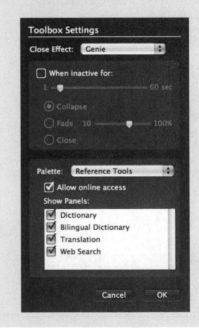

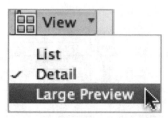

N To change the manner in which clippings are displayed, open the View drop-down menu.

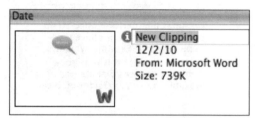

O Replace **New Clipping** with the clipping's new name.

P The Delete icon also has a drop-down menu that you can use to control deletions.

To organize Scrapbook clippings:

Do any of the following:

- To change the clipping display mode, choose an option from the View drop-down menu **N**.

- To add a descriptive name to a clipping, double-click it. Replace the selected clipping name with a name of your choosing **O**.

- To associate a selected clipping with a category or keywords, expand the Organize section at the bottom of the Scrapbook **K**. Choose categories from the drop-down lists. To add keywords, type them in the Keywords box, separated by commas. Click the Apply button when you're finished adding and editing keywords.

- To delete one or more selected clippings, click the Delete icon **M**. Confirm the deletion in the dialog box that appears.

- To delete all or just the visible clippings from the Scrapbook, click the down arrow beside the Delete icon, choose the appropriate command **P**, and confirm the deletion in the dialog box that appears.

Filtering the Clippings List

If the Scrapbook contains many clippings, you can filter it to show only those that match a criterion. Choose a command from the drop-down filter menu (see also **K**). To restore the complete list, choose All.

Compatibility Report

Many users are concerned about the cross-platform compatibility of their documents, as well as whether users of older versions of Office will be able to open documents created in the newest version. In Office 2011, you can check any document for potential compatibility issues and optionally correct them.

To create a compatibility report:

1. In Office 2011, open the document that you want to check.

2. Open the Toolbox and click the Compatibility Report tab.

3. Do one of the following:

   ▶ If you know the version of Office that the document's intended recipient uses, select it from the drop-down list. The compatibility check is performed.

   ▶ Otherwise, accept the default version range and click the Check Document button.

   Compatibility issues, if any, appear in the Results box **Q**. The button label changes to "Recheck Document."

4. One by one, select each numbered item that appears in the Results box.

   An explanation of the compatibility issue appears in the Explanation box.

5. For each compatibility issue, you can click Fix or Ignore.

   Note, however, that all issues may not be correctable in this fashion. Some must be fixed manually by following the Explanation text.

TIP Each application has Compatibility preferences where you can specify how compatibility issues will be handled, as well as which potential issues will be ignored **R**.

Select a software version   *Compatibility Report tab*

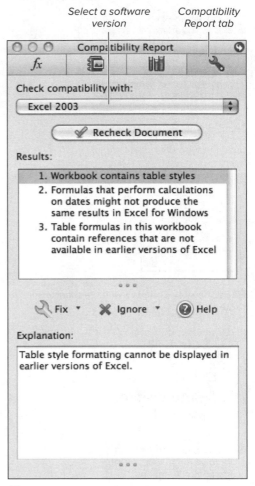

Q Use the Compatibility Report tab to determine if the current document has potential compatibility problems with other versions of Office for Mac or Windows.

R The Compatibility Report section of Excel's Compatibility Preferences.

Media Browser

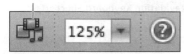

S You can click the Media Browser icon on the Standard toolbar to open or close the Media Browser.

T To view items of a particular type, click a tab at the top of the Media Browser. Select the item and drag it onto the document page.

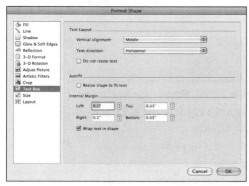

U The Format Shape dialog box.

Media Browser

The Media Browser enables you to add media (photos, clip art, movies, and audio), shapes, and symbols to any Word, Excel, or PowerPoint document. The Media Browser is also available in Outlook, but only supports photos, audio, and movies.

To insert an item from the Media Browser:

1. Open the Media Browser by clicking its icon on the Standard toolbar **S**, choosing View > Media Browser, or pressing Control-Command-M.

    The Media Browser appears **T**.

2. Click the tab of the Media Browser item that you want to add to your document.

3. When you see the desired image or item, drag it into a placeholder or empty area on a slide (PowerPoint) or onto the document page (Word and Excel).

4. To close the Media Browser, repeat step 1 or click the Media Browser's red close button.

For more detailed instructions on inserting material from the Media Browser, see "Inserting Photos and Pictures" in Chapter 3.

Dialog boxes

Dialog boxes are windows that appear when you make a choice from a menu or click a Ribbon or toolbar icon. They allow you to respond to program issues, confirm actions, or apply multiple settings to a selected item, such as text or shape formatting **U**.

In many Office dialog boxes, you set options, and then click OK to implement your choices or click Cancel to ignore them. Any menu command that ends with an ellipsis (...) will present a dialog box.

Working with Text

Text is an important part of most Office documents. In this section, you'll learn the basics of selecting, moving, and replacing text in documents.

Setting the text insertion mark

Whenever an application is ready for you to type, a blinking insertion mark appears in the document. Whatever you type appears at the text insertion mark.

To revise or add to existing text, you must move the insertion mark to the spot where you want to make the change.

To set the text insertion mark:

Do one of the following:

- Move the I-beam cursor to the spot where you want to position the insertion mark. Click to set the insertion mark Ⓐ.

- If the text insertion mark is currently set in a normal Word document, an Excel cell, or a PowerPoint text block, you can move the insertion mark by pressing the arrow keys, Page Up, Page Down, or any of the other keyboard shortcuts listed in **Table 2.1**.

> **TIP** In Excel, the text insertion mark can be in the formula bar or in the cell, depending on where you're performing edits or data entry.

TABLE 2.1 Navigation Keyboard Shortcuts

Keystroke	Movement
↑ or ↓	Up or down one line
← or →	Left or right one character
Option ← or Option →	One word to the left or right
⌘ ← or ⌘ →	Beginning or end of current line
⌘ ↑ or ⌘ ↓	Beginning of previous or next paragraph

> **Since becoming a full-time author in 1990, Steve has written almost 60 books on computer and game topics. He is Peachpit Press' primary author on Microsoft Office.** |

Text insertion mark   I-beam cursor

Ⓐ Whatever you type will appear at the text insertion mark. In this example, the text insertion mark is set to add text at the end of this paragraph.

Selected text

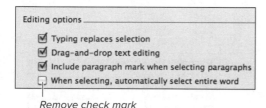

When you link rather than embed an object, the object remains in the original application's document. A *copy* of the object—linked to the original—is displayed in the second application.

B Click and drag to create a text selection. The selected text is highlighted.

Editing options

☑ Typing replaces selection
☑ Drag-and-drop text editing
☑ Include paragraph mark when selecting paragraphs
☐ When selecting, automatically select entire word

Remove check mark

C Remove the check mark from this item to simplify the process of selecting partial words.

Selecting text

Before you can edit, replace, delete, or format text, you must first select it. Any operation you then perform will affect the selected text.

To select text using the mouse:

Do any of the following:

- Click at one end of a section of text to set the text insertion mark and drag to the other end to select the text **B**. A selection can be as little as one character or can contain many consecutive paragraphs.

- To select text on consecutive lines, click to set the insertion mark at the beginning of the selection and either drag through the lines you want to select or Shift-click at the end of the selection.

- You can also make multiple, noncontiguous text selections. You might, for example, want to select several headings to simultaneously apply the same formatting to them. Hold down Command to make multiple selections.

- Double-click anywhere within a word to select it. Triple-click anywhere within a paragraph to select it.

TIP A Preferences setting (in Word and PowerPoint only) ensures that the entire first and last word of a selection are highlighted. If you want to be able to select parts of words, choose *application* > Preferences, click the Edit icon, and remove the check mark from When selecting, automatically select entire word **C**. Click OK to save the change.

TIP To select an entire line of text in a Word document, click in the left margin of the line. To select multiple consecutive lines, click in the margin to the left of a line and then drag down through the additional lines.

To select text using the keyboard:

1. Use the arrow keys or mouse to set the insertion point at one end of the text that you want to select.

2. Hold down Shift and press arrow keys (or other keys shown in Table 2.1 earlier in this chapter) to extend the selection.

TIP Use Shift-Option-Left Arrow or Shift-Option-Right Arrow to select a word at a time.

TIP Use Shift-Down Arrow or Shift-Up Arrow to select multiple lines of text.

TIP To select from the insertion mark to the beginning or end of the current line, press Shift-Command-Left Arrow or Shift-Command-Right Arrow, respectively.

Moving text

To move text in a document, you can either use Edit > Cut (Command-X) and Edit > Paste (Command-V) or drag and drop. *Drag and drop* is a simplified cut and paste, accomplished by selecting text and then dragging it to a new location in the document. You can even drag text from one document to another or from one application window to another.

To drag and drop text:

1. Select the text to be moved.

2. Place the cursor over the selected text.

   The cursor changes to an arrow pointer **D**.

3. Press and hold the mouse button, and drag the pointer to the destination.

   A text insertion mark shows the spot where the dragged text will reappear **E**.

4. Release the mouse button to drop the text at the new location **F**.

D When the cursor is moved over a text selection, it becomes an arrow pointer. (In this example, I intend to move the selected line down one line.)

Text insertion mark

E Drag the material to the destination. A text insertion mark shows where the dragged text will appear.

F Release the mouse button to drop the text. In this example, the line has been moved from the second to the third position in the list.

TIP To copy rather than move text (leaving the original text intact), press Option as you drag.

TIP A drag and drop between documents is treated as a copy rather than a cut. That is, following the operation, the original material remains in the source document.

TIP You can also use drag and drop to copy or move other kinds of objects, such as charts and graphics.

TIP You can use drag and drop to drag a text selection from Office 2011 onto the Desktop, creating a picture clipping **G**.

Replacing text

To replace text in a document or dialog box, select the text and type over it. Doing so simultaneously deletes the text and replaces it with the new text. (It isn't necessary to first delete the old text.)

◉ ◯ ◯   ⬛ Picture clipping

During his lengthy computer-industry career, Dr. Steve Schwartz has dedicated himself to educating computer users and helping them become productive with the software that's so pervasive in their business, school, and personal lives. Steve was formerly employed as Editor-in-Chief and chief methodologist for *Software Digest*, Business Editor for *MACazine*, and Technical Services Director for Funk Software—where he provided software support to a customer base of 750,000, trained Funk and Lotus Development personnel, directed QA, and wrote user manuals. In addition, he has written hundreds of articles for computer magazines such as *Macworld*, *PC World*, and *Computer World*.

Since becoming a full-time author in 1990, Steve has written almost 60 books computer and game topics. He is Peachpit Press' primary author on Microsoft Office.

Clipping contents: rich text (RTF)

G As indicated in the status area of this Picture clipping window, this text dragged from a Word document is in Rich Text Format. It can be selectively copied and pasted into other documents, retaining its formatting.

Using the Format Painter

Rather than laboriously recreate complex formatting, you can use the Format Painter to copy the formatting of selected text and objects and apply it to other text and objects.

To use the Format Painter:

Do any of the following:

- To copy character formatting from one text string to another, select the source string, click the Format Painter icon on the Standard toolbar **A**, and then drag-select the target text string. When you release the mouse button, the formatting is applied to the target text.

- To copy a paragraph format, select the entire source paragraph (including the paragraph mark at its end), click the Format Painter icon, and then click anywhere in the target paragraph (or drag through multiple paragraphs).

- To copy formatting from a picture or object, select the graphic or object whose formatting you want to copy, click the Format Painter icon, and click the destination object.

TIP To copy formatting to *multiple* objects, text strings, or paragraphs, select the source text or object and double-click the Format Painter toolbar icon **B**. One by one, apply the formatting to as many target objects, text strings, or paragraphs as you want. Click the Format Painter icon again when you're done.

TIP In Excel, you can use the Format Painter to quickly duplicate cell formatting. Examples of copied formatting include number formats (such as Currency with two decimal places), cell shading, and borders.

Format Painter

A Word, PowerPoint, and Excel support the Format Painter.

Format Painter

B Double-click the Format Painter icon to lock it.

Undo   Redo

A Undo and Redo icons can be found on the Standard toolbar.

Undo menu

Redo menu

Bold
Font
Typing "12.6" in C1
Typing "45" in B1
Typing "12" in A1

Undo 2 Actions

B Open the Undo menu and choose the actions to undo.

Repeating an Action

You'll occasionally find yourself repeating certain actions over and over. For example, if you decide to change the font, color, or style of a particular heading in a Word document, there's no need to laboriously choose the same formatting command for each additional heading. Instead, after you select a different heading, you can apply the Repeat command.

Redo and Repeat share the same keyboard shortcut: Command-Y. To apply your most recent action or command to a new selection, choose Edit > Repeat *command*.

Undoing and Redoing Actions

If you make a mistake, you can often correct it by undoing the action. You can choose Edit > Undo action or click the Undo icon on the Standard toolbar.

Office 2011 applications support unlimited undos. If you find that you made a mistake several actions ago, you can step back from the most recent action to the one you need to fix, *undoing* (reversing) each one. And if, after undoing an action, you change your mind, you can *redo* what you've undone.

To undo one or more actions:

1. To undo your most recent action, do one of the following:

    ▸ Choose Edit > Undo *action* (Command-Z).

    ▸ Click the Undo icon on the Standard toolbar **A**.

2. To undo multiple recent actions, do any of the following:

    ▸ Repeatedly choose Edit > Undo, press Command-Z, or click the Undo icon.

    ▸ Click the down arrow beside the Undo toolbar icon and select the actions you want to correct **B**.

    In order from most recent to least recent, each action is undone.

3. To reverse (*redo*) the effect of one or more Undo commands, you can:

    ▸ Choose Edit > Redo *action* (Command-Y).

    ▸ Click the Redo toolbar icon **A**.

    ▸ Click the down arrow beside the Redo toolbar icon, and choose the number of actions to redo.

Setting Magnification

The default magnification for a Word, Excel, or PowerPoint document may not always be appropriate for the task at hand. You can increase or decrease the magnification whenever you like. The magnification you set is specific to the current document and is saved with the document. Percentages greater than 100 make the material larger; percentages less than 100 make the material smaller. A setting of 100% is actual size.

To change a document's magnification:

- **Word.** Do any of the following:
  - ▸ Set a new magnification percentage on the Standard toolbar 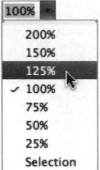.
  - ▸ Drag the slider in the status area **B**.
  - ▸ Choose View > Zoom, select a setting or type a percentage in the Zoom dialog box **C**, and click OK.

- **Excel.** Do any of the following:
  - ▸ Set a new magnification percentage on the Standard toolbar **A**.
  - ▸ Choose View > Zoom, select a setting or type a percentage in the Zoom dialog box **C**, and click OK.

- **PowerPoint.** Do any of the following:
  - ▸ Set a new magnification percentage on the Standard toolbar **A**.
  - ▸ Drag the slider in the status area **B**.
  - ▸ Choose View > Zoom > Zoom, select a setting or type a percentage in the Zoom dialog box **C**, and click OK.
  - ▸ Choose View > Zoom > Zoom In or Zoom Out to increase or decrease the magnification in 15 percent increments, respectively.

A You can choose a new magnification percentage from this drop-down menu.

B Drag the slider to change the magnification.

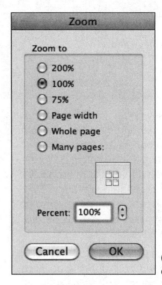

C The Zoom dialog box.

Automatic Magnification in PowerPoint

You can automatically resize the material on a PowerPoint slide to make it fill the window as much as possible. Click the tiny icon to the right of the slider in the status area. If you then resize the window, the magnification continually adjusts to the window size.

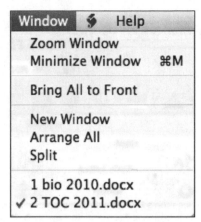

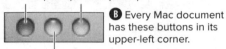

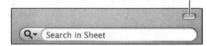

A The Window menu (Word).

Red (close) *Green (zoom)*

B Every Mac document has these buttons in its upper-left corner.

Yellow (minimize)

Hide/show toolbar area

C Click this button to roll up or reveal the toolbar area (Excel shown).

More About Zooming

The Zoom button and the Zoom Window command toggle a window between its current location and size and its previous location and size.

Managing Windows

Regardless of the Office application you're using, you'll occasionally work on multiple documents at once. You can use the Window menu **A** or click buttons to arrange, switch among, and manage the open windows.

To manage document windows:

Do any of the following:

- **Make a document active.** To make a different document active, click anywhere in its window or choose its name from the bottom of the Window menu **A**.

- **Minimize a document.** To minimize the active document to the Dock, click the yellow button in the window's upper-left corner **B**, double-click the window's title bar, choose Window > Minimize Window, or press Command-M.

  To restore a minimized document, click its Dock icon or choose its name from the Window menu.

- **Hide/show toolbars.** To hide or reveal the toolbars above the document area, click the elongated button in the upper-right corner of the document window **C**.

- **Hide/show the Ribbon.** Click the caret (^) icon above the right end of the Ribbon.

- **Arrange All.** Choose this command **A** to display all open documents at the same time. Windows are reduced as necessary to fit them onscreen.

  To work with one of the documents at its full size and position, choose Window > Zoom Window or click the green zoom button **B**. Repeat to restore the window to its Arrange All position.

- **Close a document.** Click the red close button **B**, choose File > Close, or press Command-W.

Customizing Office

Although the Office applications are pre-configured in a way that will suit the average user's needs, you're free to customize them. There are two ways you can do this:

- Modify settings in the application's Preferences dialog boxes.
- Customize toolbars, menus, keyboard shortcuts, and the Ribbon.

To change Preferences for a program:

1. With the application running, choose *application* > Preferences or press Command-, (comma).

   The Preferences dialog box appears.

2. There are two styles of dialog boxes:

   ▸ Word, Excel, and Outlook preferences are presented in the style of OS X System Preferences **A**. Click an icon to view that preference category.

   ▸ In PowerPoint **B**, preference icons are strung across the top of the dialog box. As in Word and Excel, you click an icon to view that preference category.

   The selected preference category appears in a new window (Word, Excel, and Outlook) or in the same window (PowerPoint). When you rest the cursor on a preference item in Word or Excel, an explanation appears in the bottom pane **C**.

3. Set preferences as you wish.

4. Do either of the following:

   ▸ Set preferences in other categories.

   ▸ Click OK to save the new settings (see **A** and **B**). (In Word, Excel, and Outlook, you must first return to the main window by clicking Show All.)

A In an application's Preferences dialog box, preference categories are represented by icons.

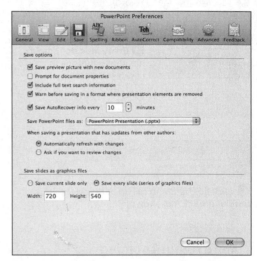

B In PowerPoint Preferences, category icons are strung across the top of the sole window.

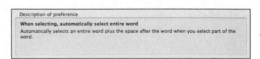

C Word and Excel Preferences provide automatic help for each preference setting.

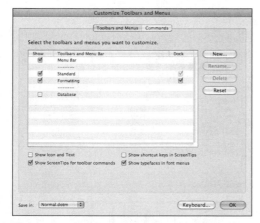

D The Toolbars and Menus tab of the Customize Toolbars and Menus dialog box (Word shown).

Categories list   *Commands list*

E When customizing toolbars or menus, you can filter the listed commands by choosing a category from the Categories list.

É Excel File Edit View Insert Format
File ▾ Edit ▾ View ▾ Insert ▾ Format ▾ Tools ▾ Data ▾ Window ▾

F When the Customize Toolbars and Menus dialog box is open, a mini-menu bar is displayed beneath the normal menu bar (Excel shown).

To set default toolbars in Word, Excel, and PowerPoint:

1. With the application running, choose View > Toolbars > Customize Toolbars and Menus.

   The Customize Toolbars and Menus dialog box appears **D**.

2. Select the Toolbars and Menus tab, and check the toolbars you want to display automatically.

   Word only: From the Save in drop-down menu **D**, choose the current document (to associate the selected toolbars with only that document) or a style sheet, such as Normal.dotm (to associate the toolbars with all Word documents based on that style sheet).

   TIP To create a toolbar from scratch, click the New button **D**.

To customize toolbars and menus in Word, Excel, and PowerPoint:

1. Choose View > Toolbars > Customize Toolbars and Menus.

2. Click the Commands tab **E**.

3. Do any of the following:

   ▸ To add an icon to a toolbar, drag it from the Commands pane to the toolbar.

   ▸ To add a command to a menu, drag the command from the Commands pane onto the menu title in the mini-menu bar **F**. The menu will drop down. Drag the command to its destination position within the menu and release the mouse button.

   TIP If you later decide to remove an added command or toolbar icon, select the Commands tab of the Customize Toolbars and Menus dialog box. Drag the command out of the mini-menu or drag the icon off the toolbar.

To customize a keyboard in Excel:

1. Choose View > Toolbars > Customize Toolbars and Menus.
2. In the Customize Toolbars and Menus dialog box **E**, click the Keyboard button.
3. Use the Customize Keyboard dialog box **G** to add or change keyboard shortcuts.

To customize a keyboard in Word:

1. Choose View > Toolbars > Customize Toolbars and Menus.
2. In the Customize Toolbars and Menus dialog box **E**, click the Keyboard button to open the Customize Keyboard dialog box **H**.
3. From the Save changes in drop-down menu **H**, choose the current document (to associate the new shortcuts with that document only) or a template (to associate the shortcuts with all documents based on that template).
4. In the Categories list, select a menu category.
5. In the Commands list, select the command whose shortcuts you want to change.
6. Do any of the following:

   ▸ To add a new shortcut, click in the Press new shortcut key/keyboard shortcut box, press the key combination, and then click Assign or Add.

   CAUTION Be sure that no other command is already associated with the key combination.

   ▸ To remove a keyboard shortcut, select it in the Current keys list and click the Remove button.

   ▸ To restore the default shortcuts, click Reset All. (In Word, you must first select the template or document name from the Save changes in menu.)

Categories list   *Commands list*

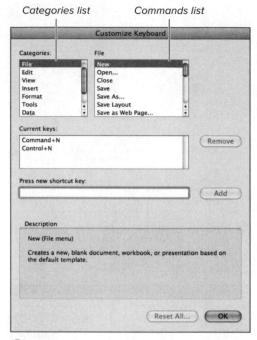

G Customize Keyboard dialog box (Excel).

Categories list   *Commands list*

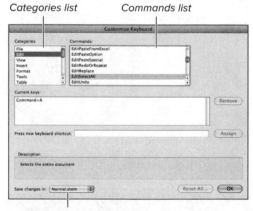

Save changes in

H Customize Keyboard dialog box (Word).

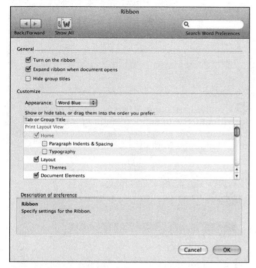

I Choose a command from this Ribbon icon to customize the Ribbon for the current application.

J The Ribbon preferences dialog box.

K The right end of the Ribbon tabs.

What About Outlook's Ribbon?

Although you can customize the Ribbon in all other Office applications, the same can't be said for Outlook. However, you can selectively hide or show the Ribbon groups and icons.

Click the caret (^) icon above the right end of the Ribbon to toggle between showing the entire Ribbon and showing only its tabs. Choosing View > Ribbon achieves the same effect. These techniques work with all Office applications.

To set Ribbon Preferences for Word, Excel, or PowerPoint:

1. Open the Office application.
2. Do one of the following:
   ▸ Choose *application* > Preferences. In the Preferences dialog box, click the Ribbon icon.
   ▸ Click the menu icon at the right side of the Ribbon and choose Ribbon Preferences **I**.
3. In the Ribbon preferences dialog box **J**, do any of the following:
   ▸ In the General section, click check boxes to enable/disable basic features.
   ▸ In the Customize section, choose a new Ribbon color scheme from the Appearance drop-down menu.
   ▸ In the Customize section, click check boxes to show/hide certain Ribbon tabs and groups. Change the order by dragging items up or down in the list.
4. Click OK to save the changes.

To change the Ribbon tab order for Word, Excel, or PowerPoint:

1. Open the Office application.
2. Click the menu icon at the right side of the Ribbon and choose Customize Ribbon Tab Order **I**.

   The tab area of the Ribbon changes **K**.
3. Do any of the following:
   ▸ To hide a tab, click its X button.
   ▸ To change the tab order, drag any tab (except Home) to a new position.
4. Click Done to accept your changes or click Reset to restore the default tab order.

Working in Other Languages

Via its Unicode language support, Office 2011 can display a variety of foreign (non-Roman) characters. You can view and edit documents in many languages, mix languages in a document, and set preferences to match the conventions and requirements of particular languages. You can also use foreign characters in filenames.

To set OS X's foreign language support:

1. Open System Preferences and click the Personal:Language & Text icon.

2. Select the Language tab of the Language & Text dialog box .

3. If the language you want to use isn't in the list box, click the Edit List button, add languages , and click OK.

   After adding a language, you can change the main list's  order by dragging items up or down to new positions.

4. Click other tabs to set your preferred date, time, and number styles (Formats); symbol substitution (Text); and keyboard layout (Input Sources). Close the dialog box to save your changes and reboot.

To mark text as a different language:

1. Select the text. Choose Tools > Language.

   The Language dialog box appears .

2. Select the text's language from the list, and then click OK.

   During spelling checks, the appropriate foreign language dictionary will be used to check the selected text.

A Use the Language & Text System Preferences to instruct OS X to support languages other than English on your computer. Choose a different sort-order language from the menu, if desired.

B Check languages that you want the operating system to support and click OK.

C You can mark text as being in a specific language. Click Default to set a new language to be used for *all* spelling checks.

A Set a follow-up date and time.

B To open the document, double-click its entry in the Office Reminders window.

Flagging Documents for Follow-Up

You can flag any Office document for follow up at a later time. For instance, if you want to be reminded to review a budget worksheet two hours before a scheduled meeting, you can flag it for follow-up. At the appointed date and time, a reminder will appear. The Office Reminders program (see Chapters 23 and 24) is responsible for displaying all Office-related reminders.

To flag a document for follow-up:

1. Make the document active in the Office program in which it was created.

2. Choose Tools > Flag for Follow Up.

   The Flag for Follow Up dialog box appears **A**.

3. Specify the date and time at which you want to be reminded, and then click OK.

   The flagged document is recorded as a new Outlook task. At the designated tIme, a reminder will appear **B**.

4. To open the document in its Office application, double-click the reminder.

TIP As with other tasks, you can use the Office Reminders window to mark a document follow-up as complete (click its check box), request that you be reminded again later (click the Snooze button), or dismiss the reminder but leave the item as incomplete in the Tasks list (click the Dismiss button).

Getting Help

Office 2011 provides several help sources:

- You can use the detailed Help system provided with each Office application.
- You can get pop-up ScreenTips (also called ToolTips) for toolbar icons, controls, and other interface elements.
- You can visit Microsoft's site for detailed help, tips, and other material.

To use application Help:

1. Choose Help > *application* Help, click the Help (**?**) icon on the Standard toolbar, or press Command-?.

   The Help system opens to its home screen **A**.

2. Do one of the following:

   - Click one of the blue help topics.

   - Enter a keyword or phrase in the Search box and press Return to search for related Help text. Potential topic matches are returned as a list. Click any item to review its Help information.

3. In the body of any Help window, blue subtopic text preceded by a triangle can be clicked to expand that subtopic. To expand all such items in the current window, click the Show All link.

   TIP Any items listed in the See also area at the bottom of the window are links to related Help topics.

4. To navigate backward and forward through multiple help screens, click the arrow icons in the toolbar. Click the Home icon to return to the main screen.

5. To dismiss Help, click the window's red close button.

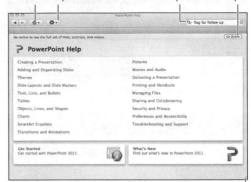

Home Options menu Search help Online help

Drag to resize window

A Your main source of help (other than this book) is each application's Help window.

Automator Workflows

Office 2011 includes Automator action sets. By employing and combining actions, you can create Automator workflows that automate complex or repetitive Office activities. To run the sample workflows included with Office, choose them from the Scripts > Sample Automator Workflows submenu. (The Scripts menu is denoted by an icon rather than the word "Scripts.")

To view the built-in Office 2011 actions, launch Automator by choosing it in the Applications folder. Then select an Office 2011 application in the Library list.

For information about using Automator to create workflows, switch to the Finder, choose Help > Mac Help, and search for **automator**. In Automator, choose Help > Automator Help.

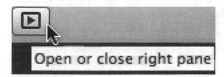

B When you rest the cursor over many Office elements, a ScreenTip appears.

C For more extensive and up-to-date help, visit Microsoft's site.

Updating Office 2011

The Help menu also contains a command that enables you to manually check for updates to the current Office program. Choose Help > Check for Updates. In the Microsoft AutoUpdate dialog box, click the Check for Updates button.

Microsoft AutoUpdate can be configured to automatically check for updates on a repeating schedule. Click the Automatically radio button and choose a schedule from the drop-down menu.

To display a ScreenTip:

Do the following:

- Move the pointer over any icon, button, or other Office element, and then wait a second or two.

  A yellow ScreenTip appears **B**.

To visit Microsoft's site for help:

1. Open the application's Help.
2. At the top of any Help screen, click the Go Online button **A**.

   Your browser launches and displays help information from Microsoft's site **C**.

TIP You can print any Help topic by clicking the Options menu icon **A** and choosing Print. Be sure to expand all topics that you want to include in the printout.

Quitting an Office Application

When you're done working in an Office application, you can exit from it—freeing up its memory for other programs and tasks.

To quit an Office application:

1. *Optional:* If any open documents contain unsaved changes, save them now (see "Saving Your Work," earlier in this chapter, for instructions).

   If you don't save, you'll be given an opportunity to save when you try to exit the program.

2. Choose *application* > Quit *application* (such as Excel > Quit Excel) or press Command-Q.

   If there are no open documents that contain unsaved changes, the application immediately quits.

3. If one or more open documents contain unsaved changes, an alert dialog box appears **A**. (An equivalent panel appears if you attempt to close a document with unsaved changes.) For each document, click one of these buttons:

   ▸ **Don't Save.** Discards the document's changes.

   ▸ **Cancel.** Aborts the exit and lets you continue working on the document.

   ▸ **Save.** If the document exists on disk, the current copy overwrites the original. If the document has never been saved, a Save As panel appears **B**. Name the document, select a location in which to save it, specify a format, and click the Save button.

   When all open documents have been handled, the program ends.

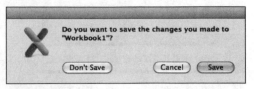

A If you attempt to quit an Office application while documents with unsaved changes are open, this dialog box appears for each such document.

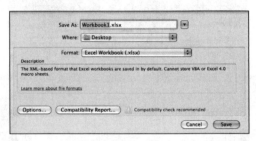

B The Save As panel (Excel shown).

3

Working with Graphics

Although many documents consist solely of pages of text or numbers, you can make your Office documents more informative and attractive by adding artwork, such as photos, clip art, movies, and WordArt.

In this chapter, you'll learn how to insert these items into your documents; embellish artwork by adding color, filters, 3-D effects, and rotation; and specify how surrounding text will wrap around them. You'll also learn how to use Office 2011's image-editing tools to correct photos.

See the following chapters for information on working with these types of objects:

- Tables (Chapters 7 and 18)
- Charts (Chapters 14 and 18)
- Text boxes (Chapter 17)
- SmartArt graphics (Chapter 17)

Instructions for adding clip art and photos to PowerPoint placeholders can be found in Chapter 17.

In This Chapter

About Adding Images and Objects

By choosing commands from the Insert menu or the Home:Insert group, you can add many types of images and objects to Office documents. There are also features that help you create your own graphics, such as WordArt, SmartArt, and common shapes.

An image can be placed inline with text or as a floating object that text wraps around. Images can be loaded from disk, copied from open documents in other programs, or dragged directly into your document from an open document in any drag-and-drop enabled program.

TIP In Internet Explorer, many images are also clickable links. If you attempt to place such an image in your document via drag and drop, the link may appear rather than the image. You can, however, use copy and paste to add such images to your documents.

Office 2011 provides its own tools for modifying and embellishing graphics. For instance, you can do the following:

- Crop an image, removing unwanted parts
- Change an image's brightness or contrast
- Recolor a picture by adding a color cast
- Add a border/frame in any combination of color, line width, and line style **A**
- Apply special effects, such as bevel, glow, 3-D rotation, and shadow or artistic filters, such as Marker, Texturizer, or Photocopy **B**
- Set text-wrap instructions for the image

Office 2011's image-editing tools are discussed at the end of this chapter. See Chapter 17 for information about adding objects to PowerPoint placeholders.

A A placed photo can be surrounded by a decorative frame.

B The same photo after applying the Photocopy filter.

A Select a photo or picture, and click Insert.

B The image in a Word document.

C Select the iPhoto image that you want to use in your document.

Inserting Photos and Pictures

You can insert almost any photo or picture into a Word, PowerPoint, or Excel document.

To insert a picture stored on disk:

1. Do one of the following:
   - **Word or PowerPoint.** Choose Home : Insert : Picture : Picture from File.
   - **Word, PowerPoint, or Excel.** Choose Insert > Photo > Picture from File.

   The Choose a Picture dialog box appears **A**.

2. Navigate to the drive and folder that contains the picture, select the picture, and click the Insert button

   The picture appears in the document **B**.

To insert a photo from iPhoto:

1. Do one of the following:
   - **Word or PowerPoint.** Choose Home : Insert : Picture : Photo Browser.
   - **Word, PowerPoint, or Excel.** Choose Insert > Photo > Photo Browser.
   - **Word, PowerPoint, or Excel.** Open the Media Browser by choosing View > Media Browser or clicking the Media Browser icon on the Standard toolbar. Select the Photos tab.

   The iPhoto library appears **C**.

2. *Optional:* To view a subclass of clip art, select a category from the drop-down menu (PowerPoint) **C** or the scrolling list (Word and Excel).

   continues on next page

3. When you see the desired image, drag it into a placeholder or empty area on a slide (PowerPoint) or onto the document page (Word and Excel).

TIP When inserting a Picture from File, the Link to File check box **A** determines whether a copy of the image is *embedded* in the document (unchecked) or the image is *linked* to the file on your hard disk (checked). Use the former when a document will be shared with others. Use the latter when the image file will be available on your computer's hard drive.

TIP You can click and drag a handle on any corner or edge of a placed picture to change its size. Drag a corner handle to resize the image proportionately **D**.

TIP You can also insert a picture via copy and paste. Open the picture or the document in which it's embedded, select the picture, and choose Edit > Copy (Command-C). Switch to the Office document, set the text insertion mark, and click Paste on the Standard toolbar or press Command-V.

TIP You can add a descriptive caption to a photo or picture by right-clicking the image and choosing Insert Caption from the contextual menu that appears **E**.

Dimensions

D As you drag to resize a photo, a ScreenTip displays the new dimensions.

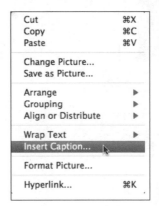

E You can optionally label a picture with a caption.

Categories

Media

Photos Audio Movies Clip Art Symbols Shapes

All Images

338 items

Thumbnail size

A The Clip Art tab of the Media Browser.

Rotation handle

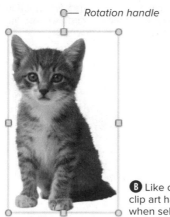

B Like other objects, clip art has handles when selected.

Adding Clip Art

Clip art images are drawings and pictures that you can use to embellish flyers, memos, brochures, party invitations, and the like. Office 2011 includes a healthy selection of clip art that you can insert from the Media Browser or the Clip Gallery. In addition to the installed clip art, you can download other images from the Microsoft Office site.

To insert clip art from the Media Browser:

1. Do one of the following:
   - **Word or PowerPoint.** Choose Home: Insert:Picture:Clip Art Browser.
   - **Word, PowerPoint, or Excel.** Choose Insert > Clip Art > Clip Art Browser.
   - **Word, PowerPoint, or Excel.** Open the Media Browser by choosing View > Media Browser or clicking the Media Browser icon on the Standard toolbar. Select the Clip Art tab.

   The Clip Art library appears **A**.

2. *Optional:* To view a particular type of clip art, select a category from the drop-down menu.

3. When you see the desired image, drag it into a placeholder (PowerPoint) or onto the document page (Word and Excel) **B**.

To insert clip art from the Clip Gallery:

1. Do one of the following:

   ▸ **Word or PowerPoint.** Choose Home: Insert:Picture:Clip Art Gallery.

   ▸ **Word, PowerPoint, or Excel.** Choose Insert > Clip Art > Clip Art Gallery.

   The Microsoft Clip Gallery application launches **C**.

2. Select an image category from the list on the left.

3. *Optional:* To find a particular image or type of image, type a search string in the Search box and click Search.

4. *Optional:* To view larger versions of the images, select an image and click the Preview check box.

5. To insert an image into the document, do one of the following:

   ▸ Select the image and click Insert.

   ▸ Double-click the image thumbnail.

   ▸ Drag the image onto the document.

6. To dismiss the Clip Gallery, do one of the following:

   ▸ Click the Close button.

   ▸ Click the window's close box (X).

   ▸ Choose Clip Gallery > Quit Clip Gallery (Command-Q).

TIP To learn more about a selected image (such as its size or file type) **D**, click the Properties button **C**.

TIP To view downloadable clip art from Microsoft's site, click the Online button **C**. To add your own images to the Clip Gallery, click the Import button.

Categories   *Search for images*

Download images

C Select an image and click the Insert button.

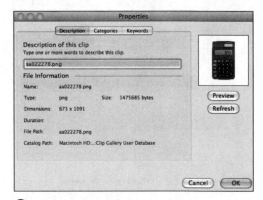

D In addition to checking an image's file type and size, you can use the Properties window to assign it to other categories and add keywords.

Categories

Thumbnail size

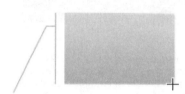

Ⓐ Shapes from the Media Browser can be inserted using drag and drop or by drawing.

Width: 1.75"
Height: 1.13"

Ⓑ When inserting a shape by drawing, a ScreenTip shows the shape's current dimensions.

Drawing Shapes and Lines

Office includes a variety of predefined shapes (such as cubes, arrows, cartoon balloons, and flowchart elements) that you can insert into documents. A shape can optionally be assigned a color, shadow, and 3-D effects, and you can insert text into many shapes.

To insert a shape or line from the Media Browser:

1. Do one of the following:
   - ▸ Choose Insert > Shape to open the Media Browser to the Shapes tab.
   - ▸ Open the Media Browser by choosing View > Media Browser or clicking the Media Browser icon on the Standard toolbar. Select the Shapes tab **Ⓐ**.

2. Select a shape category from the drop-down list, and then select the shape.

3. Do one of the following:
   - ▸ To insert the shape at its default size and dimensions, drag the shape onto the document.
   - ▸ Using the drawing cursor (**+**), click and drag in the document to create the shape **Ⓑ**. To draw a uniform shape (a circle or square rather than an ellipse or rectangle, for example), press Shift as you draw.

4. Release the mouse button to complete the shape.

To insert a shape or line from the Shape submenus:

1. In Word or PowerPoint, choose a shape or line from the Home : Insert : Shape submenus **C**.

2. Using the drawing cursor (**+**), click and drag in the document to create the shape.

   To draw a uniform shape (a circle or square rather than an ellipse or rectangle, for example), press Shift as you draw.

3. Release the mouse button to complete the shape **D**.

To edit and format a shape or line:

1. You can change the shape's size or rotation by dragging its handles **D**.

2. Format the shape by doing any of the following:

   ▸ **Apply a style.** Choose a new style **E** from the Format : Shape Styles gallery.

   ▸ **Apply a fill.** Choose a solid fill color from the Format : Shape Styles : Fill palette. To apply a texture, gradient, or pattern fill, choose Format > Shape.

   ▸ **Specify an outline.** Choose settings from the Format : Shape Styles : Line and/or Effects menus **E**.

   ▸ **Add transparency.** Drag the Transparency slider **E** to apply transparency.

   ▸ **Apply a complex style.** Open the Format Shape dialog box by choosing Format > Shape. You can apply a variety of color, line, size, rotation, and special effects to the shape.

> **TIP** Text can be added to most shapes. Some require only that you click in them and type. Right-click other shapes, and choose Add Text or Edit Text from the contextual menu. You can apply character and paragraph formatting to the text.

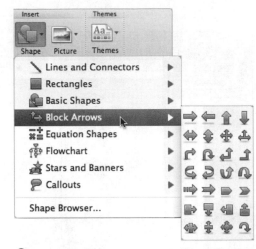

C In Word or PowerPoint, shapes can be chosen from the Shape submenus.

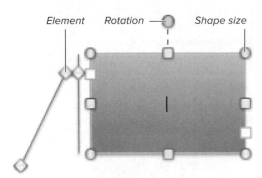

D A completed shape has colored handles that you can drag to change the shape's size (white), rotation (green), and angle or length of certain elements (yellow).

E The Shape Styles group on the Format contextual tab contains formatting controls that you can apply to change a shape's appearance.

Show all movies

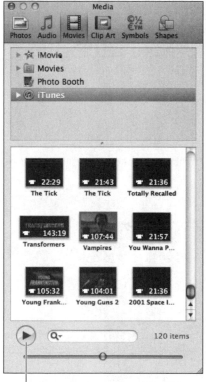

A Select a movie clip and click Choose.

B You can select a clip from iMovie, iTunes, or another movie application.

Play selected clip

Inserting Movies

In addition to photos, clip art, and shapes, you can insert movie clips into Word, Excel, and PowerPoint documents. Movies can be added that are stored in iMovie or elsewhere on your hard disk.

To insert a movie stored on disk:

1. Choose Insert > Movie > Movie from File.

   The Insert Movie or Audio dialog box appears **A**.

2. Navigate to the drive and folder that contains the movie, select its file, and click Choose.

   A black box representing the clip appears in the document.

TIP To view all movie clips on your hard disk, select Search For: All Movies in the dialog box's navigation pane **A**.

To insert a movie from iMovie or iTunes:

1. Do one of the following:

   ▶ Choose Insert > Movie > Movie Browser.

   ▶ Open the Media Browser by choosing View > Media Browser or clicking the Media Browser icon on the Standard toolbar. Select the Movies tab.

2. Select iMovie or iTunes in the top part of the Media Browser window **B**.

   All movie clips stored in the selected program are displayed in the bottom part of the window.

3. Drag the movie clip from the Media Browser onto the document page.

continues on next page

TIP When placed on a document page, movie clips may be smaller or larger than you'd like them to be. To resize the clip, select it and drag any corner handle. Doing so ensures that it will be resized proportionately.

TIP Double-click any movie clip to play it from the beginning. As it plays, a control bar appears beneath the clip window **C** (page bottom), enabling you to pause playback, go forward or backward, and adjust the volume.

TIP You can also place *audio clips* (such as songs and narratives) on document pages **D**. Like movie clips, audio clips can be selected from the Media Browser or from files stored elsewhere on your hard disk. Follow the directions for inserting a movie. Select a clip from the Audio tab of the Media Browser or from your hard disk (Insert > Audio > Audio from File). To play an audio file from the beginning, double-click its icon on the document page. Like movie clips, a playing or paused audio clip displays the same control bar and playback options.

TIP You can move a movie or audio clip to a new location by selecting and then dragging its window or icon, respectively. You can also use cut and paste to move clips between pages, documents, or Office applications.

D This tiny speaker represents an audio clip icon. Double-click it to play the audio file it represents.

Creating Artistic Text

While WordArt (described on the next page) is used to create stand-alone text objects, you can apply *text effects* to selected text to create similar effects within a Word or PowerPoint text string or paragraph.

1. Select the text within the string or paragraph that you want to format.

2. Select an effect from the Home:Font: Text Effects gallery.

Steve is a NICE guy.

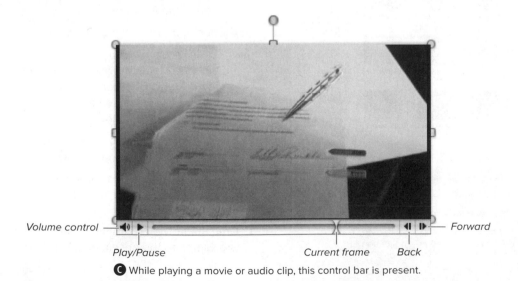

Volume control — Play/Pause — Current frame — Back — Forward

C While playing a movie or audio clip, this control bar is present.

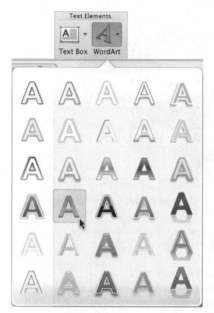

B Replace the placeholder text with your text.

C An example of WordArt (rotated).

Creating WordArt

WordArt is a decorative text object that you create by applying a special effect to text and optionally stylizing it using object-formatting commands. Although WordArt is too flashy for many business and school documents, it's great for flyers, party invitations, brochures, and PowerPoint slide text.

To create WordArt:

1. *Optional (Word and PowerPoint):* Select the text that you want to convert to WordArt.

   WordArt can be created from existing text or typed in the WordArt placeholder.

2. Do one of the following:

   ▸ **Word.** Click the Document Elements : Text Elements : WordArt icon and select a WordArt style **A**.

   ▸ **PowerPoint.** Choose Home : Insert Text > WordArt.

   ▸ **Word, PowerPoint, Excel.** Choose Insert > WordArt.

   A placeholder appears **B** or the selected text is converted to WordArt.

3. If the WordArt text box contains a placeholder (**Your Text Here**), replace it with your text by typing or pasting.

4. Using commands on the Home tab and the Formatting toolbar, set the font, size, style, and alignment for the WordArt. Additional formatting options can be selected from the Format : Text Styles group.

5. Resize the WordArt bounding box, if desired.

6. If necessary, reposition the WordArt by dragging it to a new location **C**.

Resizing, Moving, and Rotating Objects

Using the handles that surround any selected object, you can manually resize, move, or rotate the object.

To change an object's size:

1. Select the object.

   Handles appear around the object **Ⓐ**.

2. Do either of the following:

   ▸ To change only an object's height or width, drag an edge handle. Resizing an object in this manner does *not* maintain its original proportions.

   ▸ To proportionately change both the object's height and width, hold down Shift while dragging a corner handle.

TIP To proportionately resize artwork, such as a photo or clip art, it isn't necessary to hold down Shift as you drag a corner handle.

To move an object:

1. Select the object.

2. Move the cursor over the object until a cursor with arrowheads appears:

   ▸ In drawn objects, photos, and clip art, click anywhere inside the object and drag.

   ▸ In a text box, drag any edge of the box.

   ▸ In a table, drag the plus symbol that appears in the upper-left corner **Ⓑ**.

3. Release the mouse button when the object is in the desired position.

TIP In Word, you can choose a command from the Format Picture : Arrange : Position menu to position an object relative to the surrounding text.

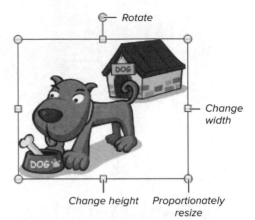

Rotate

Change width

Change height   *Proportionately resize*

Ⓐ Every selected object is surrounded by handles.

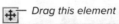

Drag this element

Name	Animal	Age
Rex	Dog	5
Fluffy	Cat	1
Tantor	Elephant	12

Ⓑ To change a selected table's position, drag here.

That Little Yellow Dot

When you select an inserted shape, you may see a tiny yellow dot around the outside of or within the shape. You can click and drag the dot to modify a property of the shape. For example, when you drag the dot in a cartoon balloon callout, you can change the direction and length of the balloon's handle.

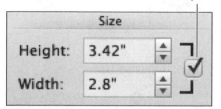

Lock Aspect Ratio

C You can also change the size of a selected object by entering dimensions in these text boxes.

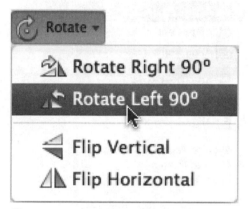

D You can rotate or reverse an object by choosing a command from the Rotate menu.

To rotate an object:

1. Select the object.

   Handles appear around the object.

2. To rotate the object, click the green rotate handle **A**, and drag left or right to the desired angle.

TIP Some objects, such as tables, cannot be rotated.

TIP You can also change the size or angle of an object by specifying exact amounts. To change an object's size, type a number or click an arrow in the Height or Width box in the Format Picture:Size group **C**. To change the angle, rotate the object in 90-degree increments by choosing a command from the Format Picture:Arrange:Rotate menu **D**.

TIP Dimensions entered in the Size group boxes **C** resize only the selected dimension or proportionately resize the object, depending on the state of the Lock Aspect Ratio check box. When checked, the object can only be resized proportionately.

Aligning and Distributing Objects

Office provides many commands that help you quickly align objects to one another and to evenly distribute the space between them. You can align shapes, WordArt, text boxes, and movie frames. Photos, clip art, and tables can't be aligned.

To align objects to one another:

1. In Word or PowerPoint, select two or more qualified objects that you want to align 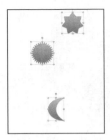.

   Click to select the first object, and Shift-click each of the others.

2. Choose an Align to command from the Format:Arrange:Align menu **B**.

   The command specifies to what the selected objects will be aligned: page edges, page margins, or each other (Word); or slide edges or each other (PowerPoint).

3. Choose an alignment command from the Format:Arrange:Align menu **B**.

   The selected objects are aligned as directed **C**.

To evenly space selected objects:

1. Select the objects that you want to evenly space.

2. Choose a Distribute command from the Format:Arrange:Align menu **B**.

   The space between objects is evenly distributed **C**.

> **TIP** PowerPoint provides two other ways to issue alignment commands. Choose from the Format:Arrange:Align menu or the Home: Format:Arrange > Align or Distribute submenu.

A Three shapes selected on a Word page.

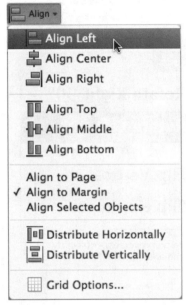

B Look at the icons to help choose the correct Align command.

C The objects' left edges are aligned to one another along the margin (left), and the space between objects (within the current margins) is vertically distributed (right).

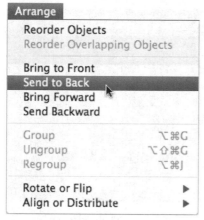

A Choose one of the commands in the center section to reorder an object in relation to others on the page.

B PowerPoint users have the added convenience of choosing a command from a standard menu.

Object Layers and Dynamic Ordering

Objects can be *layered* in Office documents. For example, you might add a callout shape that partially overlaps an Excel chart to draw attention to an important figure. Each object on a page is placed in its own layer. In addition to using the Bring Forward and Send Backward commands to change the layering of a single object, you can use the new *dynamic ordering* feature to simplify the process of working with layers. Dynamic ordering is supported in Power-Point and Word's Publishing Layout View.

To change a single object's layer:

1. Select the object whose layer you wish to change.

2. Do one of the following:

   ▸ In PowerPoint, choose a Bring or Send command from the Home : Format : Arrange, Format : Arrange : Reorder **A** or Arrange menu **B**.

   ▸ In Word, choose a Bring or Send command from the Format : Arrange : Reorder menu.

3. If moving the object one layer at a time, repeat the command, if necessary.

TIP In Word, the Reorder menu **A** has commands for reordering an object in relation to text on the page.

To reorder objects using dynamic ordering (Word and PowerPoint):

1. To reorder all objects on the page, do the following:

   ▸ **PowerPoint.** Choose Home:Format: Arrange > Reorder Objects or Arrange > Reorder Objects.

   ▸ **Word (Publishing Layout View only).** Choose Home:Arrange:Reorder > Reorder Objects.

   To reorder only particular overlapping objects on the page, select the objects and do the following:

   ▸ **PowerPoint.** Choose Home:Format: Arrange > Reorder Overlapping Objects, Format:Arrange:Reorder > Reorder Overlapping Objects, or Arrange > Reorder Overlapping Objects.

   ▸ **Word (Publishing Layout View).** Choose Format:Arrange:Reorder > Reorder Overlapping Objects.

   The dynamic ordering screen appears **C**. Object layers from highest to lowest are shown from right to left. If you move the cursor over a layer, its layer number is displayed **D**.

2. To change the layering order, drag any layer to the right to raise it to a higher level or to the left to decrease its level.

   Objects in higher layers will obscure any objects in lower layers that they overlap.

3. When you're done modifying the layering, click OK to accept the changes or Cancel to ignore the changes **C**.

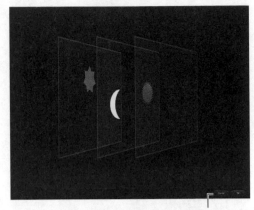

Cancel and OK buttons

C When the dynamic ordering screen appears, each object is shown in its respective layer.

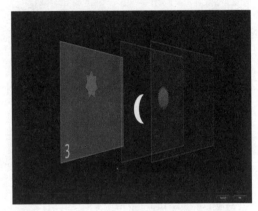

D To simplify the process of identifying and moving layers, the active layer is numbered.

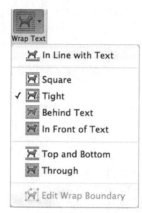

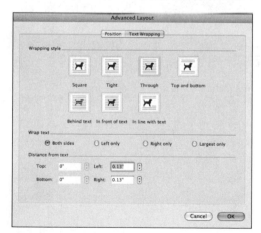

A Choose a wrap option from the Wrap Text menu.

Upgrading the Operating System

Every few years, Microsoft releases a major upgrade of the system software. In the past dozen years, we've gone from Windows 95 to Windows 7. Each version has promised new capabilities, improved speed, fewer

See a penny, pick it up, and all the day you'll have one cent.
—*Steve Schwartz, 1963*

B Specifying a text wrap setting for the quote in the text box allows surrounding text to wrap around.

C You can enter more precise wrap settings in the Advanced Layout dialog box, such as whether text will wrap only on one side and the distance of the text from the object.

Setting Text Wrap

Whether you're placing photos, charts, clip art, WordArt, SmartArt, text boxes, tables, or another object type on document pages, each object in a Word document must have a *text wrap* setting. This setting determines how surrounding text interacts with the object: whether it wraps around the object or enables the object to be placed beneath or on top of the text.

To set text wrap for an object:

1. Select the object.
2. Choose an option from the Format: Arrange:Wrap Text menu **A**.
3. Drag the object into position.

   The surrounding text wraps around the object as specified **B**.

TIP You also use the Wrap Text menu to convert an object from inline to floating or vice versa. To convert a floating object to an inline object, choose In Line with Text. To convert an inline object to a floating object, choose any command other than In Line with Text.

TIP Specific position settings can be set in the Format dialog box. To open the dialog box, select the object and choose Format > *object type*. Select the Layout tab and click the Advanced button. Enter new settings on the Text Wrapping tab of the Advanced Layout dialog box **C** and click OK. Click OK again to close the Format dialog box.

TIP You can add a watermark or stamp to a page, such as Confidential or Not for Distribution. Create a text box with large type (72 pt., for instance), set the text color to a light gray, and then choose Behind Text as the Wrap Text setting.

Image Editing

With Office 2011, you may find that it's no longer necessary to have a separate image-editing program to clean up, crop, or otherwise modify photos that you want to include in documents. Whenever you select an inserted photo, the Format Picture tab appears **Ⓐ**, providing a host of image-editing tools and enhancement options.

As you'll learn in this section, you can do the following with any photo placed in a Word, PowerPoint, or Excel document:

- Adjust the brightness, contrast, and sharpness
- Alter the color saturation or tone
- Apply artistic effects
- Apple style settings, such as a frame or border
- Crop an image to remove distracting elements or reform it to match a shape, such as a heart
- Remove the background, leaving only the photo's main subject

- Compress pictures to reduce the document's size
- Replace one picture with another
- Revert to the original photo, discarding all formatting changes

Note that edits only affect the way an image looks on the document page. The original photo on disk remains unchanged. To make permanent edits and corrections to a photo, consider using a dedicated image-editing program, such as Adobe Photoshop. Alternatively, you can right-click the image in your Office document, choose Save as Picture from the contextual menu that appears, and save the edited photo. You can overwrite the original file or save it with a new name, location, and/or file format.

TIP When experimenting with effects in a gallery, you can frequently restore the image to its previous state by selecting the first effect (labeled "None"). You can remove *all* applied edits at any time by clicking Format Picture : Adjust : Reset.

Ⓐ When a photo on a document page is selected, the Format Picture contextual tab appears.

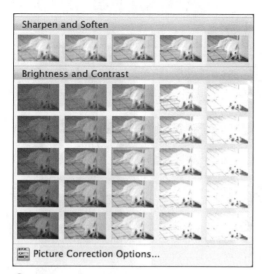

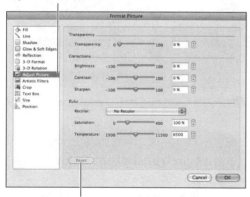

B Click a thumbnail to apply a new sharpness or brightness and contrast setting.

Adjust Picture section

Discard changes

C One advantage of using the Format Picture dialog box is that you can adjust brightness and contrast independently.

Adjusting brightness, contrast, and sharpness

Because of poor lighting conditions or inappropriate use of flash, it's not unusual for a photo to be too dark or bright, muddy looking (when shot with a Web cam, for instance), or soft (common with scanned photos). Depending on the degree of the problem, you may be able to salvage the photo by adjusting the brightness, contrast, and/or sharpness.

To adjust the brightness, contrast, or sharpness:

1. Select the inserted photo in the Word, Excel, or PowerPoint document.

   The Format Picture contextual tab appears **A**.

2. Click to select the tab.

3. Click the Format Picture:Adjust: Corrections icon.

   The Corrections gallery **B** shows brightness/contrast combinations and sharpness settings that you can apply.

4. Do either of the following:

   ▶ Click a thumbnail to apply its setting.

   ▶ For more precise corrections, choose Picture Correction Options. Use controls in the Adjust Picture section of the Format Picture dialog box **C** to adjust the Brightness, Contrast, and Sharpen settings.

5. Click OK when you're done making changes.

TIP When experimenting in the Adjust Picture section of the Format Picture dialog box, you can discard your changes by clicking the Reset button **C**.

TIP You can make changes in multiple sections of the Format Picture dialog box before clicking OK.

Setting color saturation and tone

You can also adjust the overall color saturation (density) and the color tone (temperature). Using these tools, you can brighten up a washed-out or faded shot, change a photo's mood, or create a *duotone* (a two-color picture), for example.

To change the color saturation or tone:

1. Select the inserted photo in the Word, Excel, or PowerPoint document.

   The Format Picture contextual tab appears Ⓐ.

2. Click to select the tab.

3. Click the Format Picture:Adjust:Recolor icon.

   A drop-down gallery appears Ⓓ.

4. Do any of the following:

   ▸ Click a thumbnail to apply its setting.

   ▸ To create a duotone from the photo, click an icon in the Recolor section of the gallery. To use a different recoloring shade, choose More Colors.

   ▸ For more precise corrections, choose Picture Color Options. Use controls in the Adjust Picture section of the Format Picture dialog box Ⓒ to adjust the Saturation and Temperature. Click OK when you're done making changes.

TIP To change a color photo into a black-and-white image, select the Grayscale thumbnail in the Recolor section Ⓔ. Select Sepia or an orange/tan color to create a traditional duotone image.

TIP The Black and White: 50% Recolor option provides an effect similar to Kodalith film: black and white only; no gray shades.

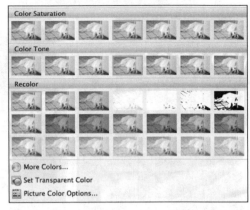

Ⓓ Select settings from the Recolor gallery to change a photo's color saturation or tone.

Grayscale   Sepia

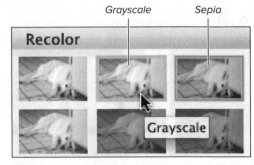

Ⓔ Grayscale and Sepia are common recoloring choices.

Setting a Transparent Color

For some images, it can be useful to set a transparent color. Areas that match the selected color will allow objects, photos, and text beneath the photo to show through. Choose Set Transparent Color from the Recolor gallery menu Ⓓ. Use the eyedropper tool to select the color in the photo that will be treated as transparent.

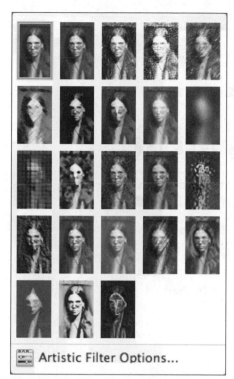

F Select an artistic filter from the gallery.

G An example of the Photocopy filter.

Applying artistic filters

Occasionally, you may want to transform a photo into something artistic or funky. Office 2011 has almost two dozen artistic filters that you can apply to photos, such as Marker, Light Screen, and Glow Edges.

To apply artistic filters:

1. Select the inserted photo in the Word, Excel, or PowerPoint document.

   The Format Picture contextual tab appears **A**.

2. Click to select the tab.

3. Click the Format Picture : Adjust : Filters icon.

   A drop-down gallery appears **F**. If you hover the cursor over a filter, its name is displayed in a ScreenTip.

4. Click a thumbnail to apply its filter to the selected photo **G**.

TIP Choosing Artistic Filter Options from the Filters menu **F** enables you to fine-tune most filters' settings. As you experiment with filters and settings, the result of each change is shown on the image—giving it a decided advantage over choosing effects from the Filters gallery.

TIP Another way to open the Format Picture dialog box is to right-click the photo and choose Format Picture from the contextual menu that appears.

Adding a border or frame

When you insert a photo into a document, it has no frame or border. While this is fine—typical, in fact—for photos inserted into email messages, photos in other Office documents often look better with a border.

To add a border or frame to a photo:

1. Select the inserted photo in the Word, Excel, or PowerPoint document.

   The Format Picture contextual tab appears **A**.

2. Click to select the tab.

3. In the Picture Styles group, do one of the following:

   ▸ To apply a solid or dashed border to the photo, click the Border icon and choose options from the drop-down menu **H**. Revisit the menu for each additional line option you wish to apply.

   ▸ Choose a decorative frame from the Picture Styles gallery **I**.

   ▸ Choose a more esoteric frame (such as a 3-D or reflection frame) from the Effects submenus.

TIP Advanced line style settings can be specified in the Line sections of the Format Picture dialog box. Choose Line Effects from the Border menu **H** to open the dialog box.

TIP You can remove a previously added line border by choosing No Line from the Border menu **H**.

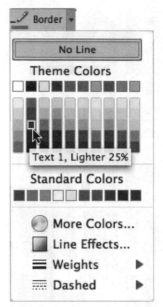

H You can choose a line color, weight, and style from the Border menu.

I Selecting Metal Frame as the Picture Style gives any two-dimensional photo a 3-D look.

J Cropping handles appear at all corners and sides of the photo.

K Drag one or more handles to show the area of the photo that you want to keep. Gray areas will be discarded.

L Only the cropped portion of the photo is retained.

Cropping photos

As framed in a camera, shots often contain extraneous material that you may wish to eliminate by judiciously *cropping* the photo. Office's image-editing tools enable you to crop manually or conform to a shape.

To crop a photo manually:

1. Select the inserted photo in the Word, Excel, or PowerPoint document.

   The Format Picture contextual tab appears **A**.

2. Click to select the tab.

3. Click the Format Picture:Adjust:Crop icon or choose Crop from its menu.

   Cropping handles appear around the picture **J**. The photo's current height and width are shown in the Size group. When the cursor is over a crop handle, its shape changes to match the handle.

4. Drag handles to remove the unwanted portions of the picture. As you drag, the dimensions of the cropped image are shown in a ScreenTip.

   The area to be removed is shown in gray **K**.

5. To complete the process **L**, click anywhere else on the page or press Esc.

TIP To crop proportionately from one corner, Shift-drag the corner handle. To crop equally from two edges, Option-drag an edge handle. To crop equally from all edges, Option-drag any corner handle.

TIP While cropping, you can also drag the image around while retaining the current crop dimensions. Click in the gray area and drag.

TIP After cropping, you can click Format Picture:Adjust:Compress to reduce the photo's size by discarding the cropped-out portions (see "Compressing pictures").

To crop to match a shape:

1. Select the inserted photo in the Word, Excel, or PowerPoint document.

   The Format Picture contextual tab appears **Ⓐ**.

2. Click to select the tab.

3. Choose a shape from a Format Picture: Adjust:Crop:Mask to Shape submenu **Ⓜ**.

   The photo is cropped to match the chosen shape.

4. *Optional:* To make additional adjustments, such as changing the part of the picture within the shape or the shape's angle, choose Crop to Fill or Crop to Fit. Drag the image and/or the cropping handles to make the adjustments.

5. To complete the process **Ⓝ**, click anywhere else on the document page or press Esc.

Ⓜ Choose a shape from one of the submenus.

Ⓝ A photo cropped to the shape of a diamond.

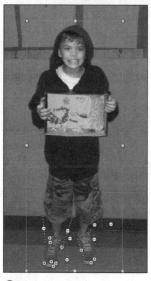

O The subject is displayed normally, while the material to be eliminated is shaded purple.

P After resizing the selection rectangle and adding points, only the subject is visible.

Q With a clearly defined subject and an uncluttered background, results can be exceptional.

Removing the background

You can use the Remove Background command to isolate part of a photo, removing all material around it. The command's effect is similar to *masking* in Photoshop.

To remove the background:

1. Select the inserted photo in the Word, Excel, or PowerPoint document.

   The Format Picture contextual tab appears **A**.

2. Click to select the tab.

3. Click the Format Picture : Adjust : Remove Background icon.

   Office guesses the photo's subject by coloring extraneous material purple **O**.

4. *Optional:* Adjust the selection marquee by dragging its handles to include less or more material.

5. If necessary, adjust the selected material by doing any of the following **P**:

   ▸ To expand the selection, click or draw in the background with the plus (**+**) cursor to denote the new areas.

   ▸ If extraneous material is selected, click or draw in the foreground with the minus (**–**) cursor to mark areas to be eliminated from the selection.

   ▸ If a point doesn't have the desired effect, click it with the delete cursor (**X**) to remove it.

6. Do one of the following:

   ▸ To complete the background removal, press Return or click anywhere outside of the photo **O**.

   ▸ To abort the process, press Esc.

TIP When adding and removing areas to keep, increasing the magnification can help.

Compressing pictures

Given the high-megapixel cameras now being sold, photos can take up considerable space in documents and presentations. Using the Compress command, you can reduce the resolution of individual photos or all photos in an Office document, shrinking the document's size.

To compress one or more pictures:

1. Select the placed photo(s) that you want to compress. (If you want to compress *all* photos in the document, it doesn't matter which photo you select.)

   The Format Picture contextual tab appears **A**.

2. Click to select the tab.

3. Click the Format Picture : Adjust : Compress icon **R**.

   The Reduce File Size dialog box appears **S**.

4. Set the following options:

   ▸ **Picture Quality.** This resolution setting determines the amount of compression to be applied to the photo(s).

   ▸ **Remove cropped picture regions.** If the selected photo(s) have been cropped, set this option to delete the cropped areas. (Cropping does not delete the cropped-out areas. It merely hides them.)

   ▸ **Apply to.** Click a radio button to compress all photos in the document or only the selected photo(s).

5. Click OK to perform the compression.

   If the results are satisfactory, save the document. If not, click the Undo icon in the Standard toolbar or press Command-Z.

Compress

Reset

R The Compress and Reset commands can be found in the Format Picture : Adjust group.

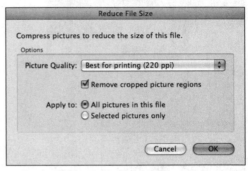

S The Reduce File Size dialog box

T Navigate to the appropriate drive and folder, and select a replacement photo.

Replacing one photo with another

You can use the Change Picture command to replace a selected photo with a different one while retaining the size and some options applied to the selected photo, such as an added border.

To replace a photo:

1. Select the inserted photo in the Word, Excel, or PowerPoint document.

   The Format Picture contextual tab appears **A**.

2. Click to select the tab.

3. Right-click the photo and choose Change Picture from the contextual menu that appears.

   The Choose a Picture dialog box appears **T**.

4. Select a replacement photo and click Insert.

   The new photo replaces the original in the document.

Resetting edits

If you've been experimenting with formatting options for an inserted photo, you can restore the original image using the Reset command.

To reset all edits for an image:

1. Select the inserted photo in the Word, Excel, or PowerPoint document.

   The Format Picture contextual tab appears Ⓐ.

2. Click to select the tab.

3. Click the Format Picture:Adjust:Reset icon Ⓡ.

   All edits are removed from the photo.

TIP You can undo a reset by choosing **Edit > Undo Reset Picture**, clicking the Undo icon on the Standard toolbar, or pressing **Command-Z**.

Introducing Word 2011

Expanding on the material in Chapter 2, this chapter covers additional elementary features that are specific to Word. While you can get along fine without mastering the material in this chapter, a familiarity with it will make your Word experience more productive.

Other chapters in Part II: Microsoft Word explain document and text formatting; designing tables; working in other views to create outlines, notebooks, and publications; and employing more advanced features to create documents for business and school.

In This Chapter

The Word Interface

If this is the first time you've used Word, begin by familiarizing yourself with the Word window and its components **Ⓐ**. They'll be referred to throughout Part II of this book.

Menu bar
Text insertion mark
Standard toolbar
Formatting toolbar
Ruler
Search box
Ribbon

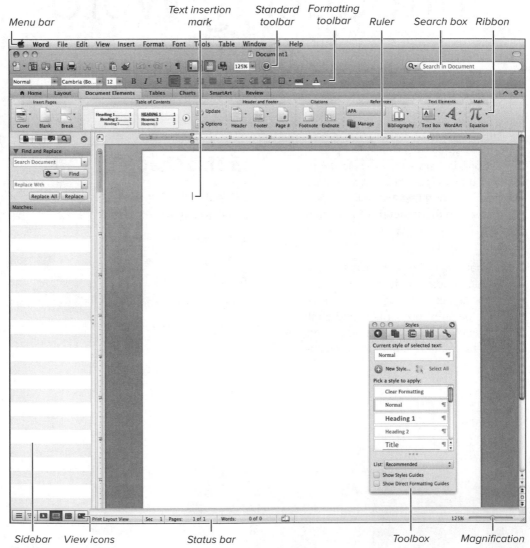

Sidebar   View icons   Status bar   Toolbox   Magnification

Ⓐ A Word 2011 document window.

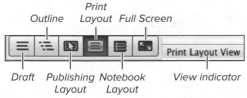

Outline   Print Layout   Full Screen

Print Layout View

Draft   Publishing Layout   Notebook Layout   View indicator

B You can switch to most views by clicking an icon at the bottom of the document window.

View

Draft
Web Layout
Outline
✓ Print Layout
Notebook Layout
Publishing Layout
Full Screen

C You can also change views by choosing a command from the top part of the View menu.

Changing views

Different views enable you to work with or view a document in different ways. You can pick from Draft, Web Layout, Outline, Print Layout, Notebook Layout, Publishing Layout, and Full Screen views (see **Table 4.1**).

To change views:

Do one of the following:

- Click an icon in the bottom-left corner of the document window **B**.

- Choose a view from the View menu **C**.

TIP Web Layout view is only accessible from the View menu.

TIP To use "click and type" (discussed later in this chapter), you must be in Print Layout, Web Layout, or Notebook Layout view.

TABLE 4.1 Word Document Views

View	Purpose
Draft	Shows text formatting in a simplified page layout that lends itself well to most standard writing tasks
Outline	Shows the document's structure and allows you to rearrange text by dragging headings
Print Layout	Shows the document as it will look when printed, including the page borders, margins, headers and footers, columns, and frames that contain images
Web Layout	Shows the document as it would appear in a Web browser
Notebook Layout	Used to quickly record notes and ideas (both in text and audio form)
Publishing Layout	Allows you to use layout tools to create complex documents, such as newsletters, brochures, and flyers
Full Screen	Dedicates the full screen to reading or editing the current Word document

Changing the magnification

Depending on the resolution setting in Displays System Preferences, what you're working on, and your eyesight, you may want to increase or decrease the magnification of the current document. Choose a new setting from the menu on the Standard toolbar 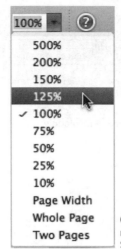, drag the slider at the bottom of the document window **Ⓐ**, or choose View > Zoom **Ⓔ**.

Showing/hiding toolbars

As is the case in all Office 2011 applications, you can show or hide individual toolbars whenever you like by choosing the toolbar's name from the View > Toolbars submenu. Checked toolbars are displayed; unchecked ones are hidden.

Using the Sidebar

In Office 2008, the navigation pane had Thumbnail and Document Map tabs that enabled you to quickly jump to key locations in the current document. In Office 2011, the navigation pane has been renamed the *Sidebar* and contains two new tabs to help you navigate documents: Reviewing Pane and Search Pane.

To use the Sidebar:

1. To show the Sidebar **Ⓐ**, choose a pane from the View > Sidebar submenu or the Sidebar icon on the Standard toolbar.

2. The Sidebar has four modes, determined by the selected tab above the pane **Ⓕ**:

   ▸ **Thumbnail Pane.** Displays miniature representations of document pages.

   ▸ **Document Map Pane.** Displays headings in the current document.

Ⓓ You can choose a new magnification from this Standard toolbar menu.

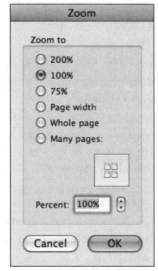

Ⓔ You can select a common magnification or set a specific one in the Zoom dialog box.

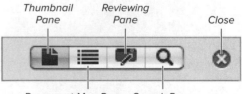

Ⓕ Click a tab to select a Sidebar component to use.

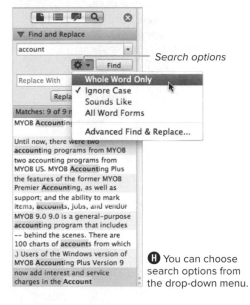

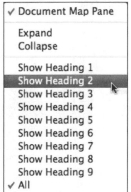

G Click the thumbnail of the page you want to view.

Search options

H You can choose search options from the drop-down menu.

I Choose a Show Heading command to specify the heading levels to be displayed.

- ▸ **Reviewing Pane.** Displays all changes made to the document when track changes is enabled.

- ▸ **Search Pane.** Search for text within a document or perform a find/replace.

3. To move to a new location in the current document, do one of the following:

- ▸ **Thumbnail Pane.** Click a page thumbnail G.

- ▸ **Document Map Pane.** Click a heading.

- ▸ **Reviewing Pane.** Double-click a change.

- ▸ **Search Pane.** Type a search string. As you type, Word lists all matches and highlights them in the document. You can restrict matches by choosing an option from the drop-down menu H. Click any match.

4. To dismiss the Sidebar, click the close icon F.

TIP To change Sidebar panes, click the tab of a different pane. You can also choose the pane from the Sidebar icon's drop-down menu on the Standard toolbar or from the View > Sidebar submenu.

TIP You can change the Sidebar's width by dragging the divider on the right side of the pane.

TIP In Document Map view, you can control the specific heading levels displayed by right-clicking in the Sidebar I. Choose a Show Heading command to display all headings at that level or higher. You can also expand and collapse heading levels as needed.

Entering Text

If you're new to computing, you'll find that entering text in a word-processing document is only a little different than using a typewriter—different but much simpler.

As in most computer programs, the blinking vertical line (called the *text insertion mark*) indicates where the next character you type will appear. Type as you would with a typewriter. The main differences include the following:

- You press Return only to begin a new paragraph—not to begin a new line in the same paragraph.

- You'll note that the lines of a paragraph are automatically adjusted to include as many words as possible. This occurs via a feature called *word wrap*. If you add or delete text in a paragraph, the entire paragraph rewraps to accommodate the changes.

- Typing a word-processing document doesn't have to be a linear process—as it must with a typewriter. For example, although you can backspace over errors by pressing Delete, you can also just *select* incorrect text and type over it. The first character you type automatically deletes the selected text.

- You can click anywhere within existing text to change the text insertion mark. Then you can insert more text at that spot, correct an error, or perform edits.

Correcting Letter Case Errors

Has this happened to you? You accidentally press Caps Lock instead of Shift and now your newly typed text reads **SUSAN JONES**. Or while entering mailing addresses, your assistant decides not to bother with capitalization.

You can fix many such errors by selecting the text and choosing a correction from the Home:Font:Change Case menu.

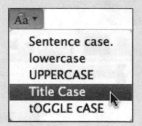

A Enable click and type in the Edit preferences.

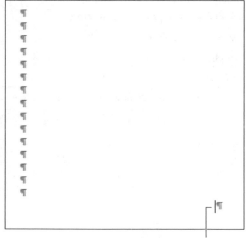

B The click and type cursor changes to show the paragraph formatting that will be applied.

Text insertion mark

C With Show all nonprinting characters enabled (as explained in the next section), you can see the blank paragraphs that Word has inserted.

Click and type

Click and type is a Word feature that you can think of as a form of automatic paragraph formatting. You can click in any blank area of your document to enter text at that spot. In a new document, for example, you could click near the right margin or halfway down the page. Click and type is available in Print Layout, Web Layout, and Notebook Layout views.

To enable and use click and type:

1. Choose Word > Preferences.

   The Word Preferences dialog box appears.

2. Click the Authoring and Proofing Tools:Edit icon to display the Edit preferences.

3. Near the bottom of the dialog box, ensure that Enable click and type is checked **A**, and click OK.

4. Switch to a view in which click and type is supported: Print Layout, Web Layout, or Notebook Layout.

5. Move the cursor to a blank spot on the page where you'd like to type.

   As you move, the cursor changes shape to reflect the type of paragraph formatting that will be applied to the text **B**. The shapes include align left, align right, center, left indent, left text wrap, and right text wrap.

6. Double-click to set the text insertion mark and begin typing.

   Word inserts the necessary blank paragraphs and tabs to fill the document to the beginning of the new text **C**.

Showing/hiding nonprinting characters

Whether you're entering, editing, or proofing text, it can be helpful to see the normally invisible, *nonprinting characters*: spaces, tabs, returns, and line breaks 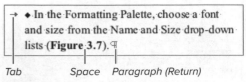. Displaying nonprinting characters is very useful when you're looking for multiple tab characters where only one should be or when you're trying to eliminate incorrect punctuation, such as blank paragraphs or extra spaces between words or sentences.

You can show or hide these characters as you work on any Word document. See Table 4.2 for a list of nonprinting characters.

To show/hide nonprinting characters:

- Click the Show all nonprinting characters icon on the Standard toolbar .

TIP The Show all nonprinting characters (¶) icon works as a toggle. Click it once to show nonprinting characters; click it again to hide them.

TIP Showing nonprinting characters is very useful in the proofing/editing stage—*after* you've finished the writing. Having these characters visible while *creating* a document, on the other hand, can be distracting.

◆ In the Formatting Palette, choose a font and size from the Name and Size drop-down lists (**Figure 3.7**). ¶

Tab   Space   Paragraph (Return)

D When displayed, nonprinting characters are a light blue.

E The Show all nonprinting characters icon is the paragraph symbol (¶).

TABLE 4.2 Nonprinting Characters

Symbol	Character
. (dot)	Space
→	Tab
↵	Line break (new line, same paragraph)
¶	End of paragraph

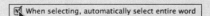
Editing: Beyond the Basics

Some basic editing techniques were discussed in Chapter 2. In this section, you'll learn to search for and replace text, use Office's AutoText feature to automatically enter text for you, and use smart buttons to speed common editing and formatting tasks.

Finding and replacing text

You can instruct Word to search for and optionally replace words or phrases. For example, if you can't remember the page on which you referred to Apple's annual report, you could perform a find on the phrase **annual report**. Or suppose your company recently changed its name from Johnson Plumbing Supplies to Widgets Inc. Using the Replace command, you can replace every instance of the old name with the new one.

There are *three* ways to conduct a search in Word 2011: using the search box at the top of the document window, performing an Advanced Find and Replace in a dialog box, or performing a find or find/replace in the Search Pane of the Sidebar. See **Table 4.3** for a list of special Find/Replace options.

TABLE 4.3 Special Find/Replace Options

Option	Description
Match case	Finds words that contain the same combination of upper- and lowercase characters
Find whole words only	Finds only complete words (for example, "art" finds only "art," not "artist")
Use wildcards	Allows you to enter a code to specify a special character combination in search strings (for example, **?** will match any single character)
Sounds like	Finds text that sounds like the search string
Find all word forms	Finds all variations of the chosen word (for example, "apple" and "apples")

To find text using the search box:

1. Click in the search box, choose Edit > Find > Find, or press Command-F.

   The cursor is positioned in the search box.

2. Type a search string **A**.

   As you type, Word highlights all matching instances in the document.

3. Scroll through the document to find the match for which you're searching or click the arrow icons to move from one match to the next.

4. To end the search, click the Clear icon.

TIP Letter case is ignored when performing a search box find and matches can be found anywhere within a word. For example, if you enter am as the search string, a match would be found in am, American, and camel.

TIP To transition to a Search Pane find or a replace, choose a command from the search box's drop-down menu **B**.

To find text using Advanced Find and Replace:

1. Choose Edit > Find > Advanced Find and Replace.

   The Find and Replace dialog box appears.

2. Type a search string in the Find what box **C**.

3. Do either of the following:

   ▶ To find the next instance of the search string, click the Find Next button.

   Word searches for the string, starting from the current text insertion mark.

   ▶ To find and highlight all matches **D**, click the Highlight all items found in check box, choose an option from its drop-down menu (such as Main Document), and click Find All.

Previous

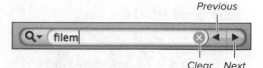

Clear   Next

A Type as many characters as necessary to correctly identify matches.

Menu

B To perform a find or find/replace in the Sidebar, choose either of these commands.

Search string

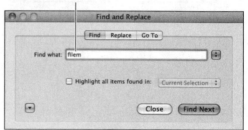

C Enter the text you want to find in the Find what box.

> • Using and Creating Databases with FileMaker Pro
> ◆ Short Description
> • Whether you want to learn how to enter data in databases created by others or how to design your own custom FileMaker Pro databases, this course—offered by Dr. Steven Schwartz, author of the bestselling FileMaker Pro Bible—will teach you what you need to know.
> ◆ Long Description
> • This course will instruct students in fundamental database concepts, the basics of entering and editing data in existing FileMaker Pro databases, constructing simple databases, constructing complex (and relational) databases, automating databases with scripts, publishing a database on the Web using Instant Web Publishing, and using FileMaker Pro in a workgroup. After completing the course, students will be able to design their own fully functioning FileMaker databases. No previous database experience is required. (Note that this is an introductory course. Advanced features, such as ODBC queries, network maintenance, and the like will not be covered.)

D Optionally, Word can highlight every match.

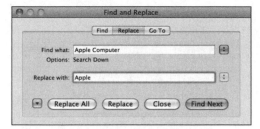

E Type the search text in the Find what box and the replacement text in the Replace with box.

Recent find strings

F When performing a find or a replace, you can select recently used search strings from the drop-down menus.

4. To search for the next occurrence of the text (when searching for individual instances), click Find Next. Repeat as necessary to find other matches.

5. When you're done searching, click the Cancel or Close button.

To replace text using Advanced Find and Replace:

1. Choose Edit > Find > Advanced Find and Replace.

   The Find and Replace dialog box appears **C**.

2. Click the Replace tab, and type a search string in the Find what box and a replacement string in the Replace with box **E**.

3. Click the Find Next button.

   Word searches for the text. If a match is found, it's highlighted in the document.

4. Do one of the following:

   ▸ Click Replace to replace the text and search for the next instance, if any.

   ▸ Click Find Next to ignore this instance and search for the next occurrence.

   ▸ Click Replace All to simultaneously replace all matches.

5. Repeat step 4 until you're done or until Word has finished searching.

6. Click Cancel or Close to dismiss the dialog box.

TIP When performing a find or find/replace, you can repeat a recent search by clicking the arrow to the right of the Find what text box **F**. Search terms you've previously used appear in a drop-down list. The arrow to the right of Replace with provides a list of the recently used replacement text strings.

continues on next page

TIP Click the triangle in the bottom-left corner of the Find and Replace dialog box to display additional search options **G**. For instance, finds are normally case-insensitive. To find terms that match a specific capitalization, click the Match case check box. To hide the extra search options, click the triangle again.

TIP To specify a search direction (down, up, or all) or to search all open documents rather than just the active one, choose an option from the drop-down menu at the top of the expanded search options **G**.

TIP You can also base a search on a font, effect, or style by choosing options from the Format drop-down menu **H**. For example, you could replace all instances of Helvetica text with Arial by specifying the fonts and leaving the Find what and Replace with boxes empty. To later clear formatting from the find or replace criteria, click the No Formatting button.

TIP To include a special character (such as a tab or paragraph mark) in a search string, choose a character from the Special menu **I**. The symbol for the character is automatically added to the search string, such as ^t for a tab.

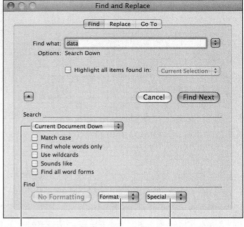

Direction   *Format menu*   *Special menu*

G Click the triangle to expand the dialog box to show advanced search options (see Table 4.3 at the beginning of this section).

H The Format drop-down menu.

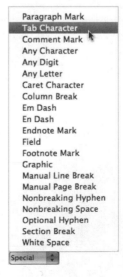

I To include a special character in a find or replace string, choose it from the Special menu.

Expand/Collapse — Find and Replace tab — Close

▼ Find and Replace

Search Document ▼

⚙ ▼ | Find

Replace With ▼

Replace All | Replace

Matches:

J Show or hide the search criteria by clicking the triangle icon.

▼ Find and Replace

student

— Special character menu

Paragraph Mark
Tab Character
Comment Mark
Any Character
Any Digit
Any Letter
Caret Character
Column Break
Em Dash
En Dash
Endnote Mark
Field
Footnote Mark
Graphic
Manual Line Break
Manual Page Break
Nonbreaking Hyphen
Nonbreaking Space
Optional Hyphen
Section Break
White Space

K You can insert special characters into a find or replace string.

▼ Find and Replace

student ▼

⚙ ▼ | Find

— Options menu

Replace With
Whole Word Only
✓ Ignore Case
Sounds Like
All Word Forms

Advanced Find & Replace...

L You can restrict the search results by choosing additional options.

To find text using the Search Pane:

1. Open the Search Pane by doing one of the following:
    ▸ Choose View > Sidebar > Search Pane.
    ▸ Choose Search Pane from the Sidebar icon on the Standard toolbar.
    ▸ If the Sidebar is already open, click the Find and Replace tab above it.

2. Expand the search area by clicking the triangle beside Find and Replace **J**.

3. Type a search string in the Find box.

    As you type, Word lists matches in the Search Pane and highlights them in the document.

4. *Optional:* To insert a special character into the search string (such as a tab or wildcard), choose it from the Find box's menu **K**.

5. *Optional:* Choose additional search criteria from the drop-down menu **L**.

6. To go to a match, do any of the following:
    ▸ To jump to a specific match, click the match text in the Search Pane.
    ▸ To review all matches in order from the text insertion mark, repeatedly click the Find button.
    ▸ To randomly review the matches, manually scroll the document.

7. To end the search, click the Sidebar's close icon **J**.

To replace text using the Search Pane:

1. Perform steps 1–5 of "To find text using the Search Pane," earlier in this section.

2. Enter a replacement text string in the Replace box ❶. Note that you can insert special characters in the replacement string in the same manner as with the find string ❶.

3. Do one of the following:

   ▸ **Step through the matches.** To find the first match (searching from the text insertion mark), click Find. If the instance is one that you want to replace, click Replace. Word replaces the text and moves to the next match.

   ▸ **Replace a particular instance.** Click the instance in the Matches section of the Search Pane and click Replace.

   ▸ **Replace all instances.** Click Replace All to simultaneously replace all matches with the replacement text.

4. When you're finished, click the Sidebar's close icon ❶.

Automatically entering text

The AutoText feature is designed to help you avoid repetitive typing. AutoText lets you quickly insert any amount of frequently used text into a document—from one word to multiple paragraphs.

To create an AutoText entry:

1. In the active document, select the text from which you want to create an Auto-Text entry.

   The selected text must consist of at least five characters.

2. Choose Insert > AutoText > New.

   The Create New AutoText dialog box appears and suggests a name ❶.

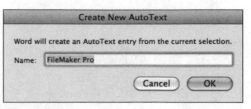

❶ The Create AutoText dialog appears and suggests a name for the new entry. Edit it as desired.

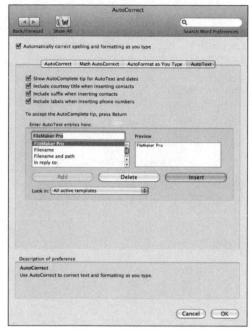

Lesson Out FileMaker Pro
1. What Is a FileMaker Database?

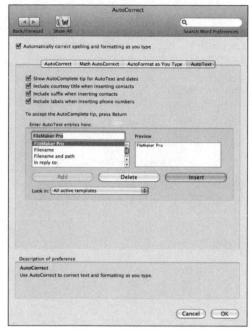 Whenever you type characters that may be an AutoText entry, you are offered the opportunity to insert it.

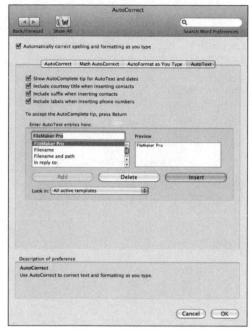 You can delete AutoText entries, as well as specify the classes of entries to use.

3. *Optional:* Edit the suggested name.

   If you want to be able to insert the entry using AutoComplete, make sure that the name contains at least four characters.

4. Click OK to add the text to the list of available AutoText entries.

To insert an AutoText entry:

As you type, Word watches for the name of an AutoText entry. When it detects one, a yellow box containing the AutoText entry's name appears 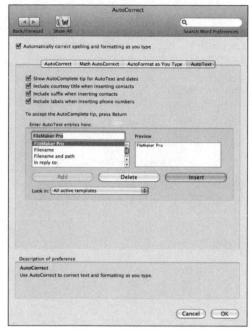. Do one of the following:

- To accept the AutoText replacement, press Return or Enter.

- To ignore the proposed AutoText replacement, continue typing.

TIP You can use AutoText to enter lengthy medical, legal, or technical terms. AutoText is also great when writing letters that use standard opening and closing lines.

TIP To delete an AutoText entry, choose Insert > AutoText > AutoText. On the AutoText tab of the AutoCorrect dialog box 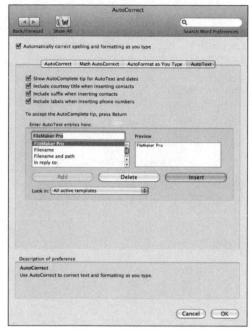, select the entry in the list box and click Delete.

TIP You can insert an AutoText entry into the current document by selecting the entry from the list box 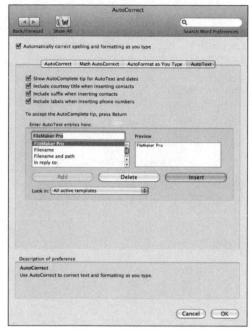 and clicking Insert.

TIP Another way to insert an AutoText entry is to choose it from one of the Insert > AutoText submenus. Word provides dozens of common AutoText entries to get you started. You'll find your personal entries in the document template in which they were stored—typically, the Normal template.

Working with smart buttons

To make certain edits more flexible, Word, Excel, and PowerPoint provide smart buttons. A *smart button* is a pop-up icon that displays a menu of options when clicked. There are two types of smart buttons: Auto-Correct Options and Paste Options.

The Replace list of words, phrases, and symbols in the AutoCorrect dialog box 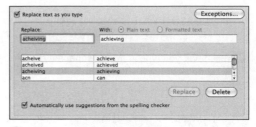 determines which text will automatically be substituted for other text as you type. For instance, if you type **(c)**, a copyright symbol (©) is substituted. Common typos, such as ones caused by transposing letters, are also corrected. After an autocorrection occurs, you can click the AutoCorrect Options button to modify the correction.

Paste Option buttons are immediately avail able after pasting or using drag and drop. You can specify that the pasted or dropped text keep its original formatting or that it adopt the formatting of surrounding text.

To use an AutoCorrect Options button:

1. After an autocorrection, move the cursor over the corrected text.

    A blue underline appears under the text.

2. Move the cursor over the blue under-line to reveal the AutoCorrect Options button, and click the button to open the menu **Q**.

3. Do one of the following:

    ▸ Choose Undo or Change back to restore the original, uncorrected text.

    ▸ Choose Stop Automatically Correcting *condition* to prevent future instances from being corrected and to delete the item from the Replace list.

    ▸ Choose Control AutoCorrect Options to change your AutoCorrect settings.

P The AutoCorrect tab of the AutoCorrect dialog box contains a Replace list of items that will automatically be corrected in your documents.

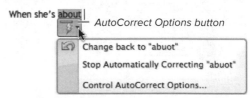

Q When the button appears, click it to open the menu.

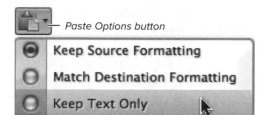
— *Paste Options button*

Keep Source Formatting

Match Destination Formatting

Keep Text Only

R Use the Paste Options button to control the formatting of pasted or dropped text.

Cut and paste options _____

☑ **Show Paste Options buttons**

S You can enable or disable Paste Options buttons in the Cut and paste options section of the Edit dialog box.

To use a Paste Options button:

1. Immediately after most paste or drag-and-drop operations, a Paste Options button appears **R**.

2. Click the button to reveal its menu, and choose one of the following:

   ▸ **Keep Source Formatting.** Keep the original formatting for the pasted or dropped text.

   ▸ **Match Destination Formatting.** Make the pasted text match the formatting of surrounding text.

   ▸ **Keep Text Only.** Strip the formatting from the pasted or dropped text. (For instance, red italicized text would be reduced to plain black text.)

TIP There isn't a time limit for clicking an AutoCorrect Options button. As long as you haven't closed and reopened the document, a button will be available for every autocorrection made during the session.

CAUTION A Paste Options button, on the other hand, must be used immediately.

TIP After undoing an autocorrection, you can later "redo" the correction by clicking the button and choosing Redo Automatic Corrections.

TIP Paste Options buttons can be a nuisance. To disable them, choose Word > Preferences, and click the Author and Proofing Tools:Edit icon. In the Edit dialog box, remove the check mark from Show Paste Options buttons **S** and click OK.

TIP You can open the AutoCorrect dialog box by choosing Tools > AutoCorrect or Insert > AutoText > AutoText. You can also choose Word > Preferences, and click the Author and Proofing Tools:AutoCorrect icon.

Proofing Your Work

It's a good idea to check your work before letting anyone else see it. Word 2011 has tools you can use to check your spelling and grammar, find synonyms when you're stuck for a word, and look up definitions.

Checking spelling and grammar

You can avoid common errors and typos by performing a spelling and grammar check on each document. Use the Thesaurus and Dictionary tools to enliven your writing and ensure that you're using words correctly.

To check spelling and grammar:

1. Choose Tools > Spelling and Grammar or press Option-Command-L.

   The Spelling and Grammar dialog box appears **A**. The spelling checker flags possible misspellings, and the grammar checker identifies questionable grammar. As it examines the document, Word stops at each questionable word or phrase.

2. For each questionable instance, do one of the following:

   ▸ To accept a selected entry in the Suggestions list, click Change. To make the same correction for all such errors in the document, click Change All.

   ▸ To leave the word or phrase as is and continue the spelling check, click Ignore. To ignore all instances of the word or phrase found in the current document, click Ignore All.

   ▸ To add the current spelling of a flagged word to your user dictionary and also accept the spelling as correct, click Add. (Adding a word to the user dictionary prevents Word from flagging it as a misspelling in other documents.)

   ▸ If this is a error you commonly make, select the correct word in the Suggestions list and click AutoCorrect. The misspelled word and its replacement are added to the AutoCorrect list.

   ▸ Manually edit the text in the upper box. Click Change to accept your edits or Undo Edit to restore the original text.

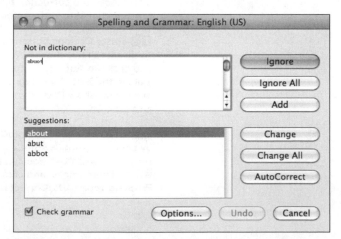

A Word suggests corrections for most spelling and grammatical issues.

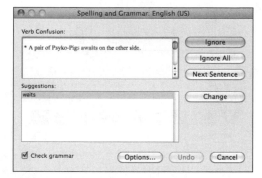

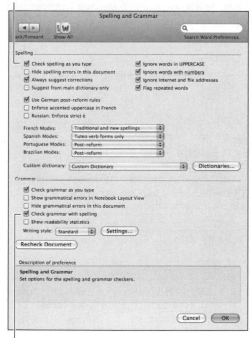

B When questionable grammar is found, you can accept a suggestion, ignore this or all instances, or skip this error and jump to the next.

Check spelling as you type

Check grammar with spelling

C Spelling and Grammar preferences.

D Any word that you commonly misspell or type incorrectly can be added to the AutoCorrect list.

When a possible grammatical error is found, the dialog box and its options change **B**.

3. For each flagged error, do one of the following:

- To ignore the error for this or all instances in the document, click Ignore or Ignore All, respectively.
- To accept a selected correction in the Suggestions box, click Change.
- To examine the next identified error (without making a judgment on the current problem), click Next Sentence.
- Manually edit the text in the upper box. Click Change to accept the edits.

An alert box appears when the spelling and grammar check is complete.

4. Click OK to dismiss the alert box.

TIP To immediately end a spelling/grammar check, click the Cancel button.

TIP To restrict a check to only part of a document, select the text prior to issuing the Spelling and Grammar command.

TIP To disable grammar checking, remove the check mark from Check grammar **A** or remove the check mark from Check grammar with spelling in Spelling and Grammar preferences **C**. Note that you can go directly to this preferences dialog box by clicking the Options button **A**.

TIP Unless you've changed the Spelling and Grammar preferences, Word automatically checks spelling as you type **C**. Suspect words are marked with a red underline.

TIP As you type, Word automatically corrects common misspellings. To add your own words to the AutoCorrect list **D**, choose Tools > AutoCorrect. Enter the misspelling in the Replace box, enter the correctly spelled word in the With box, and click the Add button.

To replace a word with a synonym:

Do one of the following:

- Select the word or phrase you want to replace. Choose Tools > Thesaurus. The Reference Tools tab of the Toolbox appears, showing information for the selected word or phrase 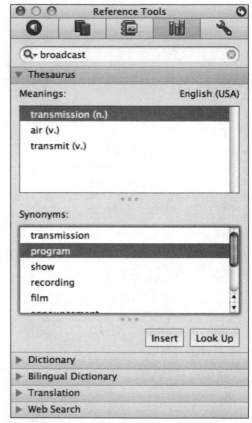. Select the closest meaning from the Meanings list, select a synonym from the Synonyms list, and click Insert.

- Display the Reference Tools tab of the Toolbox ❸. (If the Toolbox isn't open, click the Toolbox icon on the Standard toolbar or choose View > Reference Tools.) In the Thesaurus section, type or paste a word/phrase into the search box, and press Return. Select a meaning, select a synonym, and click Insert.

- Right-click the selected word or phrase, and choose a replacement from the Synonyms submenu.

TIP To view a selected synonym's definition, click Look Up and expand the Dictionary section.

To look up a word's definition:

Do one of the following:

- Select the word in your document and choose Tools > Dictionary.

- Right-click the word and choose Look Up > Definition from the contextual menu.

  The Dictionary section of the Reference Tools tab displays the definition ❺.

TIP You can also type or paste a word into the search box to view its definition.

TIP You can use the Web to expand the information available to you concerning the text in the search box by opening the Web Search section. Click links to view them in your default browser.

❺ The Reference Tools tab of the Toolbox has both a thesaurus and dictionary.

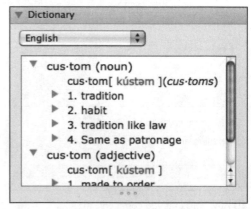

❺ You can look up a word's definition in the Dictionary section of the Reference Tools.

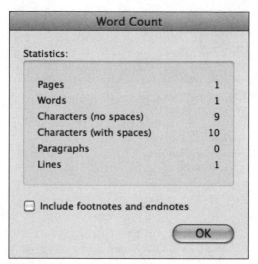

G To view a word count and other useful document statistics, choose Tools > Word Count.

Total words

Words: 264 of 729

H You can also view the word count in the status bar.

Calculating a word count

Sometimes you may need to know a document's exact word count or similar statistics. Word count is important when writing to a particular length, as is sometimes the case with magazine articles and homework assignments.

To calculate the word count:

1. Do one of the following:
   - To calculate statistics for a portion of the document, begin by selecting that part of the document.
   - To calculate statistics for an entire document, ensure that nothing is selected.

2. Choose Tools > Word Count.

   The Word Count dialog box appears **G**. It contains information about your document, including the page count and the number of words, lines, and paragraphs in your document

3. Click OK to dismiss the dialog box.

TIP At the bottom of every Word window are two numbers **H**. The first is the word in which the text insertion mark is located, counting from the beginning of the document. The second is the number of words in the document. (If text is selected, the first number is the word count for the selected words.)

Tracking Changes

On certain Word documents, you may collaborate with others. For instance, you could create a group report for school, work on a departmental budget with members of your staff, or write a magazine or article that needs to incorporate an editor's comments. As the author, you can review the comments and changes of others, as well as accept or reject each one. All tracking commands can be found on the Review tab.

To track changes to a document:

1. Click the Review:Tracking:Track Changes icon .

   When Track Changes is enabled, the icon reads ON; changes you make are recorded.

2. Choose a display option from the drop-down menu in the Tracking group 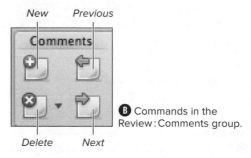:

   ▸ **Original.** Display the original, unedited document (as it would look if all changes have been rejected).

   ▸ **Original Showing Markup.** Display insertions and formatting changes in balloons. Deleted text is shown as struck through.

   ▸ **Final.** Display the document as if all changes have been accepted.

   ▸ **Final Showing Markup.** Display deletions in balloons. Insertions and formatting changes are shown in the document text.

3. To insert a comment, select the text on which you want to comment or position the text insertion mark within it. Choose Insert > Comment or click Review:Comments:New .

   A new comment balloon appears.

4. Type your comment **C**.

A Click the Track Changes control to switch tracking on or off.

B Commands in the Review:Comments group.

C Type a comment that applies to the currently selected text.

Accept

Reject

D An easy way to accept or reject an edit is to click the appropriate icon in the edit balloon.

E You can reject or accept an edit by clicking an icon. Click the Review Pane icon to show or hide the Reviewing Pane in the Sidebar.

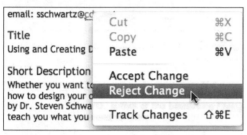

F You can also accept or reject an edit by right-clicking it and choosing a command from this contextual menu.

Comparing Document Versions

You can compare two versions of a Word document, such as an original and one that incorporates edits. Choose Tools > Track Changes > Compare Documents. In the Compare Documents dialog box, select an original and revised document to compare. Word generates and displays a comparison document that shows the differences between the two files.

5. To reject an edit or delete a comment, do one of the following:

- Click the Delete **C** or Reject **D** icon in the associated balloon.

- Position the text insertion mark in the edit or balloon. Click the Review: Changes:Reject icon **E** or the Review: Comments:Delete icon **B**, as appropriate.

- In the document or In the Reviewing Pane in the Sidebar, right-click the edit or comment. Choose Reject Change or Delete Comment from the contextual menu **F**.

6. To accept an edit, do one of the following:

- Click the Accept button in the edit balloon **D**.

- Click the Review:Changes:Accept icon **E**.

- Right-click the edit in the body of the document. Choose Accept Change from the contextual menu **F**.

TIP To show the Reviewing Pane, choose Sidebar > Reviewing Pane in the Standard toolbar. To hide the Reviewing Pane (and the Sidebar), click its close icon. You can also show or hide the Reviewing Pane by clicking the Review:Changes:Review Pane icon **E**.

TIP You can jump directly from one edit or comment to another by clicking the Next and Previous icons in the Review:Comments group **B**.

TIP During or after the review, you can email the marked-up document to team members by clicking the Review:Share:Mail icon.

TIP To alter the Track Changes preferences, choose Review:Tracking:Show Markup > Preferences.

Printing Word Documents

Like other applications in Office 2011, Word provides an assortment of printing options. The steps below discuss the options you're most likely to use.

To print a Word document:

1. Open the Word document.

2. *Optional:* To print only part of the current document, select that text.

3. Choose File > Print (Command-P).

   The Print dialog box appears **A**.

4. Select a connected printer from the Printer drop-down list.

5. Specify the number of copies and range of pages to print.

   The Selection option is only available if you preselected part of the document in step 2.

6. *Optional:* To change Page Setup options (paper size, orientation, and paper feed method), click the Page Setup button.

7. *Optional:* To set Word-specific options, choose Microsoft Word from the drop-down section menu. Choose an option from the Print What drop-down menu **B**. If you're doing two-sided printing, you can also elect to print just the odd or even pages.

   Choose Copies & Pages from the drop-down section menu to return to the main Print dialog box.

8. Turn on the printer and click Print.

   The print job is sent to the selected printer.

Quick Preview   Printer   Section menu

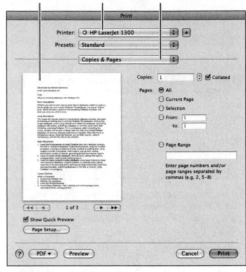

A Set options for the current print job in the Print dialog box.

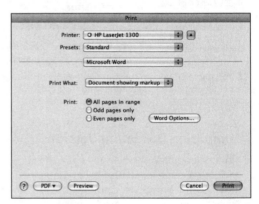

B Set Word-specific options (such as printing a document showing changes) in the Microsoft Word section of the Print dialog box.

C You can create a PDF from almost any type of Macintosh document.

TIP To preview a printout onscreen prior to printing, switch to Print Layout View. Within the Print dialog box, you can click the arrows beneath the Quick Preview area **A** to get a bird's-eye view of the printout that reflects the current print and page layout settings.

TIP To print the complete document using the current print settings, click the Print icon on the Standard toolbar. Printing commences immediately—without displaying the Print dialog box.

TIP If you save a document after printing it, the print settings are saved, too. This makes it easy to repeat complex print jobs.

TIP To share a Word document with someone who doesn't have Word, click the PDF button in the Print dialog box and choose Save as PDF **C**. A cross-platform PDF file will be generated that can be opened in Preview or Adobe Reader. The recipient will be able to read the document onscreen and print it, if desired.

TIP If change tracking has been enabled, you can include the edits and comments in the printout by choosing Review:Tracking:Final Showing Markup or Original Showing Markup (see **A** in "Tracking Changes," earlier in this chapter).

Document Formatting

Unlike character and paragraph formatting (discussed in Chapter 6), document formatting applies to an entire document (or, in some cases, to selected document sections). You can use document formatting commands to change the page orientation, set margins, or specify a custom paper size on which to print a memo or envelope, for example.

You can add columns to create a newsletter or magazine layout, divide a document into sections (as you might do for a manual or report), and force pages and columns to break exactly where you want. As you choose new settings, Word automatically adjusts the text to fit the specified orientation, margins, paper size, number of columns, and so on.

Paper Size and Orientation

Word's default printout setting is 8 ½" x 11" *portrait* (vertical orientation). The choices you make for paper size and orientation are applied to the current document only; new documents revert to the default settings. In Office 2011, you can use the Ribbon or the Page Setup dialog box to set paper size and orientation.

If you buy paper that isn't listed in the Ribbon's Size drop-down menu or in the Page Setup dialog box, you can define a *custom size*. The new paper size will be available in every program installed on your Mac, as well as in Word.

To change Page Setup options using the Ribbon:

1. Choose a paper size/type from the Layout:Page Setup:Size menu 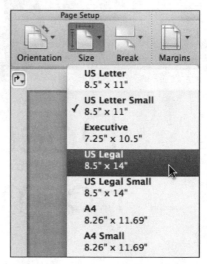.

2. Choose an orientation for the document (portrait or landscape) from the Layout:Page Setup:Orientation menu ⓑ.

   Addition options, such as scaling and the destination printer, can be set in the Page Setup and Print dialog boxes.

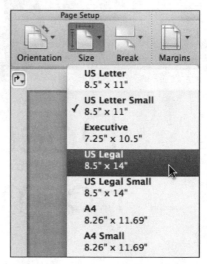

ⓐ Common paper sizes can be chosen from this drop-down menu.

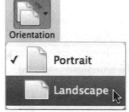

ⓑ Choose a paper orientation from this drop-down menu.

When Should I Use Landscape?

Choosing Landscape mode ⓑ results in a *wide* printout (using the 11" dimension on 8.5" x 11" paper, for example). It's often used to print fold-over brochures, cards, and church bulletins. When a document contains wide tables, using landscape mode can prevent the tables from being split between pages.

And when printing a manual or other long document, you can reduce paper waste by printing two pages per sheet, which automatically uses landscape mode. In the Print dialog box, choose Layout from the drop-down menu and set Pages per Sheet to **2**.

Select a printer   Paper type/size

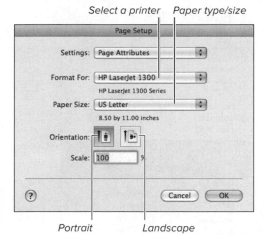

Portrait   *Landscape*

C Specify a paper size and orientation in the Page Setup dialog box.

Size name

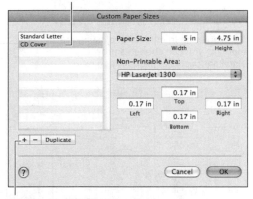

Define a new paper size

D You can define a custom paper size if you need to print on nonstandard paper.

To change Page Setup options in the Page Setup dialog box:

1. Choose File > Page Setup.

   The Page Setup dialog box appears **C**.

2. Choose Page Attributes from the Settings drop-down menu, and select a destination printer from the Format for list of installed printers.

3. To set the page orientation, click the portrait icon for a standard vertical printout or the landscape icon for a horizontal printout.

4. Do one of the following:

   ▸ Select a standard paper size from the Paper Size drop-down list **C**.

   ▸ To use a nonstandard paper size, select Manage Custom Sizes from the Paper Size drop-down list. In the Custom Page Sizes dialog box **D**, select a defined paper size and click OK.

   To define a *new* paper size, click the plus (+) icon, enter the dimensions in the Width and Height text boxes, select a target printer, specify mandatory margins, name the paper size, and click OK. Select the new size from the Paper Size drop-down list.

5. *Optional:* To proportionately scale the printout to better fit the selected paper size, enter a number in the Scale text box **C**.

6. Click OK to close the dialog box.

   The document is modified to match the new Page Setup settings.

TIP To see how the new settings will affect the printed version of the document, ensure that you're in Print Layout view (**View** > **Print Layout**).

Margins

Margins are the blank borders around each document page. Although Word has default margin settings, you can vary the margins to fit the needs of the current document—to print on odd-sized paper or to squeeze a few extra lines of text onto each page, for example.

To change the margins:

Do one of the following:

- In the Layout:Margins group **A**, choose a preset from the Margins menu or enter new Left, Right, Top, and/or Bottom margins in the text boxes.

- Choose Format > Document. On the Margins tab of the Document dialog box **B**, enter new margin settings and click OK.

    The new margin settings are applied to the document.

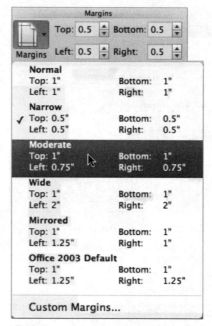

A In addition to manually adjusting the margins, you can choose a preset to simultaneously set all four margins.

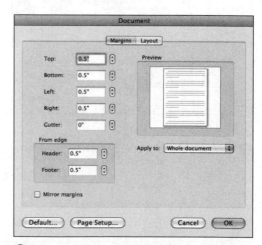

B Margin settings can also be adjusted in the Document dialog box.

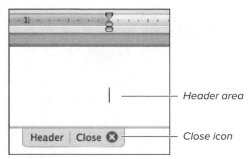

Header area

Close icon

A Create a header or footer by typing and clicking icons on the Header and Footer contextual tab.

Additional Margin Options

The Document dialog box (see **B** in "Margins" on the previous page) has other margin options that you may find useful:

- Specify a gutter margin if you're preparing the document for binding. (The *gutter* is extra space added to the edge of pages that will be bound or stapled. This prevents the binding from obscuring the printing.)

- Click the Mirror margins check box when creating a book, magazine, or other two-sided publication. This makes the outer margin on left pages match those of right pages, while also creating matching inner margins.

Headers and Footers

Headers and footers display the same reference information at the top or bottom of every document page. You can include any information you like, such as your name, document title, current date, or page numbers, for example.

To insert headers and footers:

1. Choose View > Header and Footer.

   Word switches to Print Layout view, and the Header and Footer areas are displayed **A**.

2. Select the Header and Footer contextual tab to reveal its commands **B**.

3. Decide whether you want different headers and footers to appear on odd and even pages by checking or clearing the Header and Footer: Options: Different Odd & Even Pages check box **B**.

   If this setting is enabled, you'll need to create two separate header/footer combinations: one on an odd page and the other on an even page.

4. You can edit the header or the footer. To switch between them, click the Go to Header or Go to Footer icon **B** or click in the header or the footer.

   A header or footer can contain a combination of text, graphics, and special items, such as page numbers or today's date.

continues on next page

Header and Footer contextual tab

B Select the Header and Footer contextual tab when creating or editing headers and footers.

5. Type the desired text. Insert special items by clicking icons or choosing commands from the Insert menu.

   Use tabs to separate and position header and footer elements.

6. When you're done editing, click the Close icon **A** beneath or above the header or footer area.

TIP In Print Layout view (View > Print Layout), you can create or edit a header or footer by double-clicking in the appropriate area of the page.

TIP You can insert a preformatted header or footer by selecting one from the Header and Footer:Insert:Header or Footer gallery **C**.

TIP Header and footer commands can also be found in the Document Elements:Header and Footer group.

TIP To prevent document text from distracting you while working on the header or footer, click the Header and Footer:Options:Hide Body Text check box **B**.

TIP You can insert other kinds of special text by choosing commands from the Insert > AutoText **D** submenu.

TIP You can make more room for a header or footer by adjusting Header and Footer: Position:Header from Top or Footer from Bottom **B**.

TIP To specify a different (or no) header or footer on page 1, click the Header and Footer: Options:Different First Page check box **B**. This option is often used to prevent a report title page from displaying a header or footer.

TIP To remove a header or footer, delete the header or footer text and all other elements.

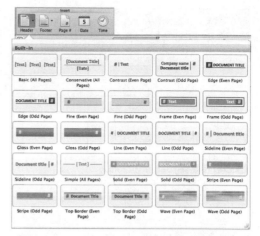

C The Header and Footer galleries contain built-in headers and footers that you can use as is or modify to suit your needs.

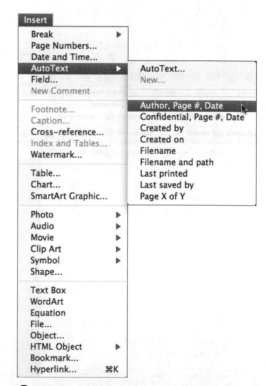

D Use the Insert > AutoText submenu to insert special text into a header or footer, such as your name, the filename, or Page X of Y.

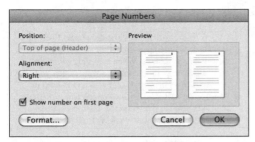

A Indicate where you want the page numbers to appear, their alignment, and whether the first page will be numbered.

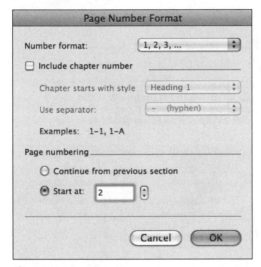

B The Page Number Format dialog box provides additional options, such as starting number and whether to use chapter-relative page numbering.

Page-Numbering Tips

You can precede each page number with the word **Page**, such as **Page 1**. Be sure to separate the **Page** text and page number placeholder with a space.

You can also insert a page number placeholder while editing the header or footer. Position the text insertion mark where you want the number to appear, and then click the Header and Footer:Insert: Page # icon.

Page Numbers

Page numbers in a header or footer can improve a document's organization and make it easy for readers to keep their place.

To number a document's pages:

1. Choose Insert > Page Numbers.

2. In the Page Numbers dialog box **A**, specify the page number's position and alignment:

    ▸ You can place numbers in the header or footer (Position) and align them to the right, left, or center (Alignment).

    ▸ The Inside and Outside alignment choices apply if you have mirrored pages, as found in books.

3. If you want the first page's number to be displayed, click the Show number on first page check box. Otherwise, the first visible number will be on the second page.

4. To set or change the page number format, click the Format button. The Page Number Format dialog box appears **B**. Do any of the following:

    ▸ Choose a numbering style from the Number format drop-down menu.

    ▸ To use chapter-relative numbering (as in 13-1, 13-2, and so on), click the Include chapter number check box, and then choose a style and separator from the two drop-down menus.

    ▸ You can also elect to continue page numbering from a previous section (as in a book, for instance) or designate a starting page number.

    Click OK to close the dialog box.

5. Click OK to close the Page Numbers dialog box.

Inserting Page Breaks

Word inserts an *automatic page break* whenever text fills a page. In Draft view, an automatic page break is shown as a thin blue line 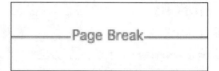. If you want a page to break *before* you've filled the page (to avoid splitting a table across two pages, for example), you can insert a *manual page break*.

To insert a manual page break:

1. Position the text insertion mark at the beginning of the line where you want the new page to begin.

2. Choose Insert > Break > Page Break, Layout : Page Setup : Break > Page, or Document Elements : Insert Pages : Break > Page. The break appears **B**.

TIP You can't delete or move an automatic page break. You can, however, insert a manual break above it. When you insert a manual page break, the positions of the automatic breaks that follow it are adjusted by Word.

TIP To delete a manual page break in Draft view **B**, select the break and press Delete. To delete a manual page break in Print Layout view, position the insertion mark just before the first character of the new page and press Delete.

TIP Use Widow/Orphan control to ensure that Word doesn't leave a single line of text at the page top or bottom when it breaks a page. Select the errant paragraph, choose Format > Paragraph, select the Line and Page Breaks tab in the Paragraph dialog box **C**, check Widow/Orphan control, and click OK. Word will repaginate as necessary to eliminate the widow or orphan text.

TIP To prevent a heading and the following paragraph from being split across two pages, select the heading and click the Keep with next check box **C**.

Automatic page break

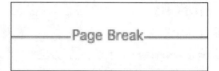

This approach has one drawback. There is no simple way to apply multiple tiers to a customer's purchases. When recording an invoice, there are no pop-up choice lists from which you can choose A-level pricing on one item and B-level on another, for example. To accomplish this, you must manually edit the prices on the customer's invoice; consulting a price list or working from memory.

A Word determines the placement of each automatic page break based on page length, margin settings, and the text. As you edit the text, the positions of automatic page breaks adjust.

——————Page Break——————

B When viewed in Draft view, a manual page break is denoted by a thin blue line with **Page Break** in its center.

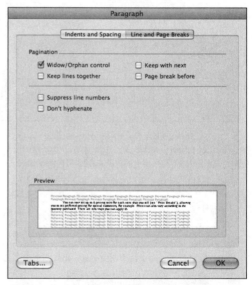

C In the Paragraph dialog box, you can instruct Word to handle widows/orphans and prevent two paragraphs from being split between pages.

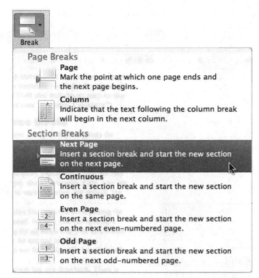

A Choose a type of section break to insert from a Ribbon icon or the Insert > Break submenu.

Section break

5/27/10		IRS	$897.00	Excess 2009 refund
6/10/10	cash	Mohave Community College	$50.00	GED testing fee
8/6/10	cash	Visions	$425.00	Theft of glasses (casualty)

Section Break (Next Page)
The information in this report is confidential and the property of Steven Schwartz.

B A new section break appears (Draft view show).

Inserting Blank Pages

Word provides an easy way for you to add a blank page. Click the Document Elements:Insert Pages:Blank icon.

Creating Multiple Sections

A document can contain multiple sections, each with different document-formatting attributes, such as margins, page numbering schemes, and headers and footers. For instance, an annual report might contain different sections for the title page, introduction, body, and financial data.

A new document contains only one section until you insert a section break. See **Table 5.1** for section break options.

To create multiple sections:

1. Place the text insertion mark where you want the new section to begin.

2. Choose Insert > Break, Layout:Page Setup:Break, or Document Elements: Insert Pages:Break, and choose a section break command from the menu **A**.

   In Draft view, Word inserts a double line marked with the text **Section Break**, followed by the break type **B**. In Print Layout view, Word displays the new section as a new page.

continues on next page

TABLE 5.1 Section Break Types

Break Type	Description
Next Page	Starts a new section at the top of the next page.
Continuous	Starts a new section without moving the text after the section break to a new page. If the previous section has multiple columns, Word evens out the column bottoms.
Even Page	If the section break falls on an odd page, Word starts the new section on the next page. Otherwise, it leaves the next odd page blank and starts the new section on the next even page.
Odd Page	If the section break falls on an even page, Word starts the new section on the next page. Otherwise, it leaves the next even page blank and starts the new section on the next odd page.

TIP Like page breaks, the Section Break indicator text and double lines are normally visible only in Draft and Outline views. However, you can also make them visible in Print Layout view by clicking the ¶ (Show all nonprinting characters) icon on the Standard toolbar.

TIP To remove a section break, switch to Draft or Outline view, select the Section Break indicator, and press Delete.

TIP To apply document-formatting options to a section, set the text insertion mark in the section and choose Format > Document. The Document dialog box appears. Click the appropriate tab, alter the layout and margin settings, choose This section from the Apply to drop-down menu **C**, and click OK.

TIP To apply document formatting to multiple sections, select some text from the sections and choose Format > Document. Specify settings in the Document dialog box, choose Selected sections from the Apply to drop-down menu **C**, and click OK.

Apply to drop-down menu

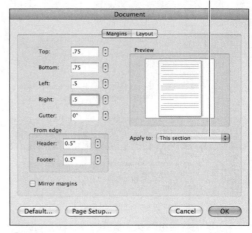

C To set new formatting for one or more selected sections, make the necessary changes on the Margins and/or Layout tab of the Document dialog box, choose This section or Selected sections from the Apply to drop-down menu, and click OK.

Setting a Document Background

Occasionally, you might like to swap the normal white page background for something more colorful:

- To apply a background color to the current document, choose a color from the Layout:Page Background:Color drop-down menu.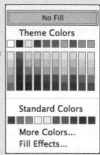

- To use a pattern, texture, gradient, or picture as the background, choose Layout:Page Background:Color > Fill Effects. Set options in the Fill Effects dialog box and click OK.

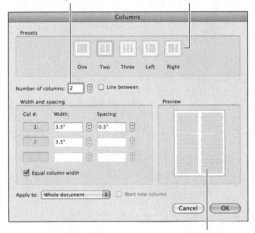

(A) You can create columns by choosing a command from the Columns icon menu.

Enter the number of columns you want...

...or click one of these presets.

Preview

(B) In addition to specifying the number of columns, you can set column widths and the space between them in the Columns dialog box.

Adding Column Breaks

Automatic pagination can sometimes result in unfortunate or unsightly breaks in a columnar layout. However, you can insert manual *column breaks* to force a break wherever you like.

Set the text insertion mark at the start of the line where you want to insert a break. Choose Insert > Break > Column, Layout: Page Setup: Break > Column, or choose Document Elements: Insert Pages: Break > Column.

Multiple Columns

A new Word document normally starts as one large column. However, if you want to lay out a newsletter or break up your text with pictures, for example, you can create additional columns.

To set up multiple columns:

1. Do either of the following:

   ▸ Choose a number, Left, or Right from the Home: Paragraph: Columns or Layout: Text Layout: Columns icon **(A)**. Your choice is instantly applied.

   Left and Right are two-column layouts, indicating the narrower of the two columns.

   ▸ To specify column settings in the Columns dialog box **(B)** (as described in the remaining steps), choose Format > Columns or choose Columns from the Columns icon **(A)**.

2. In the Columns dialog box, click one of the Presets or enter a number in the Number of columns text box.

3. *Optional:* To add a vertical line between each pair of columns, click the Line between check box.

4. In the Width and spacing section of the dialog box, specify the width and space between for each column. (To make all columns the same width, click the Equal column width check box.)

5. Choose an option from the Apply to drop-down menu and click OK.

6. Switch to Print Layout view to see the effect of the column settings.

TIP After creating multiple columns, you can change the number of columns or other column-related settings by returning to the Columns dialog box.

6

Text Formatting

In Chapter 5, you learned to apply document-level formatting, such as setting the page size, orientation, and margins. In this chapter, you'll discover the many ways you can format the *text* in your documents. There are two types of formatting that can be applied to text: character and paragraph.

- *Character formatting* refers to the font, size, styles, and color applied to—and that only affects—selected text within a paragraph.

- *Paragraph formatting* concerns itself with formatting that affects entire paragraphs. In addition to setting a default font for the paragraph, formatting can include line spacing, space before and after the paragraph, alignment, and so on.

To make it simpler to consistently format a document's text, you can define and apply character and paragraph *styles*, as explained at the end of this chapter.

Character Formatting

You can change the look of selected text by applying a different font, size, style, and color formatting. As described below, you can format text in several ways. Use any method that's convenient.

To apply character formatting:

1. Select the text that you want to format.

   Using normal selection techniques, you can select individual characters, words, paragraphs, or the entire document.

2. Do any of the following:

   ▸ Select font, size, color, highlighting, and style options from the Home:Font group **A** (page bottom) or the Formatting toolbar **B**.

   ▸ Choose Format > Font or press Command-D. On the Font tab of the Font dialog box **C**, select font, size, color, and effects, and then click OK.

   ▸ Choose a font from the Font menu.

B The most common character-formatting options can be selected from the Formatting toolbar.

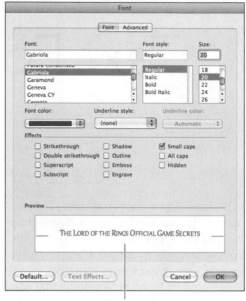

Preview of formatted text

C For more complex formatting needs, you can set options in the Font dialog box. The Preview area shows how the formatted text will look.

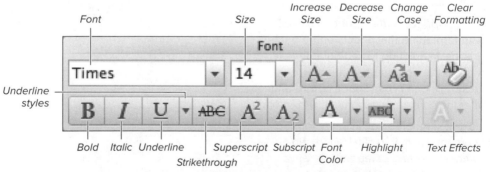

A Most character-formatting options can be selected from the Home:Font group.

TABLE 6.1 Font Effect Keyboard Shortcuts

Shortcut	Description
⌘ B	Boldface
⌘ I	Italic
⌘ U	Underline
⌘ Shift K	Small caps
⌘ Shift A	All caps
Shift F3	Cycle through case selections
⌘ Shift Z	Remove manually applied character formatting

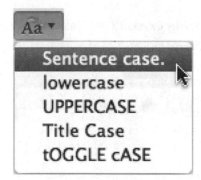

D Rather than retyping incorrectly capitalized text, you can choose a new case from the Change Case menu.

TIP To show or hide the Formatting toolbar, choose **View > Toolbars > Formatting**.

TIP To restore formatted text to the standard font and size for the paragraph, select the text and click **Home: Font: Clear Formatting** **A** or choose **Edit > Clear > Clear Formatting**.

TIP To increase or decrease the size of selected text by one size in the current font (switching from 14 to 18 points, for example), press **Command-Shift->** or **Command-Shift-<**. To increase or decrease the size by one point (switching from 14 to 15 points, for example), press **Command-]** or **Command-[**.

TIP You can use keyboard shortcuts (see Table 6.1) to apply the most common font effects to selected text.

TIP The font effect icons (such as Bold), as well as their keyboard shortcuts, work as toggles. Issue them once to apply the formatting; issue them again to remove the formatting.

TIP You can change the letter case of selected text by choosing **Format > Change Case**. Select an option from the Change Case dialog box and click OK. Alternatively, you can choose a case from the **Home: Font: Change Case** icon's menu **D**.

TIP Applying a Bold or Italic effect to text isn't the same as using the actual bold or italic version of a font, if one is available. By choosing the bold version of a font (Arial Bold or Baskerville Italic, for example), you will normally get more aesthetically pleasing and typographically correct text than you will by simply applying the Bold or Italic effect.

Paragraph Formatting

Some formatting is *paragraph-specific*. That is, rather than affecting individual words or sentences, it affects the entire paragraph. Common paragraph formatting that you can apply includes alignment, indents, tab stops, and line spacing. You can also create bulleted or numbered lists, and add borders or shading.

Setting paragraph alignment

Each paragraph in a document can be aligned left, center, right, or justified **Ⓐ**, as explained below:

- *Left* is the most common alignment setting and is the default. Text in a left-aligned paragraph is flush with the left margin and ragged on the right margin.

- *Center-aligned* paragraphs are horizontally centered between the left and right margins and are ragged on both sides. Center alignment is sometimes used for titles and section heads.

- *Right-aligned* paragraphs are flush with the right margin and ragged on the left.

- *Justified* paragraphs are aligned flush with both the left and right margins. Newspaper and magazine articles often use justified paragraphs. The spacing between words is automatically adjusted as needed to maintain the flush margins.

Left-aligned   *Center-aligned*

Right-aligned   *Justified*

Ⓐ These paragraph alignments are available in Word.

Formatting Existing vs. New Text

You can apply formats to text and paragraphs before or after you've typed them:

- When you apply a character or paragraph format to existing text, only that text is affected.

- When you apply a character format before you type, all text that follows will have the same format until you choose another character format.

- When you apply a paragraph format before you type, its format dictates the format of following paragraphs.

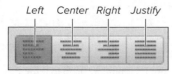

Left   Center   Right   Justify

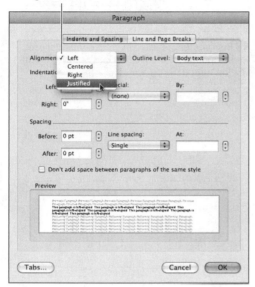

B Set the alignment for selected paragraphs by clicking an icon.

Alignment menu

C Although it's more convenient when you have multiple options to set, you can also set alignment in the Paragraph dialog box.

To set alignment for a paragraph:

1. Select one or more paragraphs whose alignment you want to change.

2. Do one of the following:

   ▸ Click an alignment icon in the Home : Paragraph group or on the Formatting toolbar **B**.

   ▸ Choose Format > Paragraph or press Option-Command-M. On the Indents and Spacing tab of the Paragraph dialog box **C**, choose an option from the Alignment drop-down menu and click OK.

   The selected paragraph(s) are aligned as directed.

TIP When you're typing and press Return to end a paragraph, the next paragraph automatically takes on the alignment of the paragraph you just completed.

Indenting paragraphs

An *indent* is space between a paragraph and the left or right margin. Indents can be used to set off quotations from surrounding text (left and right indents), format body paragraphs in a business letter or school report (first line indents), and create bulleted or numbered lists (hanging indents).

Before setting an indent, you must first select the paragraph(s). Selecting a paragraph for formatting is different from selecting a word. You don't have to select the *entire* paragraph; it's sufficient to just click somewhere within it. To select multiple contiguous paragraphs, drag through them. To select multiple noncontiguous paragraphs, Command–double-click a word in each one.

continues on next page

You can set paragraph indents using the Paragraph dialog box or the ruler. You can create the following types of indents:

- **Left.** Indents the paragraph from the left margin.

- **Right.** Indents the paragraph from the right margin.

- **First.** Indents only the first line of the paragraph.

- **Hanging.** Indents the entire paragraph except for the first line 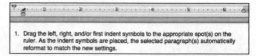.

1. Drag the left, right, and/or first indent symbols to the appropriate spot(s) on the ruler. As the indent symbols are placed, the selected paragraph(s) automatically reformat to match the new settings.

D A hanging indent is commonly used to format numbered and bulleted lists.

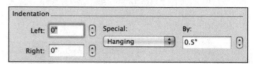

E For greater precision in setting indents, use these options on the Indents and Spacing tab of the Paragraph dialog box.

To indent paragraphs using the Paragraph dialog box:

1. Select the paragraph(s).

2. Choose Format > Paragraph or press Option-Command-M.

   The Paragraph dialog box appears **C**.

3. Select the Indents and Spacing tab.

4. Do any of the following:

   ▸ In the Indentation section **E**, change the values for Left and/or Right. The numbers correspond to the ruler that appears above the document text.

   ▸ To set a first line or hanging indent, choose First line or Hanging from the Special drop-down menu and then enter a value in the By text box.

5. Click OK to apply the new settings to the selected paragraph(s).

Left Indent
Hanging Indent
First Line Indent

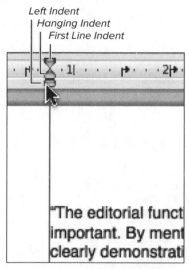

  Align these three indent markers to create a block—to format a quotation, for example.

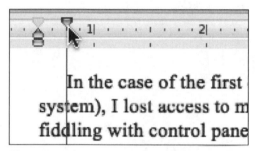

 Move the First Line Indent marker slightly to the right to create a paragraph style that is commonly used in business and education documents.

Decrease Indent

 You can click these icons to decrease or increase a paragraph's left indent.

Increase Indent

To indent paragraphs using the ruler:

- To create a uniform or flush indent, move the First Line Indent marker so it's directly above the Hanging Indent and Left Indent markers ❺. Then click and drag the square base of the Left Indent marker. The three markers will move together.

- To set a first line indent, move the First Line Indent marker ❻. Note that it moves independently of the other indent markers.

- To create a hanging indent, move the First Line Indent marker to the left of the Left Indent marker and move the Hanging Indent marker to the position where the indent will begin.

- To set the indent for the right side of a paragraph, move the Right Indent marker.

TIP Click the Decrease Indent or Increase Indent icons in the Home:Paragraph group ❼ or on the Formatting toolbar to decrease or increase the left indent to the nearest ½-inch mark on the ruler.

TIP When entering text for the first line of a paragraph that's formatted with a hanging indent, enter the bullet character or number, press Tab, and then type the paragraph text. If the paragraph has multiple lines, all lines after the first will automatically align to the Hanging Indent marker.

TIP Word also has options for *directly* creating numbered and bulleted lists, as explained later in this chapter.

Setting line spacing

Being able to modify line spacing is especially useful if you're creating a document that has space restrictions or that must follow line-spacing requirements set by an editor or teacher. The most common line spacings are single, 1.5, and double. You can also specify an exact value.

To set line spacing for a paragraph:

1. Select the paragraph or paragraphs for which you want to set line spacing.

2. Do one of the following:

   ▸ Choose an option from the Home : Paragraph : Line Spacing menu 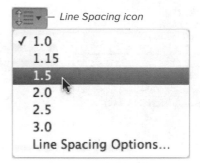.

   ▸ Choose Format > Paragraph. On the Indents and Spacing tab of the Paragraph dialog box, choose an option from the Line spacing drop-down menu 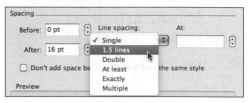, and click OK.

TIP Line spacing is a *paragraph*—not a document—formatting option. When you set line spacing, it's applied only to the currently selected paragraphs. To apply the same line spacing to an entire document, choose Edit > Select All (or press Command-A) prior to setting line spacing.

TIP The Paragraph dialog box 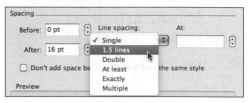 has other line spacing options. *At least* is designed to accommodate graphics and large font sizes. It sets line spacing to the minimum amount necessary to prevent clipping the tops of text. *Exactly* generates a fixed line spacing of a set amount. *Multiple* enables you to increase or decrease line spacing by a percentage. A setting of 1.2 would increase line spacing by 20 percent, for example.

TIP You can also specify the amount of blank space above and beneath a paragraph. On the Indents and Spacing tab of the Paragraph dialog box 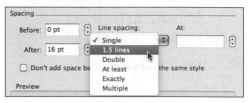, set an amount for Before and/or After (in points).

Line Spacing icon

I You can choose a line spacing from the Line Spacing menu in the Home : Paragraph group...

J ...or in the Paragraph dialog box.

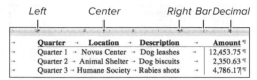

Left   Center   Right Bar Decimal

Quarter	→ Location	→ Description	→ Amount
Quarter 1	→ Novus Center	→ Dog leashes	→ 12,453.75
Quarter 2	→ Animal Shelter	→ Dog biscuits	→ 2,350.63
Quarter 3	→ Humane Society	→ Rabies shots	→ 4,786.17

K By judiciously choosing and setting tab stops, you can create perfectly aligned tables.

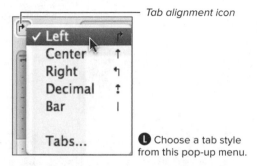

— Tab alignment icon

✓ Left
Center   ↑
Right   ↰
Decimal   ↕
Bar |

Tabs...

L Choose a tab style from this pop-up menu.

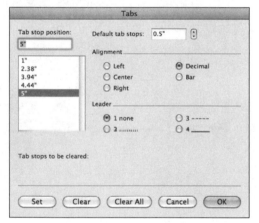

M To set tab stops precisely or specify a leader character, use the Tabs dialog box.

Setting tab stops

Tab stops are often used to align text and numbers in neat columns. For example, you can use tabs to create tables in which the entries are aligned on their left edges, right edges, centers, or decimal points **K**.

To set tabs:

1. Select the paragraph(s) for which you want to set tab stops.

2. Click the tab alignment icon to the left of the ruler and choose the type of tab you want to set **L**.

3. Click the ruler at the location where you want to place the tab stop.

   If the placement is off, drag the marker to the correct ruler position.

4. To add more tab stops for the selected paragraph(s), repeat steps 2 and 3.

5. If the selected paragraphs don't already contain tabs, insert them as necessary by pressing Tab. Affected text will conform to the new tab stops.

TIP If you need more precise tab settings, choose Format > Tabs and set tabs in the Tabs dialog box **M**. You can also select a *leader* character (such as a string of periods) that will separate the two text strings. Leaders are sometimes used to separate menu items from prices, for example.

TIP You can remove a tab stop by dragging it up or down off the ruler. To remove *all* manually placed tab stops for selected paragraphs, click Clear All in the Tabs dialog box **M**.

TIP The Bar option shown in **L** and **M** isn't for aligning text. It inserts a vertical bar at the chosen ruler location. See **K** for an example.

TIP Unless you have an overriding reason for displaying information with tab stops, consider using Word's table feature (see Chapter 7).

Bulleted and numbered lists

Bulleted lists help break text into readable chunks, making it simpler for the reader to find and digest important points. Similarly, you can create *numbered lists* to display ordered sets of points. Word 2011 also supports *multilevel lists*, enabling you to apply more sophisticated numbering or bullets to documents such as outlines and contracts. You can apply bullets, numbers, or multilevel formatting to paragraphs before or after you've typed the text.

To automatically create a list:

1. At the beginning of a new paragraph, do one of the following:

   ▸ **Bulleted list.** To create the first item, type an asterisk (*) and a space. The asterisk is converted to a bullet.

   ▸ **Numbered list.** To create the first item, type **1.** and a space. The item becomes the first in a numbered list.

2. Complete the item and press Return.

   Additional consecutive paragraphs you create by pressing Return will continue the bullets or numbering.

3. After entering the final item Ⓝ, press Return twice to end the list.

TIP You can also end a bulleted or numbered list by clicking the Bullets or Numbering icon in the Home:Paragraph group or on the Formatting toolbar.

TIP There are other characters you can type (followed by a period and a space) to automatically start a numbered list with a different numbering format, such as a., A., i., and I.

Prepare the fruit as follows:

1. Peel and chop the fresh fruit into tiny, bite-sized pieces.
2. Place in a large mixing bowl.
3. Call mom for other ingredients and instructions. ☺
4. Refrigerate

Ⓝ An example of a simple numbered list.

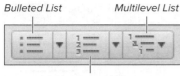

Bulleted List   *Multilevel List*

Numbered List

O Click an icon to create a list. On the Home tab, these icons have drop-down menus.

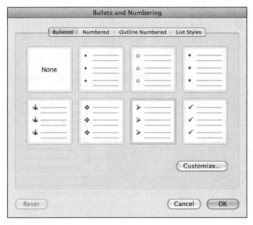

P Select one of these bullet styles. To use a different character or otherwise alter the bullet settings, click the Customize button.

Q The Decrease Indent and Increase Indent icons.

❖ **Apples**
    ● **Granny Smith**
    ● **McIntosh**
    ● **Delicious**
        ▪ **Red**
        ▪ **Golden**
❖ **Bananas**
❖ **Pears**
    ● **Anjou**
        ▪ **Red**
        ▪ **Green**

R A multilevel bulleted list.

To manually create a bulleted or numbered list:

1. Select the paragraphs to which you want to apply a bulleted or numbered format.

2. Do either of the following:
   ► To apply the most recently used bullet or number style to the paragraphs, click the Bullets or Numbering icon in the Home:Paragraph group **O** or on the Formatting toolbar.

   ► To apply a specific bullet or number style to the paragraphs, choose one from the Bullets or Numbering menu in the Home:Paragraph group **O**.

   ► Choose Format > Bullets and Numbering. On the appropriate tab of the Bullets and Numbering dialog box **P**, select a bullet or numbering style and click OK.

   The paragraph series becomes a bulleted or numbered list.

To create a multilevel list:

1. Begin an automatic or manual list by following the previous instructions in this section.

2. To enter an item at a new level, click the Increase Indent icon in the Home:Paragraph group **Q** or the Formatting toolbar.

   Additional items created at the same indent level by pressing Return will have the same bullet or number style.

3. To convert an item to a higher level, click the Decrease Indent icon **Q**.

4. To specify the bullet or number format to be applied to each level, select a style from the Home:Paragraph: Multilevel List gallery. The list is reformatted to match the gallery selection **R**.

continues on next page

TIP You can remove the bullets or numbers from selected paragraphs by clicking the Bullets or Numbering icon again.

TIP To change a list from bullets to numbers or vice versa, click the other icon in the Home : Paragraph group or on the Formatting toolbar.

TIP To type additional text directly beneath a bulleted or numbered point without interrupting the bullets or numbering, end the line by pressing Shift-Return to create a line break and type the additional text on the new line. When you press Return to end the line or paragraph, the bullets or numbering will resume.

TIP To quickly change the bullet or number style of a single-level list, double-click any bullet character or number in your text. The Bullets and Numbering dialog box will open.

TIP To change the style for one level in a multilevel list, select a point within the level (which simultaneously selects *all* points in the level), and then select a new style from the Bullets or Numbering gallery.

TIP To specify a new font and format for a numbered list, click the Customize button in the Bullets and Numbering dialog box **P**. Set options in the Customize dialog box that appears **S**, and then click OK.

TIP You can substitute other bullets for the ones in the gallery. Choose Home : Paragraph : Bulleted List > Define New Bullet or click the Customize button on the Bulleted tab of the Bullet and Numbering dialog box **P**. In the Customize Bulleted list dialog box **T**, click Bullet or Picture to select a character from an installed font (such as Symbol, Wingdings, or Webdings) or use a picture from your hard disk, respectively.

TIP Another way to change levels in a multilevel list is to press Tab and Shift-Tab.

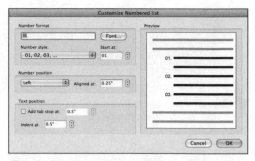

S In the Customize Numbered list dialog box, you can change the font, style, alignment, and spacing of numbered lists.

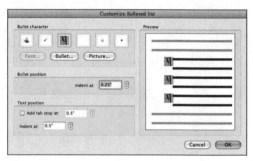

T In the Customize Bulleted list dialog box, you can define a custom bullet character based on an image or a symbol character from an installed font.

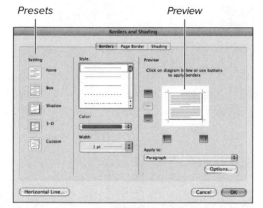

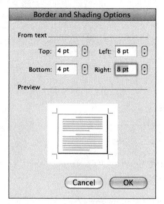

U On the Borders tab of the Borders and Shading dialog box, you can add a border to selected text or paragraphs.

V You can change the offset between each border edge and the text.

Applying borders and shading

Borders and shading can add style to a document or serve to highlight an important paragraph or block of text. You can set a border or shading around selected text, paragraphs, or pages.

To apply a border:

1. Select the text to which you'd like to add a border.

TIP To apply a border or shading to a single paragraph, it's sufficient to position the text insertion mark inside the paragraph.

2. Choose Format > Borders and Shading or click the Layout:Page Background: Borders icon.

   The Borders and Shading dialog box appears.

3. Do one of the following:
   - To create a text or paragraph border, click the Borders tab **U**.
   - To create a border around one or more pages, click the Page Border tab.

4. Select a border preset: None, Box, Shadow, 3-D, or Custom.

5. *Optional:* You can set a different line style, color, and/or width for the border.

6. *Optional:* To adjust the offset that separates the border from the text on each side, click the Options button to display the Border and Shading Options dialog box **V**.

7. From the Apply to drop-down menu, choose the part of the document to which you want to apply the border.

8. Click OK.

          continues on next page

TIP You can apply simple borders by choosing options from the Home:Paragraph: Borders menu  or the Borders palette on the Formatting toolbar. You can also choose these options *after* designing a border in the Borders and Shading dialog box.

TIP To add borders only to specific sides, switch to the Borders or Page Border tab of the Borders and Shading dialog box, and then click those sides in the Preview area ❌. You can make each side a different line style, color, and width.

TIP You can remove any line by clicking it in the Preview area of the Borders or Page Borders tab ❌. To remove all borders, select the None preset. You can also clear all borders by choosing None from the Home:Paragraph: Borders menu Ⓦ or selecting the No Border icon in the Borders palette on the Formatting toolbar.

TIP Rather than create a line border, you can use *artwork* (such as pencils, scrollwork, or trees) as the page border by choosing an image from the Art drop-down menu. To view the artwork options, select the Page Border tab of the Borders and Shading dialog box.

To apply shading:

1. Select the text to which you'd like to apply shading.

2. Choose Format > Borders and Shading or click the Layout:Page Background: Borders icon.

   The Borders and Shading dialog box appears.

3. Click the Shading tab. Select a shading color in the Fill section and a pattern in the Patterns section.

4. From the Apply to drop-down menu, choose the part of the document to which you want to apply the shading.

5. Click OK.

Ⓦ To add or remove specific border lines, choose options from this menu or the one on the Formatting toolbar.

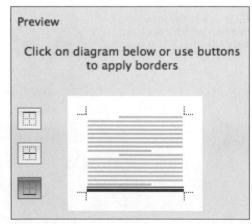

❌ To add a new line, select a style, color, and width and then click in the desired area of the preview. Click an existing line to remove it.

Styles

A You can select a style from the Formatting toolbar...

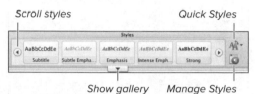

Scroll styles   Quick Styles

Show gallery   Manage Styles

B ...or from the Home:Styles gallery. You can click the arrow icon at either end to scroll through the styles or the arrow icon in the center to display the entire style gallery.

C When using styles, you'll find it useful to keep the Toolbox open with the Styles tab selected.

Using Word Styles

A *style* contains text-formatting settings. Using styles, you can quickly apply a specific combination of formatting to characters or paragraphs, ensuring consistency in the document's "look." A paragraph style named Head A might contain formatting for a heading, such as its font, size, space after, and alignment. To format selected text as that type of heading, you'd choose the Head A style from the Styles list.

Character styles contain font formatting and are applied to selected text. *Paragraph styles* are applied to entire paragraphs and contain both font and paragraph formatting. When no specific style is applied, paragraphs use the Normal style and text is formatted with the Default Paragraph Font style.

To apply a style:

1. Display the Formatting toolbar or the Home:Styles group.

2. Select characters or paragraphs to format.

3. On the Formatting toolbar **A**, Styles group **B**, or Styles tab of the Toolbox **C**, select a character or paragraph style from the Styles drop-down list, gallery, or scrolling list, respectively.

TIP On the Formatting toolbar and in the Toolbox **C**, paragraph styles are shown as ¶, while character styles are marked with an a.

TIP You can make noncontiguous text selections by Command-clicking. Doing so enables you to quickly apply the same style to selected paragraphs or text strings with one command.

TIP You can give a document an entirely different look by applying a predefined style set called a Quick Style **B**.

TIP To remove formatting from selected text, select the Clear Formatting style.

Creating a paragraph style

Generally, you should create paragraph styles when you know you'll need to use the same types of paragraphs throughout a document, such as a custom hanging indent. As explained in the following steps, all styles are easiest to create "by example."

To create a paragraph style by example using the Formatting toolbar:

1. Apply font and paragraph formatting to a paragraph, and select the paragraph.

2. Select the current style name in the Style list on the Formatting toolbar.

3. Type the new style name in place of the old one **D** and press Return.

   This sets the selected text to the newly named style and adds the new style to the Style list for the current document.

To create a paragraph style by example using the Style dialog box:

1. Apply font and paragraph formatting to a paragraph, and then select or position the text insertion mark within the paragraph.

2. Do either of the following:
   ▸ Choose Format > Style. In the Style dialog box, click the New button **E**.
   ▸ In the Styles section of the Toolbox, click the New Style button **C**.

   The New Style dialog box appears **F**.

3. Enter a name for the style in the Name box.

4. Ensure that Paragraph is the Style type and that the original style for the selected paragraph is shown as the Style based on.

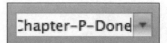

D To create a new style based on the selected paragraph, type a new name in the Style box.

E You manage styles for a document in the Style dialog box. Click New to create a new style.

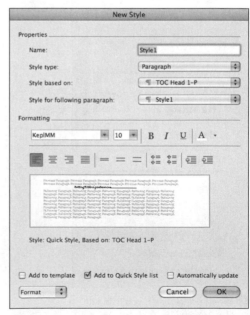

F Define new styles in the New Style dialog box.

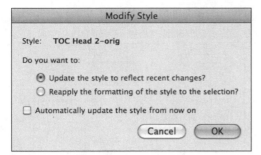

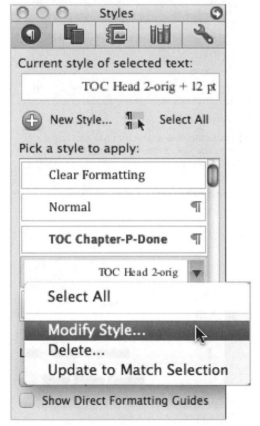

G In the Modify Style dialog box, you can update the style based on the currently selected text or reapply the original style to the selected text (to remove the new formatting).

H To change a style in the Modify Style dialog box, choose Modify Style from the style's drop-down menu in the Toolbox.

5. Select a Style for the following paragraph from the drop-down list.

This is the style Word will apply whenever you use the new style and press Return to create a new paragraph.

6. *Optional:* If there is additional character or paragraph formatting you want to include as part of the style definition, specify it in the Formatting section of the dialog box.

7. Click OK to complete the style definition.

The new style is added to the Styles lists. When you save the document, the new style is saved as part of the document.

CAUTION When you create a style in the New Style dialog box, it is not automatically applied to the original paragraph. Apply the style after you exit the dialog box.

To modify a paragraph style by example:

1. Select the paragraph. Apply desired font and/or paragraph formatting changes.

2. Select the previously applied style from the Style list on the Formatting toolbar.

The Modify Style dialog box appears **G**.

3. Select Update the style to reflect recent changes? and click OK.

Every paragraph that is currently formatted with this style will be reformatted to match the revised style definition. Other styles that are based on the modified style will also change as appropriate.

TIP You can also modify a style by clicking its drop-down menu in the Styles section of the Toolbox and choosing Update to Match Selection or Modify Style **H**.

Creating a character style

Use character styles to apply consistent formatting to selected text. You can apply character styles within a paragraph that already has a paragraph style. The character style will only affect the selected word(s) by adding formatting, such as font, size, or color.

To create a character style by example:

1. Select the formatted text from which you want to create a new character style.

2. Do either of the following:

   ▸ Choose Format > Style. In the Style dialog box, click the New button **E**.

   ▸ In the Styles section of the Toolbox, click the New Style button **H**. Or click the down arrow at the right side of the Current style of selected text box and choose New Style.

   The New Style dialog box appears **I**.

3. In the Name text box, name the new style or accept the proposed name.

4. Choose Character from the Style type drop-down menu.

5. If needed, select additional character-formatting options from the Formatting section.

6. Click OK to dismiss the dialog box and add the new style to the Styles lists.

> **TIP** You aren't required to specify *all* formatting options for a character style. For example, if you only select blue as the color while leaving the font information blank, the style will color selected text without changing the font.

> **TIP** You can make more extensive formatting changes by choosing options from the Format drop-down menu **I**. For instance, by choosing Font, you can add small caps, strikethrough, or superscript to the style definition.

Formatting options   Style type   Name the style

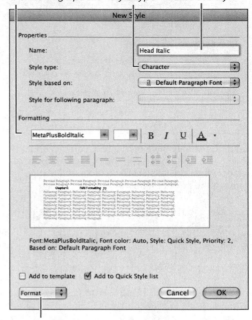

Format menu

I Name the new character style and make any desired changes to the formatting.

Defined styles for the document   *Delete*

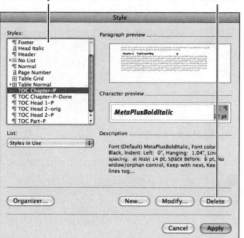

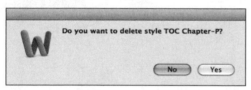

J Select a style from the Styles list and click the Delete button.

Do you want to delete style TOC Chapter-P?

No   Yes

K Click Yes to confirm the style deletion.

Deleting styles

Although there's little harm in retaining styles that aren't being used in the document, you're free to delete any style you've defined. Deleting unnecessary styles can help minimize the clutter in a lengthy Styles list. The default Word styles, however, can't be deleted.

To delete a style:

1. Do either of the following:
   - ▸ Choose Format > Style. Select the style name in the Style dialog box **J** and click Delete.
   - ▸ In the Pick style to apply section of the Styles tab of the Toolbox, click the down arrow beside the style you want to delete and choose Delete **H**.

   A confirmation dialog box appears **K**.
2. Click Yes to delete the style.
3. If the deletion was initiated in the Style dialog box (step 1), click Close to dismiss the dialog box.

Importing styles

Styles that you've defined are only available in the document(s) in which they've been saved. If you'd like to reuse some of these styles, you can *import* them into other Word documents.

To import styles:

1. Open the document or template into which you want to import styles.
2. Choose Format > Style.

   The Style dialog box appears **J**.

continues on next page

3. Click the Organizer button.

The Organizer dialog box appears 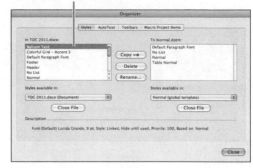, listing the document's defined styles in the left pane. (Click the Styles tab if it isn't currently selected.)

4. Click the Close File button beneath the right pane.

5. Click the Open File button beneath the right pane.

The Choose a File dialog box appears.

6. Navigate to the folder that contains the file from which you want to import styles, select the file, and click Open. The styles from this document appear in the right pane of the Organizer dialog box.

TIP By default, the Enable list is set to show Word Templates. If importing from a standard Word file rather than a template, choose Word Documents from the Enable drop-down menu.

7. In the right pane, select the styles you want to import and click the Copy button 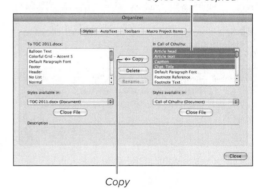.

TIP Shift-click or Command-click to select multiple styles.

8. Click Close to dismiss the dialog box.

The imported styles are now part of and available for use in the document.

TIP If you deliberately or inadvertently select a style that duplicates a style in the target document, you will be given the opportunity to overwrite duplicates, skip duplicates, or cancel the copy.

Styles in current document

L Use the Organizer dialog box to copy styles from one document or template into another.

Styles to be copied

Copy

M From the list on the right, select styles to be copied into the original document.

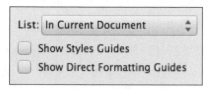

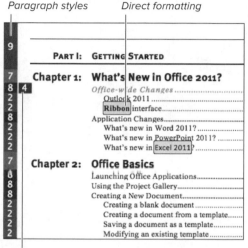

Paragraph styles   **Direct formatting**

Character style

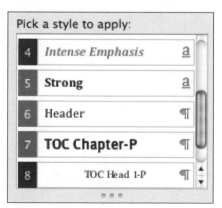

Using style guides

New in Office 2011, *style guides* are optional colored, numbered markers in the left margin that show the paragraph and character styles applied to document text. In addition to showing style-related formatting, you can highlight all instances of manually applied formatting, such as an added highlight, new color, or a font change. Enabling these options is especially useful when proofing a document to ensure that styles have been applied consistently and correctly.

To enable or disable style guides:

1. Open the Toolbox and select the Styles tab. (Click the Toolbox icon in the Standard toolbar or click the Home . Styles . Manage Styles icon **B**.)

2. In the bottom section of the Toolbox, check or clear the check boxes **N**.

   When enabled, colored guides appear in the document **O** and in the Toolbox's Styles list **P**.

N These check boxes at the bottom of the Styles tab govern the display of style and manual formatting guides.

O For each paragraph, the first number is the paragraph style. When present, a second number or plus (+) represents one or more character styles.

P With style guides enabled, paragraph and character styles in the Toolbox are numbered to match their numbering in the document.

Creating Tables

It's easy to create tables in Word documents. With little effort, you can create and begin entering information into a table. Tables can be included in sales reports, research projects, or data analyses. Or a table can consist of just a list of names and phone numbers. I'll discuss the simplest means of creating tables first and then move on to building more complex tables. Note that the material in this chapter also applies to creating and working with tables in PowerPoint.

The procedures in this chapter assume that you're working with an existing Word file. If you don't have a document open, do one of the following:

- To add a table to an existing document, choose File > Open, press Command-O, click the Open icon on the Standard toolbar, or choose the document from the File > Open Recent submenu.

- To create a table in a new document, choose File > New Blank Document, click the New Blank Document icon on the Standard toolbar, or press Command-N.

In This Chapter

Creating a Basic Table

You can create a basic table by specifying its dimensions.

To create a basic table:

1. Click to set the text insertion mark where you want the table to appear.

2. Select the Tables tab by clicking it or by choosing Insert > Table.

3. Click the Tables:Table Options:New icon **A**. In the palette that appears, drag to specify the desired number of columns and rows.

   An unformatted table appears at the text insertion mark.

4. *Optional:* To apply a predefined format to the table, select a style from the Tables:Table Styles gallery **B**.

   You can modify the formatting by clicking check boxes in the Tables:Table Options group **A**, shading the first column, for example.

> **TIP** You can also insert a table by choosing Table > Insert > Table or Tables:Table Options:New > Insert Table **A**. In the Insert Table dialog box **C**, specify the numbers of columns and rows, and set the initial column widths. If you click the Set as default for new tables check box, the dialog box will automatically propose the current settings when you create new tables.

> **TIP** You can apply table formatting at *any* point—regardless of whether you've begun entering data.

> **TIP** To show or hide the gridlines in a formatted table, select any cell in the table, and choose Table > Gridlines or click the Table Layout:Settings:Gridlines icon.

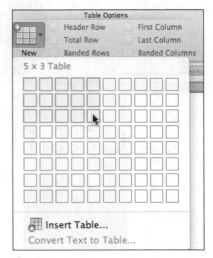

A Drag in the palette to specify the size of the table.

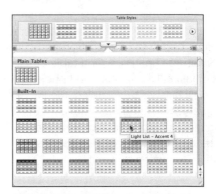

B Choose a table style from the gallery.

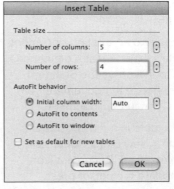

C The Insert Table dialog box.

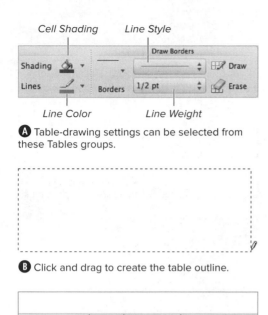

Cell Shading   *Line Style*

Line Color   *Line Weight*

A Table-drawing settings can be selected from these Tables groups.

B Click and drag to create the table outline.

C Use the Draw Table tool to complete the table by drawing the rows and columns.

Creating a Table from Scratch

If you have a complex table in mind, you can use Word's table tools to draw it.

To create a table from scratch:

1. Choose Table > Draw Table or click the Tables:Draw Borders:Draw icon.

   The Draw Table tool appears.

2. Set the line color, style, and weight by selecting options from the Draw Borders and Table Styles groups **A**.

3. Use the Draw Table tool to draw the table outline **B**.

   Click where you want one corner, drag diagonally to the opposite corner, and release the mouse button.

4. Use the Draw Table tool to draw the interior cell boundaries **C**.

5. When you're done creating the table and ready to begin entering text, click the Draw Table tool icon again to deselect it.

TIP To remove a line, click the Eraser icon in the Draw Borders group **A** and then click the line segment you want to erase. (Click and drag to erase multisegment lines.) When drawing with the Draw Table tool, you can temporarily switch to the Eraser tool by pressing Shift.

TIP To remove a line you've just drawn, choose Edit > Undo, press Command-Z, or click the Undo icon on the Standard toolbar.

Editing the Table Structure

After creating the skeleton of the table, you can fine-tune it using tools on the Tables and Table Layout tabs. Note that you can use these tools to alter *any* Word table.

To edit the table structure:

Do any of the following:

- To move a line (changing a column width or row height), drag the line to a new location 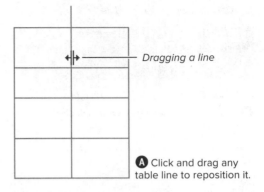 Ⓐ.

- To change the style, width, or color of a line, choose new options from the Line Style, Line Weight, and Line Color menus (see Ⓐ in "Creating a Table from Scratch" on the previous page). Click any line in the table with the Draw Table tool to apply the new settings to the line. New lines that you draw will also use these settings.

- To evenly distribute cell heights or widths, click outside the table to clear the Draw Table tool selection, and then click and drag through the cells you want to adjust. Choose a Table > AutoFit > Distribute command, or click a Table Layout:Cell Size:Distribute icon. You can also choose a command from the AutoFit drop-down menu Ⓑ.

- To precisely set row heights or column widths, select the cells you want to modify. Click the Table Layout:Settings: Properties icon or choose Table > Table Properties. On the Row or Column tab of the Table Properties dialog box Ⓒ, enter the new value and click OK.

Ⓐ Click and drag any table line to reposition it.

Dragging a line

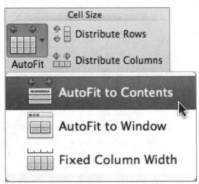

Ⓑ You can evenly distribute selected rows or columns, as well as automatically adjust them to fit the data.

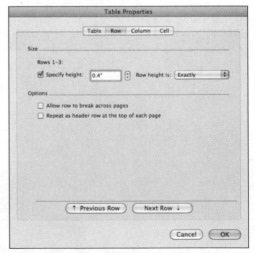

Ⓒ The Table Properties dialog box.

Preferred width

Table Properties

Table | Row | Column | Cell

Size
☑ Preferred width: 6.25"   Measure in: Inches

Alignment

Left   Center   Right

Indent from left:
0"

Text wrapping

None   Around

Positioning...

Borders and Shading...   Options...

Cancel   OK

D To resize the current table, enter a value in the
Preferred width box and click OK.

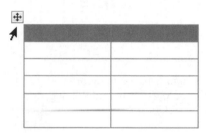

E To move a table to a new location,
click and drag this cross symbol.

- You can change the table width by entering a value in the Preferred width text box on the Table tab of the Table Properties dialog box **D**. You can also change the size of a table manually by dragging its bottom-right corner.

- To move a table, move the cursor over the table or select a cell in the table. A cross symbol appear above the table's upper-left corner **E**. Click and drag the cross symbol to move the table.

TIP **You can double-click the cross symbol E to *select* the table.**

Entering Data

After you've created a table, you can start entering your information.

To enter data into a table:

1. Click in the first table cell and then type.

   As you type, the text wraps within the cell as necessary. The entire row will become taller if it needs to accommodate multiple lines of text **A**.

2. After completing the entry in the first cell, press Tab to move to the cell to its right, and type text in that cell.

   When you reach the rightmost cell of a row, pressing Tab moves the insertion mark to the first cell of the next row.

> **TIP** Press Shift-Tab to move back one cell.

> **TIP** You can move directly to any cell by clicking in it.

> **TIP** If there is already text in a cell when you tab into it, the text is automatically selected. If you wish, you can delete the entire cell entry by pressing Delete or by typing over it.

> **TIP** When you finish entering data in the last cell of a table, pressing Tab creates a new row.

> **TIP** Use normal editing procedures to alter and format the information in cells.

> **TIP** You may be able to avoid text wrap within a cell by widening its column or by choosing Table > AutoFit and Distribute > AutoFit to Contents or AutoFit to Window.

Sorting a Table

After you've entered a few rows of data, you can sort the table. Select any cell in the table, and then do one of the following:

- Click Home:Paragraph:Sort.
- Click Table Layout:Alignment:Sort.
- Choose Table > Sort.

Set sort specifications in the Sort dialog box by choosing up to three sort fields, specifying each field *type* (text, number, or date), and selecting a sort order.

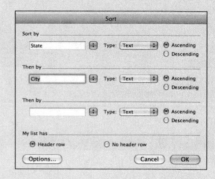

Note that empty rows, if any, are sorted, too. Header rows, on the other hand, are generally excluded.

Cell with excess text

First Name	Last Name	Address	City	State	Zip
James	Anders	2301 East Village Parkway	Flagstaff	AZ	80043

A If you enter text that's wider than the cell width, the row height expands as needed to fully display the text.

Click an icon on the Formatting toolbar or in the Home:Paragraph group to set left, centered, right, or justified alignment.

Alignment

Align   Direction   Margins

✓ Top Left

   Top Center

   Top Right

   Center Left

   Center

   Center Right

   Bottom Left

   Bottom Center

   Bottom Right

B You can also set *vertical alignment* (top, center, or bottom) for cell data.

C You can orient cell text in these three directions.

Aligning Table Data

Although the default cell formatting for content is left-aligned and horizontal, you can change the alignment or orientation.

To change the alignment or orientation of cell data:

Do any of the following:

- **Alignment.** Select the cells whose alignment you want to change. Click an alignment icon on the Formatting toolbar A or the Home:Paragraph group, or choose a command from the Table Layout:Alignment:Align drop-down menu B.

- **Orientation.** To change the orientation of data within cells, select the cells you want to orient. Choose a command from the Layout:Text Layout:Direction or the Table Layout:Alignment:Direction drop-down menu. Continue choosing rotation commands until you get the desired orientation C.

TIP You can also set text direction or alignment by right-clicking a selected cell. Choose Text Direction, or choose a command from the Cell Alignment or Alignment submenu.

TIP Another way to change text direction is to select the desired cell(s) and choose Format > Text Direction. The advantage of this approach is that you can select a specific direction in the Text Direction dialog box.

TIP To specify a *table's* alignment on the page, select any cell, and choose Table > Table Properties or click Table Layout:Settings: Properties. Select Alignment and Text wrap options on the Table tab of the Table Properties dialog box (see D in "Editing the Table Structure" earlier in this chapter).

Working with Numeric Data

Word tables have calculation capabilities that are similar to those of an Excel worksheet. You can use the AutoSum feature to total columns or rows of numeric values, as well as insert another formula into any cell.

To total a row or column:

1. Do one of the following:

   ▶ To total values in a column, click in the cell beneath the numbers you're adding, and then click the Table Layout : Data : AutoSum icon.

   ▶ To total values in a row, click in the cell to the right of the numbers you're adding, and click the Table Layout : Data : AutoSum icon.

   The Formula dialog box appears **A**.

2. If necessary, edit the formula. Click OK.

   To refer to the string of cells immediately above or to the left, AutoSum uses Above and Left, such as **=SUM(ABOVE)** or **=AVERAGE(LEFT)**.

TIP To add a blank row for totals, click in the last row and choose Table > Insert > Rows Below. To add an extra column, click in the rightmost column and choose Table > Insert > Columns to the Right.

TIP You can also create Excel-style formulas in tables. Cells in formulas are referenced as though they were in a worksheet. For example, the top five cells in the first column would be referenced as A1:A5. Click in the cell where you want to display the result, choose Table > Formula, and enter a formula in the Formula dialog box **A**. See Chapter 12 for information about creating formulas.

TIP You can insert functions by choosing them from the Paste function drop-down list **A**.

TIP To view the formula in a given cell, select the cell and choose Table > Formula.

TIP Table formulas do not recalculate automatically. To force a recalculation, reapply the AutoSum or formula to the result cell or right-click the cell and choose Update Field from the contextual menu that appears.

TIP If you need greater calculation capabilities, set up the data and formulas in Excel, and copy/paste the cells into Word as an embedded or linked table. For more information, refer to Chapter 27.

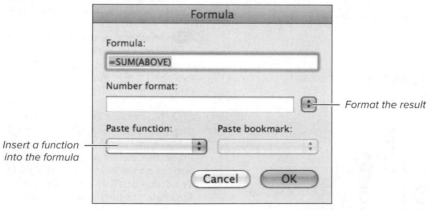

A Choose Table > Formula, and enter a formula in the Formula dialog box.

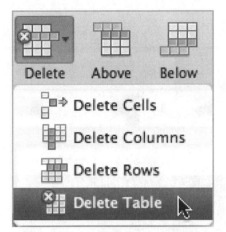

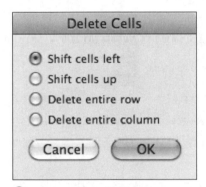

Deleting Cells

You can easily remove cells from a table by deleting the entire table, full rows or columns, or only selected cells.

To delete table cells:

Do any of the following:

- To delete an entire table, click any cell and choose Table > Delete > Table or Table Layout:Rows & Columns:Delete > Delete Table **A**.

- To delete entire rows or columns, select one or more cells from the row(s) or column(s), and choose Rows or Columns from the Table > Delete submenu or the equivalent command from the Delete icon's drop-down menu **A**.

- To delete selected cells in a table, choose Table > Delete > Cells or Table Layout:Rows & Columns:Delete > Delete Cells **A**. The Delete Cells dialog box appears **B**. You can delete the selected cells, moving the rest up or to the left (to close up the deletion), or you can delete entire rows or columns.

A All table-related deletion commands can be chosen from the Delete icon's menu.

B In the Delete Cells dialog box, indicate how surrounding cells will adjust following the deletion.

C You can also right-click selected cells and choose Delete Cells.

> **TIP** You can also open the Delete Cells dialog box by selecting the cell(s), right-clicking the selection, and choosing Delete Cells from the contextual menu **C**.

> **TIP** Deleting a cell, row, or column is not the same as simply clearing the cells' contents. The Delete commands actually remove selected cells, rows, or columns from the table. To clear one or more cells of their data, select the cells and choose Edit > Clear > Contents.

> **TIP** If you accidentally delete a table or any part of it, you can restore the deleted portions by immediately choosing the Edit > Undo command, pressing Command-Z, or clicking the Undo icon on the Standard toolbar.

Merging and Splitting Cells

Using the Merge Cells command, you can combine two or more adjacent cells into a single cell (to display an extended column or row heading, for example). Similarly, you can use the Split Cells command to split a single cell into multiple cells. Split Cells is also useful for restoring merged cells to their original multicell structure. Finally, you can use the Split Table command to divide a table into two tables.

To merge cells:

1. Select two or more adjacent cells to be merged **A**.

2. Choose Table > Merge Cells or click the Table Layout:Merge:Merge icon.

   The cells merge **B**.

To split a cell:

1. Select the cell that you want to split into multiple cells.

2. Choose Table > Split Cells or click the Table Layout:Merge:Split Cells icon.

   The Split Cells dialog box appears **C**.

3. Specify the number of columns and rows into which to split the cell. Click OK.

To split a table:

1. Select a cell in the row that will become the first row of the new table.

2. Choose Table > Split Table or click the Table Layout:Merge:Split Table icon.

   The table is split into two tables.

2010 Sales (Millions)				
	Qtr 1	Qtr 2	Qtr 3	Qtr 4
North	1.25	3.10	2.96	3.22
East	2.22	1.04	0.87	1.96
South	1.89	0.72	2.21	1.85
West	3.04	4.16	4.24	3.99

A Select the cells that you want to merge (in this case, the top row) and click the Merge icon.

Merged cells

2010 Sales (Millions)			
Qtr 1	Qtr 2	Qtr 3	Qtr 4
North	1.25	3.10	2.96	3.22
East	2.22	1.04	0.87	1.96
South	1.89	0.72	2.21	1.85
West	3.04	4.16	4.24	3.99

B The cells merge, creating a single cell in which to display the table's title.

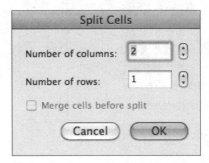

C When splitting a cell, you specify the number of resulting columns and rows.

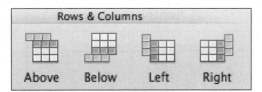

Rows & Columns

Above   Below   Left   Right

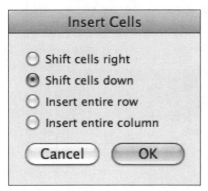

(A) You can add new rows or columns by clicking icons in the Table Layout: Rows & Columns group.

Insert Cells

○ Shift cells right
◉ Shift cells down
○ Insert entire row
○ Insert entire column

[Cancel] [OK]

(B) When you insert new cells into a table, you must indicate how the insertion will affect surrounding cells.

Adding Rows and Columns

Another way you can change a table layout is to insert new rows, columns, or cells.

To insert a new row:

1. Click a cell in the row that will serve as the reference for the new row.

2. Choose Rows Above or Rows Below from the Table > Insert submenu, or click the Above or Below icon in the Table Layout: Rows & Columns group (A).

   The new row appears.

To insert a new column:

1. Click a cell in the column that will serve as the reference for the new column.

2. Choose Columns to the Left or Columns to the Right from the Table > Insert submenu, or click the Left or Right icon in the Table Layout: Rows & Columns group (A).

   The new column appears.

To insert new cells:

1. Select the cell or cells that will serve as the reference for the new cell(s).

2. Choose Table > Insert > Cells.

   The Insert Cells dialog box appears (B).

3. Select an option and click OK.

   The new cells are inserted into the table, and the surrounding cells are adjusted as specified.

TIP To insert multiple columns or rows, select the desired number of table columns or rows and then issue the Insert command.

Nesting Tables

Nested tables are tables within tables. They can be handy if you have a special subcategory of information that the table needs to show. Inserting a nested table is similar to creating a new table.

To insert a nested table:

1. Select a cell in your current table in which to insert the nested table **A**.

2. Click the Tables:Table Options:New icon, and drag to specify the nested table's dimensions **B**.

   The nested table appears within the original table **C**.

TIP You can also insert a nested table by choosing Table > Insert > Table or by choosing Insert Table from the New icon's menu **B**. For instructions on using the Insert Table dialog box, refer to the first tip following "Creating a Basic Table," earlier in this chapter.

TIP As with other tables, you can resize a nested table by dragging its lower-right corner.

Selected cell

	Species	Jan.-June	July-Dec.
Cats	Abyssinian	37	45
	Burmese	12	17
Dogs	Retriever	52	55
	Corgi	23	18
	Total	**124**	**135**

A Select the location where the nested table will be inserted.

B Click and drag to indicate the size of the nested table (in this example, a single row with two columns).

Nested table

	Species		Jan.-June	July-Dec.
Cats	Abyssinian		37	45
	Burmese		12	17
Dogs	Retriever		52	55
	Golden	Blonde		
	Corgi		23	18
	Total		**124**	**135**

C The nested table is added to the table.

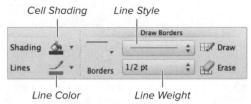

Cell Shading   *Line Style*

Line Color   *Line Weight*

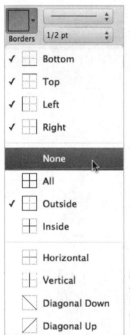

A Choose a line style, weight, and color from the Table Styles and Draw Borders groups.

B Choose borders from the Borders icon in the Draw Borders group, the Home: Paragraph group, or on the Formatting toolbar.

Date	Check #	Payee	Amount	Description
1/6/10		T Rowe Price Rollover IRA	$4,000.00	IRA withdrawal
1/15/10	Disc	Mohave Community College	$261.00	Tuition the
1/15/10	cash	Mohave Community College Bookstore	$7.95	English book
1/27/10	Disc	Mohave Community College Bookstore	$81.00	Psychology book
4/15/10		IRS	$942.00	2009 Refund applied to pay 1st Est.
5/22/10		AZ Dept. of Revenue	$18.00	2009 tax refund
5/27/10		IRS	$897.00	Excess 2009 refund
6/10/10	cash	Mohave Community College	$50.00	GED testing fee
8/6/10	cash	Visions	$425.00	Theft of glasses (casualty)

C A table with borders, varied line styles, and shading often looks more professional.

Borders and Cell Shading

Borders are the lines surrounding cells. *Shading* is a color and/or pattern fill within cells. The Table Layout:Table Styles gallery contains many attractive formats that you can apply to a table (discussed in "Creating a Basic Table," earlier in this chapter). If you prefer, you can follow the procedure below to set cell borders and shading manually.

To set borders and shading manually:

1. Select the cells whose borders or shading you want to set or change.

2. From the Tables:Table Styles and Draw Borders groups **A**, choose a line style, weight, and border color.

3. Click the Borders icon in the Draw Borders group and select the type of border (such as top, bottom, left, right, or outside) that you want to apply to the cells **B**.

4. To apply shading to the selected cells, click the Shading icon in the Table Styles group and select a color from the drop-down palette.

   The completed table can contain any combination of borders and shading **C**.

TIP Word provides another way to draw lines that you may find simpler. After selecting a line style, weight, and border color, click the Draw Table icon **A**. Each table line that you click or draw with the Draw Table tool will use the selected line settings.

TIP For more complex border and shading requirements, use the Borders and Shading dialog box. Select the cells to format, and then choose Format > Borders and Shading.

Converting Text to a Table

You can convert existing text in a Word document into a table.

To convert text to a table:

1. Select the lines of existing text you want to convert into a table **A**.

2. Choose Table > Convert > Convert Text to Table or Tables : Table Options : New > Convert Text to Table.

3. In the Table size section of the Convert Text to Table dialog box **B**, indicate the number of columns and rows that the table will contain. In the Separate text at section, select the character you used to separate data elements.

4. Click OK to generate the table.

   The selected text is converted into a table **C**. To adjust the formatting and style, see "Editing the Table Structure" and "Borders and Cell Shading," earlier in this chapter.

> **TIP** To automatically convert selected text into an appropriate table, choose Table > Insert > Table.

> **TIP** To convert multiple paragraphs into a table, select those paragraphs, choose Table > Convert > Convert Text to Table, and select Paragraphs as the text separator in the Convert Text to Table dialog box **B**.

> **TIP** If you're converting tab-delimited text into a table, make sure that the text doesn't have multiple tab characters between items that should be in adjacent columns—even if removing the extra tabs makes the spacing look wrong.

> **TIP** You can convert a table into text by choosing Table > Convert > Convert Table to Text.

A Select the text you want to convert into a table. In this instance, the text is tab-delimited.

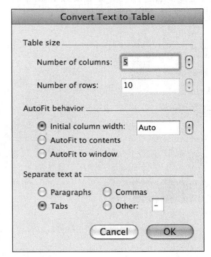

B Specify conversion options in the Convert Text to Table dialog box.

Date	Check #	Payee	Amount	Description
1/6/10		T Rowe Price Rollover IRA	$4,000.00	IRA withdrawal
1/15/10	Disc	Mohave Community College	$261.00	Tuition
1/15/10	cash	Mohave Community College Bookstore	$7.95	English book
1/27/10	Disc	Mohave Community College Bookstore	$81.00	Psychology book
4/13/10		IRS	$942.00	2009 Refund applied to pay 1st Est.
5/22/10		AZ Dept. of Revenue	$18.00	2009 tax refund
5/27/10		IRS	$897.00	Excess 2009 refund
6/10/10	cash	Mohave Community College	$50.00	GED testing fee
8/6/10	cash	Visions	$425.00	Theft of glasses (casualty)

C The selected text is converted into a Word table.

8

Working in Other Views

Many people—perhaps most—only use Word for traditional word-processing tasks, such as writing letters, memos, and the occasional report. In all but the rarest case, such work can readily be accomplished in Print Layout View (when you need to see your document formatted exactly as it will print) and Draft View (when you're more interested in generating text as fast as possible). However, Word also has other views that are more appropriate for some tasks and situations.

In this chapter, you'll learn to use these additional Word views:

- Use Outline View to create outlines.

- Use Notebook Layout View to help organize your thoughts.

- Design catalogues, newsletters, menus, and other complex publications in Publishing Layout View.

- Work in Full Screen View when you want to dedicate the entire screen to reading or editing a document.

In This Chapter

Outline View

Most of us remember creating outlines in school. Sometimes it was because we were forced to do so as part of an assignment. Other times it was because we found them useful for organizing our thoughts for a presentation, paper, or project. If you want to explore the ease with which computer-based outlines can be created and organized, you can use Outline View.

Creating an outline

When creating an outline, any document can be switched from Draft or Print Layout View into Outline View. However, it's more common to create a new document specifically for this purpose.

To create an outline:

1. In a new document, switch to Outline View by clicking the Outline View icon in the bottom-left corner of the document window **A** or by choosing View > Outline.

2. Display the Outline Tools group **B** on the Home tab.

3. Type the first item and press Return.

   Word marks it as a Level 1 item, formatted using the Heading 1 style. Each subsequent item (created by pressing Return to start a new paragraph) will be at the same level as the previous item.

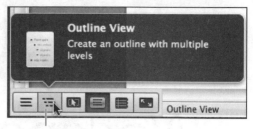

Outline View

A You can switch to Outline View by clicking its icon at the bottom of the document window.

Outline Formatting

Every point in an outline is formatted with a Heading style that corresponds to the point's level. For example, Level 1 points are formatted with the Heading 1 style. To change the formatting for a level, choose Format > Style and then modify that Heading style (see Chapter 6).

If you ever want to view an outline as single-font text (rather than displaying the default or custom formatting of the various Heading styles), click the Home:Outlining Tools:Formatting icon.

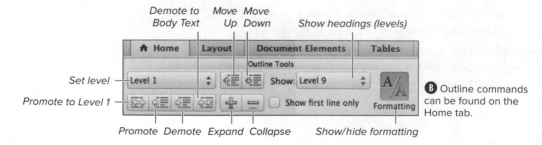

B Outline commands can be found on the Home tab.

Item to be moved

C You can promote, demote, or move an item by clicking its outline symbol and then dragging the item to a new location (up or down) or level (to the left or right).

Show: All Levels ▲▼

D To focus on material of differing levels of importance, choose a level from the Show drop-down menu.

Other Outliners

While Outline View can certainly serve your basic outlining needs, there are other very capable outliners available for Mac OS X. They have features such as multiple columns (for recording notes, dates, and other items related to each outline point), calculation capabilities, and advanced point-numbering features.

To learn more about two of my favorite Mac outliners, check out:

- NoteBook (**www.circusponies.com**)
- OmniOutliner (**www.omnigroup.com**)

Working with outlines

You can change an item's level by demoting or promoting it, rearrange and delete items, and change your view of the outline.

To change a selected item's level:

Do any of the following:

- To raise an item's level by one, click Home:Outline Tools:Promote **B** or press Control-Shift-Left Arrow.

- To lower an item's level by one, click Home:Outline Tools:Demote **B** or press Control-Shift-Right Arrow.

- To manually promote or demote an item and its subordinates, move the cursor over the item's outline symbol (**+** or **–**). When the cursor becomes a cross **C**, drag left or right to the desired level.

- Click Home:Outline Tools:Demote to Body Text **B** to change a selected item into body text. (This is useful for adding comments related to the point above.)

To move an item and subordinates:

- Select the item and drag it to its new destination in the outline.

- To delete a selected item, press Delete.

To change your view of the outline:

Do any of the following:

- To show the entire outline, choose All Levels from the Show menu **D**. Choose a specific level to show only items that are at that level or higher.

- To expand or collapse an item by one level, click the Home:Outline Tools: Expand or Collapse icon **B**. Each additional click shows or hides another level.

- To hide/show an item's subordinate items, double-click its plus (**+**) symbol.

Notebook Layout View

Notebook Layout View can help organize your thoughts concerning projects, reports, and many other activities. To facilitate note taking, you can insert pictures, freehand drawings, and audio notes. To help arrange your notes, a notebook has section tabs. Each continuously scrolling section can be as long as necessary, encompassing many pages.

To create a notebook:

Do either of the following:

- Open the Word Document Gallery 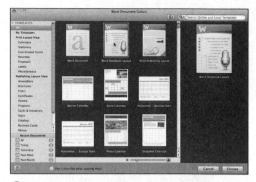 by choosing File > New From Template (Shift-Command-P). Select the All category, select the Word Notebook Layout thumbnail, and click Choose.

- With an existing Word document or a new, blank document active, click the Notebook Layout View icon **B** at the bottom of the window or choose View > Notebook Layout. In the dialog box that appears **C**, click Convert to change the current document into a notebook or click Create New to open a new notebook document.

  The Notebook Layout View Standard toolbar appears, as does the Notebook Ribbon **D**.

> **TIP** If a notebook is active, you can create a new notebook by choosing File > New Blank Notebook Layout Document (Command-N).

A To start a notebook from scratch, select its thumbnail in the Word Document Gallery.

B The Notebook Layout View icon.

C You can convert the current document to a notebook or create a new, blank notebook.

Notebook Layout View Standard toolbar

D Whenever you work on a notebook, a notebook-specific toolbar and Ribbon automatically appear.

Title   Button

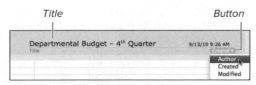

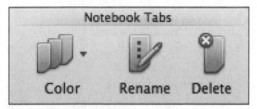

E Type the notebook's title in the space provided. Choose a notebook identifier by clicking the text button on the right.

F You can rename, delete, or change the color of any section tab (found on the notebook's edge).

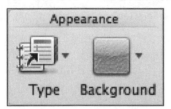

G For a ruled notebook, choose Standard from the Style drop-down menu and specify the Distance between lines. For a blank notebook, choose None from the Style menu.

H Choose a notebook style from the Type drop-down menu and background design from the Background drop-down menu.

Identification and customization

Although you can immediately start entering note text as you would in a Draft or Print Layout View document, you can improve any notebook by adding clear, identifying information and customizing the notebook's "look."

To add a title:

For each section tab, do the following:

- Type the title on the Title line at the top of the notebook **E**.
- You can change the identifying information by clicking the text button **E**.

To change the section tabs:

Do any of the following:

- To add a new section to a notebook, click the plus (**+**) section tab.
- Change the order of the section tabs by dragging them up or down.
- To rename, delete, or choose a new color for a tab, Control-click or right-click the tab or choose commands from the Appearance:Notebook Tabs group **F**.

TIP You can quickly rename a section tab by double-clicking its name and then editing.

To change a notebook's appearance:

Do any of the following:

- In the Appearance:Rule Lines group **G**, show/hide the rule lines or change their spacing.
- Choose a notebook style and background from the Appearance: Appearance:Type and Background menus **H**.

TIP You can also choose a background from the Customize Workspace icon on the status bar at the bottom of the document window.

Entering notes

Type as you do in a normal document. To start a new note, press Return. Individual notes can contain multiple lines of text and will automatically wrap as necessary.

You can use click and type to start a new note anywhere in a section. Just double-click to set the text insertion mark on the line where you want to add the new note.

Setting levels

Like outline items, notes can be indented to denote subordinate items by choosing commands from the Home:Note Levels group **I**. To indent (*demote*) a selected note, press Tab or click the Home:Note Levels:Demote icon. To promote a note to a higher level, press Shift-Tab or click Home:Note Levels:Promote. You can also demote or promote a note by choosing a specific level from the Note Level drop-down menu.

TIP You can simultaneously set a new level for multiple selected notes.

Formatting notes

Every note set—including a lone note—is considered a list and must be bulleted or numbered. To designate a note set as a bulleted or numbered list, click an icon in Home:Lists groups **J**. For each list, you can apply a different bullet or number style by choosing an option from the Home:Lists:Style drop-down menu **J**.

Notebook text can be selectively formatted. Apply formatting by choosing commands from the Home:Font group **K** or from the Format and Font menus.

TIP If change tracking marks are visible, you can hide them by choosing View > Markup.

Set level

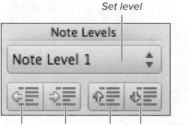

Promote Demote Move up Move down

I Select commands from the Note Levels group to change the current note's level or to move it up or down in the notebook.

Bulleted   Numbered

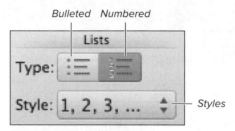

Styles

J For each note set, click Bulleted or Numbered, and choose a style.

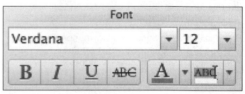

K You can format selected text by applying Font group commands.

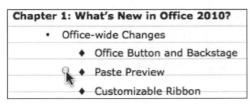

L When you move the cursor over a note's left edge, a selection symbol appears. You can click the symbol and drag the note to another location or level.

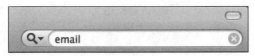

M Enter a search string and press Return. All matches found in the document are highlighted.

Dimensions (columns x rows)

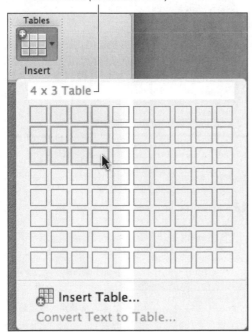

N Drag to set the table dimensions.

Reorganizing notes

In addition to cut and paste, there are techniques to help you rearrange your notes.

To rearrange notes in a section:

Do any of the following:

- To move a note and any subordinate notes to a new location, select the note by clicking the symbol to its left. Drag the note(s) to the new position **L**.

- Select a single note or a collapsed note group and click a Move icon in the Home:Note Levels group **I**.

Searching notes for text matches

To find text within a notebook, type a search string in the Quick Search box **M** and press Return. All matching instances are highlighted. (Matches in other sections are indicated by highlighted tabs.)

Inserting tables

You can add tables to display data, lists, and other tabular material.

To insert a table:

Do either of the following:

- Click Home:Tables:Insert, and drag to set the table's dimensions **N**.

- Choose Home:Tables:Insert > Insert Table. Specify the table dimensions in the Insert Table dialog box that appears.

- To manually create a table by drawing its lines, choose Table > Draw Table.

For more information about creating, modifying, and formatting tables, refer to Chapter 7.

> **TIP** If the Tables group isn't visible on the right edge of the Ribbon, widen the document.

Adding images, movies, and music

To insert these types of material, choose an item from the Insert menu ⓞ or drag a file icon onto the notebook page.

TIP Many types of material (such as photos, songs, and movies) can also be dragged from the Media Browser ⓟ onto a notebook page. Open the Media Browser by choosing View > Media Browser or by clicking the Media Browser toolbar icon.

Images, movies, and music can be inline or floating. And you can set a wrap style for any inserted item. To edit an inserted graphic, select it and choose commands from the Format Picture contextual tab.

To play an inserted movie or music clip, double-click the clip or right-click it and choose Play from the contextual menu. When playing, each clip displays a Quick-Time control bar with buttons for starting, pausing, stopping, and restarting playback; adjusting the volume; and so on.

Making freehand drawings

You can use the Scribble tool to create freehand drawings by doing the following:

- To draw in the current color and line width, click the pen icon in the Home:Scribble group. Draw by dragging on the notebook page.

- To set a new pen color and/or line width, choose new settings from the Scribble tool's drop-down menu ⓠ.

- To erase a drawn object, select the Home:Scribble:Eraser and click the object you want to erase.

TIP You can also delete a selected object by pressing Delete.

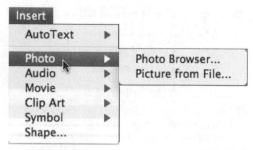

ⓞ You can insert many kinds of items by choosing a command from the Insert menu.

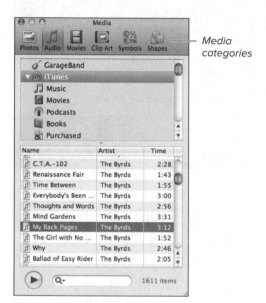

Media categories

ⓟ Add items from the Media Browser.

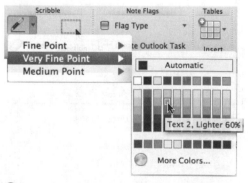

ⓠ Click the Scribble tool in the Home:Scribble group, and choose a new pen point and color.

Audio note

S Attached audio is denoted by a speaker icon.

T You can also choose recording, playback, and audio-handling commands from the Tools menu.

Recording audio

If you have a microphone-equipped Mac, you can record audio notes for any notebook. You can attach audio notes to as many notes as you like.

To record an audio note:

1. Set the text insertion mark in the note to which you want to attach a recording.

2. To access the audio tools, select the Audio Notes tab on the Ribbon **R** (page bottom).

3. Click Audio Notes:Record Audio:Record and speak into the microphone.

4. To end the recording, click Audio Notes: Record Audio:Stop.

   When the Audio Notes:Advanced:Show icon is selected, a speaker icon appears beside each audio note **S**. Otherwise, the icon appears only when the cursor is moved over or into the note.

5. To listen to audio notes, do either of the following:

   ▸ To play a specific audio note, click the speaker icon in the note's margin **S**.

   ▸ To play all notes in the order they were recorded, click Audio Notes:Audio Playback:Play or click the speaker icon of the first recorded audio note. Word automatically flips to the proper page as it plays each audio note.

   Control playback by clicking buttons **R** or by choosing commands from the Tools > Audio Notes submenu **T**.

Status indicator *Level indicator*   *Controls*   *Show audio notes*

R Use the tools on the Audio Notes tab to create and play audio notes.

Publishing Layout View

You can use Publishing Layout View for simple desktop publishing tasks, such as creating newsletters, flyers, and brochures. In the past, people used Print Layout View to create such material. However, the following Publishing Layout View tools can help you overcome many of the difficulties of doing layout work in Print Layout View:

- **Master pages.** Behind every document page is a master page that contains static material for the page, such as a corporate logo or page numbers. You can create different masters for odd and even pages, as well as make a separate one that applies only to the first page.

- **Guides.** To make it easier to place text boxes, photos, and other objects, you can add *guides* (lines) to master or content pages. When you print, the guides disappear.

- **Text boxes.** Rather than click and type as you do in other Word documents, you indicate where you want text to appear on each page by drawing text boxes. You can also create links between text boxes to specify how the text should flow from one text box to the next.

Templates vs. Blank Publications

Although you can create publications from scratch, you'll find it simpler and less confusing to start by using and experimenting with some of the provided templates. Substitute your own photos or clip art images for the ones in the template, replace the placeholder text with your copy, and experiment with the layout features, such as adding guides, inserting and removing pages, and creating and linking text boxes.

When you feel that you have a handle on the basics, you'll be better prepared to create your own publications from scratch.

Categories *Selected thumbnail* *Preview*

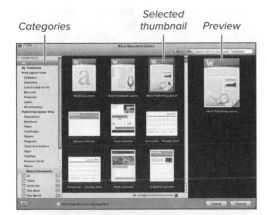

A The most straightforward way to create a blank publication is to select its thumbnail in the gallery.

B If the current document is new, you can change it into a publication by clicking the Publishing Layout View icon at the bottom of the window.

C This easily accessible dialog box enables you to convert the current document to Publishing Layout View or to create a blank publication.

Starting a publication

There are a number of ways to start a new publication. Use whichever method is convenient for you.

To create a blank publication:

If you want to design a publication and its master page(s) from scratch, do one of the following:

- Open the Word Document Gallery **A** by choosing File > New From Template, (Shift-Command-P). Select the All category, select the Word Publishing Layout thumbnail, and click Choose. Or select the Publishing Layout View category and open the Blank template.

- Create a new blank document. Click the Publishing Layout View icon in the lower-left corner of the document window **B** or choose View > Publishing Layout. Click OK in response to the Welcome dialog box.

- If a publication is open, you can choose File > New Blank Publishing Layout Document (Command-N).

To create a publication from a template:

1. Open the Word Document Gallery (see the previous step list).

2. Select a template from the Publishing Layout View category or one of its subcategories.

3. Click the Choose button or double-click the template's thumbnail.

    TIP You can also convert an open Word document into a publication. Click the Publishing Layout View icon **B** or choose View > Publishing Layout. In the dialog box that appears **C**, click Continue to convert the document into a publication or click Create New to create a blank publication.

Master and content pages

Every publication page has two layers. In the top layer are *content* pages. That's where you'll place most of the document's text and photos. Beneath the content layer of every page is a *master* page. Static items, such as running heads, page numbers, logos, and boilerplate text are generally placed on master pages. Unless covered by solid material in the content layer, master page items show through.

When you create a blank publication, the initial master page is also blank, allowing you to create it and others from scratch (or ignore them, if they aren't needed). When you select a publication template, on the other hand, its master pages often contain material. However, you can replace their contents, change the formatting, or whatever you like.

A publication can have one master page or different masters for even and odd pages (as is the case with many two-sided documents, such as magazines and books). The first page can also have its own master.

To view or edit a master page:

1. *Optional:* To view a specific master page, scroll to its content page.

2. Click the Master Pages tab in the lower-right corner of the window **D**.

   The master page for the current page is shown **E**. Each master page is labeled in its upper-left corner. To view others, scroll using the vertical scroll bar.

   You can add graphics to any master page as you do in other Word documents. To add text, you must create text boxes (as explained later in this section).

3. When you're done viewing and editing master pages, click the All Contents tab.

D Click a tab to switch between viewing content and master pages.

Master page identifier

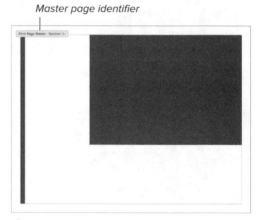

E This master page for a brochure template contains only this graphic background.

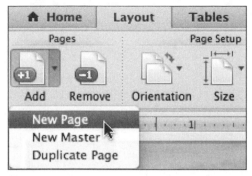

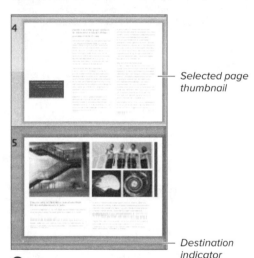

Selected page thumbnail

Destination indicator

G To move a page, drag its thumbnail up or down. The solid line indicates the destination.

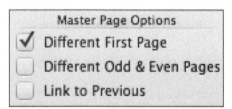

H Select master page types by clicking check boxes in the Master Page Options group.

To insert a new content page:

1. In the All Contents layer, display or select material on the page immediately above where you want to add the content page.

   For example, to create a new page 3, display content page 2.

2. Choose Insert > New Page or choose Layout : Pages : Add > New Page **F**.

   The new content page appears.

To insert a new master page:

1. In the All Contents layer, display or select material on the page immediately above where you want to add the master page.

   Note that when inserting a new master, a new content page is also created.

2. Choose Insert > New Master or choose Layout : Pages : Add > New Master **F**.

   A new content page is inserted immediately after the current page, along with a new master to be used with the page.

To delete a content page:

1. In the All Contents layer, display or select material on the page you want to delete.

2. Click the Layout : Pages : Remove icon **F**.

   The page is deleted from the publication.

> **TIP** Although you can insert a page in the middle of a publication, it's more common to expand a publication by adding pages to its end.

> **TIP** If you need to reorganize pages, choose View > Sidebar > Thumbnail Pane. Select the thumbnail of the page you want to move and drag it up or down in the page list **G**.

> **TIP** You can specify the types of master pages needed in a publication by clicking the Master Pages tab **D** and then checking options in the Layout : Master Page Options group **H**.

F On the Layout tab, click the Add icon and choose New Page from the drop-down menu.

Working with guides

Guides are nonprinting lines that help you align objects and create precisely sized and placed text boxes in a publication. There are three types of guides: margin, static, and dynamic.

Margin guides show the page margins (top, bottom, left, and right) as a blue bounding rectangle. If you change the margins in the Layout:Margins group or by choosing Format > Document, the margin guides adjust automatically.

Static guides are manually positioned vertical or horizontal lines that can be added in any quantity to content or master pages 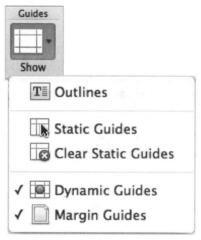. Their purpose is to help you align placed objects and text boxes. Such items automatically snap to the guides. If you place static guides on a master page, they are repeated on all master pages of the same type (for example, Even Page Masters). Static guides placed on a master page are pink; ones placed on a content page are blue.

Dynamic guides appear as you drag an object. They make it easy to precisely place an object by appearing automatically whenever a side or center of the object aligns with something else on the page, such as the page's horizontal or vertical center or the edge or center of another object.

TIP Unless you find the dynamic guides intrusive, you should leave them enabled.

To enable or disable a guide type:

- Click the Layout:Guides:Show icon and choose a guide type from the drop-down menu 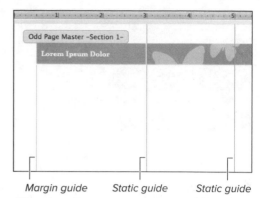.

  Enabled guides are checked; disabled guides are unchecked.

Margin guide   Static guide   Static guide

I The ever-present margin guides show the page margins. Static guides enable you to easily and accurately position placed objects and text.

J Items on the Show icon's menu work as toggles. Each guide type can be enabled or disabled.

K To place a static guide, drag from the vertical (left) or horizontal (right) ruler.

To place static guides:

1. Switch to the layer in which you want to add guides by clicking the All Contents or Master Pages tab **D**.

   Static guides placed in the content layer are specific to the page on which they're placed. Those placed on a master page appear on all master pages of the same type, such as Even Page Master.

2. To add a static guide to the page, move the cursor over the horizontal or vertical ruler. When the cursor changes shape, drag down or across to place the guide.

   As you drag, a ScreenTip shows the guide's exact position **K**.

TIP To reposition a static guide, switch to the layer (content or master) in which the guide exists and move the cursor over the guide. When the cursor changes shape **K**, you can drag the guide to a new position on the page.

TIP To remove a static guide, drag it off the page. You can also remove a static guide by displaying the appropriate content or master page and then choosing Clear Static Guides from the Show icon's menu **J**.

TIP To temporarily hide *all* static guides (regardless of whether they're on a content or master page), remove the check mark from the Static Guides command on the Show icon's menu **J**.

Creating text boxes

Because text can be added anywhere to a Publishing Layout (including inside objects), text is bounded by a rectangular box. Either these text boxes already exist (templates often include text placeholders) or you can create, size, and position them as required.

To create a text box:

1. Do one of the following:

   ▸ To create a text box, select the Text Box tool 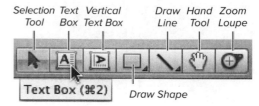, choose Insert > Text Box, choose Home:Insert:Text Box > Text Box, or press Command-2.

   ▸ To draw a box that displays text vertically, select the Vertical Text Box tool , choose Home:Insert:Text Box > Vertical Text Box, or press Command-3.

2. Display the content or master page on which you want to create the text box.

3. Click and drag to create the rectangular text box . Release the mouse button to complete the box.

   The text insertion mark appears within the box, ready for you to start typing.

4. Type or paste text into the box.

   The text automatically wraps as needed to fit within the text box's bounds.

TIP You can format selected text within the box by choosing commands from the Format menu or from the Font, Paragraph, and Typography groups on the Home tab.

TIP To apply a single format to *all* text within a text box, select the box with the Selection Tool and then apply the formatting .

Selection Tool *Text Box* *Vertical Text Box* *Draw Line* *Hand Tool* *Zoom Loupe*

Text Box (⌘2)   *Draw Shape*

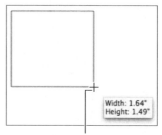

To draw a text box, select the Text Box or Vertical Text Box tool on the toolbar.

Text Box cursor

Width: 1.64"
Height: 1.49"

As you drag to create a text box, a ScreenTip shows its current dimensions.

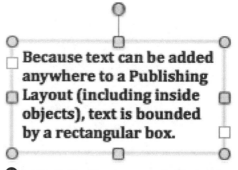

Because text can be added anywhere to a Publishing Layout (including inside objects), text is bounded by a rectangular box.

A selected text box is surrounded by handles.

Resizing and Moving Text Boxes

To change a text box's size, drag any handle. To resize it proportionally, Shift-drag a corner handle. To move a box to a new location, select the Selection Tool and drag the box's center.

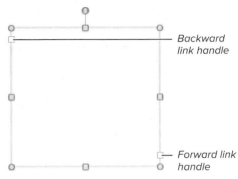

Backward
link handle

Forward link
handle

O To create a link, begin by clicking a link handle.

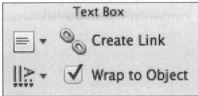

P Use this cursor to draw the new text box to which you'll link.

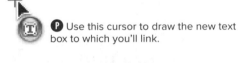

Q To link to an existing empty text box, start by clicking the Create Link icon.

R Use this cursor to select the existing empty text box to which you'll link.

Linking text boxes

Although you are never required to do so, you can instruct text to flow from one box to another. For example, in an article that's spread across multiple columns or extended over many pages, you can make the text flow from one box to the next—creating as many linked text boxes as needed. If you edit, delete, or add to the text, the flow is adjusted automatically—just as word wrap occurs automatically in a normal Word document. Linked text boxes constitute a *story*.

At most, a text box can have two links: one forward and one backwards. Thus, each text box has both a forward and a backward link handle **O**. The text box from which you are creating the link can be empty or it can contain text. The text box to which you're linking, on the other hand, must be empty.

To link text boxes:

1. Select the text box from which you want to link.

2. Do one of the following:

   ▶ **Link to a new text box.** Click the first box's forward or backward link handle. Draw the new text box with the special cursor that appears **P**.

   ▶ **Link to an existing text box.** Click Format:Text Box:Create Link **Q**. Move the special cursor **R** over the empty text box to which you want to link, and then click the box.

   A number appears in the upper-left corner of each linked box to indicate its linking order in the story. Whenever the cursor passes over a linked text box, the number becomes visible.

3. To create additional links, repeat step 2.

TIP If you change your mind about creating a link, press Esc. If you've just created an unwanted link, choose Edit > Undo or Edit > Undo Text Box Linking (Command-Z).

TIP If a story contains more text than can fit in the final text box, a special symbol appears beneath the box **S**. To view the additional text, increase the size of one or more of the story's text boxes or create additional linked boxes to hold the overflow text.

TIP The purpose of links is to ensure that text flows between the text boxes. If you discover that text in the initial box breaks badly (ending in the middle of a paragraph or showing only the first line of a paragraph), you can often correct the problem by adjusting the box's height—making it shorter or taller so the break comes at the desired spot.

TIP If a story is long, you may prefer to create it in a normal Word document. Then use copy and paste or drag and drop to insert it into the Publishing Layout text boxes.

TIP If it becomes necessary, you can *break* links, creating two sets of links where there is currently one. (Breaking a link is a useful first step when you need to insert a text box in the middle of an existing story.) Select the text box that will be the new final link in the story and click the Format:Text Box:Break Link icon **T**. All boxes following the selected one will now be empty.

TIP To remove a linked text box, select it and press Delete. Doing so deletes only the box—not the story text that the box contains.

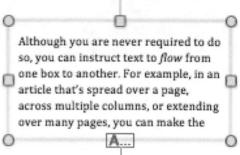

Although you are never required to do so, you can instruct text to *flow* from one box to another. For example, in an article that's spread over a page, across multiple columns, or extending over many pages, you can make the

Overflow indicator

S If you see this indicator beneath a story's final text box, it means that there's additional text for you to place.

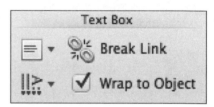

T Click the Break Link icon to break a previously set link between boxes.

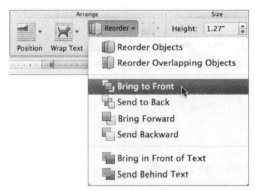

U To move an object forward or backward in the layering order, choose a command from a Reorder icon's drop-down menu.

V Drag the Zoom control to a new position to change the magnification.

Additional Publishing Layout tips

Here are some other Publishing Layout techniques and tips that you may find useful.

Grouping objects. To prevent two or more objects from moving in relation to one another, you can group them so Word will treat them as one object. Select the objects and choose Home:Arrange:Group > Group. Moving one will now cause all to move. If you later need to work individually with the grouped objects, choose Ungroup from the same drop-down menu.

Nudging objects. You can nudge a selected text box or object by pressing arrow keys.

Working in layers. If two or more objects overlap, you can specify their layering by selecting an object and choosing a command from the Home·Arrange:Reorder **U** or Format Picture:Arrange:Reorder menu. Or you can choose Format > Reorder Overlapping Objects to visually manipulate the object layers (see Chapter 3).

More tools. The Publishing Layout View Standard toolbar **L** has other useful tools:

- To switch from a tool, such as the Hand Tool or Zoom Loupe, click the Selection Tool.

- You can create common shapes and line types by choosing items from the Draw Shape or Draw Line drop-down menus and then dragging to draw.

- Use the Hand Tool to move around a page by clicking and dragging. It's more precise than using the scroll bars.

- Use the Zoom Loupe to change the magnification. Drag right or down to increase the magnification; drag left or up to decrease the magnification. You can also set the magnification by dragging the Zoom control **V** at the bottom of the document window.

Full Screen View

Have you ever wished for a way to read or perform basic edits without having to deal with the menus, toolbars, and Ribbon and without the distraction of the Desktop, shortcut icons, and other unnecessary program and document windows? The new Full Screen View 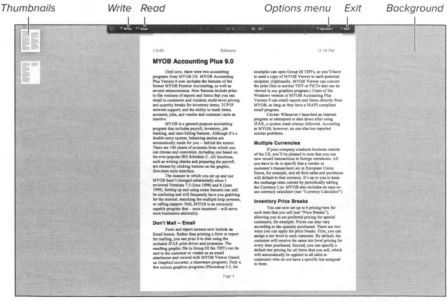 can be used with any Word document other than notebooks.

In Full Screen View, a toolbar stretches across the top of the screen and vanishes when not in use. To make it reappear, move the cursor to the top of the screen.

To view the current document in Full Screen View:

1. Choose View > Full Screen or click the Full Screen View icon at the bottom of the document window.

2. *Optional:* Choose a background from the Options menu on the toolbar.

3. Do either of the following:

   ▸ **Reading view.** To read the document, click the Read toolbar icon. Navigate by clicking thumbnails or toolbar icons; using the vertical scroll bar or the mouse's scroll wheel; or by pressing the Page Up, Page Down, Home, and End keys.

   ▸ **Writing view.** To edit the document, click the Write toolbar icon. Edit as you normally would, choosing commands from the toolbar.

4. To restore the normal document view, click the Exit toolbar icon or press Esc.

Thumbnails   Write Read   Options menu   Exit   Background

Ⓐ In Reading view, the toolbar and thumbnails are dedicated to reading activities.

9

Other Word Features

Many people—perhaps most—only use Word for traditional word-processing tasks, such as writing letters, memos, and an occasional report. However, Word also has a host of ancillary features and capabilities that you may occasionally find useful. In this chapter, you'll learn to do the following:

- Add a cover page from a Document Elements gallery.

- Create labels and print envelopes.

- Use the Mail Merge Manager to create merge documents, such as personalized form letters.

In This Chapter

Adding a Cover Page

To dress up a report or any other important Word document, you can select a cover page from the Cover gallery. An inserted cover page automatically becomes the document's first page. Every cover page has placeholders for important text, such as the document title, date, and so on.

To insert a cover page:

1. Switch to Print Layout View.

   Although you can also insert a cover in Draft or Outline View, you need to be in Print Layout View to view the cover design and edit its text.

2. Select a cover design from the Document Elements : Insert Pages : Cover gallery **A**.

   The chosen cover page becomes the document's first page.

3. Replace the text placeholders **B**, and delete the ones you don't need.

4. *Optional:* To specify a page-numbering format (such as Roman numerals or chapter-relative numbering), click the icon at the top of the cover page and choose Format Page Numbers **C**. Specify settings in the Page Number Format dialog box and click OK.

   See "Page Numbers" in Chapter 5 for instructions on adding page numbers to a Word document.

> **TIP** If you change your mind, you can eliminate a document's cover page by choosing Remove Cover Page **C**.

> **TIP** You can replace an existing cover page by choosing a different design from the Cover gallery. Placeholder text that you've already added will often carry over to the new design.

Cover icon

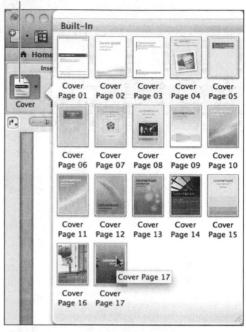

A Select a cover page design from the Cover icon's gallery.

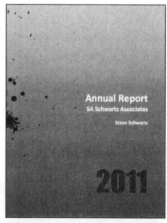

B Cover pages have placeholders that you can replace with your own text.

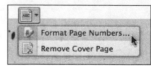

C Use this icon menu to specify a numbering format or delete the cover page.

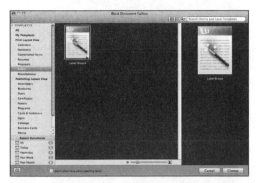

Ⓐ Select the Labels wizard icon and click Choose, or simply double-click the icon.

Ⓑ The Labels dialog box.

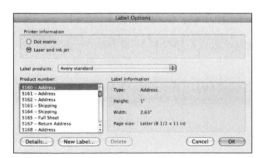

Ⓒ Specify a printer type and the label stock in the Label Options dialog box.

Creating Labels

Word provides templates that you can use to create many kinds of labels, such as mailing labels and name badges. Using the Labels wizard, you can generate a single label or an entire sheet of the same label that will print on popular label stock.

To create labels:

1. Start the Labels wizard by doing either of the following:

   ▶ Open the Word Document Gallery **Ⓐ** by choosing File > New from Template (Shift-Command-P). Select Labels in the Category list, and double-click the Label Wizard icon.

   ▶ Create a new blank document by choosing File > New Blank Document (Command-N), and then choose Tools > Labels.

   The Labels dialog box appears **Ⓑ**.

2. Click the Options button to open the Label Options dialog box **Ⓒ**. Specify the type of printer you'll use, the label manufacturer, and the label's part number. Click OK to dismiss the dialog box.

3. Enter the address or other appropriate text in the Address box of the Labels dialog box **Ⓑ**.

   TIP To create a return address label, you can insert your address from Outlook Contacts by clicking the Use my address check box.

4. Click a radio button in the Number of Labels section **Ⓑ** to indicate what you want to print: Full page of the same label or Single label. If the latter, you must also specify the label row and column on which to print.

continues on next page

5. *Optional:* Click Font ⓑ to alter the font, size, and style of selected text in the Address box. Choose settings in the Font dialog box ⓓ and click OK.

6. *Optional:* To specify a custom paper size or label feed method, click Customize.

7. Click OK to create a label document or click Print to immediately route the labels to the printer.

TIP This procedure is for printing a single label once or many times. If you want to generate labels with different text, such as address labels, see "Creating a Mail Merge," later in this chapter.

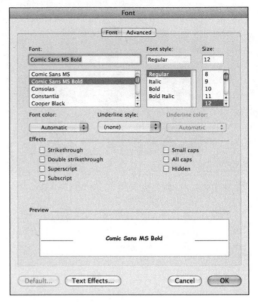

ⓓ To change the font, size, or style of selected text in the Address box ⓑ, choose settings in the Font dialog box.

Categories Templates   Color and font themes

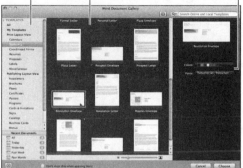

A Select the Stationery category and an envelope design.

B The envelope appears as a new document. Replace the placeholder text with the recipient's address.

Matching Stationery

After creating an envelope from a template, you can complete the effect by also picking matching letterhead from the Stationery category **A**. Each letter template includes placeholders for key components, such as the date, the recipient's name and address, and the letter body (including paragraph formatting).

You can type the placeholder text or choose appropriate commands, such as:

- *Letter date:* Insert > Date and Time
- *Recipient name/address:* Tools > Contacts

If you need help creating a letter, try the Letter Wizard (Tools > Letter Wizard).

Printing Envelopes

Word provides two ways for you to print an envelope:

- You can use an envelope template. Many of the templates include colorful graphics that are excellent for dressing up a plain white envelope.

- The Envelope wizard can extract the mailing address from a Word letter and format it so you can print an envelope. You can also use the wizard to create and print any envelope; it doesn't matter whether the address is extracted from an open document, chosen from the Office or Apple Address Book, or typed by hand. The Envelope wizard can also be used to print on envelopes that have a preprinted return address.

To create an envelope using a template:

1. Open the Word Document Gallery **A** by choosing File > New from Template (Shift-Command-P).

2. Select the Stationery category from the list on the left side of the dialog box.

3. Double-click an envelope thumbnail (such as Revolution Envelope), or select a thumbnail and click Choose.

   The envelope template opens as a new document **B**.

TIP You can optionally choose a different color and font theme from the drop-down menus on the right side of the dialog box **A**.

4. Replace the placeholder text with the recipient's name and address. If necessary, you can also enter or edit the return address.

To create an envelope using the Envelope wizard:

1. Choose Tools > Envelopes.

   The Envelope wizard appears **C**.

2. Type or paste the recipient's address into the Delivery address box, or select the address from the Office or Apple Address Book by clicking the icon beside the box.

   TIP If the active document contains an obvious address, the Envelope wizard may automatically insert the address into the Delivery address box.

3. To specify a return address in the Return address box, do one of the following:

   ▸ Click the Use my address check box to use your address from the Office Address Book as the return address.

   ▸ Type or paste a return address into the Return address box.

   ▸ Click the Address Book icon to select a return address from the Office or Apple Address Book.

   ▸ Click the Omit check box if you're using preprinted envelopes that already have a return address.

4. *Optional:* Click the Font and Position buttons to make changes to the format and position of the delivery and/or return addresses.

5. In the Printing Options section of the wizard, click a radio button to indicate that the envelope will be printed using standard settings for your printer or, in the case of an unsupported envelope size, that custom settings are necessary.

Delivery address   *Address Book*

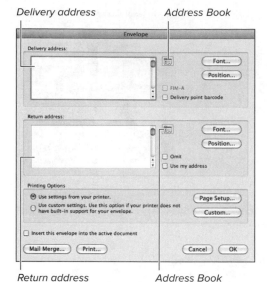

Return address   *Address Book*

C Specify the delivery address, return address (if desired), and formatting options.

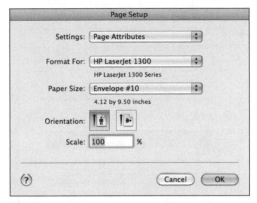

D Choose a printer (Format For), envelope type (Paper Size), and feed direction (Orientation).

Delivery point bar code   FIM-A bar code

E If you want an opportunity to review or edit the envelope, click OK rather than Print.

6. Click the Page Setup button to specify the printer to use, envelope size, and feed method; then click OK **D**.

TIP In the Paper Size drop-down list **D**, Envelope #10 is a standard business envelope.

7. Do either of the following:

‣ If you're satisfied with the formatting and are ready to print the envelope, click Print.

‣ If you want to make further changes to the envelope (reducing the line spacing in the addresses or adding a logo, for example), click OK. The envelope is displayed as a new Word document **E**. Make the desired changes and then print.

TIP The Delivery point bar code option **A** prints a machine-readable version of the Zip Code on the envelope **E** to help the post office process the letter. If you're creating reply envelopes, you can also print a *FIM* (Facing Identification Mark) code by clicking the FIM-A check box. FIM codes are necessary only for business reply mail. Check with the post office for more information.

TIP You can apply fonts selectively. To use a different font or style for only the recipient's name, for example, select the name before clicking the Font button **A**.

TIP Addresses chosen from the Office Address Book routinely include the country. For mail within your country, you'll probably want to delete this line from the return and delivery addresses. Click OK (rather than Print) to create a Word document, make the edits, and then print.

Creating a Mail Merge

Word provides help for creating mail merge letters, labels, and envelopes. It can assist you in creating the main document (containing placeholders for the information that changes with each copy), creating or opening the data source (for example, a collection of names and addresses), and printing the merged documents. In this example, you'll learn how to create form letters using records in the Office Address Book as the data source.

To generate a merge:

1. Create or open the document you'll use as the main document **A**.

    You can use a form letter, a label layout, or an envelope layout, for example.

2. Choose Tools > Mail Merge Manager.

    The Mail Merge Manager appears.

3. In the Select Document Type section **B**, click Create New and choose a merge type (in this example, Form Letters) from the drop-down menu that appears. The name of the current document is inserted as the Main document.

4. Expand the Select Recipients List section **C**, click the Get List icon, and choose one of the following from the drop-down menu:

    ▸ **New Data Source** steps you through the process of creating a data source from scratch.

    ▸ **Open Data Source** lets you use data from a Word or Excel document.

    ▸ **Office Address Book** uses contact information from Outlook Contacts.

    ▸ **Apple Address Book** takes its data from Address Book, a utility included as part of Mac OS X.

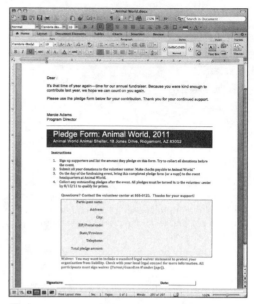

A This form letter will serve as the main document. Space has been left at the top for the recipient's address and the salutation.

B The first section shows the main document's name and the type of merge.

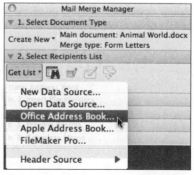

C Choose a data source for the merge.

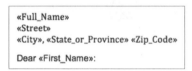

D After you select the data source, its list of fields appears. Drag fields into position in the document.

```
«Full_Name»
«Street»
«City», «State_or_Province» «Zip_Code»

Dear «First_Name»:
```

E The merge field placeholders are placed in the main document.

View Merged Data   *View placeholders*

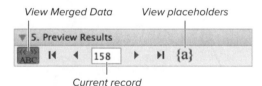

Current record

F You can preview the merge using actual data. Click the arrow icons to display the first, previous, next, or last record, respectively. Type a number in the box to view a specific record.

James Anders
1800 Highway 7
Bemidji, MN 56601

Dear James:

G Using Preview Results, the merge fields are replaced by data from the selected source.

▸ **FileMaker Pro** lets you import data from selected fields in an existing FileMaker Pro 7.0 or higher database.

After you've created or opened the data source, the Insert Placeholders section expands to display the fields in the data source—in this example, the Office Address Book **D**.

5. Drag merge fields from the Insert Placeholders section into position in the main document **E**.

The merge fields are placeholders for data from the data source. You can place merge fields on separate lines, together on a line, or embedded within the body of the main document.

6. If necessary, format the merge fields and add any required spaces and punctuation.

For example, for the last line of an address, you'd separate City, State, and Zip Code merge fields with a comma and spaces **E**.

7. *Optional:* To merge only particular records or ones that match a criterion, expand the Filter Recipients section and click its Options button. (Filtering options vary by data source. For example, Office Address Book records can be filtered by Outlook category.)

8. To substitute your actual data for the merge fields in the main document, expand the Preview Results section **F**, and click the View Merged Data icon. Click the arrow icons to move through the data, while viewing the results in the main document **G**.

continues on next page

9. In the Complete Merge section **H**, specify the records to merge by choosing an option from the drop-down menu:

   ▸ **All.** Create the merge using all records in the data source.

   ▸ **Current Record.** Merge only the record number shown in the Preview Results section **F**.

   ▸ **Custom.** In the From and To boxes, specify a range of records to merge.

10. When the merge document is satisfactory, click one of these buttons in the Complete Merge section **H**:

    ▸ **Merge to Printer.** Routes the merge directly to the printer.

    ▸ **Merge to New Document.** Creates a Word merge document that you can edit and print later.

> **TIP** If you're uncertain whether you've chosen the correct records or think some may be incomplete, click Merge to New Document **H**. Examine the document, delete unwanted records, edit incomplete ones, and then print.

    ▸ **Merge to Email.** Sends the merge document(s) to Outlook's Outbox for transmission as email. Fill in the Mail Recipient dialog box **I** (being certain to select an email field for the To item), and click Mail Merge To Outbox. A separate email message is generated for each recipient.

> **CAUTION** When merging to email, set Outlook to offline mode prior to generating the merge (choose Outlook > Work Offline). Examine the messages in the Outbox, and make any necessary edits and deletions. When you're ready to send the messages, choose Outlook > Work Offline again.

11. To dismiss the Mail Merge Manager, click its close button or choose Tools > Mail Merge Manager.

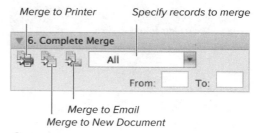

Merge to Printer   Specify records to merge

Merge to Email
Merge to New Document

H In the Complete Merge section, specify the records you want to include in the merge.

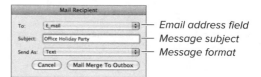

Email address field
Message subject
Message format

I Set options in the Mail Recipient dialog box prior to merging to email.

Spreadsheet Essentials

Excel is Office 2011's spreadsheet application. By working in a grid of columns and rows called a *worksheet*, you can create lists, perform complex calculations, and graph important data.

In this chapter, we'll explore the basic topics you'll need to understand in order to begin using Excel, as well as a few advanced ones that you'll want to refer to later:

- Creating new workbooks
- Understanding the interface and views
- Entering data into cells and navigating a worksheet
- Using AutoFill to intelligently fill ranges
- Editing cell contents and performing Find/Replace procedures
- Documenting cells with comments
- Naming cell ranges
- Importing text files
- Working with workbooks and worksheets
- Printing workbooks, sheets, and ranges

In This Chapter

Creating a New Workbook

An Excel document is called a *workbook*. Every workbook consists of one or multiple pages known as *sheets* or *worksheets*. In addition to creating new, blank workbooks, you can base a new workbook on a template selected from the Excel Workbook Gallery.

To create a new, blank workbook:

Do either of the following:

- When you launch Excel, the Excel Workbook Gallery appears **Ⓐ**. By default, the All category and the Excel Workbook thumbnail are selected. Double-click the thumbnail, press Return, or click the Choose button.

- If Excel is already running, choose File > New Workbook, press Command-N, or click the New Workbook icon **Ⓑ** on the Standard toolbar.

    A new workbook appears **Ⓒ**.

> **TIP** On Excel's launch, if you close the Excel Workbook Gallery without opening a new or existing workbook or click the Cancel button, a new workbook is automatically created.

Template Selected
categories thumbnail   *Preview*

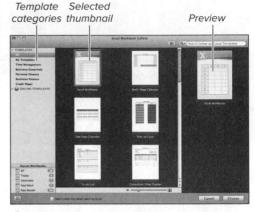

Ⓐ On launch, you can create a new workbook in the Excel Workbook Gallery by pressing Return.

Ⓑ Click the New Workbook icon when Excel is currently running.

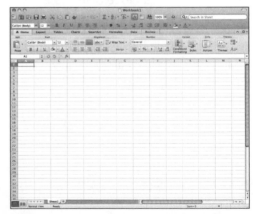

Ⓒ A new, blank workbook appears.

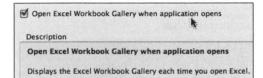

D This check box determines whether the Excel Workbook Gallery automatically appears each time you launch Excel.

To create a workbook from a template:

1. Choose File > New from Template, press Shift-Command-P, or click the New from Template icon on the Standard toolbar.

   The Excel Workbook Gallery appears **A**.

2. Select a template category from the list on the left.

   My Templates are the templates you've created and saved; Online Templates are ones you can download from Microsoft Office Online; and other categories (such as Time Management and Business Essentials) contain templates that were installed as part of Office 2011.

3. Select a template thumbnail in the right side of the window and click Choose.

   Excel creates and opens a new workbook based on the selected template.

TIP Whether the Excel Workbook Gallery appears at startup is determined by a Preferences setting **D**. Choose Excel > Preferences, and click the General icon. You can also disable the gallery by clicking the Don't show this when opening Excel check box at the bottom of the Excel Workbook Gallery **A**.

TIP It isn't necessary to close an open workbook before creating a new one.

The Excel Interface

The Excel interface components with which you'll need to be familiar are shown in **A**.

Menu bar. Like other Macintosh applications, commands can be chosen by clicking a menu bar heading. For example, to save changes to the current workbook, you click the File menu and choose Save.

Scripts menu. Click this menu bar icon to run installed AppleScripts and Automator workflows **B**.

Toolbars. A toolbar presents common Excel features grouped by function. Each toolbar appears above the worksheet area. You execute toolbar commands by clicking icons and choosing options from drop-down menus. To show or hide a toolbar, choose its name from the View > Toolbars submenu.

B Excel includes many Automator workflows that you can choose from the Scripts menu or execute by pressing the assigned keyboard shortcut.

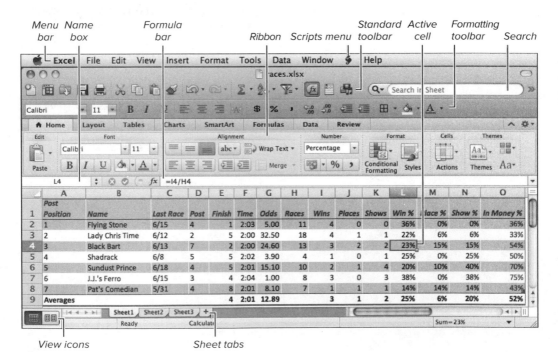

Menu bar · Name box · Formula bar · Ribbon · Scripts menu · Standard toolbar · Active cell · Formatting toolbar · Search

View icons · Sheet tabs

A The Excel 2011 interface.

D Type the address or range that you want to select and press Return.

Cancel Enter

E To accept the cell entry or edit, click Enter or press Return. To reject the cell entry or edit, click Cancel or press Esc.

Ribbon. New in Excel 2011, the Ribbon **C** (page bottom) provides access to the most frequently used commands and can be used instead of or in addition to the menus. Similar commands and procedures are listed together on *tabs*. Within each tab, procedures are further divided into *groups*, based on similarity of function.

Name box. Part of the formula bar, the Name box **D** shows the active cell's address. You can also create English-like names in the Name box that you can use in formulas as shorthand for the cell or range it represents, such as **=SUM(Sales)** rather than **=SUM(A5:A27)**. Finally, you can enter a cell address or range in the Name box and press Return to immediately go to and select that cell or range in the workbook.

Formula bar. The formula bar **E** has two purposes. First, it displays the contents of the active cell. Second, you can use it to enter and edit data and formulas. To show or hide the formula bar, choose View > Formula Bar. When hidden, you can only enter and edit data in the cells.

Active cell. This is another name for the currently selected cell. The cell's address is the intersection of the column and row in which it is located (column L and row 4 in **A**, for example). Excel automatically highlights the appropriate column and row headings. The cell address is displayed in the name box, and the cell contents (data or a formula) are shown in the formula bar.

Function group   *Formulas tab*

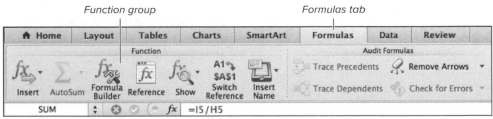

C Part of the Excel Ribbon.

View icons. You can work with the current sheet in either of two views: Normal or Page Layout. In Page Layout view (the default), the sheet is shown as it will print—with margins and page breaks. In Normal view 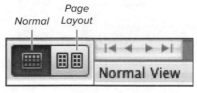 (the preferred view for entering and editing data), columns and rows are displayed without breaks. Dashed lines show where pages will break when you print.

You can switch views whenever you like by clicking a view icon **F** or choosing Normal or Page Layout from the View menu. If a workbook has multiple sheets, each one can be set to a different view. You can set the *default* view (Preferred view for new sheets) in the View section of Preferences.

Sheet tabs. You use the sheet tabs **G** to add, delete, name, and switch between worksheets. For information on sheets and sheet tabs, see "Working with Workbooks," later in this chapter.

> **TIP** To change the magnification, choose a setting from the Zoom drop-down menu on the Standard toolbar. Note that Zoom settings are sheet-specific. Each sheet can have a different magnification, if you like.

> **TIP** Click the Toolbox icon on the Standard toolbar to show or hide the Toolbox. As you learned in Chapter 2, each Office application makes different tools available on the Toolbox's tabs, such as the Formula Builder in Excel. You can also open the Toolbox by choosing a specific Toolbox tab from the View menu.

F You can switch views by clicking one of these icons or by choosing a command from the View menu.

G A workbook can have many sheets. To make a different sheet active, click its tab. If the sheet name isn't visible, click the navigation icons.

Setting Preferences

It's a good idea to review Excel customization options in Preferences. Because there are so many, the Preferences dialog box was made to look and work like System Preferences. After choosing Excel > Preferences, click icons to view the different categories. Here are some options you should examine:

- **Authoring:General.** Number of sheets in a new workbook, default font and size, user name.

- **Authoring:View.** Settings (show formula bar, preferred view for new sheets), Window options (show page breaks, show formulas, show gridlines).

- **Authoring:Edit.** Double-click allows in-cell editing, direction to move after pressing Return, number of decimal places to display.

- **Sharing and Privacy:Save.** The AutoRecover time interval.

- **Sharing and Privacy:Compatibility.** Default file format.

- **Sharing and Privacy:Security.** Remove personal information from the current file on save.

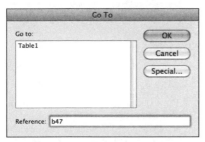

Active cell (A1)

	A	B	C
1			
2			
3			
4			
5			

A In a standard worksheet, each column is named by letter and each row by number. A cell address, such as A1 or BW723, is named for the intersection of the cell's row and column.

B Type a cell address and click OK. (If the address was recently used, you can select it from the Go to list.)

TABLE 10.1 Keyboard Navigation Shortcuts

Shortcut	Action
↑, ↓, ←, →	Move to the adjacent cell (up, down, left, or right)
Pg Up, Pg Dn	Move up or down one screen
Option Pg Dn, Option Pg Up	Move right or left one screen
Tab, Shift Tab	Move right or left one cell
Enter, Shift Enter, Return, Shift Return	Move down or up one cell
Home	Move to first cell of row
Control + arrow key	Move to edge of current data
Control Home	Move to cell A1
Control End	Move to last cell in use

Worksheet Navigation

Excel windows work as they do in most other Macintosh applications—with some additional tricks to get you where you want to go.

A sheet is divided into a grid of columns and rows **A**. The intersection of a column and row is a *cell*. Every column is labeled with a letter (shown in its heading) and every row with a number. The combination of a column letter and row number uniquely identifies each cell, such as G7 or D103. This combination is known as a *cell address*.

To move to a cell:

Do one of the following:

- Scroll as necessary to display the desired cell, and then click the cell.

- Use the keyboard to navigate to the cell, as explained in **Table 10.1**.

- Type the cell address in the Name box (see **D** in "The Excel Interface" earlier in this chapter), and then press Return or Enter.

- Choose Edit > Go To (Control-G). In the Go To dialog box **B**, enter the address in the Reference box or select it from the Go to list. Click OK.

  The cell you click or move to becomes the active cell. The address appears in the Name box, and the corresponding column letter and row number are highlighted.

TIP You can use the scroll bars to scroll through a worksheet without changing the active cell.

TIP When scrolling, press Control-Delete to return immediately to the active cell.

Entering Data

As explained in the following steps, data entry is essentially a click-and-type procedure.

To enter data into a cell:

1. Click in a cell to make it active **Ⓐ**.

2. In the cell or the formula bar, type the text, number, date, or formula **Ⓑ**.

   Formulas must begin with an equal sign (=), as explained in Chapter 12.

3. Complete the entry by pressing a navigation key, such as Return or Enter to move down or Tab to move right.

   Excel evaluates the cell contents and then formats it appropriately.

TIP To complete a cell entry, you can also use the keyboard shortcuts listed in Table 10.1 earlier in this chapter.

TIP If you change your mind about a cell entry, press Esc or click the Cancel icon (X) on the formula bar **Ⓑ**. If the cell was originally empty, it's cleared; if it contained data or a formula, the data or formula is restored.

TIP If a text entry you're typing matches one or more others in the same column, Excel provides a drop-down AutoComplete list of matches **Ⓒ**. Click one to accept it, or keep typing to ignore the list. (If you don't find the lists helpful, you can disable AutoComplete in the AutoComplete section of Preferences.)

TIP Some numbers, such as zip codes, are best treated as text rather than as numbers. Doing so enables you to preserve any leading zeros, such as 01701. (If recorded as a number, Excel drops leading zeros.) To prevent this, format the cells as Text prior to entering the data. See Chapter 11 for formatting instructions.

TIP You can also start a formula by clicking the fx icon on the formula bar. This also has the effect of opening the Formula Builder.

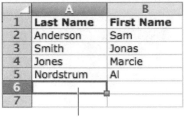

Active cell (A6)

Ⓐ The current (or active) cell is surrounded by a thick, blue border. Its column and row heading are highlighted.

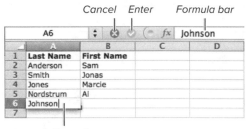

Active cell

Ⓑ You can type directly into the active cell or into the text box on the formula bar.

Ⓒ An AutoComplete list appears when Excel finds matching text in the column. Depending on the AutoComplete settings in Preferences, the list can appear after as little as one character is typed.

Entering Data into a Range

If you know the range into which you'll be entering data, you can speed up the process by preselecting the range.

After you finish each cell entry, press Tab to move to the cell to the right or press Return or Enter to move to the cell below. When a row or column of the range has been completed, the cursor automatically moves to the beginning of the next row or column.

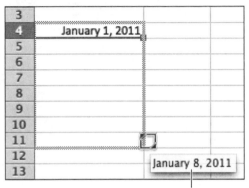

A Move the cursor over the cell's lower-right corner. It becomes a fill handle.

AutoFill ScreenTip

B Drag to select the range you want to fill.

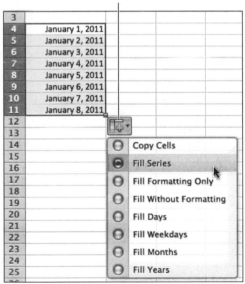

AutoFill Options

C When you release the mouse button, the new data appears.

Filling Cells with a Series

When you need to fill a cell range with consecutive numbers, dates, days of the week, or items that follow a specific pattern (such as every four days), you can use AutoFill to automatically enter the sequence.

To AutoFill a range of cells:

1. In the first cell, type the first number, word, or date of the series.

   Examples include **105**, **Sunday**, **March**, **6/30/10**, **April 1, 2011**, or **Qtr 1**.

2. If the series isn't apparent from the initial cell entry, enter the next item in the series in an adjacent cell (the column to the right or the row below).

3. Select the initial cell or cells. Then move the pointer over the lower-right corner of the lowest or rightmost cell. It becomes a fill handle **A**. Drag to extend the sequence, as desired **B**.

   As you drag past each cell, the value that will be filled in the current cell is shown in a ScreenTip.

4. Release the mouse button when the destination cells have been selected.

   The sequence appears in the selected cells **C**.

5. *Optional:* Click the AutoFill Options icon **C** to choose an option, such as Fill Weekdays.

> **TIP** You can also use this procured to fill a series of cells with the *same* text or numeric data, such as CA or 0.082.

> **TIP** Another way to fill a selected cell range is to choose a command from the Edit > Fill submenu.

Editing Cell Data

The easiest way to change a cell's contents is to select the cell and type over the current data. But if the cell contains a formula or a lengthy text string, it's often faster to edit the current contents than to retype.

To edit a cell's contents:

1. Do one of the following:

   ▸ Click the cell to select it. (Selecting a cell automatically selects its entire contents.) Type to replace/overwrite the contents.

   ▸ Double-click the cell to set the text insertion mark in the cell text **A**.

   ▸ Click the cell to select it. Set the text insertion mark in the text displayed in the formula bar **B**.

2. Edit the contents in the cell or in the formula bar using the same techniques as you would if editing text in Word.

   For example, you can delete the previous character or a selection by pressing Delete, insert additional characters, or move left or right within the contents by pressing the left- or right-arrow key.

3. To complete the edit, you can move to another cell by pressing Return, Enter, Tab, or another navigation key; or you can click the Enter button on the formula bar (see **B** in "Entering Data" earlier in this chapter).

TIP To cancel a revision and leave the original contents of the cell intact, press Esc or click the Cancel icon on the formula bar.

TIP If you edit a formula or data that is referenced by a formula, all affected cells are recalculated when you complete the edit.

B	C
First Name	**Street Address**
Edna	1807 Oak Park Drive
John	907 Janes Street

A You can edit cell data directly in the cell...

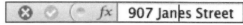

B ...or in the text box on the formula bar.

Search string   Replacement string

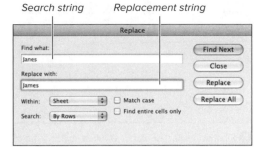

A Enter Find what and Replace with strings in the text boxes.

B	C
First Name	**Street Address**
Edna	1807 Oak Park Drive
John	907 Janes Street

Selected match

B When a match is found, Excel scrolls to the cell and selects it.

Using the Search Box

If you want to perform a simple Find, the quickest way is to use the Search box in the upper-right corner of the workbook. Type a search string and click the arrow icons to move from one match to the next. The search starts from the active cell, moves downward by row, and then wraps around to the beginning of the sheet. If no match is found, an alert dialog box appears.

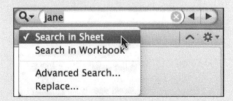

To perform a replace or a more complex search, click the magnifying glass icon and choose a search option.

Finding and Replacing Data

Another way to edit a worksheet is to use the Replace command to search for a string and replace it with another.

To perform a Find/Replace:

1. *Optional:* To restrict your search to part of the worksheet, select the range.

2. Choose Edit > Replace.

   The Replace dialog box appears **A**.

3. Enter a search string in the Find what text box and a replacement string in the Replace with text box.

4. From the Within drop-down menu, choose Sheet to search only the active sheet or Workbook to search all sheets.

5. From the Search drop-down menu, choose By Rows or By Columns, depending on how the data is arranged.

   For example, to replace an old company name or address with a new one in a worksheet that restricts those items to one or two columns, a By Columns search is best. If the text could be found in any column, on the other hand, a By Rows search might be better.

6. *Optional:* Click one or both check boxes to restrict matches to those with identical letter case (Match case) or where the Find what string is the only data in the found cell (Find entire cells only).

7. To begin the search, click Find Next.

   If a match is found, Excel selects its cell **B**.

   continues on next page

8. For each match, do one of the following:

▸ To replace this match with the Replace with string, click Replace.

▸ To skip this match and look for the next one, click Find Next.

▸ To skip this match and end the search immediately, click Close.

Repeat this step to find and handle any additional matches in the sheet or workbook.

9. Click the Close button to dismiss the dialog box.

TIP To simultaneously search for and replace *all* instances of the match, you can click Replace All at any time. Note, however, that you will not be given an opportunity to view the changes individually because they are made *en masse*.

TIP You can undo a Replace All by immediately choosing Edit > Undo Replace (Command-Z).

TIP The Find what string can also include wild card characters. You can use a question mark (?) as a substitute for any single character. For example, s?ng would find sang, sing, song, and sung. An asterisk (*) can substitute for any number of characters (including none). j*n would find Jan, John, Jones, and AJ Loans—that is, any text string that includes a J followed by an N.

TIP If you want to find certain data but not replace it, choose Edit > Find (Command-F). The Find dialog box **C** is similar to the Replace dialog box and offers similar advanced search options.

TIP As a sanity check following a Replace All, you may wish to perform a Find, search for the replacement string, and see if the entries look appropriate.

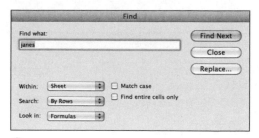

C Find works like Replace. You can switch from a Find to a Find/Replace by clicking the Replace button.

Sorting Data

Many sheets or certain ranges are organized as rectangular data arrays in which every row is the equivalent of a record and every column is a field. In Excel, such an array can be defined as a table or analyzed using database tools. Whether or not you formally declare an array to be a table, you can periodically sort it by one or several fields. For instructions on sorting using the Sort dialog box, see Chapter 15 and Chapter 13.

You can use the Sort toolbar icon to sort any rectangular data array based on the contents of one of its columns:

1. Do one of the following:

▸ To sort the entire array, select any cell within the column on which the sort will be based.

▸ To sort only one column of data while ignoring the surrounding columns, select the column's cells.

2. Do one of the following:

▸ Click the Sort icon on the Standard toolbar to perform an ascending sort.

▸ To perform a different type of sort (such as Descending), click the Sort icon and choose an option from its menu.

Ⓐ A text box appears in which you can type the comment.

Comment indicator

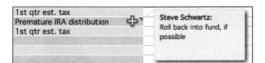

Ⓑ The presence of a comment is indicated by a tiny triangle in the cell's upper-right corner.

Ⓒ A comment appears when you move the cursor over the cell to which it's attached.

Comments
New   Delete   Previous   Next   Show   Show All

Ⓓ Comment-related commands can also be selected from the Review:Comments group.

> ### Edit Comment
> ### Delete Comment
> ### Show Comment

Ⓔ You can right-click a cell that contains a comment to edit, delete, or display the comment.

Adding Cell Comments

To document the assumptions underlying a calculation or explain the meaning of a complex formula, you can attach a *comment* to any cell. Comments are visible only when you want them to be.

To create and manage comments:

1. To attach a comment to a selected cell, choose Insert > New Comment or click the Review:Comments:New icon.

   A text box appears **Ⓐ**. If you've entered a User Name in the General section of Excel Preferences, the name appears in the text box to identify the comment's author. You can delete it, if you wish.

2. Enter your comment in the box. When you're finished, click any other cell.

   The comment box closes and a small triangle appears in the cell's upper-right corner **Ⓑ**.

3. To view comments, do the following:

   ▸ To view a specific comment, rest the cursor over its cell **Ⓒ**.

   ▸ To view all comments, choose View > Comments or click Review:Comments: Show All. (To hide the comments, choose the command again.)

TIP You can resize a comment box by dragging any of its surrounding handles **Ⓐ**. You can also drag the box to a new location.

TIP To delete a comment, select the cell, and click **Review:Comments:Delete Ⓓ**. Or right-click the cell and choose **Delete Comment** from the contextual menu **Ⓔ**.

TIP Because a comment is an object, you can format it (changing its color or font, for example). Choose **View > Comments**, select the comment, and choose **Format > Comment**.

Naming Cell Ranges

To make it easy to find a particular cell range, create a chart from it, or reference it in a formula, you can assign a name to any cell or range. Such names are called *range names*, *named ranges*, or *names*.

For example, you could assign the name **April** to a column of April sales figures and refer to it in formulas by name: **=SUM(April)** rather than **=SUM(D3:D14)**. You can assign a name to a single cell, part of a column or row, a group of cells that spans several rows or columns, or a group of nonadjacent cells. A name can be referenced from any sheet in the workbook and may contain up to 255 characters.

To name a cell range:

1. Select the cell(s) you want to name.

2. In the Name box on the formula bar 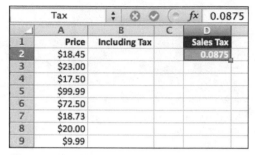, enter the name you want to assign to the selected cell(s), and press Enter or Return.

CAUTION The first character of a name must be a letter or an underscore (_). Names may consist of multiple words, but they can't contain spaces. Use an underscore or period instead, such as Sales.Tax.Pct or Sales_Tax_Pct. Note that letter case is ignored in names; for example, SALES, Sales, and sales are all considered the same name.

CAUTION You can't name a cell while you're changing its contents.

TIP You can assign a name to a constant, such as defining Tax as .0875 Ⓐ.

TIP You can also define names by choosing Insert > Name > Define. In the Define Name dialog box Ⓑ, enter a name, specify a range or constant in the Refers to box, and click Add. Click OK when you're done.

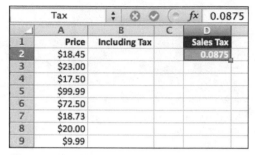

Ⓐ In the Name box, enter a name for the selected cell or cell range. In this example, the sales tax percentage in D2 is named **Tax**.

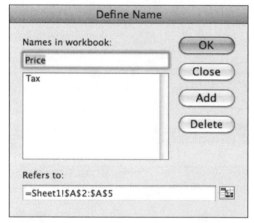

Ⓑ You can use the Define name dialog box to create or delete names, as well as change the cell or range to which a previously defined name refers.

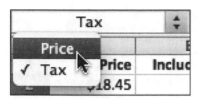

C To go to or select a named range, you can select it from the Name box's drop-down list.

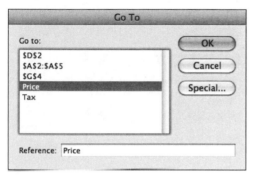

D You can also go to or select a named range by selecting its name in the Go To dialog box.

A Practical Naming Example

By naming a range, you can simplify formulas that refer to elements in that range. For example, by naming the data in column A as **Price** **A**, you could total the column's data with the formula **=SUM(Price)**.

To calculate each total price including the sales tax (column B), the formula **=Price+(Price*Tax)** could be entered in cell B2 and then filled down into the remaining cells (B3:B6). Rather than each cell in column B showing a relative reference, such as **=A2+(A2*.0875)**, they'd all show the formula **=Price+(Price*Tax)**.

TIP To edit a name's cell or range reference, select it in the list in the **Define Name** dialog box **B**, edit the range in the **Refers to** box, and click OK.

CAUTION If you delete a name in the **Define Name** dialog box **B** that's in use in one or more formulas in the workbook, those formulas become undefined.

TIP Another reason to create names is to enable you to quickly jump to key areas of a sheet or workbook. For example, you can name important summary figures, lists, and data areas. To go to and select a named range, do any of the following:

- Select the name from the **Name** box's drop-down list **C**.

- Type the name in the **Name** box.

- Choose **Edit > Go To** or press **Control-G**. In the **Go To** dialog box **D**, select the name and click OK.

TIP In a multisheet workbook, names can enable you to move directly to areas on different sheets. For example, suppose you're tracking sales or expenses by creating a new sheet each month. The totals are likely to be in a different range on each sheet. Assign a name to each month's total range, and then you can jump to any of those ranges—regardless of the sheet that's currently displayed.

Importing Data from a Text File

Typing data isn't the only way to fill cells. You can import data from a variety of external sources. Chapter 15 discusses procedures for importing data from FileMaker Pro databases and from Web pages. In this section, you'll learn to import data from text files. Since most major applications can save or export data as tab-delimited text files, it's a very common format for data exchange.

To import data from a text file:

1. In the source program (such as a database, spreadsheet, or word-processing program), export or save the file in a delimited format, such as tab- or comma-delimited.

   In a delimited file, fields are separated from one another by a special character, such as a tab or comma. Each record is a single paragraph, ending with a Return character.

2. Drag the icon of the exported file onto the Excel program icon. (If Excel is in the Dock, you can drag it onto that icon, for example.)

   Excel attempts to open and interpret the file as a new worksheet .

3. If the resulting worksheet is satisfactory, save it as a normal Excel file. Choose File > Save As, and change the Format setting to Excel Workbook (.xlsx) or Excel 97-2004 Workbook (.xls).

	A	B
1	1/9/10	Doctors, dentists
2	1/12/10	Health insurance premiums
3	2/9/10	Health insurance premiums
4	3/3/10	Doctors, dentists
5	3/6/10	Health insurance premiums
6	3/10/10	Doctors, dentists

Ⓐ Check the new worksheet to see if the data seems to have been reasonably interpreted by Excel.

Ⓑ The Outlook 2011 Export wizard.

Try It Yourself

To see how importing a text file works, you can create an Excel worksheet from your Outlook Address Book contacts:

1. In Outlook, choose File > Export.

   The Export wizard appears Ⓑ.

2. Select Contacts to a list (tab-delimited text). Click the right-arrow icon.

3. In the Save dialog box, name the export file, select a convenient location for it (such as the Desktop), and click Save.

4. Drag the resulting tab-delimited text file onto the Excel icon (found in the Dock or in the Applications: Microsoft Office 2011 folder).

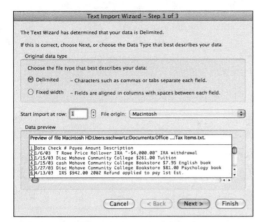

C The Text Import Wizard presents a series of dialog boxes in which you specify the format of the data being imported.

D In the Open dialog box, open the Enable menu to view a list of Excel-compatible file types.

TIP If the result of the drag-and-drop procedure is not satisfactory, you can import the data using the Text Import Wizard. Choose Data > Get External Data > Import Text File or click Data : External Data Sources : Text. Select the text file and follow the wizard's instructions **C**. The Text Import Wizard can import virtually any consistently delimited file, as well as those in which the data consists of fixed-width fields.

TIP You can also start the Text Import Wizard by choosing File > Import. Select Text file in the Import dialog box.

TIP If you use the File > Open command to open a text file, the Text Import Wizard is automatically invoked.

TIP When data is exported as text from most applications, any formulas contained in the source data are lost. Instead, the results are exported. Following the import into Excel, you may need to reconstruct those formulas in the worksheet.

TIP Excel can also open some types of files in their native format, such as FileMaker Pro databases and AppleWorks worksheets. When available as an option, this is the preferred method of importing data into Excel. For a list of compatible file types, choose File > Open and click the Enable pop-up menu in the Open dialog box **D**.

Working with Workbooks

An Excel file is a called a *workbook*. By default, every new workbook contains the number of worksheets (or sheets) specified in the Authoring:General section of Preferences 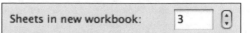. As you'll learn in this section, you can add sheets as needed and delete unnecessary ones, switch from one sheet to another, rename sheets, reference data in any sheet from any other sheet, and consolidate multiple sheets.

Naming sheets

You can replace the default sheet names (Sheet1, Sheet2, and so on) with descriptive names, such as Advertising, July, Personnel, or Budget Summary.

To name or rename a sheet:

1. At the bottom of the workbook window, double-click the tab of the sheet you want to rename.

   The sheet name is selected .

2. Type a new sheet name or edit the current name.

3. To complete the process, click anywhere else in the sheet or press Return or Enter .

   Sheet names can contain a maximum of 31 characters and may include spaces.

> **TIP** To select the current sheet's name for editing or renaming, you can also choose **Format > Sheet > Rename**. Or you can right-click the sheet tab and choose Rename from the contextual menu 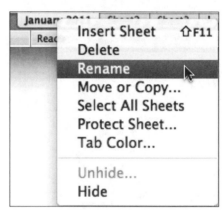.

Ⓐ You can specify the number of sheets in each new workbook.

Ⓑ Double-click a sheet name to select it for renaming.

Ⓒ You can rename as many or as few sheets as you like—as often as you like,

Ⓓ You can right-click a sheet tab to reveal commands for changing or deleting the tab, changing its color, and so on.

TIP Because sheet names are also used in formulas to indicate where a given cell or range is located, you may want to keep the names relatively short. For instance, =Income!A17-Expenses!A17 is preferable to ='Income Statement FY 2011'!A17-'Expense Items FY 2011'!A17.

TIP In a formula, any sheet name that contains a space must be surrounded by single quotes, such as 'Income Statement'.

TIP If you rename a sheet, the name that appears in any affected formulas is automatically changed by Excel to match.

Switching and rearranging sheets

Many of your workbooks will consist of only one sheet or only one that you're using. But when you're using multiple sheets, it's simple to switch from one to another or change their order.

To change the active sheet:

- At the bottom of the workbook window, click the tab of the sheet you want to display **E**.

  The selected sheet becomes active.

TIP If the sheet's tab isn't visible, click the navigation icons to scroll through the tabs.

To rearrange sheets:

- Drag a sheet tab left or right to a new position in the sheet tabs. Release the mouse button to complete the move.

Navigation icons   *Active sheet*   *Add sheet*

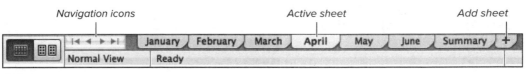

E To make a different sheet active, click its tab at the bottom of the document window.

Adding and deleting sheets

There are several methods you can use to add or delete sheets.

To add a sheet:

Do one of the following:

- Click the Insert Sheet (+) icon to the right of the sheet tabs 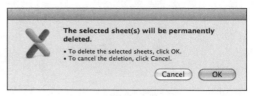.

- Choose Insert > Sheet > Blank Sheet.

- Right-click a sheet tab and choose Insert Sheet ⓓ from the contextual menu.

  A new sheet is added to the workbook. If you clicked the Insert Sheet (+) icon, the sheet is appended to the sheet list. If you used one of the other methods to add the sheet, it is inserted to the right of the current sheet.

TIP **Although you can keep adding sheets to a single workbook, it's more common to create a new workbook for each new project.**

TIP **You can't undo a sheet insertion. If the new sheet is unwanted, you can either ignore or delete it.**

To delete a sheet:

Do one of the following:

- Make the sheet active and choose Edit > Delete Sheet.

- Right-click the sheet's tab and choose Delete from the contextual menu ⓓ.

  Confirm the deletion by clicking OK in the dialog box that appears ⓕ.

ⓕ Whether the current sheet is empty or packed with data, you must confirm its deletion by clicking OK. Click Cancel if you've changed your mind.

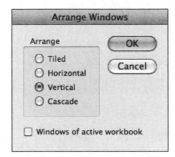

G Window-related commands can be chosen from the Layout:Window group.

H Select an arrangement option and click OK.

I This example shows three tiled windows.

Viewing multiple sheets

Sometimes it can be helpful to view several worksheets at the same time. You can accomplish this by opening each sheet in a separate window and then arranging the windows so you can see them all. Because each window is simply another instance of the same workbook, you can make edits in any instance—that is, changes made in one window are simultaneously made in all.

To view multiple sheets:

1. Choose Window > New Window or click the Layout:Window:New icon **G**.

   A copy of the workbook opens in a new window. Each copy name has a number appended to it, such as **Sales:1**, **Sales:2**, and **Sales:3**. As desired, repeat this step for additional copies.

2. In each copy, click the tab **E** of the sheet you want to view.

3. Choose Window > Arrange or Layout: Window:Arrange > Arrange Windows.

   The Arrange Windows dialog box appears **H**.

4. Select one of the following window arrangements and click OK.

   ▸ **Tiled.** Arrange windows so that all are visible and as large as possible **I**.

   ▸ **Horizontal, Vertical.** Arrange windows in horizontal or vertical strips.

   ▸ **Cascade.** Display all windows at full size, cascading down and to the right. Each window overlaps the next, leaving an edge exposed so you can switch between them by clicking the visible edge.

5. To work in a window, click in it to make it active.

continues on next page

TIP You can also use the window arrangement commands to arrange different open workbooks—not just multiple copies of the same workbook.

TIP To make the active workbook fill the screen, click the zoom icon (the green plus) in its title bar. Click the zoom icon again to restore the window to its previous size and screen position.

TIP To temporarily minimize the active window to the Dock, click the minimize icon (the yellow minus) in the title bar, double-click the window's title bar, choose Window > Minimize Window, or press Command-M. To restore a minimized window, click its icon in the Dock. You can also hide a window. Choose Window > Hide. To restore a hidden window, choose Window > Unhide. In the Unhide dialog box 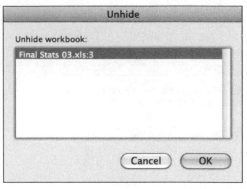, select the window that you want to reveal and click OK.

TIP If one or more Excel windows are covered by other programs' windows, you can reveal them by choosing Window > Bring All to Front.

TIP The names of all open workbooks and copies are listed at the bottom of the Window menu ⓚ. You can make any open workbook or copy active by choosing its name from this menu.

TIP In addition to opening multiple copies of a workbook to view different parts or sheets at the same time, you can split a sheet—dividing it into two or four panes. See "Working with Large Sheets" in Chapter 11 for instructions.

TIP You can toggle a window between its current size/position and full screen by choosing Window > Zoom Window ⓚ or clicking the zoom icon (the green plus) in the window's title bar.

ⓙ Select a window to unhide and click OK.

ⓚ Any open workbook or copy can be made active by choosing its name from the Window menu.

```
=DB!G25
```

E	F	G
	WEEK 1	**WEEK 2**
	POINTS	**POINTS**
DA BAERS	51	52

Active cell

L This formula refers to cell G25 on sheet DB.

Referring to data on other sheets

Formulas (see Chapter 12) aren't restricted to cell references to the current worksheet. They can also reference data from other sheets in the workbook.

To reference another sheet:

1. Click the cell in which you want to create the formula. Type an equal sign (=) to start the formula.

2. As necessary within the formula, you can refer to a cell or range in another sheet by doing either of the following:

   ▸ Switch to the appropriate sheet, and select the cell or range.

   ▸ Type the cell reference in the form *sheet!range*.

   For example, **August!C17** refers to cell C17 on the worksheet named August.

3. If it isn't finished, continue building the formula. To add references to other sheets, repeat step 2.

4. To complete the formula **L**, press Return or Enter.

TIP If there are named ranges in other sheets, you can enter their names in formulas without worrying about which sheet the data is on. Excel will find the range on any sheet in the current workbook. See "Naming Cell Ranges" earlier in this chapter.

Consolidating worksheets

When various workbook sheets contain data that you want to summarize, you can total or perform other calculations across those sheets, recording results in a *consolidation sheet*. Recordkeeping workbooks are often organized in a way that makes them amenable to such calculations. For example, a bookkeeping workbook might have a separate sheet for each month of the year, followed by a single sheet in which totals and averages across all sheets are displayed.

Depending on how the data on your sheets is organized, you can consolidate manually (by position) or using the Consolidate dialog box:

- **Manually (by position).** The data to be consolidated must be identically organized on each sheet. That is, to consolidate a monthly sales total, it must be located in the same cell (G72, for example) on every sheet. You must create the formula for each cell or range that you want to consolidate.

- **Consolidate dialog box.** There is no requirement that the sheets be identically organized. Rather than creating the formulas manually, you select a function (such as Sum or Average) and the specific cell or range to be used from each sheet.

The following examples show how these two consolidation techniques work.

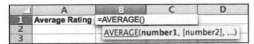

M Start the formula as you normally do, but be sure to restrict it to the supported consolidation functions.

N Double-click the cell to see the formula. Or to view it in the formula bar as shown here, single-click the cell.

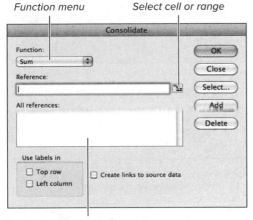

Function menu   *Select cell or range*

Cell and range references

O Create the necessary formulas and select sheet ranges in the Consolidate dialog box.

To consolidate manually (by position):

1. Create or select a sheet for the consolidation. On that sheet, select the destination cell for the formula. Type an equal sign (=) to begin the formula.

2. Enter a supported function, followed by an open parenthesis **M**.

   Supported functions include AVERAGE, AVERAGEA, COUNT, COUNTA, MAX, MAXA, MIN, MINA, PRODUCT, STDEV, STDEVA, STDEVP, STDEVPA, SUM, VAR, VARA, VARP, and VARPA.

3. Click the tab of the first sheet in the consecutive set of sheets. Select the cell or range to include in the formula.

4. Hold down Shift and click the tab of the last consecutive sheet that you want to include in the calculation.

   This assumes, of course, that each sheet in the set contains the same data in the selected cell or range.

5. Press Return or Enter to complete the formula.

   Double-click the formula cell in the consolidation sheet to view the formula **N** or examine it in the formula bar.

To create a consolidation formula using the Consolidate dialog box:

1. Click the upper-left cell of the range in the worksheet where you want to consolidate the data.

2. Choose Data > Consolidate or click the Data : Tools : Consolidate icon.

   The Consolidate dialog box appears **O**.

3. Choose a function from the Function drop-down menu.

continues on next page

4. For each sheet that you want to include in the consolidation, enter a reference to the pertinent cell or range in the Reference text box.

You can type the reference (or a range name) or select the cell(s) **P** after clicking the selection icon **O**.

TIP If the referenced data is arranged in the same manner and location in each sheet, Excel will automatically select it for you as you add each sheet to the All references list.

5. After entering or selecting each reference, click Add.

The new reference is added to the list in the All references box **Q**.

6. *Optional:* If you're identifying ranges by column and/or row labels, click the appropriate radio button in the Use labels in section of the dialog box.

7. *Optional:* To maintain a link between the referenced cells and the consolidation formula, click the Create links to source data check box.

Doing so will cause the consolidation formula to automatically update if any of the referenced cells change. Do not check this box if you want the current result to remain unchanged.

8. Click OK.

The consolidated data appears in the consolidation sheet **R**.

TIP The Consolidate dialog box for each workbook retains the most recently used references. To create additional formulas that reference other cells, you'll need to delete or edit the entries in the All references list **O**.

TIP To apply a different function to the same references, select a new destination cell, choose the new function, and click OK **S**.

⊿	A	B	C
1	January		
2		Expenses	
3	Advertising	15000	
4	Freight	4300	
5	Salaries	62500	
6			

P Each sheet contains monthly totals. Because the labels are selected as part of the range and Top row and Left column are checked in the Consolidate dialog box **O**, the labels will appear in the consolidation sheet.

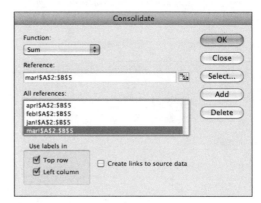

Q References are added to the sheets that contain the January–April expenses.

⊿	A	B
1		**Expenses**
2	**Advertising**	**$55,250.00**
3	**Freight**	**$16,625.00**
4	**Salaries**	**$250,000.00**

R This sheet uses a SUM consolidation formula to total expenses across the monthly worksheets.

⊿	A	B	C	D	E
1	TOTALS			AVERAGES	
2		Expenses			Expenses
3	Advertising	$55,250.00		Advertising	$13,812.50
4	Freight	$16,625.00		Freight	$4,156.25
5	Salaries	$250,000.00		Salaries	$62,500.00

S A second consolidation of the same monthly data using the AVERAGE function was generated, using D2 as the start of the destination range.

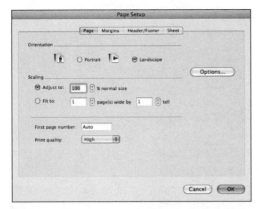

A The Page tab of Excel's Page Setup dialog box.

Selected printer

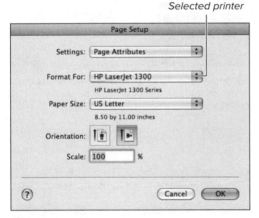

B The printer you select can affect other print settings, such as margins and print quality.

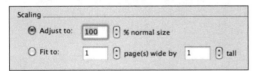

C You can specify a magnification/reduction percentage or force the printout to scale as needed to fit a specific number of pages.

Printing Worksheets and Workbooks

Excel provides tools and options to ensure that you can print exactly what you want. For example, in Page Layout view, page breaks are shown onscreen as new physical pages. In Normal view, they're indicated by dashed lines.

Printing is a two-step process: setting Page Setup options (in the Page Setup dialog box or on the Layout tab) and printing.

To set Page Setup options in the Page Setup dialog box:

1. Choose File > Page Setup.

    Excel's Page Setup dialog box appears.

2. On the Page tab of the Page Setup dialog box **A**, set any of the following:

    ▸ **Printer.** Click the Options button to select a printer to use (in the Mac OS X Page Setup dialog box **B**). Click OK to return to the Excel Page Setup dialog box.

    ▸ **Orientation.** Click the Portrait or Landscape radio button. Changing the orientation changes the amount of material that will fit per page, as well as where page breaks will occur.

    ▸ **Scaling.** To make the printout easier to read or to squeeze additional data onto each page, change one of the Scaling settings **C**.

    ▸ **First page number.** If this printout is a continuation of another printout or it will be inserted into another numbered publication, enter a starting number.

    ▸ **Print quality.** You can choose a quality setting from this drop-down menu.

    continues on next page

3. On the Margins tab of the Page Setup dialog box **D**, you can change the page margins and indicate whether you want to center the output on each printed page.

4. To specify a header or footer to print on each page, click the Header/Footer tab and select options from the Header and/or Footer drop-down lists.

5. Click the Sheet tab to set the following print options:

   ▸ **Print titles.** To repeat row and/or column labels on each page (making it easier to interpret the printout), select or type the rows and/or columns that contain the labels **E**.

   ▸ **Print.** You can set any of these display options **F**: *Print area* (select or type the range to print), *Gridlines* (print the lines that make up the cell grid), *Black and white* (ignore color), *Draft quality* (print at reduced quality and ignore graphics, such as charts), *Row and column headings* (print the row numbers and column letters), *Comments* (include cell comments in the printout).

6. When you're done changing settings in the Page Setup dialog box, click OK.

7. Switch to Page Layout view to see the effects of the new settings.

TIP To avoid awkward breaks in the printout (splitting a chart in two, for example), you can insert manual page breaks. Select the cell that will begin the new page. Choose Insert > Page Break or Layout:Page Setup:Breaks > Insert Page Break.

TIP You can also create or edit a header or footer manually. In Page Layout view, simply click in the header or footer area of any page and make the changes.

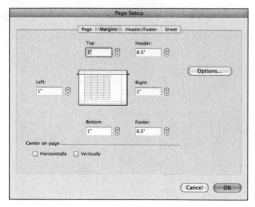

D If desired, you can change the printout margins by entering new numbers in the text boxes.

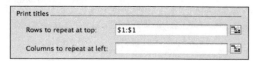

E On the worksheet, select the row and column headings that will repeat on each page. In this example, material in row 1 will repeat.

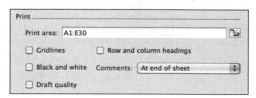

F You can set additional options in the Print section of the Sheet tab. In this example, the print range is specified and cell comments will print.

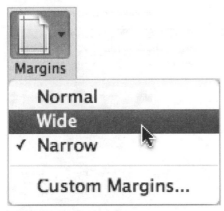

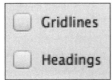

H If one of the basic margin settings (Normal, Wide, or Narrow) doesn't suffice, choose Custom Margins to set exact margins.

I You can optionally add gridlines and headings to the printout by clicking these check boxes in the Layout:Print group.

To set Page Setup options using the Ribbon:

1. Select the Layout tab **G** (page bottom), and click Layout:View:Page Layout.

   Page Layout view automatically shows the effect of new page setup settings.

2. Choose an orientation (Portrait or Landscape) from the Layout:Page Setup:Orientation drop-down menu.

   Changing the orientation changes the amount of material that will fit per page, as well as where page breaks will occur.

3. Open the Layout:Page Setup:Size menu and ensure that the proper paper size is selected.

4. *Optional:* Change margins by choosing a general setting from the Layout:Page Setup:Margins menu **H** or choose Custom Margins to enter exact settings in the Page Setup dialog box **D**.

5. *Optional:* To add or edit the header or footer, click the Layout:Page Setup: Header & Footer icon and make changes in the Page Layout dialog box.

6. *Optional:* To add a background image to the printout, click the Layout:Page Setup:Background icon, select an image in the Choose a Picture dialog box, and click Insert. (If you don't care for the effect, click the Background icon again to remove the picture.)

7. *Optional:* To add gridlines or headings (column letters and row numbers) to the printout, click their check boxes in the Layout:Print group **I**.

G Options on the Layout tab duplicate those in the Page Setup dialog box, but have the advantage of immediately showing the effect of changed settings.

To print a selected range, worksheet, or workbook:

1. *Optional:* To print only part of the active sheet, select the area. If you intend to print an entire worksheet, the whole workbook, or a saved print area, you can skip this step.

> **TIP** If you want to save the selection as the sheet's new print area (so it will be remembered the next time you print), choose **File > Print Area > Set Print Area.**

2. Choose File > Print (Command-P).

   The Print dialog box appears, open to the Copies & Pages section 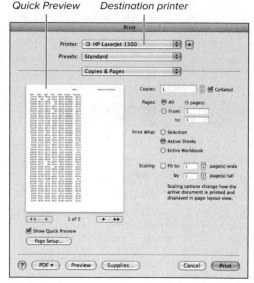.

3. Select the destination printer from the Printer drop-down list.

4. Specify the number of copies and range of pages to print.

5. Click a radio button (Selection, Active Sheets, or Entire Workbook) to specify the Print What setting.

6. *Optional:* The Quick Preview area shows the pages as they will print—reflecting the printer, Print settings, and Page Setup settings. Click the arrow icons under the Quick Preview to view the pages, margins, and page breaks.

> **TIP** If it's necessary to revisit the Page Setup dialog box, click the Page Setup button.

7. Ensure that the chosen printer is on, and click the Print button.

   The print job is routed to the printer.

> **TIP** To print immediately using the current settings (bypassing the Print dialog box), click the Print icon on the Standard toolbar.

> **TIP** Another way to preview a printout is to click the Layout:Print:Preview icon, creating a PDF file that will open in Apple's Preview or Adobe Reader.

Quick Preview   *Destination printer*

J Set options in the Print dialog box.

Modifying Worksheets

Raw data typed in a monospaced font into fixed-width columns is satisfactory for many worksheets, but it isn't fine for all worksheets. Excel provides a variety of formatting tools and procedures that you can apply to dress up any worksheet. With minimal effort, you can turn the ordinary into presentation-quality material.

In addition to formatting a sheet, you can alter its structure by changing the widths and heights of selected columns and rows; adding or deleting rows, columns, and cells; and moving or copying data to different areas of the sheet. You can also insert shapes (such as callout balloons), clip art, photos, SmartArt, and other kinds of graphics.

Setting Column and Row Sizes

You can change the width of selected columns and the height of selected rows as the data dictates. This is particularly useful when a lengthy text string spills into the adjacent columns, for instance.

To manually adjust a column's width:

1. Move the pointer over the right edge of the column's heading.

   The pointer becomes a double arrow **A**.

2. Click and drag to the right or left.

   As you drag, a ScreenTip appears **B**, showing the current width of the column in characters (approximate) and in the default unit of measurement.

3. Release the mouse button to complete the procedure.

To manually adjust a row's height:

1. Move the pointer over the bottom edge of the row.

   The pointer changes to a double arrow.

2. Click and drag up or down.

   As you drag, a ScreenTip appears **C**, showing the current height of the row in points and in the default unit of measurement. (There are 72 points per inch.)

3. Release the mouse button to complete the procedure.

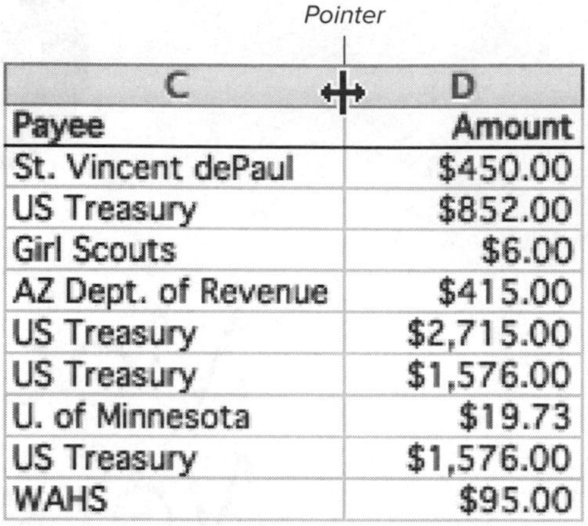

Pointer

A Move the pointer over the right edge of the column header (in this example, column C). The pointer changes to a double arrow.

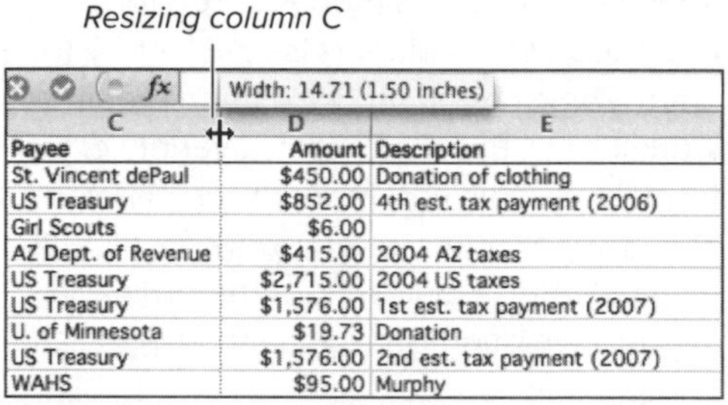

Resizing column C

B Drag to the right or left to set the new column width.

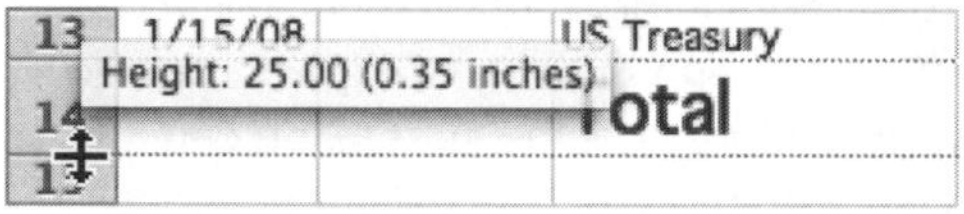

C You can change a row's height in the same manner as changing a column's width.

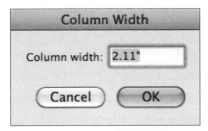

Column Width

Column width: 2.11"

Cancel   OK

D Use the Column Width (or Row Height) dialog box to enter a precise width or height.

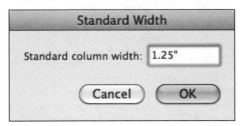

Standard Width

Standard column width: 1.25"

Cancel   OK

E You can define a new default column width that will automatically be applied to blank and new columns.

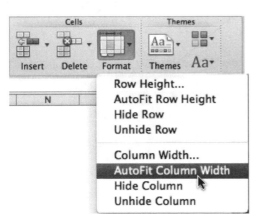

Cells   Themes

Insert Delete Format Themes Aa

Row Height...
AutoFit Row Height
Hide Row
Unhide Row

Column Width...
AutoFit Column Width
Hide Column
Unhide Column

F Commands to resize rows and columns are also available on the Ribbon.

To make other column width and row height adjustments:

Do any of the following:

- To set a column width to the width required to fully display the longest text string, select the column heading and choose Format > Column > AutoFit Selection. To set the column width to that of a specific cell, select the cell and choose the same command.

- To precisely set the width or height of selected columns or rows, choose Format > Column > Width or Format > Row > Height. In the dialog box that appears **D**, enter the new size (in the default measurement unit), and click OK. (You can also open these dialog boxes by right-clicking a column or row header and choosing Column Width or Row Height, respectively.)

- To set a new default column width for the worksheet, choose Format > Column > Standard Width, enter the new width **E**, and click OK. The standard width is applied to every column whose width you haven't changed.

TIP To adjust a column width or row height to automatically accommodate its contents (the widest or highest entry, respectively), double-click the column heading's right border or the row heading's bottom border.

TIP To set multiple columns or rows to the same width or height, select the columns or rows by dragging across their headings. Then drag the edge of any selected column or row heading. All selected columns or rows will change uniformly.

TIP Equivalent commands can also be chosen from the Home:Cells:Format menu **F**.

Reorganizing a Worksheet

To make room for additional data, you can insert and delete rows, columns, and cells. You can also copy or move data from one area of a worksheet to another.

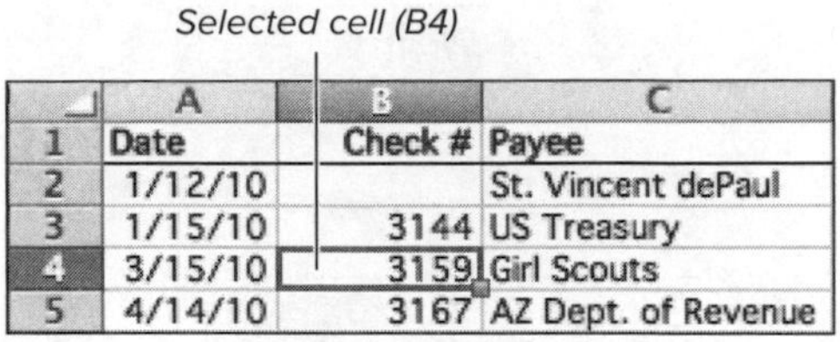

Inserting and deleting columns and rows

With a single command, you can insert or delete one or multiple rows or columns.

To insert new rows or columns:

1. Do one of the following:

   ▸ To insert a single row or column, select any cell in the row or column where you'd like the new row or column to appear Ⓐ.

   ▸ To insert multiple rows or columns, select contiguous cells where you'd like the new rows or columns to appear.

2. Choose Insert > Rows, Insert > Columns, or a command from the Home:Cells:Insert drop-down menu.

   The new rows or columns appear. The worksheet adjusts to accommodate them Ⓑ.

TIP Rather than selecting one or more cells prior to inserting rows or columns, you may find it less confusing to select row or column headings.

Selected cell (B4)

	A	B	C
1	Date	Check #	Payee
2	1/12/10		St. Vincent dePaul
3	1/15/10	3144	US Treasury
4	3/15/10	3159	Girl Scouts
5	4/14/10	3167	AZ Dept. of Revenue

Ⓐ Select the cell where you want to insert the column or row. With cell B4 selected, you could insert a blank column in B or a blank row in 4.

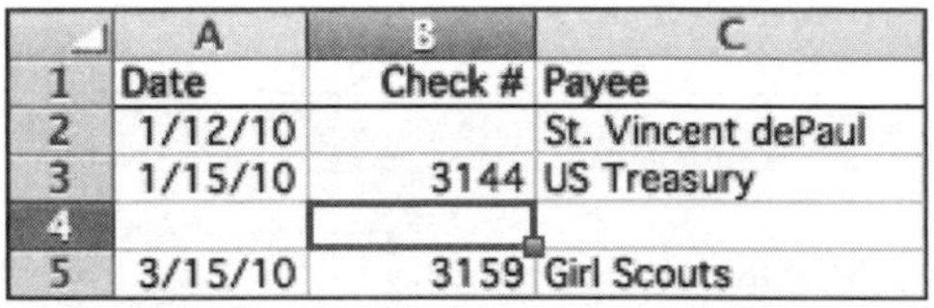

	A	B	C
1	Date	Check #	Payee
2	1/12/10		St. Vincent dePaul
3	1/15/10	3144	US Treasury
4			
5	3/15/10	3159	Girl Scouts

Ⓑ Inserting a new row 4 allows you to insert a missed transaction into the data array.

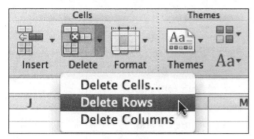

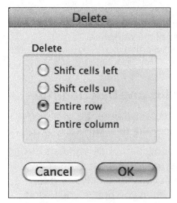

C You can delete cells, rows, or columns by choosing a command from the Home:Cells:Delete drop-down menu.

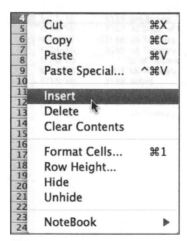

D Indicate whether you'd like to delete the entire row or the entire column.

E Right-click a row or column heading to quickly insert or delete a row or column.

To delete rows or columns:

1. Do one of the following:

   ▶ To delete a single row or column, select any cell in the row or column that you want to delete.

   ▶ To delete multiple rows or columns, select contiguous cells in the rows or columns that you want to delete.

2. Do one of the following:

   ▶ Choose a command from the Home:Cells:Delete icon **C**.

   ▶ Choose Edit > Delete. The Delete dialog box appears **D**. Select Entire row or Entire column. Click OK.

   The worksheet adjusts to accommodate the deleted row(s) or column(s).

   TIP Although it's sufficient to select cells prior to deleting rows or columns, it's more expedient to select entire rows or columns by clicking their heading. When you choose Edit > Delete, the selected rows or columns are instantly deleted—without displaying the Delete dialog box.

   TIP You can also right-click a column or row heading, and choose Insert or Delete from the contextual menu **E**. You can use this technique for multiple insertions and deletions, too. Simply select more than one row or column before right-clicking one of them.

Inserting and deleting cells

When you insert or delete one or more cells, Excel needs to know how to adjust the data in adjacent cells. You indicate your choice in the Insert or the Delete dialog box.

To insert blank cells:

1. Select a cell or a contiguous group of cells where you want to insert empty cells.

2. Do one of the following:

   ▶ Choose Home:Cells:Insert > Insert Cells or Insert > Cells.

   ▶ Right-click one of the selected cells and choose Insert from the contextual menu.

   The Insert dialog box appears **F**.

3. Select either Shift cells right or Shift cells down (referring to how the sheet will be adjusted following the insertion).

4. Click OK.

   New, blank cells appear to replace the selected cells. Existing affected cells are shifted down or right, as directed.

To delete selected cells:

1. Select a cell or a contiguous group of cells that you want to delete.

2. Do one of the following:

   ▶ Choose Home:Cells:Delete > Delete Cells or Edit > Delete.

   ▶ Right-click one of the selected cells, and choose Delete from the contextual menu.

   The Delete dialog box appears **D**.

3. Select Shift cells left or Shift cells up, and click OK.

   The worksheet adjusts to fill in the hole left by the deleted cell or cells.

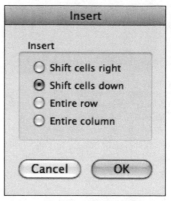

F Select a shift option to apply to affected areas of the worksheet following the cell insertion.

Cell Insertion and Deletion Tips

Before deleting a cell or range, you should consider the following:

- The need to insert or delete cells is a rare occurrence for most users. One situation in which you may need to do this is when you notice you've left out a single piece of data in a lengthy record (row) or that you've accidentally duplicated a cell's data in the next cell.

- You can clear a cell's contents rather than deleting the cell. Press Delete or choose a command from the Edit > Clear submenu or the Home:Edit: Clear menu.

Health insurance premiums	BlueCross BlueShield of AZ
Health insurance premiums	BlueCross BlueShield of AZ
Health insurance premiums	BlueCross BlueShield of AZ

G An open hand signifies a move operation.

Health insurance premiums	BlueCross BlueShield of AZ
Health insurance premiums	BlueCross BlueShield of AZ
Health insurance premiums	BlueCross BlueShield of AZ

H A closed hand stamped with a plus symbol signifies a copy operation.

Source range

19	9/7/10	Health insurance premiums	BlueCross BlueShield of AZ	209.00
20	9/22/10	Health insurance premiums	BlueCross BlueShield of AZ	258.00
21	10/2/10	Health insurance premiums	BlueCross BlueShield of AZ	229.00
22	10/23/10	Doctors, dentists	Dr. Lundin	127.00
23	10/29/10	Doctors, dentists	Dr. Garrett	25.00
24	11/4/10	Health insurance premiums		229.00
25	12/11/10	Health insurance premiums		229.00
26	12/30/10	Health insurance premiums		258.00
27				
28			C24:C26	

Destination   Destination
range   ScreenTip

I Rather than retype **BlueCross BlueShield of AZ** three times, it's faster to copy the contents of C19:C21 to C24:C26.

Copying and moving data

Excel's support of drag and drop makes it easy to move or copy data.

A drag-and-drop copy is a nondestructive procedure; the original cells remain unaltered. A drag-and-drop move, on the other hand, *is* a destructive procedure. It is the same as performing a cut followed by a paste—that is, the contents of the original cells are deleted.

To move or copy a cell range using drag and drop:

1. Select a cell range to move or copy.

2. Move the pointer over the edge of the range. It becomes an open hand **G**.

3. Do one of the following:

   ▸ To move the cells, drag them to the destination.

   ▸ To copy the cells, press Option while dragging to the destination. A plus sign (+) appears inside the hand pointer to indicate that you're copying the data rather than moving it **H**.

   A yellow ScreenTip appears to show the destination range.

4. Release the mouse button to copy or move the cell range to the destination **I**.

TIP When copying or moving data, make sure that the destination range is empty. Copied or moved data always replaces existing data in the destination range.

TIP If you're more comfortable using cut and paste or copy and paste, select the source range, choose Edit > Cut (Command-X) or Edit > Copy (Command-C). Select the cell that will be in the upper-left corner of the destination. To complete the move or copy, press Enter or Command-V, choose Edit > Paste, or click the Home:Edit:Paste icon.

Working with Large Sheets

To simplify the process of working with large worksheets, you can freeze columns and/or rows, as well as split a sheet into multiple panes. Freezing columns and rows prevents data from moving offscreen when you scroll. For instance, you could freeze row 1 to ensure that its column headings were always visible.

Splitting a sheet into multiple panes enables you to display and independently scroll through two or four worksheet regions. A sheet can be split horizontally, vertically, or in both directions.

To freeze column and/or row headings:

1. Do one of the following 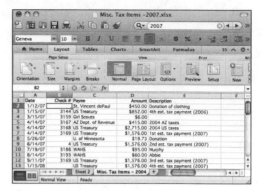:

   ▸ To freeze only rows, click the row heading that is immediately beneath the rows you want to freeze.

   ▸ To freeze columns, click the column heading that is immediately to the right of the columns you want to freeze.

   ▸ To freeze both rows and columns, select the cell immediately below and to the right of the rows and columns you want to freeze.

2. Choose Window > Freeze Panes or Layout:Window > Freeze Panes **B**.

   Gray lines appear in the worksheet to mark the frozen areas **C**. To unfreeze the panes, choose Window > Unfreeze Panes or Layout:Window > Unfreeze Panes **B**.

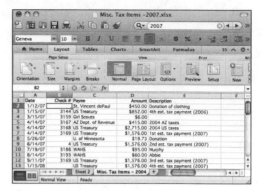

A To freeze the top row of column headings, select row 2. To freeze the Date column (A), select column B. To freeze both, select cell B2.

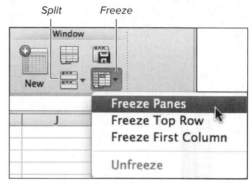

B Choose commands from this icon in the Layout: Window group to freeze or unfreeze panes.

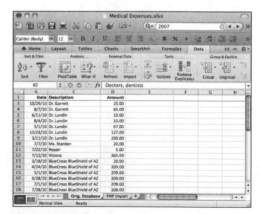

C Row 1 and column A are both frozen. No matter which direction you scroll, row 1 and column A will remain onscreen.

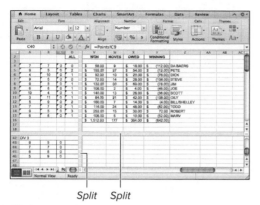

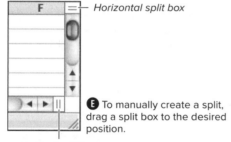

Split *Split*

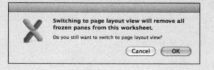

D A worksheet can be split into two or four panes.

— *Horizontal split box*

E To manually create a split, drag a split box to the desired position.

Vertical split box

Frozen Pane Tips

- You can quickly freeze just the top row or first column by choosing a command from the Layout:Window group **B**.

- When you've created frozen panes, pressing Control-Home selects the cell in the upper-left corner of the unfrozen data range rather than A1.

- Frozen panes aren't supported in Page Layout View. If frozen, they'll be unfrozen if you attempt to switch to Page Layout View.

> **X** Switching to page layout view will remove all frozen panes from this worksheet.
> Do you still want to switch to page layout view?
>
> Cancel   OK

To automatically split a worksheet into four panes:

1. Click the cell that you want to become the upper-left corner of the bottom-right pane.

2. Choose Window > Split or click the Layout:Window:Split icon **B**.

   The worksheet is split into four panes **D**.

To manually split a worksheet into multiple panes:

1. Decide whether you want to split the worksheet into two vertical panes, two horizontal panes, or four panes.

   Each sheet has two split boxes—found at the top of the vertical scroll bar and the right end of the horizontal scroll bar **E**.

2. Do any of the following:

   ▸ Drag the horizontal split box downward to split the worksheet into two horizontal panes.

   ▸ Drag the vertical split box to the left to split the worksheet into two vertical panes.

   A ghost of the split bar appears as you drag.

3. Release the mouse button when the split bar is positioned correctly.

TIP To adjust any split, click and drag its split bar or split box to a new position.

TIP To remove all splits, click the Layout: Window:Split icon **B** or choose Window > Remove Split. To remove an individual split, drag its split bar or box off the right edge or top edge of the worksheet.

Worksheet Formatting

The remainder of this chapter discusses ways you can make your worksheets more readable and attractive by applying formatting and adding objects and pictures.

Formatting text

Excel offers a wide range of formatting that you can apply to text. You can specify a font, color, styles (such as boldface or italic), and an alignment to selected cells.

To format text:

1. Select a cell or range to format.

   TIP You can also apply formatting to selected text within a cell, such as applying italic to a word or phrase.

2. Do any of the following:

   ▶ Choose Format > Cells, press Command-1, or right-click one of the selected cells and choose Format Cells from the contextual menu. In the Format Cells dialog box **Ⓐ**, set formatting options on the Alignment and Font tabs, and click OK.

   ▶ Apply formatting by choosing commands from the Home : Font and Alignment groups **Ⓑ** or the Formatting toolbar. (If the Formatting toolbar isn't visible, choose View > Toolbars > Formatting.)

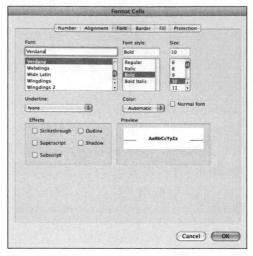

Ⓐ Select font and alignment settings from the tabs of the Format Cells dialog box. Click OK to apply the chosen settings.

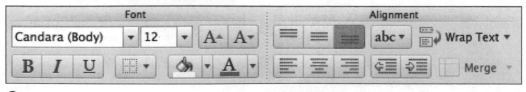

Ⓑ Text-formatting commands are readily available on the Ribbon's Home tab.

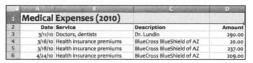

Medical Expenses (2010)			
Date	Service	Description	Amount
3/11/10	Doctors, dentists	Dr. Lundin	290.00
3/18/10	Health insurance premiums	BlueCross BlueShield of AZ	20.00
3/18/10	Health insurance premiums	BlueCross BlueShield of AZ	237.00
4/24/10	Health insurance premiums	BlueCross BlueShield of AZ	209.00

C Select the group of cells within which the text will be centered—in this case, A1:D1.

D After selecting the cells, click the Merge and Center toolbar icon.

		Medical Expenses (2010)	
Date	Service	Description	Amount
3/11/10	Doctors, dentists	Dr. Lundin	290.00
3/18/10	Health insurance premiums	BlueCross BlueShield of AZ	20.00
3/18/10	Health insurance premiums	BlueCross BlueShield of AZ	237.00
4/24/10	Health insurance premiums	BlueCross BlueShield of AZ	209.00

E The Merge and Center results in a single cell (in this case, A1) containing the centered text string.

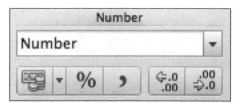

F Extensive number-formatting commands are available in the Home:Number group.

Making Text Fit within a Cell

There are three ways to make text fit entirely within a cell when it would otherwise spill into adjacent cells:

- Manually reduce the text's point size.
- Enable text wrap for the cell by choosing Home:Alignment:Wrap Text > Wrap Text.
- Automatically reduce the point size as needed by choosing Home:Alignment:Wrap Text > Shrink Text to Fit.

To center text across a group of cells:

1. Type a title or other text into the leftmost cell of the cell group.

2. Select the cell group **C**—that is, the cells within which you want to center the text.

3. Click the Merge and Center icon on the Formatting toolbar **D** or choose Home:Alignment:Merge > Merge and Center.

   The selected cells are merged into a single cell and the text is centered within it **E**. To restore merged cells to individual cells, repeat the command.

Formatting numbers, dates, and times

Worksheets often contain columns of numbers, dates, and times. While Excel's default formatting will sometimes suffice, you can also apply specific number, date, or time formatting to such cells.

To format numbers, dates, or times:

Select cells that contain a number, date, or time, and do one of the following:

- Select a number-formatting command from the Home:Number group **F** or the Formatting toolbar.

- Choose Format > Cells (Command-1). On the Number tab of the Format Cells dialog box, select a category and set formatting options.

TIP Number formatting is in addition to any text formatting applied to the cells.

TIP Unless you select a specific number format, Excel applies the General format.

TIP If you enter a number preceded by a dollar sign ($), Excel automatically applies Currency formatting. If you enter a number followed by a percent sign (%), Excel applies Percentage formatting.

Adding cell borders and shading

A *border* is a line (or lines) at the edge of a cell. You can use borders to divide information on the sheet into logical regions. *Shading* is a color or pattern used to fill selected cells.

To apply a border to a cell or range:

1. Select the cell or range to which you want to apply a border.

2. Do one of the following:

   ▸ To apply the most recently used border to the selected cell(s), click the Borders icon on the Formatting toolbar.

   ▸ Choose a border from the Borders icon on the Formatting toolbar or in the Home:Font group.

   ▸ Choose Format > Cells (Command-1). On the Border tab of the Format Cells dialog box 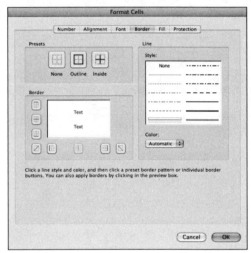, select borders, a line style, and a color. Click OK to apply the border(s) to the cells.

TIP To remove borders from a selected range, select the No Border icon from the Borders gallery on the Formatting toolbar **G** or the Home:Font group. Alternatively, in the Format Cells dialog box **H**, click the None preset.

TIP You can go directly to the Border tab of the Format Cells dialog box by choosing Home:Font:Borders > Border Options.

No Border

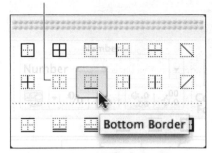

G You can quickly choose a border style from the Borders gallery on the Formatting toolbar.

H Select one or more borders by clicking icons, specify a line style, and choose a border color.

Fill Color icon

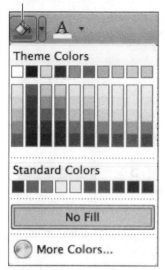

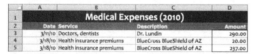

I Select a color to apply to the selected cells.

A	B	C	D
1	Medical Expenses (2010)		
2	Date Service	Description	Amount
3	3/11/10 Doctors, dentists	Dr. Lundin	290.00
4	3/18/10 Health insurance premiums	BlueCross BlueShield of AZ	20.00
5	3/18/10 Health insurance premiums	BlueCross BlueShield of AZ	237.00

J As shown in the titles in rows 1 and 2, white text is legible and stands out nicely with dark fill colors.

Using Office Themes

You can quickly alter the look of a worksheet by applying a new theme to it. A theme consists of a font and color set, designed to impart a consistent appearance to sheet elements.

To apply a different theme to the current worksheet, choose options from the Home:Themes group. Choosing a new color scheme, for example, is instantly noticeable because the colors are applied to all tables, charts, and shapes.

To apply shading to a cell or range:

1. Select the cell or range to which you want to apply shading.

2. Choose a solid color from the Fill Color icon on the Formatting toolbar **I** or in the Home:Font group.

   The color is applied to the selected cell or range.

TIP You can create a gray or colored pattern fill on the Fill tab of the Format Cells dialog box. To open the dialog box, choose Format > Cells or press Command-1.

TIP A handful of preset fill styles can be chosen from the Home:Format gallery.

TIP If shading makes it difficult to read a cell's contents, choose a text color that contrasts with the shading. For example, white or light-colored text works well with a dark cell shading **J**.

Creating and applying styles

A *style* in Excel serves the same purpose as it does in Word. After formatting a cell with a combination of properties (number format, font, alignment, border, fill, and protection), you can save the settings as a style and then apply the style to other cells or ranges in the workbook. In addition to these custom styles, Excel includes built-in styles that you can use.

To create a style:

1. Format a cell as desired and select it.

2. Choose Format > Style or Home : Format : Styles > New Cell Style.

   The New Cell Style dialog box appears, showing the attributes with which the selected cell is formatted **K**.

3. Enter a name for the style in the Style name box.

4. To remove attributes from the style definition, clear their check marks.

   Any attribute that you won't want to apply to every cell should be removed. If an attribute isn't included in the definition, any cell to which the style is applied will retain its original settings for that attribute.

5. *Optional:* To modify the formatting of any attribute, select it in the New Cell Style dialog box and click Format.

   The Format Cells dialog box appears. If necessary, click the appropriate tab. Make any desired changes and click OK.

6. Click OK to save the style definition.

   The style is added to the Custom section of the Styles gallery **L** for the workbook. Be sure to save the workbook to retain the new style definitions.

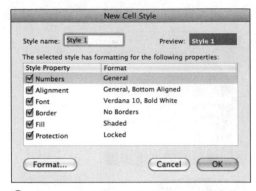

K When creating a style, Excel automatically displays the formatting attributes that will be part of the style based on the selected cell's formatting.

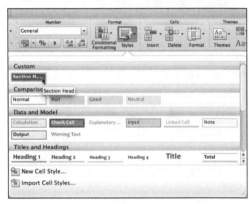

L The style is added to the Custom section of the Home : Format : Styles gallery, where it can be applied to any cell or range in the workbook.

What About the Format Painter?

Although they can be tremendous time savers and ensure consistency in your worksheet formatting, styles aren't for everyone. Another approach you can use is to duplicate formatting using the Format Painter.

Select a cell whose formatting you want to copy, click the Format Painter icon in the Standard toolbar, and then click the destination cell or drag through the destination range to apply the formatting.

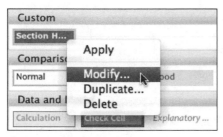

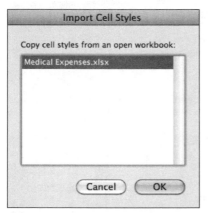

M To modify or delete a style, right-click its name in the Styles gallery.

N Select the workbook whose styles you want to import, and then click OK.

![Alert dialog]

O If any import style exists in the destination workbook, click Skip to ignore the duplicates and import the others, click Replace to replace the existing styles with the imports, or click Cancel to abort the import.

To apply a style:

1. Select the cell or range to which you want to apply formatting.

2. Select a style from the Home:Format: Styles gallery **L**.

   The style is applied to the cell or range. If you like, you can apply other formatting to the cell or range, as well as change attributes that are part of the style definition.

TIP When a [0] follows a style name in the Styles gallery, Excel formats the data with zero decimal places.

TIP To modify a style, open the Styles gallery, right-click the style name, and choose Modify from the contextual menu **M**. In the Modify Cell Styles dialog box (identical to **K**), specify new formatting attributes and click OK. Cells to which the style has been applied are updated.

TIP By default, Excel assigns cells the Normal style unless you specify a different style. To change the default cell formatting, modify the Normal style.

TIP You can import styles from another workbook into the current one. Open the workbook whose styles you want to import, and choose Home:Format:Styles > Import Cell Styles. Select the workbook's name in the Import Cell Styles dialog box **N** and click OK. If any of the import styles already exist in the current workbook, an additional dialog box appears **O**.

CAUTION You can delete styles that you no longer need by right-clicking them in the Styles gallery and choosing Delete **M**. Note, however, that you can't delete the Normal style. And if you delete the Comma, Currency, or Percent style, it will no longer be available on the Formatting toolbar. In general, it's best to restrict style deletions to the ones you've created.

CAUTION If you delete a style that's in use in the worksheet, applicable style-related formatting will be removed from any affected cells.

Conditional formatting

By specifying *conditional formatting* (formatting that's applied only when specified criteria are met), you can make important data stand out from other elements in a data set. Conditional formatting options  allow you to do the following:

- Overlay every member of the data set with a data bar, color, or icon that shows its position in the distribution.

- Apply a color highlight to a specific number of items that are highest, lowest, above average, or below average.

- Apply a color highlight to items identified by a rule, such as bowling scores greater than 200.

Unlike manually applied formatting, conditional formatting updates itself as required. That is, if the data that has been conditionally formatted changes, the items formatted in this manner (highlighted in green, for instance) will automatically change, too.

To apply data bars, color scales, or icon sets to data:

1. Select the cell range to which you want to apply conditional formatting.

2. Click the Home:Format:Conditional Formatting icon and choose an option from the Data Bars, Color Scales, or Icon Sets submenu **Q**.

   The conditional formatting is applied to the range.

P Choose conditional formatting from this drop-down menu in the Home:Format group.

Result		Result		Result	
	2.4		2.4	⇨	2.4
	2.8		2.8	⇨	2.8
	3.8		3.8	⬆	3.8
	1.6		1.6	⬇	1.6
	3.6		3.6	⬆	3.6
	4.0		4.0	⬆	4.0
	1.2		1.2	⬇	1.2
	3.8		3.8	⬆	3.8
	3.0		3.0	⇨	3.0

Data Bars   *Color Scales*   *Icon Sets*

Q You can show the relative size of every item in a data distribution by formatting with data bars, a color scale, or an icon set.

Custom Conditional Formatting

In addition to simply choosing an option from one of the Conditional Formatting submenus, you can customize the settings for any conditional formatting to show only particular values in a specified manner. Choose More Rules from the bottom of the appropriate Conditional Formatting submenu. Depending on the rule type, you can specify a minimum and/or maximum value or indicate how negative values will be displayed, for example.

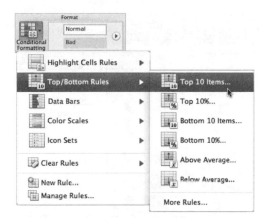

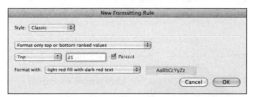

® Choose an option from the Top/Bottom Rules submenu to select the highest/lowest items or those above/below the average for the data set.

⑤ Set options for the rule and click OK.

① The Highlight Cell Rules support more complex criteria than the Top/Bottom Rules.

To apply a Top/Bottom Rule to data:

1. Select the cell range to which you want to apply a Top/Bottom Rule.

2. Click the Conditional Formatting icon and choose an option from the Top/Bottom Rules submenu **®**.

3. Set options in the dialog box that appears:

   ▸ For Average rules, the dialog box allows you to select fill and text colors.

   ▸ For Top and Bottom rules **⑤**, you can also set the cutoff point (as a number or percentage), highlighting only the lowest five scores, for example.

4. Click OK to apply the rule to the selected cell range.

To apply a Highlight Cells Rule to data:

1. Select the cell range to which you want to apply a Highlight Cells Rule.

2. Click the Conditional Formatting icon and choose an option from the Highlight Cells Rules submenu **①**.

3. In the dialog box that appears, set options and click OK to apply the rule.

TIP You can apply multiple types of conditional formatting to any range. To view and manage conditional formatting rules, select the range and choose Format > Conditional Formatting.

TIP To remove conditional formatting from a selected range, open the Conditional Formatting menu **①**, and choose Clear Rules > Clear Rules from Selected Cells.

TIP You can copy conditional formats to other cells using the Format Painter tool.

Shapes and Pictures

Although it doesn't come up often in most worksheets, Excel provides many ways for you to enliven worksheets for inclusion in presentations or reports, for example. You can add any of the following items to a worksheet:

- AutoShapes
- Clip art and photos
- Special symbols, such as fractions and ©
- WordArt, SmartArt objects, movies and audio files (see Chapter 3)

In this section and the next, you'll learn how to insert shapes, clip art, photos, and special characters into your worksheets.

AutoShapes

An *AutoShape* is a defined Office object that you can move, resize, and rotate. After placing an AutoShape, you can change its formatting by choosing a new color or gradient fill, altering its 3D properties, or setting a transparency level. Some AutoShapes can also accept text.

To add a shape to a worksheet:

1. Open the Media Browser by choosing View > Media Browser, clicking the Media Browser icon on the Standard toolbar, or choosing Insert > Shape.

2. Click the Shapes tab on the Media Browser, and choose All Shapes or a specific shape category from the drop-down menu **Ⓐ**.

3. Drag the shape from the Media Browser onto the worksheet **Ⓑ**.

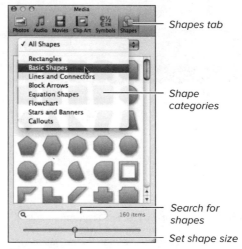

Shapes tab

Shape categories

Search for shapes

Set shape size

Ⓐ Pick a shape to add to the worksheet.

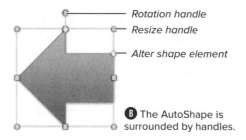

Rotation handle

Resize handle

Alter shape element

Ⓑ The AutoShape is surrounded by handles.

Resizing Objects Exactly

Sometimes just "smaller" or "bigger" isn't sufficient when resizing a shape, clip art image, photo, or other object. To resize a selected object to a specific height or width, enter the new dimension in the Format Picture:Size group. To resize proportionately (to avoid stretching one dimension), be sure the box is checked.

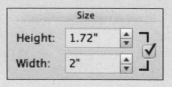

Cut	⌘X
Copy	⌘C
Paste	⌘V
Edit Text	
Edit Points	
Save as Picture...	
Grouping	▶
Arrange	▶
Assign Macro...	
Set as Default Shape	
Format Text...	
Format Shape...	
Hyperlink...	⌘K

C You can insert text inside some AutoShapes.

These sales figures make me sad.

D Excel supports object layering, such as this AutoShape placed on a photo.

4. You can do any of the following:

- ▸ Click inside the shape and drag it to a new location on the worksheet.

- ▸ To resize the shape proportionately, press Shift as you drag a corner handle. To resize from the shape's center, press Option as you drag.

- ▸ To flip the shape, drag a side, top, or bottom handle across the shape.

- ▸ Drag the green rotation handle to change the shape's angle on the page.

- ▸ Drag a yellow handle to modify that element of the shape.

- ▸ To alter the shape's formatting, select new settings from the Format contextual tab. Or choose Format > Shape (Command-1) to open the Format Shape dialog box.

- ▸ If the AutoShape can accept text, right-click it and choose Edit Text from the contextual menu **C**. A text insertion mark appears in the object. (If the shape can't accept text, the text insertion mark won't appear.) Type the text. To format the text, select it and choose settings from the Formatting toolbar or the Home:Font and Alignment groups.

- ▸ If the shape will be placed in a stack with other shapes or graphics **D**, you can change its layering by choosing an option from the Format:Arrange: Reorder menu, such as Send to Back.

- ▸ To remove the shape from the worksheet, select it and press Delete.

TIP **Unlike with shapes, you can proportionately resize clip art or a photo without having to hold down Shift as you drag a corner handle.**

Clip art and photos

You can also dress up worksheets by inserting Office clip art (from the Media Browser or Microsoft Clip Gallery) or photos (stored in iPhoto or as files on disk).

To insert clip art from the Microsoft Clip Gallery application:

1. Choose Insert > Clip Art > Clip Art Gallery. Clip Gallery launches **E**.

2. Locate the desired clip art image by selecting a category, scrolling through the thumbnails, or entering a text string in the Search box and clicking Search.

   To preview images in a separate window, click the Preview check box.

3. To add the selected clip art image to your worksheet, click Insert.

4. When you're finished, click Close.

TIP To view free clip art images at Office Online, click the Online button. Your default browser launches and opens to the site.

To insert clip art from the Media Browser:

1. Open the Media Browser by choosing View > Media Browser, clicking the Media Browser icon on the Standard toolbar, or choosing Insert > Clip Art > Clip Art Browser.

2. Click the Clip Art tab on the Media Browser **F**, and choose All Images or a specific category from the drop-down menu.

3. Drag a clip art image onto the sheet **G**.

Categories　　　*Search box*

Visit Microsoft's site　　　*Preview check box*

E The Microsoft Clip Gallery application.

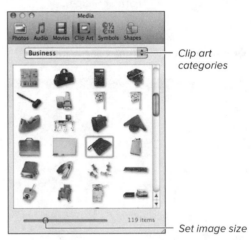

Clip art categories

Set image size

F Drag a clip art image onto the worksheet.

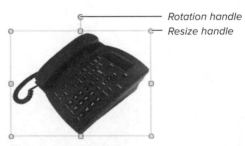

Rotation handle
Resize handle

G Like other inserted objects, a clip art image is surrounded by handles.

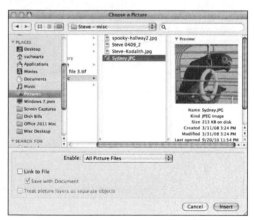

H The Media Browser's Photos tab works like the Shapes tab. In addition to changing the thumbnail size, you can search for photos by filename.

I Select a stored photo to insert.

To insert a photo from your iPhoto library:

1. Open the Media Browser by choosing View > Media Browser, clicking the Media Browser icon on the Standard toolbar, or choosing Insert > Photo > Photo Browser.

2. Click the Photos tab to display the images stored in iPhoto **H**.

3. Find the desired image by doing any combination of the following:

   ▸ Choose a library or folder from the scrolling list.

   ▸ Enter a search string to find images with matching filenames in the current folder. To search all of iPhoto, select iPhoto at the top of the scrolling list.

   ▸ Scroll through the thumbnail list.

4. Drag a photo onto the worksheet.

To insert other photos and pictures:

1. Choose Insert > Photo > Picture From File.

   The Choose a Picture dialog box appears **I**.

2. Navigate to the drive/folder that contains the file you want to insert and select the image's filename.

3. *Optional:* To maintain a link to the file (allowing Excel to automatically show edits), click the Link to File check box.

4. Click Insert.

   The image appears on the worksheet, surrounded by normal object handles.

TIP To replace inserted clip art or a photo, you don't have to delete the original. Right-click the image on the worksheet and choose Change Picture from the contextual menu.

Special Characters

Excel makes it easy to insert special characters into cell text. Rather than hunting for "magic" key combinations that will enable you to type a copyright symbol, a fraction, or a foreign language character, you can select the character from the Symbols tab on the Media Browser.

To insert a special character:

1. Open the Media Browser by choosing View > Media Browser, clicking the Media Browser icon on the Standard toolbar, or choosing Insert > Symbol.

2. Click the Symbols tab on the Media Browser to view the list of supported symbol characters **A**.

3. Set the text insertion mark at the spot within the cell where you want to add the symbol or special character.

4. Choose a symbol category from the drop-down menu.

5. Click the character or symbol you want to insert.

   The character or symbol appears in the cell at the text insertion mark **B**.

> **CAUTION** Resist the temptation to add currency symbols by selecting them from the Symbols tab. If you intend to treat the currency as a number (so it can be used in a formula), choose Format > Cells and select the currency type on the Number tab of the Format Cells dialog box.

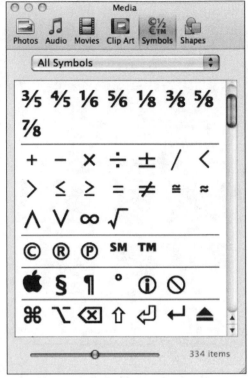

A You can insert special characters into cell text by selecting them from the Symbols tab of the Media Browser.

Press ⌘V to paste.

B The cell text now includes the Command symbol.

Formulas and Functions

Calculations are the way that Excel "does the math." Even if you're only using Excel to keep lists, you may have numbers on which you'd like to perform some calculations (for example, totaling the number of items sold or computing bowling averages). Excel excels at calculations of this sort and provides tools to save you time and effort.

For instance, suppose you want to calculate the total of a column of numbers. You would create a formula in the cell beneath the column. The formula might look like this: `=SUM(B2:B12)`

All formulas begin with an equal sign (=), which enables Excel to distinguish them from text or a number. When you've finished entering the formula and move to another cell, Excel evaluates the formula based on any functions used (such as SUM) and the data to which it refers (cells B2 through B12). What's now shown in the cell is no longer the formula but its result—in this case, the total of the numbers in the specified cells.

In This Chapter

Formula Basics

To add two numbers, you could select a cell and type **=23+43**. To add the contents of two cells, you use their *addresses* in the formula, as in **=B3+B4**. (The addresses are referred to as *cell references*—that is, you're referring to the cells by their addresses.) The cell into which you type the formula displays the calculation result as soon as you move to a different cell.

If data in any referenced cell changes, the result instantly changes. This quick recalculation lets you perform what-if analyses. Just change any of the numbers in the referenced cells to see how the changes affect the results.

Formulas can consist of any combination of data, cell references, functions, and operators (such as +, −, and /). The following steps show how to create a basic formula.

To create a simple formula:

1. *Optional:* You can create or edit formulas in the cell or in the formula bar, whichever you find convenient.

2. Select the cell in which you want to create the formula and type an equal sign (=), either in the cell or in the formula bar **Ⓐ**.

3. Do either of the following:

   ▸ Type the first number or cell reference to include in the formula.

   ▸ Click the first cell you want to reference in the formula. (When creating or editing a formula, clicking a cell results in the clicked cell's address being inserted into the formula.)

4. Type an operator, such as + or /.

   See **Table 12.1** on the following page for a list of common arithmetic operators.

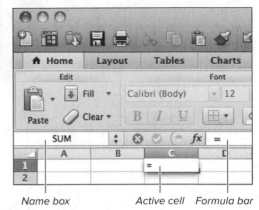

Name box   *Active cell* *Formula bar*

Ⓐ You can create or edit a formula in its cell or in the formula bar.

Creating Formulas

When entering a formula, you can use any combination of these techniques:

- Type the formula, including cell references, range references, and names,

- Add a cell or range reference by clicking the cell or drag-selecting the range.

- Choose functions from the Name box **Ⓐ** or Formula AutoComplete lists. To dismiss a Formula AutoComplete list, continue typing rather than selecting a function name. Formula AutoComplete lists are discussed in "Using Functions" later in this chapter.

- Design the formula in Formula Builder, as explained in "Working with Formula Builder," later in this chapter.

TABLE 12.1 Arithmetic Operators

Operator	Action
+	Addition
–	Subtraction
*	Multiplication
/	Division
%	Percentage
^	Exponentiation

Formula for selected cell (E2)

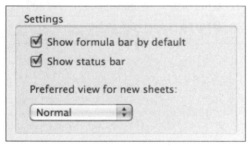

	A	B	C	D	E	F
1		Test 1	Test 2	Test 3	Avg Score	
2	Michelle	15	14	16	=AVERAGE(B2:D2)	
3	Thomas	18	16	19	17.67	
4	Adrian	14	9	11	11.33	
5	Anthony	17	14	18	16.33	
6	Jonas	20	20	18	19.33	
7	Heidi	13	15	16	14.67	

SUM · fx =AVERAGE(B2:D2)

Formula

B A cell normally displays the result rather than the formula. To view the formula, double-click the cell or select the cell and examine the formula bar.

Settings

☑ Show formula bar by default

☑ Show status bar

Preferred view for new sheets:

| Normal |

C The formula bar can be shown or hidden automatically whenever you open a workbook or create a new one.

5. Do one of the following:

 ▸ Type the final number or cell reference that you want to include in the formula.

 ▸ Click the final cell that you want to reference in the formula.

6. Press Return or Enter to complete the formula and view the result.

TIP You can combine numbers (*constants*) and cell references in a formula, such as =C2*2.5 (the contents of cell C2 multiplied by 2.5).

TIP After the initial element in a formula has been typed or inserted, clicking a cell automatically adds the contents of the cell to the current formula. For example, if a formula currently contains =17 and you click cell A4, the formula becomes =17+A4.

TIP To view a cell's formula rather than its result, double-click the cell or check the formula bar **B**. When you're done examining the formula, press Esc to restore the cell to its normal state.

TIP If adjacent cells require a similar formula, you can copy the formula from cell to cell. See "Copying a Formula to Adjacent Cells," later in this chapter.

TIP Unlike in Excel 2008, the formula bar is now shown by default in all new workbooks. If you prefer not to use it, choose Excel > Preferences, click the View icon in the Authoring section of Excel Preferences, remove the check mark from the option to Show formula bar by default **C**, and click OK.

TIP You can manually show or hide the formula bar for the current workbook by choosing View > Formula Bar. When the Formula Bar command is preceded by a check mark, it is displayed.

About Precedence

Here's a fact of spreadsheet life. Few formulas consist only of two cell references or numbers separated by an operator. They're often much more complex. And while it might make your life simpler if formulas were evaluated from left to right, that isn't necessarily the case. Instead, spreadsheets follow established rules of precedence when evaluating formulas. These strict rules determine the order in which a formula's components are combined.

Suppose that you see the following formula:

= 3 + 7 * 2

If evaluated from left to right, the result would be 20. The actual result, however, is 17. This is because operators with a higher precedence (such as multiplication) are always evaluated before operators with a lower precedence (such as addition). Thus, our example is calculated by multiplying 7 times 2 and then adding 3, resulting in 17. **Table 12.2** shows the precedence of the various operators.

To avoid forcing you to rearrange numbers, cell references, and operators, Excel lets you alter the evaluation order for a formula by enclosing items in parentheses. Such items are automatically given higher precedence. If you use multiple sets of nested parentheses, they are evaluated from innermost to the outermost set.

By adding parentheses to your formula, as in **=(3 + 7) * 2**, you can force it to be evaluated from left to right. Although addition is of lower precedence than multiplication, the parentheses will make it be evaluated by first adding 3 and 7 and then multiplying that result by 2, yielding 20. See **Table 12.3** for additional examples.

TABLE 12.2 Operator Precedence (from Highest to Lowest)

Operator	Meaning
–	Negation (–5, for example)
%	Percentage
^	Exponentiation
* and /	Multiplication, division
+ and –	Addition, subtraction
&	Concatenation (for combining text strings)
=, <, >, <=, >=, <>	Comparison (equal, less than, greater than, less than or equal, greater than or equal, not equal)

TABLE 12.3 Precedence Examples

Example	Evaluation	Result
2 * 3 + 4	(6) + 4	10
2 + 3 * 4	2 + (12)	14
2 * (3 + 4)	2 * (7)	14
(7 – 2) * (3 * 4)	(5) * (12)	60
30 – (2 * 3) * 4	30 - (6 * 4)	6

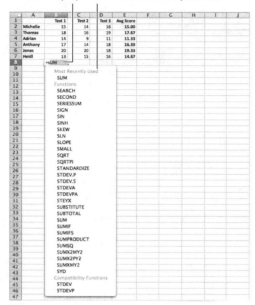

Active cell (B8)   *Formula AutoComplete list*

A Select the cell, type =, and then begin entering the function. The AutoComplete list appears, showing all functions that start with the typed letters.

	A	B	C	D	E
1		Test 1	Test 2	Test 3	Avg Score
2	Michelle	15	14	16	15.00
3	Thomas	18	16	19	17.67
4	Adrian	14	9	11	11.33
5	Anthony	17	14	18	16.33
6	Jonas	20	20	18	19.33
7	Heidi	13	15	16	14.67
8		=SUM(B2:B7)			
9		SUM(number1, [number2], ...)			
10					

B Drag to select the cells you want to total with the Sum function—in this case, cells B2 through B7.

	A	B
1		Test 1
2	Michelle	15
3	Thomas	18
4	Adrian	14
5	Anthony	17
6	Jonas	20
7	Heidi	13
8		97

C After completing the formula, the total of cells B2 through B7 (97) is displayed in cell B8.

Using Functions

Functions are shortcuts for calculations that would be difficult to create with a basic formula. Excel's 300+ built-in functions can be included in formulas to help you easily perform financial, statistical, engineering, logical, and text-based computations.

Functions accept values called *arguments*, perform an operation on them, and then return one or more values. See the end of this chapter for a list of common functions.

Totaling a column with SUM

Perhaps the simplest function-based calculation you can perform—and certainly the most common—is to total a column of numbers using the Sum function. Sum can also be used to total rows or a combination of adjacent and nonadjacent cells.

To total a column using Sum:

1. Click the cell in which you want the sum to appear.

   Although this will generally be the cell immediately beneath the column of numbers, you can choose any cell.

2. Enter **=s** to begin the formula. Excel displays a Formula AutoComplete list of functions that begin with the letter S **A**. Select SUM from the list.

   Excel adds parentheses, displaying **=SUM()** and placing the text insertion mark between the parentheses.

3. Drag down the column of numbers you want to total **B**.

4. Press Return or Enter to complete the formula.

   The result is displayed in the cell **C** and the formula is shown in the formula bar.

Using AutoSum

To make it easier to perform the most common computations on a column or row, Excel provides the AutoSum feature. When used directly beneath a column or to the right of a row, AutoSum determines the desired cell range by examining the data.

To perform a column or row calculation using AutoSum:

1. Click the empty cell directly beneath a column or to the right of a row.

2. Do one of the following:

   ▸ To calculate a column or row total using the Sum function, click the AutoSum icon on the Standard tool-bar **D**.

   ▸ Click the down arrow beside the AutoSum icon. Choose a function (such as Average or Max) from the drop-down menu.

   The complete formula is shown **E**.

3. Do one of the following:

   ▸ Press Return or Enter to accept the selected range and display the result.

   ▸ Edit the formula (changing the range, for example). Then press Return or Enter to display the result.

TIP AutoSum defaults to operating on columns. If it finds suitable data above the destination cell, it performs a column calculation. If not, it attempts to operate on a row.

TIP To quickly perform a calculation for a set of adjacent columns, select the empty cell beneath each of the columns before choosing an AutoSum function. Excel will insert a formula in each selected cell.

TIP You can also insert an AutoSum by selecting the data to be summarized and then choosing an AutoSum function.

AutoSum icon

D Click the AutoSum icon to calculate a Sum, or click the down arrow to choose a function.

Selected range

D	E
Test 3	
16	
19	
11	
18	
18	
16	
=SUM(D2:D7)	

Resulting formula

E The formula (including the range selected by AutoSum) is displayed in the cell.

Text insertion mark

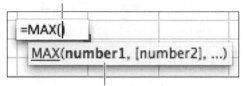

Function syntax and arguments

F When you select a function from a Formula AutoComplete list, the opening and closing parentheses are automatically provided for you.

Nonadjacent references as function arguments

While column- and row-based calculations are commonplace, there's no requirement that a formula operate on adjacent cells. Referenced cells can be scattered all over a worksheet or workbook. The following example shows how to enter nonadjacent references as arguments to a function, such as `=MAX(A3,A5,D12:D17)`. Note that references are separated by commas (**,**).

To include nonadjacent references as arguments to a function:

1. Click the cell in which you want to place the formula.

2. Type an equal sign (=), followed by the first letter or two of the function name.

3. Select the function name from the Formula AutoComplete list that appears **A**.

   The function appears in the cell. The text insertion mark is positioned between the provided parentheses **F**.

4. Click the cell or select the range that will serve as the first argument to the function. If you prefer, you can type the cell or range reference, such as **G17** or **B12:B16**.

5. Type a comma (**,**).

6. Click the next cell or select the next range whose values you want to include in the formula. You can also type this cell or range reference.

7. Repeat Steps 5 and 6 until you've included the necessary references.

8. Press Return or Enter to complete the formula.

Working with Formula Builder

Formula Builder is a Toolbox utility designed to help construct and edit formulas. It's especially useful if you're uncertain of a function's syntax or are unfamiliar with the process of creating formulas.

To create a formula using Formula Builder:

1. Select a cell to contain the formula.

2. If the Toolbox is currently open, click the Formula Builder tab **A**. Otherwise, click Formulas : Function : Formula Builder or choose View > Toolbox > Formula Builder.

3. Do one of the following:

   ▸ If the formula begins with a function, double-click its name in Formula Builder. The equal sign, function name, and parentheses are inserted into the cell **A**.

   ▸ If the formula begins with data or a cell/range reference, type =, the data or reference, and the first operator in the cell or formula bar (for example, **=A17+**).

4. Do one of the following:

   ▸ If you inserted a function, boxes for its arguments appear **A**. For each argument, select a reference on the sheet or type the data or reference.

   ▸ When following an operator, such as +, −, or *, type the data or reference, or select the reference on the sheet.

   As you add arguments and elements, Formula Builder evaluates the data and displays the current result **B**.

Formula   *Formula Builder tab*   *Selected function*

A The Formula Builder tab of the Toolbox.

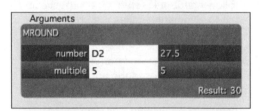

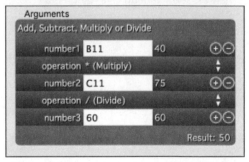

B Formula Builder displays each argument and calculates the result so far. These examples show a function (top) and a simple calculation (bottom).

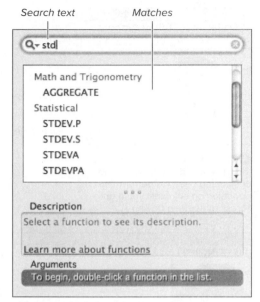

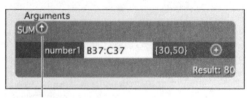

Up arrow

C To find a function, type its name, part of the name, or some descriptive text.

D In this formula, a SUM function is an argument to the main function. Click the up arrow to resume editing the main function.

5. Add the functions, arguments, and/or elements needed to finish the formula.

6. Press Return or Enter to complete the formula.

7. If you no longer need Formula Builder, you can close the Toolbox.

TIP If the formula cell is near the end of a row or bottom of a column and the formula is function-based, Formula Builder may treat it as an AutoSum and insert the range for you. If the range is incorrect, you can change it by typing or selecting the correct range. For information about creating an AutoSum, see "Using AutoSum," earlier in this chapter.

TIP Rather than scroll through the entire function list, you can enter search text in the box at the top of Formula Builder. As you type, potential matches are listed **C**.

TIP To insert a function as an argument to the current function (known as a *nested function*), double-click the function's name in the list. When a formula contains multiple functions, you work with each function separately. To switch between the functions, click the up-arrow icon **D** or click the function name in the cell or formula bar.

Copying a Formula to Adjacent Cells

You'll sometimes want to perform the same calculation for several columns or rows. For example, in a worksheet that shows sales by region, you may want to display a total for every column of sales figures. Rather than rebuild the formula from scratch, you can copy it to adjacent cells. Excel changes the formula automatically to refer to the data in each destination column or row.

To copy a formula to adjacent cells:

1. Select the cell containing the formula.

2. Drag the fill handle at the lower-right corner of the cell across the adjacent cells to which you want to copy the formula **A**.

   The formula's results appear in the cells, and the Auto Fill Options button appears **B**.

3. *Optional:* To specify the format of the destination cells, click the Auto Fill Options button and choose a formatting option from the drop-down menu **B**.

TIP Check copied formulas for accuracy if they reference cells in columns or rows other than the ones containing the formula. Excel sometimes guesses incorrectly about your intentions.

TIP This copy operation can also be accomplished using a Fill command. Select the first cell, drag to select the destination cells, and then choose Home:Edit:Fill > *direction* or Edit > Fill > *direction*.

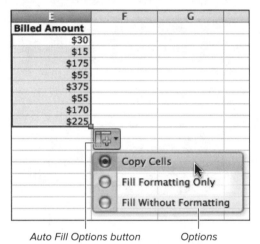

D	E
Dollar Amt.	**Billed Amount**
$27.50	$30
$12.50	
$175.00	
$56.25	
$375.00	
$56.25	
$168.75	
$225.00	

Original cell

Fill handle

A Click the original cell and drag the fill handle down to select the destination cells. (To perform this operation on columns, you'd drag across rather than down.)

E	F	G
Billed Amount		
$30		
$15		
$175		
$55		
$375		
$55		
$170		
$225		

Copy Cells
Fill Formatting Only
Fill Without Formatting

Auto Fill Options button   *Options*

B The results appear in the destination cells. Click the Auto Fill Options button to review formatting options.

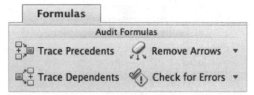

A The Formulas : Audit Formulas group on the Ribbon.

Finding Invalid Data

Another type of error check that Excel can perform is to identify invalid data. You can specify validation criteria to indicate that only certain data should be allowed in a given cell, range, or table column. For instance, you could specify that dates must fall between two values or that numbers must be larger than a particular value. When you enter new data in those cells, Excel prevents you from entering data that violates the criterion.

1. To set a validation criterion, select the cell/range and choose Data > Validation.

2. Repeat step 1 as needed to set criteria for other ranges.

3. To check a sheet for cells that violate validation criteria, choose Data : Tools : Validate > Circle Invalid Data.

   Any cell that contains invalid data is circled. (To view the criterion that a circled cell is violating, select the cell and choose Data > Validation or Data : Tools : Validate > Data Validation.)

4. *Optional:* Correct the errors by editing the data, changing the validation criterion, or removing the criterion.

5. Remove the invalid data circles by choosing Data : Tools : Validate > Clear Validation Circle.

Correcting Formula Errors

To prevent erroneous results from incorrect formulas, Excel supplies a comprehensive set of auditing and troubleshooting tools. For instance, you can do the following:

- **Worksheet auditing.** By selecting a cell and then choosing the appropriate command, you can locate the following in a worksheet:

  - *Precedents.* Cells that provide data to the selected formula.

  - *Dependents.* Formulas that draw data from the selected cell.

  - *Errors.* To identify the source of a marked error (such as **#VALUE**), you can find all cells that provide data to the selected formula.

  Auditing commands can be selected from the Formulas : Audit Formulas group **A** or chosen from the Tools > Auditing submenu.

- **Error checking.** Automatically scan a worksheet and step through the process of correcting each identified error.

To audit a worksheet:

1. Do any of the following:

- To locate precedents, select the cell that contains the formula. Click Formulas : Audit Formulas : Trace Precedents **Ⓐ** or choose Tools > Auditing > Trace Precedents. Arrows appear on the sheet, showing the formula dependencies **Ⓑ**.

- To locate dependents, select the data cell. Click Formulas : Audit Formulas : Trace Dependents **Ⓐ** or choose Tools > Auditing > Trace Dependents. Arrows appear, showing all formulas in which the cell is referenced **Ⓒ**.

- To trace an error, select the cell that contains an error indicator. To identify the error type, rest the cursor on the Error button that appears **Ⓓ**. With the error cell selected, you can identify the cell(s) involved in the error by choosing the Trace Error command from the Formulas : Audit Formulas : Check for Errors submenu, the Tools > Auditing submenu, or from the Error button's drop-down menu **Ⓔ**.

2. To remove arrows placed by the audit commands, do the following:

- *All arrows.* Click Formulas : Audit Formulas : Remove Arrows or choose Tools > Auditing > Remove All Arrows.

- *Dependent or precedent arrows.* Select the appropriate cell. Choose Formulas : Audit Formulas : Remove Arrows > Remove Dependent Arrows (or Remove Precedent Arrows).

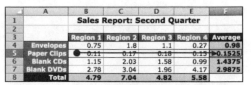

Ⓑ The arrow shows that the formula in cell F5 depends on data in the cells in the range B5:E5.

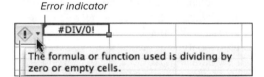

Ⓒ The arrows show that the selected cell (C5) is used in two formulas, found in C8 and F5.

Error indicator

> #DIV/0!

> The formula or function used is dividing by zero or empty cells.

Error button

Ⓓ A ScreenTip explains the error.

Error indicator   *Detected error*

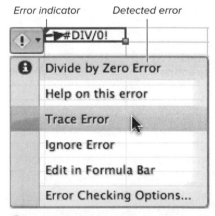

Ⓔ Open the error button's menu to choose an error-handling command.

Handling Circular References

A *circular reference* occurs when a formula directly or indirectly refers to the cell that contains the formula. For instance, if cell A7 contained the formula **=C3/A7**, it would constitute a circular reference. Similarly, two formulas that rely on one another is another example of a circular reference. Until a circular reference is corrected, Excel displays the result as **0** (zero).

If at least one circular references exists in a worksheet, it is shown in the status bar **G**. To correct it, you must edit the formula in one or both cells to eliminate the error. If additional circular references exist, the next one will be displayed in the status bar.

Circular: H4

G Circular references are noted in the status bar at the bottom of the sheet.

To perform an error check for a worksheet:

1. Click Formulas : Audit Formulas : Check for Errors **A** or choose Tools > Error Checking.

   If no errors are found, a notification box appears. Click OK to dismiss it. Otherwise, the Error Checking dialog box appears, highlighting the first error **F**.

2. For each identified error, you can do any of the following:

   ▸ Click Help on this error to consult Excel Help for an explanation.

   ▸ Click Trace *error* to display arrows on the sheet that identify the other cells (if any) that are related to the error.

   ▸ Click Ignore Error to skip this error.

   ▸ Click Edit in Formula Bar to manually correct the error.

3. Click Next to view the next error, if any, and repeat step 2.

4. When all errors have been displayed, close the final dialog box by clicking OK.

Formula containing the error

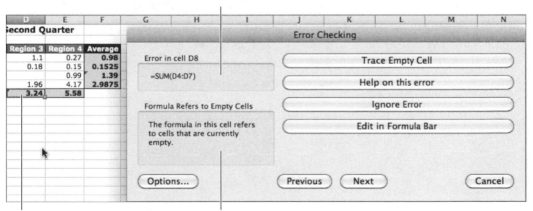

Cell containing the error (D8) Error description

F The Error Checking dialog box displays the first error. The erroneous cell (D8) is selected on the sheet.

Common Excel Functions

Table 12.4 lists common functions used in Excel.

TABLE 12.4 Common Excel Functions

Syntax	Definition
AVERAGE (number1, number2, ...)[†]	Calculates the average (arithmetic mean) of the arguments
DAYS360 (start_date, end_date, method)	Calculates the number of days between two dates based on a 360-day year (used in some accounting functions)
DDB (cost, salvage, life, period, factor)	Provides the depreciation of an asset for a specified period using the double-declining balance method or another specified method
FV (rate, nper, pmt, pv, type)	Calculates the future value of an investment
IF (logical_test, value_if_true, value_if_false)	Performs a test that when true returns one value and when false returns another value
IRR (values, guess)	Provides the internal rate of return for a series of cash flows
MAX (number1, number2, ...)	Calculates the maximum value in a list of arguments
MEDIAN (number1, number2, ...)	Calculates the median (the middle value) of the given numbers
MIN (number1, number2, ...)	Calculates the smallest number in the list of arguments
NOW ( )	Provides the serial number of the current date and time
NPV (rate, value1, value2, ...)	Calculates the net present value of an investment based on a series of periodic cash flows and a discount rate
PMT (rate, nper, pv, fv, type)	Calculates the periodic payment for an annuity or loan
PV (rate, nper, pmt, fv, type)	Calculates the present value of an investment
ROUND (number, num_digits)	Rounds a number to a specified number of digits
SUM (number1, number2, ...)	Calculates the sum of all numbers in the list of arguments
STDEV (number1, number2, ...)	Estimates the standard deviation based on a sample
TODAY ( )	Provides the serial number of today's date
VALUE (text)	Converts a text string that represents a number into a number

[†]The expression (number1, number2, ...) can also be specified as a range, such as C25:C47.

Working with Tables

Many worksheets are simply lists of information, such as address data and club membership rosters. Such lists typically include few calculations, if any. A spreadsheet program is very adept at managing lists—considerably more so than a word processing program, for instance.

Because so many people use spreadsheets to create and manage lists, Microsoft introduced list management features in Excel 2001. In Excel 2011, lists are now called *tables*, adapting the Office 2007 (Windows) convention. More powerful than the tables available to Word and PowerPoint documents, Excel tables can simplify many cumbersome tasks, such as sorting, filtering, totaling data, and performing complex calculations.

Excel tables are essentially databases. If you intend to create tables in Excel, you'll also want to learn about Excel's database features, discussed in Chapter 15.

In This Chapter

About Tables

An *Excel table* **A** is a rectangular array that is independent of the rest of the worksheet. That is, you can perform most actions within a table without affecting data elsewhere. A table is basically a database in which columns are *fields* and rows are *records*. To create a table, you need only concern yourself with finding an empty area of sufficient size in which to place the table.

A table has the following advantages over a normal worksheet range:

- You can add or delete rows/columns without worrying about inadvertently damaging the worksheet's integrity.

- You can sort the entire table on any field. Data above and below the table is unaffected by sorting.

- To focus on specific records or those that match a criterion (such as **>4**), you can filter the data. (Filtering is a record-selection technique similar to a find.)

- Even after you've created a table, you easily increase its size—as long as there are contiguous empty cells into which it can be expanded.

- You can add a total row to the bottom of any table, using it to calculate an Excel function (such as SUM or AVERAGE) for designated columns.

- If you enter a formula in any cell, you can optionally propagate it to every cell in the column by designating the column a calculated column. If you later add new records, the formula will automatically be applied to the new data.

Menu icon   *Field label*   *Calculated column*

	Today's Post	Name	Last Race	Post	Finish	Time	Odds	Races	Wins	Places	Shows	In the Money %
2	1	Flying Stone	Jun-15	4	1	2:03	5.0	11	4	0	0	36%
3	2	Lady Chris Time	Jun-12	2	5	2:00	32.5	18	4	1	1	33%
4	3	Black Bart	Jun-13	7	2	2:00	24.6	13	3	2	2	54%
5	4	Shadrack	Jun-08	5	5	2:02	3.9	4	1	0	1	50%
6	5	Sundust Prince	Jun-18	4	5	2:01	15.1	10	2	1	4	70%
7	6	J.J.'s Ferro	Jun-15	3	4	2:04	1.0	8	3	0	3	75%
8	7	Pat's Comedian	May-31	4	8	2:01	8.1	7	1	1	1	43%
9	Average				4.29	2:01	12.9	10.14	2.57	0.71	1.71	52%

Total Row

A This typical table shows some standard and optional table features. Each labeled column (*field*) has a menu from which you can choose sorting and filtering commands.

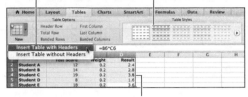

New menu   Table Styles gallery

Selected range (A1:D6)

A Two ways to use the Ribbon to create a table from a selected range are to choose an Insert Table command or select a Table Style.

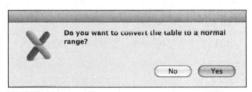

B The selected range is converted into a table.

> Do you want to convert the table to a normal range?
>
> No   Yes

C Click Yes to convert the table into a normal worksheet range.

Moving a Table

You can relocate any Excel table. Start by selecting the entire table (including its header labels and total row). Move the cursor over any edge of the table. When it becomes an open hand, drag the table to its new location.

You can also use cut and paste to move a table—to another workbook or sheet, for example. Select the table, and choose Edit > Cut (Command-X). Select a destination cell for the table, ensuring that there are sufficient empty cells to receive the table. Choose Edit > Paste (Command-V) or press Enter.

Creating a Table

You can create a table in a blank range or convert existing data to a table.

To create a table:

1. Do one of the following:

   ▸ Select a blank range where you want to insert the table.

   ▸ Select a range containing data that you want to convert to a table.

2. Do one of the following:

   ▸ Click Tables : Table Options : New and choose an Insert Table command **A**.

   ▸ Select a table format from the Tables : Table Styles gallery **A**.

   ▸ Choose Insert > Table (Control-T)

   The data or blank range is converted to a table **B**.

   If the table range was blank or you chose Tables : Table Options : New > Insert Table without Headers, each column has a generic label of the form Column1, Column2, and so on.

3. Double-click each label and type a new name.

   You are ready to begin entering data or formatting the table (as described later in this chapter).

> **TIP** The menu icon in each column header can obscure its label **B**. You may want to widen the columns, change the paragraph alignment, or apply text wrap to the headers.

> **TIP** To convert a table back to normal data, select the table or any table cell and click Tables : Tools : Convert to Range. Confirm the conversion by clicking Yes in the dialog box that appears **C**. (Note that workbooks that contain tables can't be shared. Use the Convert to Range procedure prior to sharing.)

Entering and Editing Data

Cells in a table are the same as other worksheet cells. You can use normal editing techniques to enter, delete, and modify table cell contents. See "Entering Data" and "Editing Cell Data" in Chapter 10 for basic data-entry and editing techniques. In addition, you may find the following procedures useful.

To enter and edit table data:

- To add new data to a table, you can use any of the following techniques:

  ▸ Type data into each cell and edit as you would in any worksheet. Press Tab or Shift-Tab to move to the next or previous cell.

  ▸ Select any cell within the table and choose Data > Form. Use the Form dialog box **A** to edit existing records, enter new records, or delete records.

- To create a new *record* (table row), select the final cell in the last record and press Tab.

TIP As you begin typing a cell entry, a list of previous entries for the column that begin with the same characters appears **B**. This is the column's AutoComplete list. You can select one of the items as a data-entry shortcut.

TIP To display a column's entire AutoComplete list, press Option-Down Arrow.

TIP To clear the contents of a row without deleting it, select the entire row. Choose Home:Edit:Clear > Contents or choose Edit > Clear > Contents.

TIP See Chapter 15 for more information about using forms for data entry and editing.

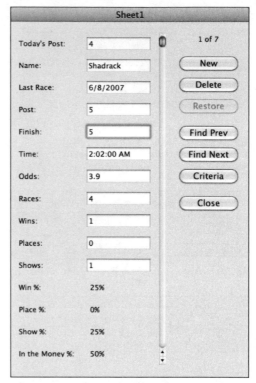

A You can optionally use a form to create new records, edit existing records, or delete records. Click Close when you're done.

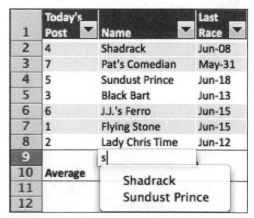

B The two horses whose names begin with S appear the moment you type the **S**. You can choose a drop-down list item or continue typing.

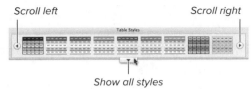

Scroll left   Scroll right

Show all styles

A You can choose a basic table style from this scrolling gallery.

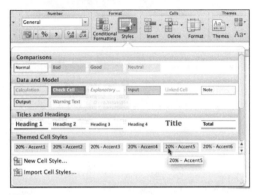

B You can select pre-formatted cell styles from the Home:Format:Styles drop-down gallery.

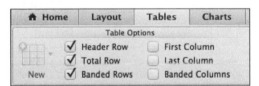

C Click check boxes in the Table Options group to hide, show, and format table components.

Selecting Table Rows or Columns

To select a table column rather than an entire worksheet column, move the cursor over the top edge of the column header. When the cursor changes to a black down-pointing arrow, click to select the table column.

Similarly, to select a table row, move the cursor over the left edge of the row. When the cursor changes to a black arrow that points right, click to select the table row.

Formatting a Table

A table is just another worksheet range. As such, if you aren't thrilled with the default formatting, you can format individual cells, rows, columns, or the entire table any way that you like.

To format a table:

Do any of the following:

- **Format the entire table.** Select any cell in the table. On the Tables tab, select a style from the Table Styles gallery **A**.

- **Format a selected row, column, or range.** Choose a format from the Home: Format:Styles drop-down menu **B**.

  You can also apply a fill color, fill pattern, and/or borders to specific cells. Choose Format > Cells and set options in the Format Cells dialog box. You can also choose settings from the Formatting toolbar and the Home tab.

- **Format the first or last column.** The first column often contains record identifiers and the last column is frequently used to summarize each record's data. To apply distinctive formatting to these columns (boldface and, in some cases, a background color), click the First Column and/or Last Column check boxes in the Tables:Table Options group **C**.

- **Create alternating rows or columns.** Click Banded Rows or Banded Columns in the Tables:Table Options group **C**.

TIP The effect of selecting First Column and Last Column in the Table Options group depends on the table's current formatting. For instance, if the entire table is formatted with a single color, only boldface will be applied to the column.

Changing a Table's Size

Table contents can change over time. In addition to editing the data, you may want to add or delete columns, as well as add or delete rows.

To change a table's size:

- **Insert rows.** Select a cell in the row beneath where you want to insert the new row. (To insert multiple rows in the same spot, select that number of cells in adjacent rows.) Choose Tables : Cells : Insert > Table Rows Above **A**.

- **Insert columns.** Select a cell in the column to the right of where you want to insert a new column. (To insert multiple columns in the same spot, select that number of cells in adjacent columns.) Choose Tables : Cells : Insert > Table Columns to the Left.

- **Increase a table's size by dragging.** Move the cursor over the lower-right corner of the table. When the cursor changes shape **B**, drag to the right to add columns or drag down to add rows.

- **Delete rows.** Select one or more cells in the row or rows that you want to delete. Choose Tables : Cells : Delete > Table Rows.

- **Delete columns.** Select one or more cells in the column or columns that you want to delete. Choose Tables : Cells : Delete > Table Columns.

TIP You can also use the Home : Cells : Delete commands to modify a table. However, unlike the equivalent table commands, these commands also affect data outside the table.

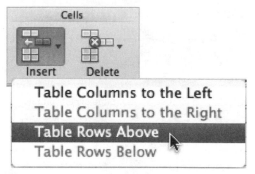

A To insert or delete table rows or columns, choose a command from the Tables : Cells group. Although rows are normally inserted above the selection and columns to the left, some selections allow them to be inserted below or to the right.

	A	B	C	D	E	F
1	Student	Sex	Test Sc	Weight	Result	
2	Marci	F	12	0.2	19.90	
3	Joni	F	14	0.2	20.30	
4	Jason	M	19	0.2	21.30	
5	Jeremy	M	8	0.2	19.10	
6	Stan	M	18	0.2	21.10	
7	Chris	M	20	0.2	21.50	
8	Kendra	F	6	0.2	18.70	
9	Michelle	F	19	0.2	21.30	
10	Sammy	M	15	0.2	20.50	
11	Average		14.56		20.41	
12						

Resize cursor

B You can append rows or columns to a table by dragging the table's lower-right corner.

Stay Inside the Lines!

When adding new records (rows) or fields (columns) to a table, be sure you're adding them within the table, rather than beneath or beside it. For Excel to treat new data as part of a table, it has to be within the table's bounds.

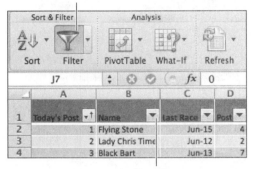

Filter icon

Arrow icon

Ⓐ Click the Filter icon to enable/disable filtering and sorting. To specify a filtering criterion, click a field's arrow icon. Additional filtering options can be found in the Filter icon's menu.

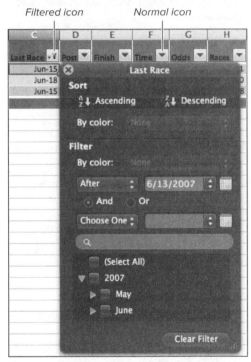

Filtered icon   Normal icon

Ⓑ Clicking a field's icon displays this window. Set the filter criterion for the field by choosing options and/or typing. Fields that are currently being used to filter the table display a slightly different icon.

Filtering a Table

As your table grows, you may occasionally want to view only records that match certain criteria. You can filter a table in this manner to generate a data subset for printing, charting, record deletion, or calculating special totals, for example. Filtering criteria can be based on the contents of one or multiple fields.

To filter a table:

1. If arrow icons aren't visible beside each column header **Ⓐ**, choose Data > Filter, or click the Filter icon on the Standard toolbar or in the Data:Sort & Filter group.

2. Click the icon beside the column on which you want to filter. Specify the filtering criterion in the window that appears **Ⓑ**.

   Changes are displayed instantly. The records that match the criterion are shown; others are temporarily hidden.

3. *Optional:* To further filter the table, choose additional criteria from other columns or modify any current criteria.

4. To restore all or some of the hidden records, do one of the following:

   ▸ To show all table records, choose Data > Filter or click the Data:Sort & Filter:Filter icon.

   ▸ To remove some but not all filters, select a cell in a column whose filter you want to remove, and choose Data:Sort & Filter:Filter > Clear Filter. Alternately, you can click the column's icon and then click the Clear Filter button **Ⓑ**.

TIP You can click check boxes in the bottom of a field's criterion window **Ⓑ** to manually select the records you want to view.

Sorting a Table

You can sort the entire table by the values in one or more columns. When sorting on multiple columns, each additional column serves as a tie-breaker. For instance, you could sort on State and on City. This would group each state's records together, while breaking them into subgroups for each city. Note that when the data set is filtered, only the visible records are sorted.

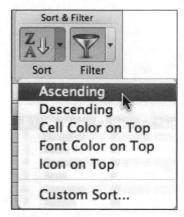

Ⓐ Set the sort order. Ascending or Descending are commonly chosen.

To perform a one-column sort:

Do one of the following:

- Click any cell in the column on which you want to sort. Choose a sort order from the Sort icon's drop-down menu in the Data:Sort & Filter:Sort group Ⓐ or on the Standard toolbar.

- With filtering enabled (as explained in the previous step list), click the arrow icon of the column on which you want to sort. Choose Ascending or Descending in the window that appears (see Ⓑ in "Filtering a Table" earlier in this chapter).

  The table rows are reordered.

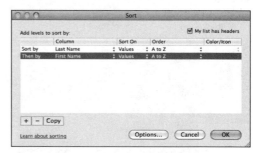

Ⓑ Specify sort fields in order of their importance. Click the + and – icons to add or remove fields, respectively. You can change the field order by dragging a field up or down in the Sort By list.

To perform a complex sort:

1. Select any cell in the table.

2. Choose Data > Sort, or choose Sort > Custom Sort on the Standard toolbar or in the Data:Sort & Filter group.

   The Sort dialog box appears Ⓑ.

3. Select the primary sort field from the Column drop-down list and select an order from the Order drop-down list.

4. *Optional:* Add Then By sort fields by clicking the plus (+) icon, selecting a column, and selecting a sort order.

5. Click OK to perform the specified sorts.

Sorting and Filtering Shortcuts

In certain instances, you can speed up the sorting or filtering process by taking advantage of contextual menus.

- To perform a one-column sort, right-click a cell within the column on which you want to sort and choose Sort > Ascending or Sort > Descending.

- To filter a table so it only shows records that are identical to a certain cell's contents, right-click the cell and choose Filter > By Cell Value.

Calculated Columns

Formulas in a table work differently than ones elsewhere in the worksheet. Any column can contain a mixture of formulas and data. However, you also can insert the same formula into every cell of a column. This is known as a *calculated column*. If you later add rows to the table, the formula is automatically copied to the new cells in the column.

To create a calculated column:

1. If necessary, insert a new column in the table in which to place the formula.

   A calculated column can be defined in a column that contains data, but the column's cells will be overwritten by the formula results. It's usually desirable to start with a new or an empty column.

2. *Optional:* Clear all filters that you've applied to table columns (see "Filtering a Table," earlier in this chapter).

   If the table is filtered when you create a calculated column, the formula propagates only to the visible cells.

3. Select a cell in the column. Create the formula by any combination of typing, pasting, and clicking other cells. Complete the formula by pressing Return.

   The formula is copied to all cells in the column **A**. If you later edit the formula, it automatically replaces the original formula throughout the column.

TIP If you replace the formula with data in any cell in a calculated column, Excel marks the cell as an exception. Click the indicator beside the cell to see the nature of the exception and either restore the formula or instruct Excel to ignore the inconsistency.

TIP To prevent a formula entered in a blank column from creating a calculated column, click the icon that appears and choose Stop Automatically Creating Calculated Column.

Calculated column formula

	E2	$\updownarrow$	⊗ ⊘ ⌃	fx	=[@[Test Score]]*[@Weight]	
	A	B	C	D	E	F
1	Student	Sex	Test Sc	Weight	Result	
2	Marci	F	12	0.2	2.40	
3	Joni	F	14	0.2	2.80	
4	Jason	M	19	0.2	3.80	
5	Jeremy	M	8	0.2	1.60	
6	Stan	M	18	0.2	3.60	
7	Chris	M	20	0.2	4.00	
8	Kendra	F	6	0.2	1.20	
9	Michelle	F	19	0.2	3.80	
10	Sammy	M	15	0.2	3.00	

A The formula created in cell E2 automatically propagates to the other column E table cells. Created by pointing to cells C2 and D2, the formula uses structured references rather than normal cell references.

Adding a Total Row

A table can optionally have a single total row at its bottom, enabling you to calculate summary statistics for selected columns in the table. Each column can display a different statistic or none at all. In a donations table, for example, you could compute total donations and the average of the most recent donations.

To add a total row to a table:

1. Select a cell in the table to make the table active.

2. In the Tables:Table Options group, click the Total Row check box.

   The total row appears at the bottom of the table 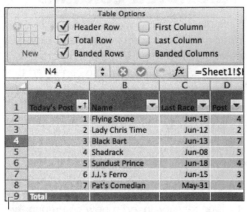.

3. *Optional:* Edit or delete the **Total** label in the leftmost cell of the total row.

4. To display a summary statistic for a column, click the total row cell beneath the column. Click the icon that appears beside the cell and choose a statistic from the drop-down menu .

5. Repeat step 4 for each additional column that you want to summarize.

6. Format the total row cells as desired.

TIP If the function you need isn't shown in the drop-down menu, choose More Functions. To eliminate the summary statistic for a column, choose None.

TIP You can disable or enable the total row as needed by clicking the Total Row check box. When you re-enable the total row, any statistic previously set for a column reappears.

Total Row check box

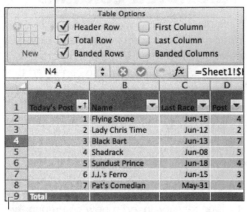

Total row

A When enabled, the total row is displayed at the bottom of the table.

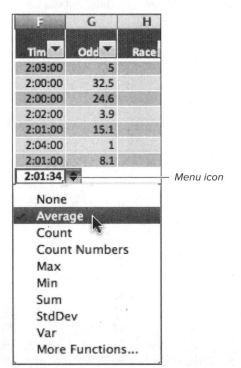

— *Menu icon*

B Each cell in the total row has a menu from which you can choose a statistical function.

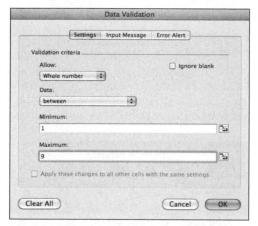

A Specify a validation criterion on the Settings tab of the dialog box (in this case, that the post position for a horse must be between 1 and 9).

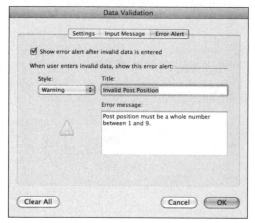

B Because the validation criterion might not be obvious, supplying an error alert is often wise.

Data Validation

Excel allows you to specify a validation criterion for any column's cells to ensure that only valid data is entered. For example, a Zip Code column could be restricted to entries of exactly five digits. Validation tests are automatically applied to new data as it's added to the table.

To set validation options:

1. Select cells in the table column for which you'd like to set a validation criterion.

2. Choose Data > Validation or Data: Tools: Validate > Data Validation.

   The Data Validation dialog box appears.

3. On the Settings tab of the dialog box **A**, set a validation criterion by making choices from the drop-down menus and typing in the text box(es).

4. *Optional:* To treat a blank entry in the column as an error, remove the check mark from Ignore blank.

5. *Optional:* If you want a pop-up box to appear whenever you select a cell in the column, click the Input Message tab. Enter a title and message text.

6. *Optional:* Enter an error message that will appear whenever validation fails. Click the Error Alert tab **B**, enter a title and message text, and choose an alert style from the Style drop-down menu:

   ▸ **Stop.** Prevent further work until the error is corrected.

   ▸ **Warning.** Offer a choice of correcting or accepting the entered data.

   ▸ **Information.** Display only explanatory text.

continues on next page

Click OK when you're finished. If an incorrect value is later entered into a cell, the alert message appears **C** and presents options.

CAUTION Applying a validation criterion to cells that already contain data won't result in error messages appearing if the data is invalid. To view *all* invalid data on a sheet (including preexisting errors), choose Data : Tools : Validate > Circle Invalid Data **D**. To remove the circles, choose Data : Tools : Validate > Clear Validation Circle.

TIP To edit validation criterion, select the same cells and choose Data > Validation or Data : Tools : Validate > Data Validation.

TIP If you can't remember which cells have validation criteria, choose Edit > Go To. In the Go To dialog box, click Special. In the Go To Special dialog box that appears **E**, select Data Validation and All, and click OK. Excel highlights all cells for which a data validation criterion has been set or displays a "No cells were found" message.

C A warning alert allows the user to override the validation criterion by clicking Yes.

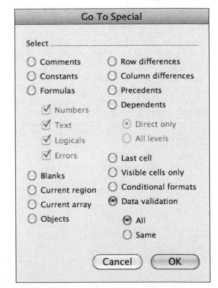

D You can elect to circle all invalid data, making validation errors stand out.

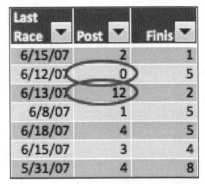

E Select Data Validation and All to identify the cells for which you've set a validation criterion.

Charts and Graphs

Numeric information is often easiest to understand when presented graphically. In Excel 2011, you can create 73 different styles of charts, including bar, column, line, area, pie, scatter, bubble, radar, and stock charts—and many of them can be 3-D.

After Excel has generated a chart, you can tailor it to suit your needs. You can add, edit, or delete a title, axis and data labels, legends, and gridlines. You can also add, change, or remove color, patterns, or shading, as well as change the scale, labeling, and look of the axes. If you later edit a chart's source data, the chart will automatically reflect the new values.

In this chapter, you'll learn to create charts from existing data and display them in the current worksheet. Chapter 18 explains the process of creating charts to embellish a PowerPoint presentation. (These same techniques apply equally to adding a chart to a Word document.) Chapter 27 offers assistance in pasting, embedding, and linking existing Excel charts into Word documents and PowerPoint presentations.

In This Chapter

Chart Elements

Designing a chart is similar to creating art. You can freely add or remove elements, move them to new positions, and change their size, shape, and formatting. (Of course, you can accept the default elements and formatting used in a newly created chart, but you're unlikely to do so often.)

Because you'll spend so much time working with chart elements **A**, it's important to be able to identify them. Note that many of the elements shown are optional.

Chart Element Definitions

The *chart area* is the chart's background. The *plot area* varies, depending on the chart style. In some, it is the background of the chart itself; in others, it refers only to the area immediately around the axis labels. (3-D column charts refer to the background areas as *walls*.) *Gridlines* are lines in the plot area denoting axis values. The *title*, *axes*, and *legend* are text identifiers used to label parts of the chart.

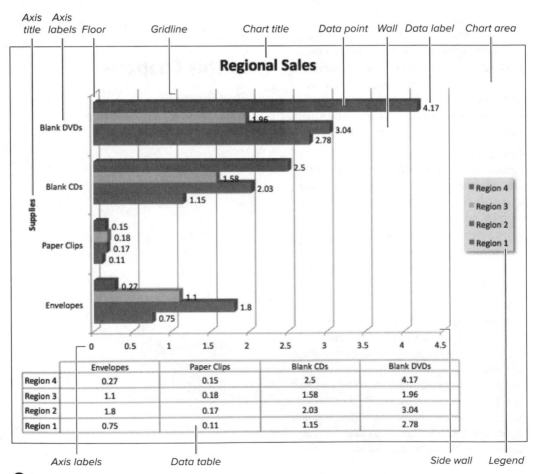

A A chart and its elements.

	A	B	C	D	E	F
1		Sales Report: Second Quarter				
2						
3		Region 1	Region 2	Region 3	Region 4	Average
4	Envelopes	0.75	1.8	1.1	0.27	0.98
5	Paper Clips	0.11	0.17	0.18	0.15	0.1525
6	Blank CDs	1.15	2.03	1.58	0.99	1.4375
7	Blank DVDs	2.78	3.04	1.96	4.17	2.9875
8	Total	4.79	7.04	4.82	5.58	

A The selections are A3:E4 and A6:E7 (skipping the data for paper clip sales, but including the column and row labels).

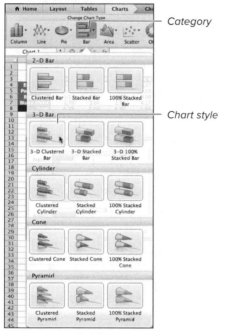

Category

Chart style

B Select a chart category by clicking its icon, and then pick a style by clicking its thumbnail.

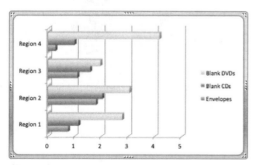

C The chart appears (with default formatting and options).

Creating Charts

As in former versions of Excel, you can easily create a clustered column chart (the default chart type) from selected data as a new chart sheet. Rather than appearing as a floating object on the same sheet as the data, a new sheet tab that's dedicated to the chart is added to the workbook.

In most cases, though, you'll begin by selecting a specific chart style from the Charts:Insert Chart group. Such charts are added to the worksheet as floating objects.

To create a chart by selecting a style:

1. Select the data from which you want to create the chart **A**.

   To chart nonadjacent data, press Command while drag-selecting cell ranges.

2. In the Charts:Insert Chart group, select a chart category by clicking its icon. In the gallery that appears, choose a style of chart by clicking its thumbnail **B**.

   The completed chart appears as a floating object on the same sheet as the source data **C**.

TIP To change a Chart Sheet chart to a floating chart (or vice versa), choose Chart > Move Chart. In the Move Chart dialog box, you can move a Chart Sheet chart onto a designated worksheet as a new floating object or move a floating chart onto a new Chart Sheet.

TIP Note that you can also use the Move Chart command to simply move a chart from one worksheet to another or from one Chart Sheet to another. There's no requirement that you change from one destination type to the other.

To create a default column chart:

1. Select the data from which you want to create the chart.

   If they're relevant, be sure to include labels in the selected data. They're used when generating the chart.

2. Choose Insert > Sheet > Chart Sheet.

   The clustered column chart appears on a new Chart Sheet **D**.

3. Modify and customize the chart by following the instructions in "Modifying Charts," later in this chapter.

General Charting Tips

- Don't be afraid to experiment with options you don't completely understand. You can undo almost any modification by choosing Edit > Undo or by clicking the Undo icon on the Standard toolbar.

- Creating charts in all Office applications requires the use of Excel. In fact, if Excel 2011 isn't installed on your Mac, you won't be able to create charts.

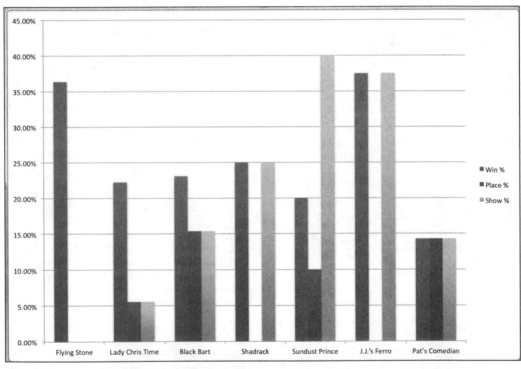

D A column chart with colored bars, axis labels, and a legend is generated.

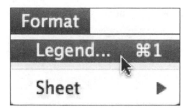

A The wording of the first Format command changes to reflect the currently selected object(s).

Chart object list

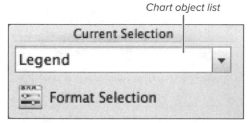

B The Format:Current Selection group.

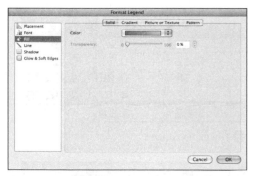

C A Format dialog box specific to the selected object(s) appears. Note that you can select options from multiple categories before clicking OK.

Objects and Charts

You can embellish worksheets and charts by inserting objects, such as shapes, photos, clip art, SmartArt, and text boxes. For additional instructions on inserting, resizing, moving, and rotating objects, refer to Chapter 3.

Modifying Charts

Although the initial chart may be perfect for your needs, you can also modify or embellish it as you like. Using a variety of techniques, you can change virtually any chart element, the data series, or even the chart type/style.

To modify a chart element:

1. To open a Format dialog box for a given chart object, you can:

   ▶ Double-click the chart object.

   ▶ Select the chart object. Choose the first command in the Format menu or press Command-1 **A**.

   ▶ Right-click the chart object, and choose Format *object type* from the contextual menu that appears.

   ▶ With the chart or any part of it selected, select the object you want to modify from the drop-down list in the Format:Current Selection group. Then click the Format Selection icon **B**.

2. In the Format *object* dialog box **C**, make the desired changes and click OK.

> **TIP** You can make many changes by simply choosing settings from the Format contextual tab. For instance, you can apply Quick Styles to the legend or a variety of Chart Element Styles to graphic elements.

> **TIP** To resize a chart, click and drag any corner of its bounding frame. You can also resize or move some chart elements, such as the legend, title, and plot area. To resize a selected element, drag one of its handles. To move an element, click an edge and drag. (Although most elements can be moved, only certain ones can be resized.)

> **TIP** To add a title, choose a position from the Chart Layout:Labels:Chart Title menu. Enter the title in the text box that appears.

To change a chart's type, style, or layout:

1. Make the chart active by selecting it or one of its elements.

2. Select a new chart type, style, or layout from one of the following galleries on the Charts tab: Change Chart Type, Chart Styles, Chart Quick Layouts.

   The chart is transformed as specified.

TIP You can change the rotation of a 3-D chart in the Chart Layout : 3-D Rotation group.

To change the data source for a chart:

Do any of the following:

- To change any value in the current data range so it's reflected in the chart, edit the source data.

- To change the data range, select the chart. (Click in the area around the chart or choose Chart Area from the Current Selection list on the Chart Layout or Format contextual tab **D**.) The current source data and labels are indicated by colored selection rectangles **E**. Then do any of the following:

  ▸ To select a different contiguous data set of the same size, move the cursor over an edge of the blue source data rectangle. When the cursor changes to a hand, drag the rectangle to select a new range of the same size **F**.

  ▸ To change the data range's size, move the cursor over a corner of the blue source data rectangle and drag **G**.

- To remove a single data series from the chart, select the series in the chart and press Delete.

Current Selection menu

D You can quickly (and accurately) select any chart object with the Current Selection menu.

Row labels
(A4:A7)   *Column labels*
                    (B3:E3)

	A	B	C	D	E	F
1		**Sales Report: Second Quarter**				
2						
3		Region 1	Region 2	Region 3	Region 4	Average
4	Envelopes	0.75	1.8	1.1	0.27	0.98
5	Paper Clips	0.11	0.17	0.18	0.15	0.1525
6	Blank CDs	1.15	2.03	1.58	0.99	1.4375
7	Blank DVDs	2.78	3.04	1.96	4.17	2.9875
8	Total	4.79	7.04	4.82	5.58	

Data (B4:E7)

E When you select a chart that's on the same sheet as the source data, the source data and labels are surrounded by colored rectangles.

Region 3	Region 4	Average
1.1	0.27	0.98
0.18	0.15	0.1525
1.58	0.99	1.4375
1.96	4.17	2.9875
4.82	5.58	

F The move cursor.

Region 3	Region 4	Average
1.1	0.27	0.98
0.18	0.15	0.1525
1.58	0.99	1.4375
1.96	4.17	2.9875
4.82	5.58	

G The resize cursor.

Add Data

Select the new data you wish to add to the chart.

Include the cells containing row or column labels if you want those labels to appear on the chart.

Range: [   ]

Cancel   OK

H You can use the Add Data dialog box to specify additional ranges to include in the data set.

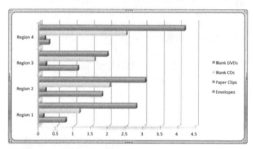

I You can swap rows and columns to view your data in a different way. When reversed, this chart would group by item rather than region.

Series list   *Chart data range*

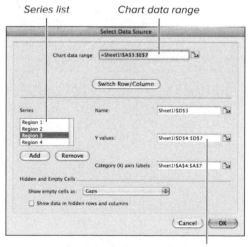

Data range for selected series

J The Select Data Source dialog box.

- To add another range to the data set, select the chart and choose Chart > Add Data. In the Add Data dialog box **H**, type or select the additional range, and then click OK.

- Click a Charts:Data:Switch Plot icon to reverse how the data is graphed, swapping columns for rows and vice versa **I**.

TIP You can select any data series or chart element from the drop-down list in the Chart Layout:Current Selection group **D**.

To change the data source in the Select Data Source dialog box:

1. Choose Chart > Source Data or click the Charts:Data:Select icon.

   The Select Data Source dialog box appears **J**.

2. Do any of the following:

   - Enter a new range or select the range in the worksheet.

   - To edit a single data series, select the series in the Series list box and edit the Y values range. If you'd rather select the new range, click the Y values icon **J**, select the range on the worksheet, and click the icon again.

   - To remove a series, select it in the Series list box and click Remove **J**.

   - To add a series to the chart, click the Add button. Click the icon beside the Y values box, select the new data values in the sheet, and click the icon again. Finally, name the series in the Name box or click the icon to the right of the box and select the name or label in the worksheet. (Note that it may be simpler to change the Chart data range **J** to encompass all of the data than to add the new series.)

To format all data or a selected data series:

Do any of the following:

- To change the color of all data series, select the chart or any object on it and then select a new color scheme from the Charts:Chart Styles gallery **K**.

- To format a single data series, select the series on the chart or by name from the Current Selection drop-down list **D** on the Chart Layout or Format contextual tab. Do any of the following:

  ▸ Select new settings from the Format:Chart Element Styles group **L**, such as fill color, line properties, and transparency.

  ▸ Select new settings in the Format Data Series dialog box **M**, and click OK.

    To open the Format Data Series dialog box, double-click an element in the data series, select a series element and choose Format > Data Series (Command-1), select a series element and click Format:Current Selection:Format Selection, or right-click an element in the data series and choose Format Data Series from the contextual menu.

K You can pick a new color scheme by clicking a thumbnail in the Charts:Chart Styles gallery.

L Select new chart element settings from the Format:Chart Element Styles group. Note that some settings, such as Transparency, can only be applied to certain objects.

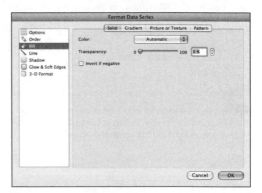

M To format a single data series, you can set options in the Format Data Series dialog box.

Categories *Category tabs* *Preview*

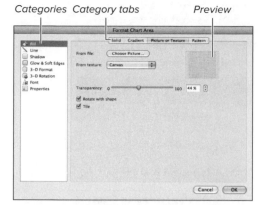

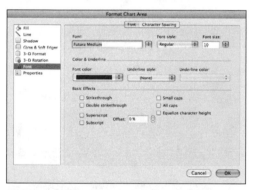

N You can alter the formatting of the chart area (background) in the Format Chart Area dialog box. As you alter settings, a preview is displayed on the chart. Click OK to apply all changes.

O Chart text (titles and labels) can be formatted with a different font, style, size, or color.

P The Format contextual tab.

To format the chart area (background):

Format the chart area by doing any of the following:

- **Format Chart Area dialog box.** Open the dialog box **N** by double-clicking the chart area, right-clicking the chart area and choosing Format Chat Area, selecting the chart area and choosing Format > Chart Area (Command-1), or selecting the chart area and clicking the Format Selection icon in the Current Selection group of the Chart Layout or Format tab.

  Select the Fill category **N** to set the fill color and transparency for the area surrounding the chart. By clicking tabs, you can choose a solid color, gradient, picture, texture, or pattern. Line category options apply to the border around the chart. Select the Font category **O** to alter the font for the axis labels, legend, and chart title.

- **Format contextual tab** **P**. You can pick an attractive, 3-D background from the Chart Element Styles gallery. You can also apply settings from the Text Styles group and the Fill, Line, and Effects drop-down menus.

TIP As you'll quickly discover, you can use the same techniques to format any chart element. Click the element or select it from the drop-down list in the Current Selection group of the Chart Layout or Format tab. Then click the Format Selection icon or select options from the Format : Chart Element Styles group.

TIP Format the most general elements (such as the chart area) first and then the individual elements within that area (such as axis labels).

To add or remove other chart elements:

Do any of the following:

- You can delete any chart element (even a data series) by selecting it on the chart and pressing Delete.

- Other chart elements can be displayed or removed by choosing commands from these icons in the Chart Layout: Labels and Chart Layout: Axes groups:

  ▸ **Chart Title.** Display or remove the title, and specify whether it will be above the chart or overlap the data.

  ▸ **Axis Titles.** Display or remove the horizontal or vertical axis title.

  ▸ **Legend.** Display or remove the legend, specify its position, and indicate whether it will overlap data **Q**.

  ▸ **Data Labels.** Optionally label each data point with its value, series name, or category name **R**.

  ▸ **Data Table.** Optionally display the source data with the chart (see **A** in "Chart Elements," at the beginning of this chapter). You can also combine the data table with the chart's legend.

  ▸ **Axes.** Set axes labels, units, and location.

  ▸ **Gridlines.** Display or remove major or minor gridlines for the axes.

To apply other formatting to these elements, choose *element name* Options from the bottom of the element's drop-down menu **Q**.

> **TIP** The chart title, axes titles, and legend can be repositioned by dragging. Select the text box or bounding box, move the cursor over any edge, and drag the object to the desired location.

Q You can add, remove, or move the legend by choosing a command from the Legend drop-down menu.

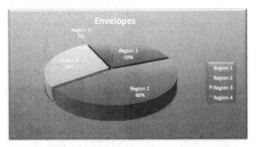

R The slices in this pie chart were labeled by choosing Chart Layout: Data Labels > Category Name and Percentage. Note that different chart types offer different labeling options.

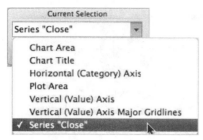

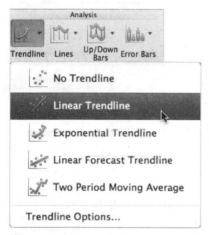

Adding Trendlines

A *trendline* is a straight line or curve drawn through the points of a data series to show a trend. In order to provide additional information and make it easier to interpret the data, you can add a trendline to any chart in which the data changes over time.

To display a trendline for a data series:

1. Select a data series to which you want to add a trendline.

   Select the series by clicking one of its data points or by selecting the series name from the Current Selection drop-down list on the Chart Layout or Format contextual tab **A**.

2. Do one of the following:

   ▸ Choose a basic trendline type from the Chart Layout:Analysis:Trendline drop-down menu **B**.

   ▸ To view additional trendline types and options, choose Trendline Options **B**. The Format Trendline dialog box appears. Select a category from the left side of the dialog box. Specify a trendline type, line type and characteristics, and other options, and then click OK.

   The trendline appears on the chart **C**.

3. *Optional:* To replace the current trendline, choose another from the Trendline menu or the Format Trendline dialog box.

A If you have difficulty selecting a data series by clicking, you can select one from the Current Selection list.

B To test basic trendline types, choose one from the Trendline drop-down menu.

TIP To remove the trendline, choose **No Trendline** from the **Trendline** menu **B** or select it on the chart and press **Delete**.

TIP To change the settings for a trendline, double-click it. Make changes in the Format Trendline dialog box and click OK.

Polynomial trendline R^2 value

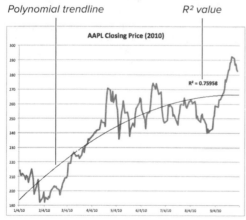

C You can add a variety of trendline types and options to charts. In this example, a polynomial trendline is applied to stock price data.

Creating Sparklines

Introduced in Office 2010 for Windows, *sparklines* are tiny charts that display and summarize data. Unlike normal charts that are floating, resizable objects, sparklines are presented in individual cells, visually linking them with their data. A sparkline can be one of three styles: Line, Column, or Win/Loss.

To add sparklines:

1. Select the sparklines' data range or location range.

2. In the Charts:Insert Sparklines group, click a sparkline format icon **A**.

   The Insert Sparklines dialog box appears **B**.

3. Fill in the two range text boxes by typing or selecting the worksheet ranges.

   The data or location range selected in step 1 will already be specified in the dialog box. Edit them, if necessary.

4. Click OK.

   The sparklines appear in the designated range **C**.

TIP As with other Excel charts, if you edit the data on which sparklines are based, the sparklines update automatically.

TIP To change the style or formatting for a selected sparkline or sparkline group, set options on the Sparklines contextual tab. For example, you can click a different icon in the Change Type group, add data-point markers by clicking check boxes in the Markers group, or choose a new color scheme from the Format gallery.

TIP You can enter text in a sparkline cell.

TIP To remove all or selected sparklines, choose a command from the Sparklines:Edit: Clear drop-down menu.

A Select a sparkline format by clicking an icon.

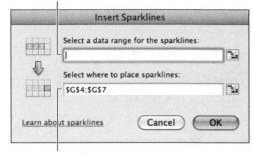

B Specify the data range and location range for the sparklines.

C In this example, column sparklines show the sales for each item in the four regions. (To make it easier to see the sparklines, you can increase their row height as shown here.)

Database Techniques

Office 2011 doesn't include a database application. However, unless you work with extremely large data sets or need a complex or relational database, Excel can probably provide all the database power you'll need.

In Excel, you enter data in rows. Each row is a *record* (one complete set of information). Each column is a *field* that contains one type of information for the record, such as a last name, Social Security number, or salary, for example. It isn't necessary to define a data array as a database. In Excel's eyes, any rectangular array of data can be treated as a database.

Rather than enter information directly into worksheet cells, you can use an Excel "fill-in-the-blanks" form to make it easier to enter, edit, delete, and search for data. You can also import data from other programs, such as FileMaker Pro.

After you enter the data, you can sort it, view only the information that matches certain criteria, and calculate group totals and other summary statistics.

Creating a Database

There are two ways to create a database in a worksheet. First, as explained in Chapter 13, you can create a table. Second, you can manually create a database by entering the data in contiguous rows and columns, as explained below.

Note that any area of a worksheet can be considered a database as long as every column has a label (which is treated as the field name) and the rows and columns are contiguous. A single blank row or column—even in the middle of an extensive data set—marks the edge of the database. Records beneath a blank row or fields to the right of a blank column are not considered part of the database.

To manually create a database:

1. In either a new or an existing worksheet, enter the field names at the top of a group of adjacent columns.

2. Enter the data into the rows below the field names **A**, creating each new record directly beneath the last data row.

TIP You can speed data entry by preselecting a range; click and drag to make the selection. Press Tab after each cell entry to move through the range from left to right. When you reach the end of a row, you'll move to the start of the next row. If you don't preselect a range, the cell you initially select is treated as the start of your data-entry range. Press Tab after each cell entry to move to the cell to the right. When you complete the entry in the last cell of a row, press Return to move to the beginning of the next row (directly beneath the starting cell).

TIP You don't have to dedicate an entire worksheet to a database. You can create a database as a separate area within any sheet or include multiple databases in a single sheet.

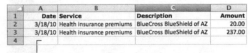

Next record

A Add a new record in the blank row immediately beneath the last record.

Database to Table

If you later decide that a *table* is what you need, you can easily change an existing database into a table. Select the database (including its headers), and choose Tables : Table Options : New > Insert Table with Headers.

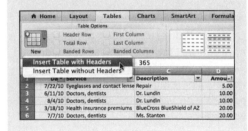

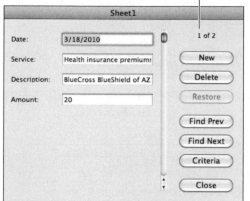

Current record

A You can use a form to view records, create new records, edit data in existing records, and delete unwanted records.

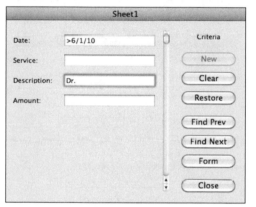

B Enter search criteria in one or more fields. In this example, only records in which the Date is after **6/1/2010** and the Description starts with **Dr.** will be identified as matches.

Using a Form for Data Entry

You can use forms to speed data entry and make the process more like working with a traditional database. A form can display up to 32 fields.

To use a form for data entry:

1. Click any cell in the database.

2. Choose Data > Form.

   The data-entry form for the first record appears **A**.

3. Do any of the following:

   ▸ To flip through the records in their current sort order, click Find Next, Find Prev, or the up and down arrows at the bottom of the scroll bar. To go directly to a record of interest, drag the scroll box.

   ▸ To create a new record, click the New button or drag the scroll box down to the blank record at the end of the database (labeled New Record). Enter the new data by typing and tabbing from field to field. When you're done, press Return/Enter to add the record.

   ▸ To edit a record, display it, make the changes, and press Return/Enter.

   ▸ Click Delete to delete the current record. Confirm the deletion.

   ▸ To view only specific records, click Criteria. In the form that appears **B**, enter search criteria. Repeatedly click Find Next and Find Prev to view the matching records. To resume working with the entire database, click Criteria, Clear, and Form.

4. To dismiss the form and record any changes you've made, click Close.

Database Operations

In any database, you can sort the records, *filter* (display only records that match criteria), and calculate subtotals.

To sort a database on a single field:

1. Select a cell in the column on which you want to sort the database.

2. Choose a sort order from the Sort icon's drop-down menu in the Data : Sort & Filter : Sort group or on the Standard toolbar 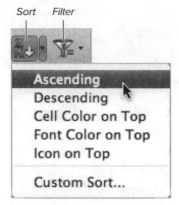.

> **TIP** If arrow icons are visible beside each column header, you can perform a one-field sort by clicking the field's icon and choosing a sort order from the window that appears. Choose Data > Filter to enable or disable the icons.

To sort a database on multiple fields:

1. Select any cell in the table.

2. Choose Data > Sort, Sort > Custom Sort on the Standard toolbar, or Data : Sort & Filter : Sort > Custom Sort.

   The Sort dialog box appears **B**.

3. Select the primary sort field from the Column drop-down list and select an order from the Order drop-down list.

4. *Optional:* Add Then By sort fields by clicking the plus (+) icon, selecting a column, and selecting a sort order.

5. Click OK to perform the specified sorts.

> **TIP** When sorting on multiple fields **B**, specify fields in order of their importance. The additional fields are tie breakers. For example, if you sort on Last Name, you could use First Name as the second sort field. If you sorted only on Last Name, all Johnsons would be grouped together, but their first names wouldn't be in a useful order.

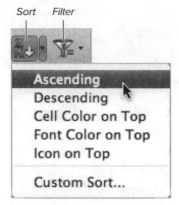

A One-field sorts are performed by choosing a sort order.

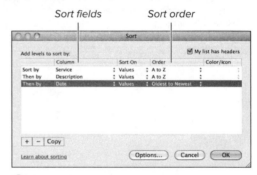

B Specify sort criteria in the Sort dialog box. In this example, the database is sorted on three fields: Service, Description, and Date.

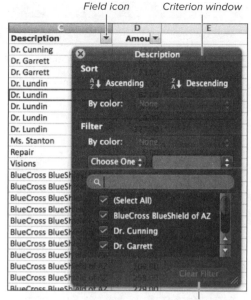

Field icon   Criterion window

C Specify a filtering criterion in this window.

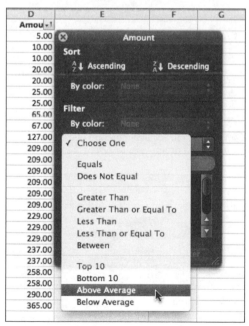

Remove filter

D Depending on the type of data in the selected field, the Choose One list may include useful predefined groups.

To filter a database:

1. If arrow icons aren't visible beside each column header, choose Data > Filter, or click the Filter icon on the Standard toolbar or in the Data : Sort & Filter group.

2. Click the icon of the column on which you want to filter. Specify a filtering criterion in the window that appears **C**.

   Changes are displayed instantly. The records that match the criterion are shown; others are temporarily hidden.

3. *Optional:* To further filter the table, choose additional criteria from other columns or modify the current criteria.

4. To restore all or some of the hidden records, do one of the following:

   ▸ To show all table records, choose Data > Filter or click the Data : Sort & Filter : Filter icon.

   ▸ To remove some but not all filters, select a cell in a column whose filter you want to remove, and choose Data : Sort & Filter : Filter > Clear Filter. Alternately, you can click the column's icon and click the Clear Filter button.

   Filtering is also discussed in Chapter 13.

   TIP In a filtered database, row numbers of extracted records appear in blue.

   TIP After filtering the database, you can sort the visible records by any field. Follow the step lists on the previous page, or click the sort field's arrow icon and specify a sort order.

   TIP A useful criterion can often simply be chosen from the Choose One list. For example, a numeric field can be filtered to display the 10 highest values or those that are below the field's average value **D**. Other field types, such as dates and text fields, offer different filtering options in the Choose One list.

To display subtotals or other grouping statistics:

1. Sort the database by the appropriate field(s) to create the groups of data on which to calculate subtotals or another statistic.

2. Select any cell in the database, and then choose Data > Subtotals.

    The Subtotal dialog box appears 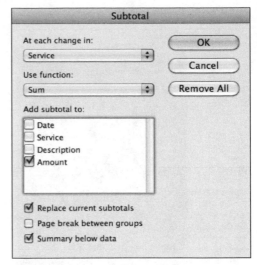.

3. Select a *break* (grouping) field from the At each change in drop-down list.

    A subtotal or other statistic will appear each time this field's value changes. The break field is normally one of the fields on which you sorted in step 1.

4. Select the mathematical or statistical function to calculate from the Use function drop-down list.

5. In the list box, click the check box for each field to which the function will be applied.

6. Make any desired changes in the remaining options and click OK.

    The function is applied to each subgroup in the database 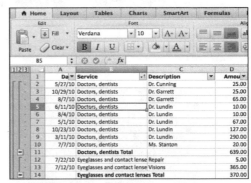.

TIP You can click the level controls to the left of the database to show only the grand total, only subtotals, or a mixture of subtotals and data 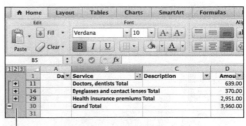. You can also selectively collapse and expand groups.

TIP To eliminate the subtotals, choose Data > Subtotals, click the Remove All button **E**, and then click OK.

E Set subtotal options.

F The function is calculated and displayed in bold for each data group.

Level controls

G Click controls to choose what to display. In this example, all groups have been collapsed to show only their totals.

Working with External Databases

As you learned in Chapter 10, you can open or import text files into Excel. Excel also provides tools to import data directly from FileMaker Pro 5 through 11 databases and to retrieve data from the Web.

Importing from FileMaker Pro

Keep the following in mind when importing FileMaker Pro data into Excel 2011:

- Files from FileMaker Pro 5.0 and higher can be imported. In addition to the database file, you must have a working copy of an appropriate version of FileMaker Pro installed on the same computer as Excel 2011:

  - To import a FileMaker .fp5 file, you must have FileMaker Pro 5.0–6.0.

  - To import a FileMaker .fp7 file, you must have FileMaker Pro 7.0–11.0.

- If the database doesn't permit exporting data from some user accounts, you must first open the database using an account that allows exporting.

- Only calculation results are imported, not the actual formulas. You may want to reconstruct the formulas in Excel.

- The worksheet will probably need to be sorted following the import because Excel doesn't recognize the current FileMaker sort order, if any.

- If the number of records or fields in the database exceeds Excel's maximum rows or columns, the additional records or fields will be discarded.

- If any cell contains more than 35,767 characters, the additional characters will be truncated.

- Imported FileMaker Pro databases automatically become tables 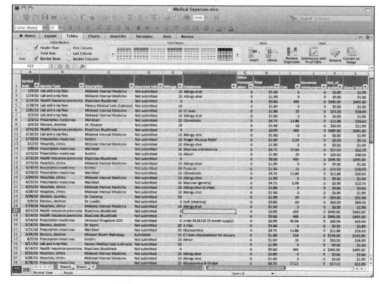. To learn about Excel tables, see Chapter 13. To convert the table into an Excel database, select any table cell and click Tables : Tools : Convert to Range.

A This is an example of an imported FileMaker database. Note that field names become column labels on import.

To import a FileMaker Pro database:

1. Launch FileMaker Pro, and do one of the following:

   ▸ In Excel, choose File > Open. Select the database in the Open dialog box.

   ▸ Choose File > Import. Select FileMaker Pro database in the Import dialog box, click Import, and select the database in the Choose a Database dialog box.

   ▸ Choose Data > Get External Data > Import from FileMaker Pro or choose Data:External Data Sources:FileMaker. Select the database in the Choose a Database dialog box. (This procedure requires that a workbook be open.)

   FileMaker launches, the database opens, and the FileMaker Pro Import Wizard appears **B**.

2. From the Layouts or Tables drop-down list, select a layout or table in which the fields to be imported appear. Add a field to the Import these fields list by selecting it and clicking Add. To simultaneously move all fields from a layout or table, click Add All.

   Fields are imported in the order listed.

3. To change the position of a field in the Import these fields list, select the field and click the up or down button. Click Next to continue.

4. In the Step 2 screen **C**, you can optionally specify up to three criteria for record selection.

5. Click Finish.

   If you used File > Open in step 1, a new sheet is automatically created. If you used File > Import or Get External Data, a dialog box appears **D**, allowing you to create a new sheet or add the imported data to the current sheet starting in a cell of your choice.

Layouts   *Tables*

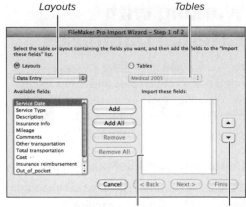

Fields to import   *Move up/down*

B In the wizard's first screen, specify the fields to import and their order.

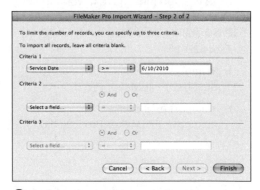

C If you don't want to import the entire database, you can enter record-selection criteria. Otherwise, leave the criteria blank and click Finish.

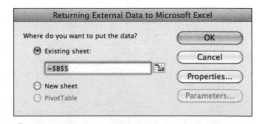

D Specify where to place the imported data.

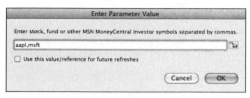

E Enter symbols for the stocks and mutual funds, separated by commas. (If you want to be able to easily update the data, click the check box. To fetch new data, select any cell in the query results and choose Data:Refresh > Refresh Data.)

F Excel connects to the Web site, downloads the data, and adds it to the worksheet.

Creating Queries

To create your own database query, choose Data > Get External Data > New Database Query. Note that you must first install the required ODBC (Open Database Connectivity) driver. For additional information, review "Import data from a database" in Excel Help.

Importing data from the Web

You can copy selected data from a table on a Web page and paste it into an Excel worksheet, but it doesn't always work as expected. A more precise method of retrieving data from the Web is to create a Web query using HTML forms.

Office includes three sample queries you can use. They can be found in the Microsoft Office 2011:Office:Queries folder. The following example shows how to use one of the sample queries to retrieve stock data from the Web.

To retrieve Web data using a query:

1. Choose Data > Get External Data > Run Saved Query.

   The Choose a Query dialog box appears, open to the Queries folder.

2. Select the MSN MoneyCentral Stock Quotes query, and click Get Data.

   The Returning External Data to Microsoft Excel dialog box appears **D**.

3. Do one of the following:

   ▸ To import the data into the current worksheet, click the Existing sheet radio button. Type or select the starting cell address of the range that will receive the imported data.

   ▸ To import the data into a new, empty worksheet, click New sheet.

4. Click OK to continue.

   The Enter Parameter Value dialog box appears **E**.

5. Enter stock or mutual fund symbols separated by commas, and click OK.

   The query report appears in the worksheet **F**.

Sharing Workbooks

Individuals in workgroups often need to share workbooks. Excel provides tools to distribute workbooks on the Web or a network, protect parts of workbooks that shouldn't be changed, and track and review changes that have been made.

Note that Excel, PowerPoint, and Word files can also be shared over the Internet using SkyDrive and the Office Web Apps (as discussed in Chapter 29).

In This Chapter

Publishing Excel Data on the Web

Excel makes it easy to save workbooks or worksheets for display on the Web. One advantage of publishing in this manner is that those who only need to view the contents don't need Excel to open the file. All they need is a browser. You can also preview any Excel file as it will look if saved as a Web page.

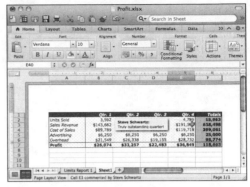

A Create or open a workbook.

To preview a file's Web appearance:

1. Open the workbook in Excel **A**.

2. Choose File > Web Page Preview.

   The worksheet opens in your browser as it would appear on the Web **B**.

> **TIP** To avoid surprises, it's a good idea to use Web Page Preview until you're satisfied with the file's appearance and formatting. Then save it as a Web page. (Note, however, that the preview doesn't always produce identical results to saving the file as a Web page.)

> **TIP** Comment indicators are displayed in a preview as bracketed numbers **B**. Click a comment indicator to go to the spot on the Web page where the comment is explained.

Comment

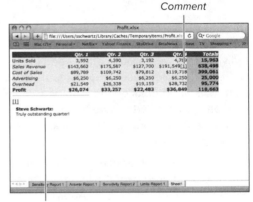

Comment text

B A temporary HTML file is created and opens in your default browser.

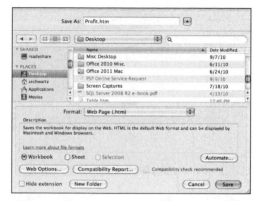

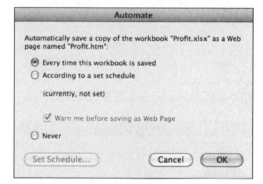

G Specify the filename, destination, and options.

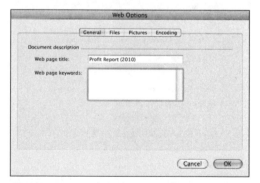

D Indicate the condition under which a new HTML file will automatically be generated.

Web Options

E Click the Web Options button **G** to enter a title for the generated Web page and set other options.

To save a file as a Web page:

1. *Optional:* To save a specific sheet or only a range as a Web page, select the worksheet and/or range.

2. Choose File > Save As Web Page.

   A Save As panel appears **G**. The Web Page (.htm) format is automatically selected.

3. Click a radio button to indicate whether you want to save the entire workbook, only the active worksheet, or only the currently selected cell range.

4. *Optional:* If this material is updated regularly, you can instruct Excel to automatically create a new HTML file whenever you save the workbook or according to a schedule. Click the Automate button.

   The Automate dialog box appears **D**. Select one of the following:

   ▶ **Every time this workbook is saved.** Automatically generate a new HTML file whenever you save the workbook.

   ▶ **According to a set schedule.** Generate a new HTML file daily, weekly, or on some other schedule. Click the Set Schedule button to set the schedule.

   ▶ **Never.** Disable the automatic generation of new HTML files.

   Click OK to close the Automate dialog box.

5. *Optional:* Click the Web Options button to set Web-specific settings **E**, such as the page title and keywords that will be used by search engines. Review the information on the various tabs and click OK.

6. *Optional:* Click Compatibility Report to check for potential problems.

7. Click Save to create the HTML file and a folder of supporting files.

Sharing Workbooks on a Network

When sharing has been enabled for a workbook, other network users can simultaneously view and edit the workbook.

To enable sharing for a workbook:

1. Choose Tools > Share Workbook or Review:Share:Share Workbook > Share Workbook.

   The Share Workbook dialog box appears **A**.

2. On the Editing tab, click Allow changes by more than one user at the same time.

3. Click the Advanced tab to review or set options for managing changes by multiple users **B**.

4. Click OK to dismiss the dialog box.

   A confirmation dialog box appears.

5. Click OK to save the workbook and enable sharing.

6. Save or copy the workbook file to a shared network folder so it can be accessed by authorized users. For assistance, contact your network administrator.

> **TIP** To later disable sharing for a workbook, choose the Share Workbook command again, remove the check mark from **Allow changes by more than one user at the same time A**, click OK to close the dialog box, and then click Yes in the confirmation dialog box.

> **TIP** Sharing is primarily intended for viewing and working with workbook data. While a workbook is being shared, you can't add certain elements, such as pictures, charts, PivotTable reports, or subtotals. Such items must be added before you elect to share the workbook.

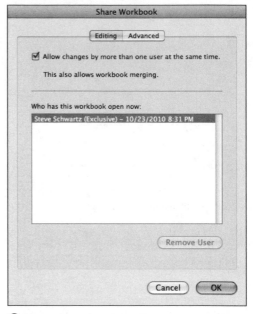

A Enable sharing by clicking the check box.

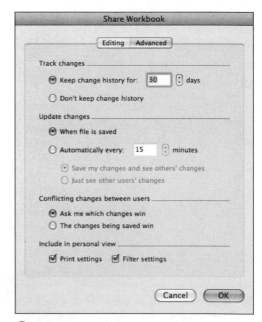

B Advanced tab settings determine how often the file is updated and how conflicting changes are resolved.

(A) Set criteria for tracking and displaying changes.

Changed data

(B) To view the details for a given change, move the cursor over the changed cell.

Document Properties

To add identifying information to a workbook (such as the workbook name, author, company name, and custom identifiers), choose File > Properties. Make the desired additions and changes on the tabs of the Properties dialog box, and then click OK. To record this information, save the workbook.

Tracking Changes

When sharing a workbook, changes made by users are tracked and recorded in a change history. (View the Advanced tab of the Share Workbook dialog box **(B)** in "Sharing Workbooks on a Network" on the previous page for change history options.) When you enable change tracking, Excel marks each modified cell with an indicator and provides an explanation of the change. You can then review and accept or reject each change.

To enable change highlighting:

1. Choose Tools > Track Changes > Highlight Changes or Review : Share : Track Changes > Highlight Changes.

   The Highlight Changes dialog box appears **(A)**.

2. Click the Track changes while editing check box.

3. Set any of these tracking options:

   ▸ **When.** Specify which changes to track, based on a time period or a save.

   ▸ **Who.** Indicate whose changes to track.

   ▸ **Where.** If you're interested in only a particular cell range, click this check box and drag-select the range.

4. Click OK. If a save confirmation dialog box appears, click OK.

   Modified cells will have a colored triangle added to their upper-left corner. To view a change explanation, move the pointer over the changed cell **(B)**.

TIP Workbook sharing and change tracking go hand in hand. Enabling one enables the other. When you elect to share a workbook, you should also review the settings in step 3.

To review changes:

1. Choose Tools > Track Changes > Accept or Reject Changes or Review:Share: Track Changes > Accept or Reject Changes. If the workbook contains unsaved changes, you will be prompted to save before proceeding.

   The Select Changes to Accept or Reject dialog box appears **C**.

2. Use the When, Who, and Where criteria to specify the changes you want to review, and click OK.

   The Accept or Reject Changes dialog box appears **D**. Excel displays each change, while simultaneously selecting the affected cell in the worksheet.

3. Do either of the following:

   ▸ For each proposed change, click Accept, Reject, Accept All, or Reject All.

   ▸ To end the review process immediately (even if there are still changes remaining to be reviewed), click Close.

TIP To indicate a cell range for the Where criterion **C**, you can drag-select the desired range in the workbook.

TIP You can also track and highlight changes when you're the sole user of a workbook. Although the workbook will automatically be shared, you don't have to store it in a location that's accessible to others.

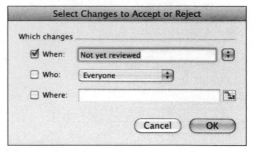

C Specify criteria for the changes you want to review.

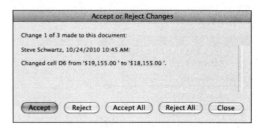

D For each change, click a button to indicate how you want to handle it.

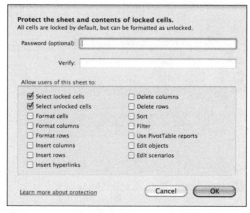

A The Protect Sheet pane.

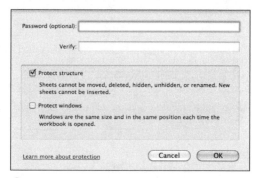

B The Protect Workbook pane.

C The Protect Shared Workbook dialog box.

Protecting Your Data

If you work in a sharing environment or are afraid others might be able to view your data without permission, you can prevent certain types of changes and optionally require a password for entire workbooks or individual worksheets. On the other hand, if your concern is only to ensure that others can't open a workbook, password-protect the file and skip the protection settings.

To protect a workbook or worksheet:

1. If the workbook is currently open in shared mode, temporarily disable sharing by following the tip at the end of "Sharing Workbooks on a Network" earlier in this chapter

2. Do one of the following:

   ▸ To protect only the current sheet, choose Tools > Protection > Protect Sheet or click the Review:Protection: Sheet icon.

   ▸ To protect the entire workbook, choose Tools > Protection > Protect Workbook or click the Review: Protection:Workbook icon.

   ▸ To simultaneously protect a workbook and enable sharing, choose Review:Share:Share Workbook > Protect and Share Workbook or Tools > Protection > Protect and Share Workbook.

3. Do one of the following:

   ▸ If protecting a worksheet **A** or workbook **B**, click the check boxes of the elements you want to protect.

   ▸ If protecting and sharing a workbook **C**, click the Sharing with track changes check box.

continues on next page

4. *Optional:* To add password protection to a protected worksheet or workbook, enter a password in the box (**A** or **B**).

A password is an additional layer of protection. In addition to preventing the changes specified in step 3, each user must supply the password whenever accessing the worksheet or workbook.

5. Click OK to dismiss the dialog box and enable the new protection settings. If you assigned a password, you'll be prompted to re-enter it.

When sheet or workbook is a protected, its icon in the Review:Protection group is darkened/selected **D**.

TIP Protecting a worksheet or workbook is more about preventing inadvertent or malicious changes than about security. Use protection to keep critical data from being altered. To prevent others from opening and viewing a workbook or sheet, assign a password.

TIP To remove protection, click the darkened Sheet or Workbook icon in the Review: Protection group **D**. If you also assigned a password to the sheet or workbook, you'll be prompted to supply it **E**. Otherwise, the protection will be removed immediately.

TIP Unprotecting a shared workbook does not disable sharing. If you wish to do this, too, choose Tools > Share Workbook. In the Share Workbook dialog box (see **A** in "Sharing Workbooks on a Network," earlier in this chapter), remove the check mark from Allow changes by more than one user at the same time, click OK to close the dialog box, and then click Yes in the confirmation dialog box.

D The darkened Sheet icon shows that the current sheet is protected.

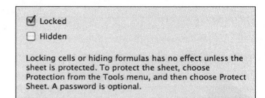

E To unprotect a sheet or workbook that has a password associated with it, you must supply the password.

> ☑ Locked
> ☐ Hidden
>
> Locking cells or hiding formulas has no effect unless the sheet is protected. To protect the sheet, choose Protection from the Tools menu, and then choose Protect Sheet. A password is optional.

F To make selected cells modifiable, clear the check mark from Locked.

Working with Locked Cells

By default, every worksheet cell is locked. This locked status has no effect unless you also protect the sheet or workbook. To allow some cells to be modified in a protected sheet or workbook, you must unlock them.

Unprotect the sheet (if it's protected), select the cells to unlock, and choose Format > Cells. In the Format Cells dialog box, click the Protection tab, remove the check mark from Locked **F**, and click OK. Finish by protecting the sheet.

G Enter a password in the appropriate text box or boxes and click OK.

H This dialog box appears when a password to open has been set for a workbook.

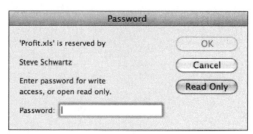

I This dialog box appears when a password to modify has been set for a workbook.

To password-protect an Excel file:

1. Click the Review:Protection:Passwords icon **D**.

2. In the File Passwords dialog box **G**, do either or both of the following:

   ▸ **Open protection.** To prevent unauthorized users from opening the workbook, enter a password in the Password to open box.

   ▸ **Modify protection.** To prevent unauthorized users from modifying the workbook but still let them view it, enter a password in the Password to modify box. Users who cannot supply the password will only be allowed to view the workbook.

3. Click OK to close the dialog box.

4. Verify each password that you entered in step 2.

To open a password-protected file:

1. Open the Excel workbook file.

2. Depending on the type(s) of password protection associated with the file (open or modify), one of the following occurs:

   ▸ **Open protection.** A Password dialog box appears **H**. Enter the password and click OK. If the password is incorrect or Cancel is clicked, the workbook does not open.

   ▸ **Modify protection.** A Password dialog box appears **I**. Enter the password for permission to modify the workbook and click OK.

   If you only want permission to view the workbook but not change it (or if you don't know the password), click Read Only.

To remove or change a password:

1. As follows, open the workbook by sup-plying the password:

   ▸ **Open protection.** A Password dialog box appears ⒣. Enter the password and click OK. If the password is incor-rect or Cancel is clicked, the work-book does not open.

   ▸ **Modify protection.** A Password dialog box appears ⒤. Enter the password for permission to modify the workbook.

2. Click Review : Protection : Passwords ⒟.

3. In the File Passwords dialog box ⒢, do the following:

   ▸ To eliminate a password, delete it from the appropriate Password text box.

   ▸ To change a password, delete the old password, type a new one, and then confirm the change.

4. Save the file by choosing File > Save, clicking the Save icon on the Standard toolbar, or pressing Command-S.

   Any edits made to passwords, as well as password deletions, are recorded in the saved file. The edits and deletions will be in effect the next time you open the file.

TIP Save an unprotected copy of the work-book to CD or another type of removable media—in case you forget the password(s).

TIP Use the Password to modify option when one or more users need to view a workbook but not change it. Restrict access to that pass-word to those few users (or only yourself) who have permission to change the data.

TIP If you assign both types of password to a workbook, be sure to use different passwords.

Information Rights Management

The Office 2011 support for Information Rights Management (IRM) will enable certain users to set permissions for workbooks on a per-person or per-group basis. Three permission levels are avail-able: read, change, and full control.

To use IRM, you must have access to an Active Directory Rights Management Services (AD RMS) server. Such servers and server software are most frequently found in large corporations, educational institutions, and government offices. If IRM is available to you, start by reviewing these Excel Help topics:

- About restricting access with Informa-tion Rights Management

- Restrict permission to content in a file

- Set permission levels manually

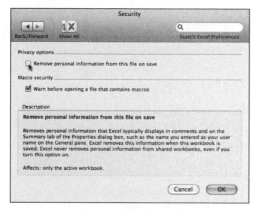

A Click the top check box to remove identifying information from the current workbook.

User name: Steve Schwartz

B You can add, edit, or remove your Office user name.

Removing Personal Information

When you save a new workbook, identifying information is also saved with the file. At a minimum, this includes your user name as specified in the Authoring:General preferences. To protect your privacy, you can remove the user name and other types of identifying information from selected workbooks.

To remove identifying information:

1. Open the workbook.

2. Choose Excel > Preferences or press Command-, (comma).

   The Excel Preferences dialog box appears.

3. Click the Sharing and Privacy:Security icon.

   The Security dialog box appears **A**.

4. Click the check box in the Privacy options section of the Security dialog box, click OK, and save the workbook.

   Your user name and other identifying information (such as names of reviewers and comment authors, and data on the Summary and Statistics tabs of the Properties dialog box) are removed from the workbook file.

TIP To set or change your user name **B**, click the Authoring:General icon in the Excel Preferences dialog box.

Creating a Presentation

PowerPoint provides you the tools necessary to create impressive slide presentations. You can choose among a variety of professional themes designed to help you create a presentation with a compelling visual message.

The first part of this chapter explains the essentials of creating a new presentation, working in different views, adding and deleting slides, and working with text and graphics. The second part shows how to use slide masters to add a background design, static images, and color to your presentation. You'll find that customizing presentations in PowerPoint is as straightforward as it has always been.

Starting a Presentation

A theme, template, or a blank document can serve as the starting point for a new presentation.

To create a new presentation:

1. Open the PowerPoint Presentation Gallery **A** by launching PowerPoint, choosing File > New from Template, or pressing Shift-Command-P.

2. Do one of the following:

   ▸ To create a presentation without a theme (background, colors, and fonts), select Themes: All and select the White or Black thumbnail **A**.

   ▸ To create a presentation with a theme, select Themes: All or My Themes, and select a thumbnail.

   ▸ To create a presentation from a template, select an option in the Templates category, and select a thumbnail.

3. Click the Choose button.

   The presentation appears. If you picked a template, the presentation contains explanatory slides. If you selected a themeless or theme-based presentation, it contains a single slide **B**.

TIP You can also start a blank White presentation by choosing File > New Presentation (Command-N). (If you've removed the check mark from Open PowerPoint Presentation Gallery when application opens in General Preferences, a blank presentation is created automatically at each PowerPoint launch.)

TIP You can set or change the theme at any time by selecting a new one from the Themes: Themes group. Also see "Slide Backgrounds," later in this chapter.

Categories   Thumbnails   *Preview*

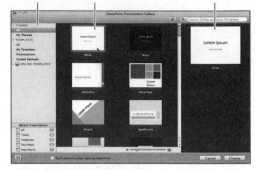

A To start a presentation, select a category and a thumbnail. The White and Black themes are equivalent to a Blank Presentation in Office 2008.

B The new presentation appears.

Slide Size

When creating a presentation, the slide size is set to Standard (4:3), suitable for television. If the presentation will be given on a widescreen display, however, you can design it specifically for that display. Choose Themes:Page Setup:Slide Size > Widescreen (16:9). In general, it is best to set this option before adding content to the slides.

Navigation pane tabs

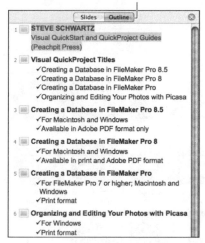

A In Normal view, you can click a slide thumbnail or outline element to display its slide.

B Slide Sorter view.

C You can switch views by clicking an icon. The name of the current view is displayed.

About Views

PowerPoint provides six views that you'll use while creating, preparing for, and giving a presentation. Each view has a particular purpose. For instance, you can rearrange slides in Slide Sorter view.

- *Normal view* (see **B** in "Starting a Presentation" on the previous page) displays the text, slide, and notes, enabling you to work on all parts of your presentation in one window. The navigation pane in Normal view can display slide thumbnails or an outline of each slide's key points **A**.

- *Slide Sorter view* **B** displays slide thumbnails. You can reorganize the slides by clicking and dragging or go directly to any slide by double clicking its thumbnail. You can also use this view to add and edit effects within and between slides.

- *Notes Page view* lets you conveniently enter and edit speaker notes that will accompany the slides.

- *Presenter view* contains tools to help you prepare to give the presentation.

- *Slide Show view* displays the presentation as an onscreen slide show.

- *Master view* is used to place a background and static objects and text that will appear on a particular slide layout or on all slides. In addition to the Slide Master view, there are Notes Master and Handout Master views.

You'll learn more about the different views in the next two chapters.

To switch views:

- Click an icon in the lower-left corner of the document window **C** or choose a command from the View menu.

Adding and Deleting Slides

Designing presentations is seldom a linear process. Along the way, you'll have many occasions when you'll need to add or delete slides. You can do so in any view other than Slide Show or Presenter.

To add a slide:

1. Select or display the slide after which you want the new slide to appear.

   A new slide is always inserted after the currently active slide.

2. Do one of the following:

   ▸ To insert a slide of the same type as the selected slide, click the Home: Slides:New Slide icon, choose Insert > New Slide, or press Shift-Command-N.

   ▸ To insert a slide with a different layout, select a slide layout from the Home:Slides:New Slide gallery **Ⓐ**.

To delete a slide:

1. Select or display the slide that you want to delete.

2. Choose Edit > Delete Slide or press Delete.

   The active slide is immediately deleted.

TIP To recover a slide you mistakenly deleted, choose Edit > Undo Delete Slide or press Command-Z.

TIP Rather than select a slide, you can right-click a slide and choose New Slide or Delete Slide from the contextual menu that appears **Ⓑ**.

TIP You can change the layout of any slide by choosing another from the Home:Slides: Layout gallery—even if the slide already contains text and other objects.

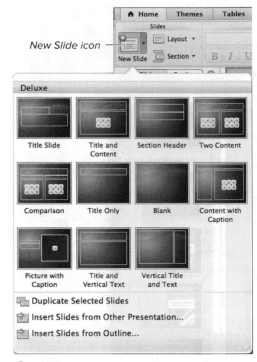

New Slide icon

Ⓐ You can choose a specific layout for the new slide from the New Slide gallery.

Ⓑ You can choose many useful commands from this contextual menu.

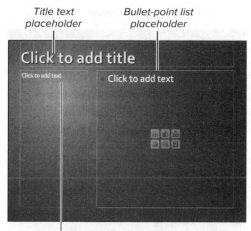

Title text placeholder   *Bullet-point list placeholder*

Click to add title

Click to add text   Click to add text

Body text placeholder

Ⓐ The new slide appears, ready for you to enter text into the placeholders.

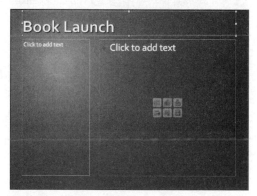

Book Launch

Click to add text   Click to add text

Ⓑ Click each text placeholder and type or paste your text.

Duplicating Slides

After you've created several slides, one of the fastest ways to move the creation process along is to duplicate slides and edit the duplicates, rather than design every new slide from scratch.

To duplicate a slide, select its thumbnail in the current view and choose Home:Slides: New Slide > Duplicate Selected Slides.

Adding Text to Slides

Most slide layouts contain text placeholders into which you can enter a title or other text.

To create a new text slide:

1. Select or display the slide after which you want the new slide to appear.

   A new slide is always inserted after the currently active slide.

2. Do one of the following:

   ▸ To insert a slide of the same type as the selected slide (assuming it has text placeholders), click the Home: Slides: New Slide icon, choose Insert > New Slide, or press Shift-Command-N.

   ▸ To insert a slide with a different text layout, select a layout in the Home: Slides: New Slide gallery (see Ⓐ in "Adding and Deleting Slides," earlier in this chapter).

   The new slide appears Ⓐ.

3. Click a Click to add title or Click to add text placeholder and type the text Ⓑ.

> **TIP** To format text, set paragraph alignment, or create additional bulleted or numbered lists, you can choose commands from the Format menu, the Formatting toolbar, or the Home tab. Character formatting can be applied to only selected text or—if the text box itself is selected—to all text within the box.

> **TIP** If you don't need a particular text placeholder, you can leave it blank or delete it.

> **TIP** If there's a blank area on a slide into which you want to add text (as found on the Blank layout, for instance), you can add a text box to the slide. Choose Insert > Text Box or Home: Insert: Text > Text Box. Using the A-shaped cursor that appears, click and drag to create the text box. For information on working with placeholder or user-created text boxes, see the following section.

Working with Text Boxes

You can select characters, words, or paragraphs within a text box the same way you do in a Word document (see "Working with Text" in Chapter 2). However, PowerPoint differs a bit in the manner in which you move and format text boxes.

To select a text box:

- Click its edge or inside the text box.

  The text box 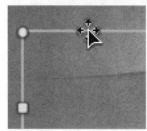 is surrounded by handles, enabling you to move and resize it as desired.

To move or resize a text box:

- To move a selected text box, move the cursor over any edge until it changes to a cross **B**, and then drag the box to a new position on the slide.

- Drag a handle to resize the box. Text inside the box automatically rewraps to fit the box's new size.

TIP To resize a text box proportionately, hold down Shift as you drag a corner handle. To resize a text box from its center, hold down Option as you drag a corner handle. If the box was originally centered on the slide, this will keep it centered.

TIP To edit text within a text box, you can simply click in it to set the text insertion mark. You can select text within the box (to format or delete it, for example) using normal editing procedures.

TIP You can drag a text box's rotation handle to change its angle on the page **A**.

Rotation handle

Text insertion mark

A Whether it's a placeholder or manually drawn, every text box is an object. When selected, handles appear around its edges.

B The cursor takes this shape when it's moved over the edge of a text box.

Adding Slides from Other Presentations

Slides that you've created for another presentation can sometimes be useful in the current presentation. You can add them to the presentation by doing either of the following:

- Choose Insert > Slide From > Other Presentation. Select the presentation and specify the slide(s) to insert.

- Select the thumbnail of the slide you want to copy and choose Edit > Copy. Switch to the destination presentation and choose Edit > Paste.

Using the current theme as the background, PowerPoint places the content from the copied slides on new slides.

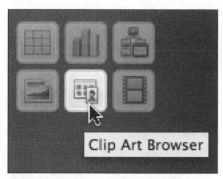

Categories menu

Adding Images to Slides

You can make your slides more interesting by adding clip art from the Clip Art Gallery or Clip Art Browser or by using photos and other image files. As an example, the steps below explain how to add clip art to a slide. Information on adding other types of graphic elements can be found in these chapters:

- **SmartArt graphics.** See the following section ("Adding SmartArt Graphics").
- **Charts and tables.** Chapter 18.
- **Movies.** Chapter 3.
- **WordArt.** Chapter 3.

To add clip art to a slide:

1. Create a new slide, selecting a layout that includes a clip art placeholder.

   The new slide appears.

2. Click the Clip Art Browser icon in the placeholder **A**.

   The Media Browser opens with the Clip Art tab selected **B**.

3. *Optional:* Choose a clip art category from the drop-down menu.

4. Select an image and drag it into the placeholder frame.

   The clip art image is inserted into the placeholder.

A Icons show the object types a placeholder can accept. The top row has table, chart, and SmartArt icons. The bottom row icons are for photos, clip art, and movies.

B Choose a category and drag the clip art onto the slide.

C When the image is selected, you can click these icons to move, crop, or resize it within the placeholder frame.

TIP Every image (including clip art) inserted into a placeholder can be repositioned, cropped, or resized to better fit the frame. Select the image and click an icon beneath it **C**.

TIP iPhoto pictures and iMovie movies can also be placed by dragging them from the Photos or Movies tab of the Media Browser.

continues on next page

TIP You can also insert an image from the Clip Art Gallery. Choose Insert > Clip Art > Clip Art Gallery, select an image **D**, and click the Insert button.

TIP Even if you haven't created a slide with a clip art placeholder, you can manually add clip art to any slide.

TIP To insert a photo from your hard disk that isn't stored in iPhoto, create a new slide that contains a picture placeholder. When you double-click the placeholder, the Choose a Picture dialog box appears **E**, allowing you to select any picture or photo from your hard disk.

TIP You can also insert any compatible image by dragging its file icon onto a placeholder or a blank area on the slide.

TIP Commands for inserting clip art, photos, movies, and shapes can also be found in the Home:Insert group.

TIP If you want to edit a selected picture, you can select options from the Format Picture contextual tab. You can also choose Format > Picture and set options in the Format Picture dialog box. For more information about image editing, see Chapter 3.

TIP You can substitute one image for another by right-clicking it on the slide and choosing Change Picture from the contextual menu **F**.

CAUTION Don't insert or drag multiple pictures onto the same placeholder. Rather than replacing the previous image, any new image is placed atop the old one. Be sure to delete the original image first.

Categories   Search box

D You can insert an image from the Clip Gallery.

E You can insert an image file from your hard disk by selecting it in the Choose a Picture dialog box (Mac OS X 10.6.5/Snow Leopard shown).

F To replace one image with another, right-click the placed image and choose Change Picture.

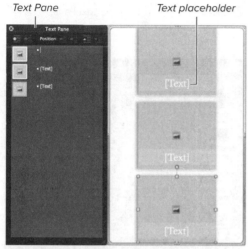

A If the placeholder contains a SmartArt icon, you can click it to select the SmartArt tab on the Ribbon.

Text Pane   *Text placeholder*

B Enter text into the placeholders or in the Text Pane. Notice that this SmartArt graphic has placeholders for both text and images.

C The completed slide with SmartArt in place.

Adding SmartArt Graphics

Available on the SmartArt tab, *SmartArt graphics* are colorful combinations of text and graphics that you can insert to create eye-catching bullet lists, processes, hierarchies, organizational charts, and so on. Although SmartArt is also available in Word and Excel, it's more commonly used in PowerPoint presentations. All SmartArt is selected from the SmartArt tab.

To insert a SmartArt graphic:

1. With the destination slide selected, do one of the following:

   ▸ Click the SmartArt icon in the destination placeholder **A**. The SmartArt tab is automatically selected.

   ▸ Select the destination placeholder, and then select the SmartArt tab.

   ▸ On a slide without a placeholder, select the SmartArt tab.

TIP The Insert > SmartArt command also selects the SmartArt tab.

2. Choose a graphic from the Smart Art:Insert SmartArt Graphic group.

   The SmartArt graphic is added to the slide **B**.

3. Enter text into the [Text] placeholders.

   You can type directly into the placeholders or into the Text Pane.

4. If the SmartArt graphic has picture placeholders **C**, click each icon and select a photo or other picture from your hard disk.

continues on next page

TIP You aren't required to select a place-holder before inserting SmartArt. If you neglect to do so, the Smart Art will be placed as a floating graphic or in the graphic placeholder furthest to the left.

TIP Click the icon in the top-left corner of a SmartArt graphic **D** to open the Text Pane **E**, which contains additional controls for managing the graphic's text blocks.

TIP You can replace a SmartArt graphic at any time by choosing another from the SmartArt:Change SmartArt Graphic group. Any text you've added will be retained.

TIP You can modify SmartArt by selecting a new style or color from the SmartArt:SmartArt Graphic Styles group **F**. Icons in the SmartArt: Edit SmartArt group can be used to flip the SmartArt horizontally (Right to Left) or change the shape of a selected component. Choose commands from the Format contextual tab to change the fill, transparency, and effects of selected SmartArt shapes or text. At any time, you can click Reset Graphic to restore the SmartArt to its original style and color.

TIP Choose settings from the Formatting toolbar to change the font, style, and size of selected text.

Show Text Pane

D Click this icon to display the Text Pane.

Close   *Toolbar*

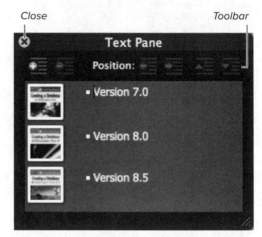

E The Text Pane has a toolbar with controls for managing a SmartArt graphic's text.

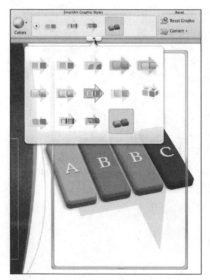

F You can change the SmartArt's style.

Rotation handle

Click to add title

A When selected, every placeholder has handles along its edges that you can drag to resize it.

B When this cursor appears, you can drag the placeholder to a new spot.

Adding Shapes and Lines

In addition to adding a variety of image types, you can embellish slides by adding lines and shapes from the Media Browser's Shapes tab or the Home:Insert:Shapes submenus. Many shapes, such as callout balloons, can accept text.

Precise Object Positioning

When adding items to a slide, Office 2011 has tools to ensure accurate positioning— aligning objects to one another or to the slide's center.

- **Align commands.** Select the objects that you want to align to one another, and choose a command from the Format:Format:Arrange:Align or Distribute submenu or the Arrange > Align or Distribute submenu.

- **Guides.** Enable View > Guides > Dynamic Guides. As you drag an object, guidelines show when it's aligned with the edge or center of another object, as well as the slide's center.

Working with Placeholders

In the previous sections, you saw that most slide layouts have placeholders for some combination of text, photos, charts, tables, clip art, movies, and the like. Placeholders have two purposes. First, clicking an icon in a placeholder enables you to easily add that type of material to the layout. Second, preformatted text within placeholders ensures consistency among the slides.

Because you'll be spending a lot of time working with placeholders, here are some additional facts and tips that may be helpful:

- You can resize, move, or delete placeholders:
  - ▸ To change a placeholder's size or shape, drag a handle **A**.
  - ▸ To move a selected placeholder, position the cursor over any edge **B**, click, and then drag.
  - ▸ To rotate a placeholder, drag its green rotation handle **A**.
  - ▸ To delete a selected placeholder, press Delete.

- You can selectively set formatting within a text placeholder or apply the format-ting to all of the placeholder's text. To do the latter (such as changing the bullet symbol, paragraph alignment, or font, for example), select the place-holder by clicking one of its edges and then apply the formatting.

- Most built-in themes contain a layout without placeholders (Blank). If you want more control over slide layouts in your presentation, you can add your own text boxes, photos, and SmartArt to the Blank layout.

Slide Backgrounds

In addition to selecting a presentation theme from the PowerPoint Presentation Gallery or the Themes tab, you can create your own theme by judiciously choosing background graphics and colors.

Creating a picture background

There are two ways to quickly add a background image to the slides in your presentation. First, you can place the image on a slide master. Second, you can use the Format > Slide Background command. In either case, you can choose graphics from the art collections included with Office or use your own images.

To add an image to a slide master:

1. Choose View > Master > Slide Master or press Shift as you click the Normal view icon at the bottom of the document.

   The Slide Master window appears **Ⓐ**.

2. In the navigation pane on the left, select a slide layout as follows:

   ▸ To apply the image to a specific slide layout, select that layout.

   ▸ To apply the image to all layouts, select the first layout (Office Theme Slide Master).

3. Choose a command from the Insert > Photo or Insert > Clip Art submenu, or click the Home:Insert:Picture icon and choose a command from its menu.

   The Media Browser, Choose a Picture dialog box, or Clip Gallery appears.

4. In the former case, drag an image onto the slide. In either of the latter cases, select an image and click Insert.

   The picture appears on the slide master **Ⓑ**.

Office Theme Slide Master   Close   Close

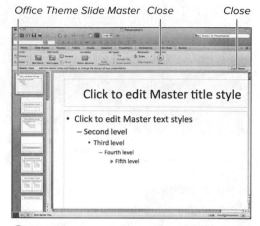

Ⓐ Graphics and text added to a slide master can appear on every slide in the presentation.

Ⓑ Depending on its dimensions and orientation, the placed image will either fill the slide or appear as a smaller floating object.

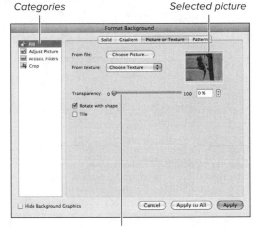

C When resized, this winter image from the Media Browser's Clip Art tab fills the background.

Categories   *Selected picture*

Transparency slider

D The selected image file is displayed.

5. As necessary, modify, resize, or move the image **C**.

6. To exit Slide Master view, click either of the Close buttons **A**, click a View icon, or choose a View menu command.

TIP You can also enter Slide Master view by choosing Themes: Master Views: Edit Master > Slide Master.

To use a picture as the background:

1. Choose Format > Slide Background.

   The Format Background dialog box appears.

2. Select the Fill category in the pane on the left, and click the Picture or Texture tab.

3. Click the Choose Picture button

4. In the Choose a Picture dialog box, select an image file and click Insert.

   The image appears in the dialog box **D** and on the current slide.

5. *Optional:* Make the image transparent by dragging the Transparency slider or by typing a percentage in the text box.

6. *Optional:* If the selected image doesn't fill the slide as you'd like, click the Tile check box to repeat the image as many times as necessary to fill the slide.

7. To add the image to the background of all slides in the presentation, click Apply to All. To apply it only to the current slide, click Apply.

TIP Graphics already on the slide master as part of a template background may need to be ungrouped before you can alter or delete them.

TIP You can copy and paste a graphic image from another program onto the slide master, as well as copy and paste graphics from the slide master of another presentation onto the slide master of the current presentation.

Applying a background color, gradient, texture, or pattern

The Format Background dialog box **D** also can be used to apply a solid color, gradient, texture, or pattern to the background. Background formatting can be applied to one or all slides in a presentation.

To set a background color, gradient, texture, or pattern:

1. *Optional:* To set the background for only one slide, select that slide in Slide Master view.

> **TIP** When applying a background to all slides in a presentation, it doesn't matter which slide you select.

2. Do one of the following:
   - ▸ Choose Format > Slide Background.
   - ▸ Choose Themes : Theme Options : Background > Format Background.

   The Format Background dialog box appears.

3. Ensure that the Fill category is selected **D**, and click one of these tabs:
   - ▸ **Solid.** Select a color from the drop-down menu **E**. If you don't see the color you want, choose More Colors to set a color using a color picker.
   - ▸ **Gradient.** Select a gradient style from the Style drop-down menu. Use the controls to create the gradient **F**.
   - ▸ **Picture or Texture.** Select a texture from the From texture pop-up list **G**.
   - ▸ **Pattern.** Select a pattern from the grid, as well as foreground and background colors.

   A preview of the effect is applied to the current slide.

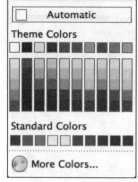

E You can choose a solid fill color from the drop-down menu.

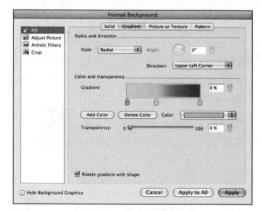

F After selecting a gradient style, you can alter the gradient by using the arrows and other controls beneath the Gradient preview.

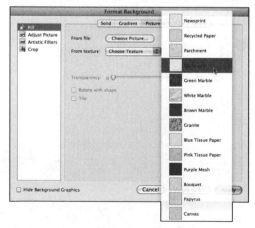

G Select a texture thumbnail from the list.

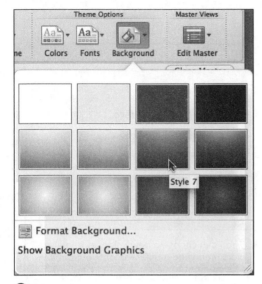

H You can use the Background menu to select a basic background or open the Format Background dialog box.

I If graphics inserted onto a slide master don't cover the slide, you can combine them with a background format, such as this gradient.

4. Do one of the following:

▸ To apply the new background to only the current slide, click Apply.

▸ To apply the background to all slides in the presentation, click Apply to All.

TIP When formatting the background, you can apply a solid color, gradient, texture, or pattern; they're mutually exclusive. If you set a new background, it replaces the current background.

TIP If you preselect a color on the Solid tab before creating a gradient, the gradient is based on the selected color.

TIP You can also choose a variety of gradients from the Themes:Theme Options: Background gallery **H**.

TIP The Format Background dialog box **F** and the Background icon's menu **H** both have an option that enables you to hide background objects/graphics. If the current slide theme has graphics on the slide master, use this option to enable your color, gradient, or texture background to be seen while hiding the slide master graphics. As an alternative, you can edit the slide master and delete the graphics.

TIP Even if a slide master contains graphics, you can still use the Format Background dialog box to specify a background color, gradient, or texture—but only if the graphics don't completely cover the slide **I**.

Changing Theme Colors or Fonts

You can add consistency to a presentation by specifying a *color scheme* (theme colors) and/or set of fonts. The eight colors in a color scheme are applied to all elements on slides in the presentation. You can pick one of the built-in color schemes or create one of your own. Similarly, you can replace any theme's fonts.

To specify a new color or font theme:

Do either or both of the following:

- Choose a color scheme from the Themes: Theme Options: Colors menu 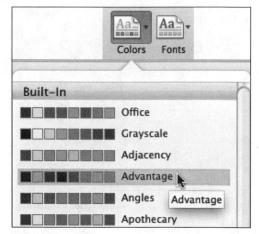.

- Choose a new font set from the Themes: Theme Options: Fonts menu Ⓐ.

  The new color scheme and/or fonts are applied to the entire presentation.

TIP To customize the current color scheme, choose Format > Theme Colors or Theme: Theme Options: Colors > Create Theme Colors. In the Create Theme Colors dialog box Ⓑ, select new colors by clicking an element's color box and then clicking the Change Color button. The effects of the change (if any) are shown in the preview area. When you're done, name the color scheme and click Apply to All.

TIP Custom color themes that you create in PowerPoint will also be available to you in Word and Excel.

TIP To replace one or more fonts in the current font set, choose Format > Replace Fonts, make the changes in the Replace Font dialog box, and click Close.

TIP If you choose a different theme from the Themes tab on the Ribbon, the color scheme and font set automatically change, too.

Ⓐ You can choose a new color set from the Colors menu and a different font set from the Fonts menu.

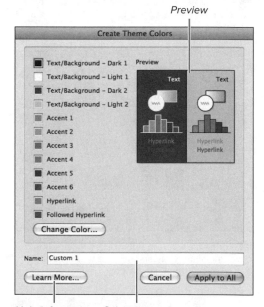

Ⓑ You can customize the current color scheme by choosing new colors for the various elements.

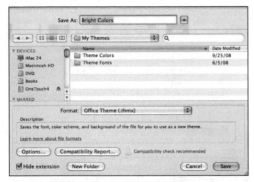

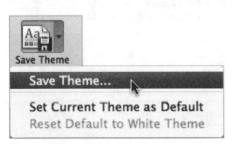

A You can save the current presentation as a reusable PowerPoint Template or a custom theme.

B To directly save a theme, choose the Save Theme > Save Theme command.

Organizing with Sections

Although you've gotten along without them for many years, PowerPoint 2011 lets you group slides into logical *sections*. Because you can expand or collapse a section in Normal or Slide Sorter view, sections are especially useful for focusing on specific parts of a large presentation.

To insert a section, select the slide that will be the first one in the new section, and choose Home:Slides:Section > Add Section. Name the section in the Rename Section dialog box that appears.

You can collapse or expand a section by clicking the triangle that precedes the section name. Commands in the Section icon's menu enable you to to expand or collapse all sections, as well as remove or rename sections.

Saving and Reusing a Custom Design

After spending hours modifying a Power-Point template or creating a presentation from scratch, you can optionally save its design as a custom template or theme that you can use as the basis for future presentations.

To save a presentation as a template or theme:

1. Choose File > Save As.

   The Save As panel appears **A**.

2. Choose PowerPoint Template (.potx) or Office Theme (.thmx) from the Format drop-down menu.

3. Name the template or theme, and click the Save button.

   Templates are stored in the My Templates folder; custom themes are stored in the My Themes folder. Either can be selected for use in other presentations from the My Templates or My Themes category in the PowerPoint Presentation Gallery.

> **TIP** A faster way to save a custom theme is to choose Themes:Themes:Save Theme > Save Theme **B**. Doing so automatically chooses the Office Theme format and My Themes folder.

Saving Presentations

Don't forget to save the presentation on which you're working. In addition to saving it as a standard presentation that can be opened, viewed, and edited in PowerPoint, you can save in a variety of formats for different purposes and audiences, such as the following:

- **PDF.** This output can be viewed in Preview, Adobe Reader, and similar utilities.

- **QuickTime movie.** This option lets people view the presentation as it might appear during a live presentation.

- **iPhoto images.** Saves the presentation as a series of JPEG or PNG images, allowing it to be viewed on an iPod.

PowerPoint supports a variety of save formats 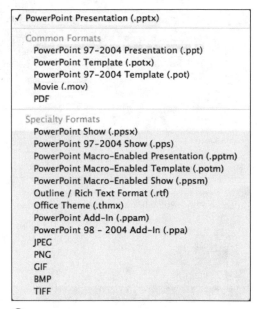. See Chapter 19 for an in-depth discussion of some useful Save options.

To save a presentation:

Do one of the following:

- Choose File > Save.

- Press Command-S.

- Click the Save icon on the Standard toolbar.

One of the following occurs:

- If this is the first time you've saved, a Save As panel appears **B**. Name the presentation, specify a format, select a location on disk, and click Save.

- If you've previously saved the presentation, this version overwrites the previous one. Continue working.

TIP To save a previously saved presentation with a new name, a different format, or in another location on disk, choose File > Save As (Shift-Command-S) rather than File > Save.

A When saving a presentation for the first time or when using Save As, these file formats can be chosen from the Format drop-down menu.

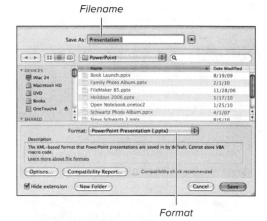

B Name the file, specify a save location and file format, and click Save.

18

Charts and Tables

A chart or graph can make complex numerical information easier to interpret by expressing it visually. To create or edit a chart, PowerPoint and Word 2011 use Excel. When creating a new chart or editing an existing one, you temporarily leave Power-Point and work in Excel. Note the following:

- Information in this chapter concerning the process of creating charts in Power-Point is also applicable to creating them in Word.

- If you've already created and format-ted a chart in Excel, you don't need to follow the instructions in this chapter. See "Copying, Linking, and Embedding" in Chapter 27 for help transferring the chart into PowerPoint.

- In Office 2008 and earlier, organization charts were created in the Organization Chart application. In Office 2011, org charts are SmartArt graphics and can be chosen from the SmartArt:Insert SmartArt Graphic:Hierarchy gallery.

- See Chapter 14 for additional informa-tion about creating, editing, and format-ting charts.

Creating a Chart

You can add a chart to an existing slide or to a new slide.

To add a chart to a slide:

1. *Optional:* Create a new slide by clicking the Home : Slides : New Slide icon, choosing Insert > New Slide, or pressing Shift-Command-N.

   The new slide's layout duplicates that of the initially selected slide. If desired, you can choose a different layout from the Home : Slides : Layout gallery.

2. Do one of the following:

   ▸ If the slide contains a chart placeholder icon , click the icon.

   ▸ If the slide contains a placeholder for another type of object (such as a picture), select the placeholder.

   ▸ If the slide has no suitable placeholder but has a blank area large enough to receive the chart, do nothing.

3. If the Charts tab isn't selected, click it or choose Insert > Chart.

   The chart types are displayed in the Charts : Insert Chart galleries **B**.

4. Click a chart category icon, and then click the thumbnail of the chart style that you want to create.

   Excel launches and displays a worksheet with sample data **C**.

5. Replace the sample data with your own by typing or pasting. Drag the lower-right corner to match the range of your data.

6. When you're finished editing the worksheet data, click the worksheet's close button (X).

   The chart appears on the slide **D**.

A Some placeholders have an icon for a chart.

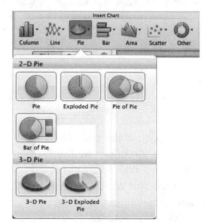

B Choose a chart style thumbnail from a chart category.

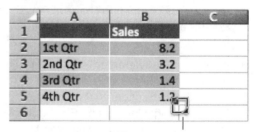

	A	B	C
1		**Sales**	
2	1st Qtr	8.2	
3	2nd Qtr	3.2	
4	3rd Qtr	1.4	
5	4th Qtr	1.3	
6			

Drag to change the range

C Replace the sample labels and data with your own information.

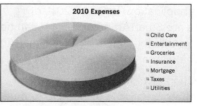

D The new chart appears on the slide.

Transpose data

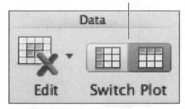

E In the Charts:Data group, you can edit the data or transpose rows and columns.

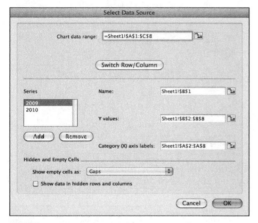

F In the Select Data Source dialog box, you can change the data range, add or remove a series, transpose the array, or specify new worksheet locations from which to draw the title and labels.

TIP If you have a large screen or dual monitors, you can see the effects of your edits in step 5 as you enter the data. PowerPoint builds and updates the chart as you work in Excel. If you want to play with the chart labels and data arrangement before committing to the chart, it isn't necessary to close the Excel worksheet.

TIP If your data is in another worksheet, copy it, select cell A1 in the sample worksheet, and paste over the sample data.

TIP After creating a chart, you can change its type or style by selecting the chart (or any part of it) on the slide and then choosing a new thumbnail from the Charts:Change Series Chart Type galleries **B**.

CAUTION Not every chart type is appropriate for every data set. It's important to select a suitable type when creating or changing charts. For example, a column or bar chart is typically created from multiple data series. If you later convert such a chart to a pie chart (which is based on a single data series), unexpected results will likely ensue.

TIP After creating a chart, you can modify its data or labels by editing the worksheet. Select the chart and click the Charts:Data:Edit icon **E**, or right-click the chart and choose Edit > Data from the contextual menu that appears.

TIP You can also make changes in the Select Data Source dialog box **F**. Choose Charts:Data:Edit > Select Data in Excel. You can transpose the data by clicking Switch Rows/Columns or remove selected series from the chart. Click OK when you're ready to edit the worksheet data.

TIP The simplest way to transpose data (switching from plotting a data series by rows to columns or vice versa) is to click the other Switch Plot icon in the Charts:Data group **F**.

Chart Appearance Options

Every chart type and style has predefined options that may or may not be precisely what you want. You can embellish charts and make them easier to interpret by adding a legend, gridlines, data point labels, chart data, and chart or axis titles. You can change the formatting for many of these elements if you aren't satisfied with the default appearance.

Legends

A *legend* graphically differentiates the data series on a chart.

To show or hide the legend:

With the chart or any part of it selected:

- Choose a legend position from the Chart Layout:Labels:Legend menu 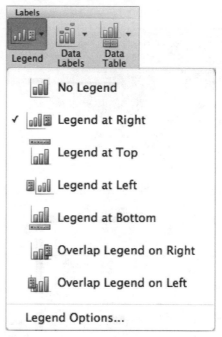 **A**.

- Choose No Legend to remove the legend from the chart.

To modify the legend:

You can do any of the following:

- To move the legend, click in its center and drag it to a new position.

- To change the legend's size or shape, drag a handle.

- To change the legend series labels, edit them in the worksheet.

- You can set a new font, size, and style for the legend text on the Formatting toolbar, or on the Font tab of the Format Legend **B** or Format Text dialog box.

TIP You can also remove the legend by selecting it on the chart and pressing Delete.

A You can position or remove the legend by choosing an option from this menu.

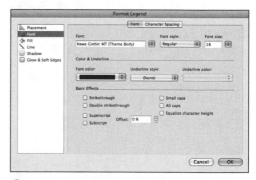

B You can also set position and formatting for the legend in the Format Legend dialog box. To open the dialog box, double-click the legend or select it and choose Format > Legend.

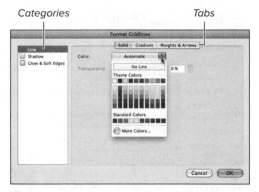

Categories   *Tabs*

G With the Line category selected, you can choose a new line color on the Solid tab.

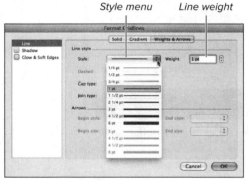

Style menu   *Line weight*

D You can also change the line style and weight.

Opening the Format Dialog Box

You need to open the correct Format *item type* dialog box in order to format a chart element. If you're having difficulty doing this, the simplest options are:

- Double-click the item on the chart.
- In the Chart Layout : Current Selection group, select the item type from the drop-down menu and then click the Format Selection icon.

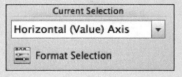

Gridlines

Gridlines can help viewers interpret the data by making it easier to see the approximate size or value of each data point. You can add gridlines to most chart types.

To show or hide gridlines:

Do the following:

- Choose commands from the Chart Layout : Axes : Gridlines menu.

  You can display any combination of major, minor, vertical, and horizontal gridlines.

To format a gridline set:

1. On the chart, select a gridline of the type (major or minor) that you want to format and choose Format > Gridlines. Alternatively, you can double-click the gridline.

   The Format Gridlines dialog box appears **G**.

2. Select the Line category, and do any of the following:

   ▸ To change the line color, select the Solid tab and choose a color from the drop-down Color palette **G**.

   ▸ To change the line thickness or style, select the Weights & Arrows tab **D**.

TIP You can also open the Format Gridlines dialog box by opening the Chart Layout : Axes : Gridlines menu and choosing Gridlines Options from either of the submenus.

Data point labels

You can label the data values in your chart to highlight the differences between them or to make it easier for viewers to interpret the chart 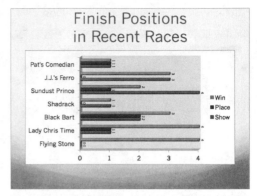.

To label data points:

Do one of the following:

- **Label all data points.** Select the chart or any part of it. Choose a label option from the Chart Layout:Labels:Data Labels drop-down menu **F**.

- **Label a single data series.** Select an element of the series on the chart or select the series name from the Chart Layout:Current Selection list. Choose a label option from the Chart Layout: Labels:Data Labels drop-down menu **F**.

TIP You can also specify a label for a single data point, labeling only the highest and lowest values, for example. After clicking once to select the series, click the specific data element within the series and choose an option from the Data Labels drop-down menu **F**.

TIP To remove all data labels from a chart, select the chart and choose **No Data Labels** from the Data Labels drop-down menu **F**. To remove data labels from only one series, select the series on the chart and choose **No Data Labels**.

TIP Data labels take on the formatting of other chart text. To change the font, size, or color of the labels, you must format them one series at a time. For example, the data labels in **E** were reduced in size and rotated to prevent them from overlapping.

TIP The numeric format of the labels (such as the number of decimal places) is determined by cell formatting in the worksheet.

E Data point labels let viewers immediately determine the size of any data element.

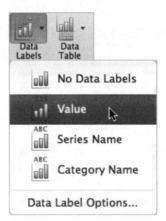

F The Data Labels menu.

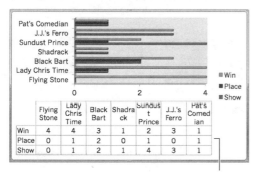

G Choose a display option from the Data Table drop-down menu.

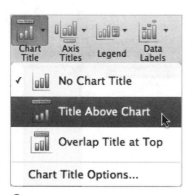

Data table

H An example of a chart with a data table.

I For a slide layout without a title placeholder, you can elect to add a title text box.

Chart data

In many types of charts, it's impractical—and ugly—to label the data points. As an alternative, you can display the chart data (called the *data table*) beneath the chart.

To display the chart data:

With the chart or any part of it selected:

- Choose an option from the Chart Layout: Labels: Data Table menu **G**.

  The data table appears beneath the chart **H**.

TIP If the effect isn't what you had in mind, you can remove the data table by choosing **No Data Table G** or the alternative option.

TIP If you choose Data Table with Legend Key, the normal legend becomes superfluous. You can remove the legend by selecting it and pressing Delete. Or you can choose Chart Layout: Labels: Legend > No Legend.

Chart titles

In general, a chart should have a title that clearly explains what's being shown. If the chart slide doesn't have a title placeholder, you can add a title to the chart itself.

To add a chart title:

1. Select the chart or any part of it.

2. Choose an option from the Chart Layout: Labels: Chart Title menu **I**.

3. Type or paste the chart title in the text box.

   The title appears at the top of the chart. If desired, you can drag the title by any edge to a new location on the chart.

TIP You can also add a vertical or horizontal axis title to most charts. Choose an option from the Chart Layout: Labels: Axis Titles menu and then type the title in the text box.

Formatting Chart Elements

You can change the appearance of any chart element, such as a single set of bars, a line, or an axis. You can also change the style of any data series in the chart by formatting the series.

To format a chart element using a Format dialog box:

1. Select the chart element that you want to format and then double-click it.

   The dialog box for the element appears, such as Format Chart Area (with the entire chart selected), Format Axis, Format Data Series 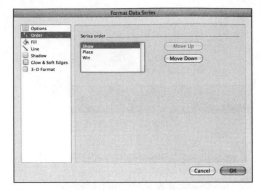, Format Legend, or Format Title.

2. Set formatting options and click OK.

TIP To avoid opening the wrong Format dialog box, right-click the element and choose the command from the contextual menu that appears **B**.

To format a chart element using the Ribbon:

1. Select the chart element that you want to format.

2. Click the Format contextual tab.

3. Select formatting options from the Chart Element Styles and/or Text Styles group **C**.

TIP If you don't care for the formatting you just applied to a chart element, you can remove its effect by immediately choosing Edit > Undo *formatting effect* or by clicking the Undo icon on the Standard toolbar.

A In the Order category of the Format Data Series dialog box, you can change the order of the bars in a bar chart—without rearranging the worksheet data.

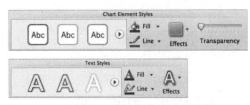

B Right-clicking is one of the easiest ways to open the correct Format dialog box.

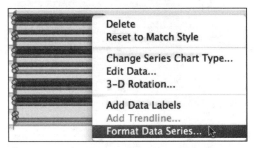

C Element (top) and text formatting (bottom) options can also be selected from the Format contextual tab.

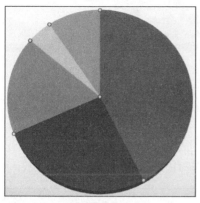

A When a pie is selected, each slice has handles.

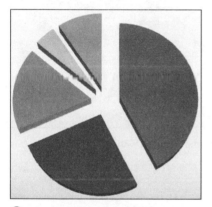

B Drag outward to explode the entire pie.

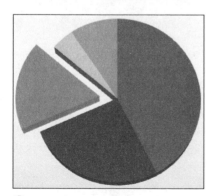

C If you select and drag a single slice, you can separate the slice from the rest of the pie.

Exploding a Pie Chart

If you've created a pie chart, you can *explode* the chart (pull all pieces out from the center to make it more visually interesting) or pull out an individual piece to emphasize a data value.

To explode or cut a pie chart:

1. Click to select the pie in the chart.

2. To explode the pie, do either of the following:

   ▸ Choose the Exploded Pie or 3-D Exploded Pie thumbnail from the Charts:Change Chart Type:Pie gallery. The original pie chart is replaced by an exploded pie chart.

   ▸ Click once to select the plot area **A** and then drag a slice outward **B**.

   TIP When exploding by dragging a slice, the distance you drag determines how far *all* slices will be exploded.

3. To cut/explode a single slice, click once to select the plot area **A**; click a second time to select only the slice that you want to cut; and then drag the selected slice outward **C**.

   TIP To rejoin a cut slice with the pie, drag the slice back to the center of the pie. To rejoin an exploded pie, drag any slice back to the center of the pie.

Creating Stock Charts

Stock charts (also known as high-low-close charts) can display daily prices and, optionally, the opening price and daily volume for a stock. Stock charts can also be used to present other types of numeric data, such as temperatures or barometric pressures.

To create a stock chart:

1. Depending on the type of chart you want, arrange the columns to match one of the following:

   ▸ Date, High, Low, Close

   ▸ Date, Open, High, Low, Close

   ▸ Date, Volume, High, Low, Close

   ▸ Date, Volume, Open, High, Low

2. In the Excel worksheet or other source document, select and copy the data from which the chart will be created (Edit > Copy or Command-C).

3. In PowerPoint, select or create the slide on which you'll insert the stock chart.

4. Follow the instructions in "Creating a Chart" earlier in this chapter to create the chart.

5. Click the Charts:Insert Chart:Other icon and select a stock chart thumbnail 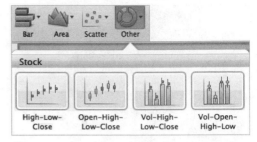.

   Excel launches and displays a worksheet with sample data.

6. Paste (Edit > Paste or Command-V) the stock data into cell A1 and, if necessary, resize the range to encompass the pasted data.

7. Close the worksheet.

8. Format the chart **B**.

   You can remove the legend and adjust the vertical axis to display a tighter data range, for example.

A Stock chart styles are presented in the top section of the Other gallery.

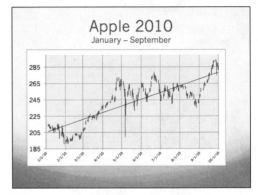

B The formatted chart with an added linear trendline.

C Enter a ticker symbol or company name, and click Get quotes.

	A	B	C	D	E	F
1	Date	Open	High	Low	Close	Volume
2	10-Dec-10	27.19	27.4	27.11	27.34	37629009
3	9-Dec-10	27.28	27.34	27.01	27.08	47148284
4	8-Dec-10	26.83	27.24	26.8	27.23	41666716
5	7-Dec-10	27.08	27.13	26.85	26.87	57860447
6	6-Dec-10	26.93	26.98	26.76	26.84	36273877
7	3-Dec-10	26.81	27.06	26.78	27.02	52621910
8	2-Dec-10	26.24	26.98	26.2	26.89	91798687
9	1-Dec-10	25.57	26.25	25.56	26.04	74123490
10	30-Nov-10	25.05	25.47	25	25.26	75282094
11	29-Nov-10	25.19	25.42	24.93	25.31	56608148
12	26-Nov-10	25.21	25.41	25.17	25.25	21356527

D Each historical data record downloads in the form: date, open, high, low, close, volume. If necessary, rearrange the columns to conform to the field order in the selected stock chart.

Gathering stock data

You can download historical stock data from many of the bigger financial sites. As an example, these steps explain how to get data from Google.

To download stock data from Google:

1. Go to **http://www.google.com/finance** in your Web browser.

2. Request a quote for the company in which you're interested **C**, and click the Historical prices link on the new page.

   A year of historical data is presented.

3. If desired, change the date range and click Update.

4. In the Export section, click the Download to spreadsheet link.

   A comma-separated values file named data.csv downloads to your Mac.

5. Double-click the downloaded file to open it in Excel **D**. (If the file opens in another program, launch Excel and open the file using File > Open.)

6. Select the historical data in Excel and copy it (Edit > Copy or Command-C).

7. Continue with step 5 of the previous step list ("To create a stock chart").

TIP The more data you plot, the more difficult it becomes to see the data points. You can improve the chart's readability by dragging its lower-right corner to resize it.

TIP Another approach to this problem is to reduce the amount of data. For instance, you could use weekly rather than daily quotes. Or you might consider charting data over a shorter time period.

Adding a Table to a Slide

Tables help present information efficiently. Creating and formatting a table in Power-Point is similar to working with tables in Word. See Chapter 7 for more details.

To add a table to a new slide:

1. Create a new slide or select an existing slide on which to insert the table.

   Several slide layouts include an Insert Table placeholder icon .

2. Do either of the following:

   ▸ Click the slide's Insert Table place-holder icon, if it has one.

   ▸ To place a table manually (on a blank slide, for example), choose Insert > Table.

   The Insert Table dialog box appears **B**.

3. Specify the number of columns and rows, and then click OK.

   The table appears on the slide **C**.

4. Enter the table's text and/or data. Format the cells and table as desired.

   To aid in formatting the table and its contents, select options from the Tables tab or choose Format > Table to open the Format Table dialog box.

TIP Another way to add a table to a slide is to click the Tables:Table Options:New icon and drag to specify the desired number of rows and columns **D**.

TIP To remove a table, select its frame and press Delete. Or select the table or any of its cells, and choose Table Layout:Rows & Columns:Delete > Delete Table.

A Although it isn't essential, you may want to select a slide layout that contains an Insert Table placeholder icon.

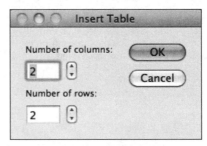

B Specify the number of table columns and rows.

C A blank table with the specified number of columns and rows appears on the slide. Enter the text, format the cells, and modify the table.

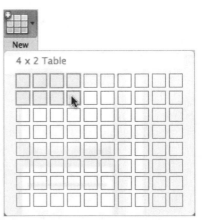

D Drag to set the table's dimensions.

Wrapping up a Presentation

When you've finished constructing a presentation, it's time to get it ready to be viewed by an audience. This is when you make final decisions about details such as slide order and design, and whether to also save the presentation as a QuickTime movie or for presentation on the Web.

The first part of the chapter discusses preparing the presentation. The second part covers some options and tools for giving and sharing the presentation.

Using the Slide Sorter

Use Slide Sorter view to get an overview of your presentation. It's similar to viewing 35mm slides on a light table. You can reorder the slides, switch themes to change the presentation's look, and delete or duplicate slides in Slide Sorter view.

To switch to Slide Sorter view:

Do the following:

- Choose View > Slide Sorter, press Command-2, or click the Slide Sorter view icon in the bottom-left corner of the PowerPoint document window **A**.

TIP To revert to viewing a single slide, double-click the slide in **Slide Sorter view** or select the slide and click the **Normal view** icon **A**.

To reorder slides in a presentation:

1. Click the slide that you want to move and drag it to a new position **B**.
2. Release the mouse button to drop the slide into its new position.

TIP To move a contiguous group of slides, click and drag the mouse across their thumbnails to select them **C**, and then drag the group to the new position. If you find it easier, you can select the slides by Shift-clicking the first and last thumbnail in the contiguous group.

TIP To move a noncontiguous group of slides, Command-click each slide and drag the group to the new position. The slides will appear in sequence and in the same relative order.

TIP If you've created multiple versions of a presentation, you can click the Review : Compare : Compare icon open the Compare Changes window **D** and view all differences between a prior version and the current version.

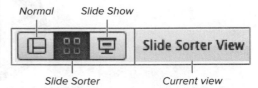

Normal   *Slide Show*

Slide Sorter   *Current view*

A One way to switch to Slide Sorter view is to click its icon at the bottom of the document window.

Destination   *Slide being moved*

B The slide about to be moved appears as a ghost and then disappears when you complete the move.

C You can click and drag the mouse across multiple slides and then move them as a group. In this example, all three slides are selected.

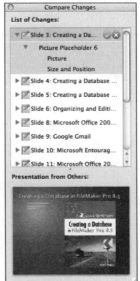

D The Compare Changes window.

Cut	⌘X
Copy	⌘C
Paste	⌘V
Select All	⌘A
New Slide	⇧⌘N
Duplicate Slide	⇧⌘D
Delete Slide	
Add Section	
Format Background...	
Transitions...	
Hide Slide	
Zoom...	
View Slide Show	

E If you don't remember the command, try right-clicking the slide or other object.

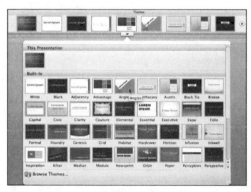

F Click a thumbnail to apply the new theme to the selected slides.

Section 1   *Section 2*

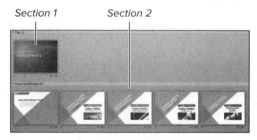

G Slides in the second section now have a style that distinguishes them from slides in other sections.

To delete or duplicate slides:

1. Select the slide(s) that you want to delete or duplicate.

2. Do one of the following:
   ▸ To delete the slide(s), choose Edit > Delete Slide or press Delete.
   ▸ To duplicate the slide(s), choose Edit > Duplicate, press Command-D, or press Shift-Command-D.
   ▸ Right-click a slide, and choose Delete Slide or Duplicate Slide from the contextual menu that appears **E**.

TIP You can reverse the effects of a slide deletion or duplication by immediately choosing Edit > Undo or pressing Command-Z.

To apply a new theme to selected slides:

1. Select the slides to which you want to apply the new theme.

   Select slides by clicking, Command-clicking, Shift-clicking, or dragging through them.

2. Scroll or expand the Themes : Themes gallery **F**. Click the thumbnail of the theme you want to apply to the selected slides.

   The slides adapt the selected theme **G**.

TIP To quickly select all slides in the presentation, choose Edit > Select All or press Command-A.

TIP This technique can also be used in Normal view to change the theme of selected slides.

Adding Transitions

Transitions are visual effects, such as dissolves, splits, and wipes, used to transition between slides. You can apply different transitions to different slides. Note that an applied transition appears as you switch *to* the slide—not *from* it.

To add a transition to a slide:

1. In Normal view, select the slide to which you want to add a transition.

2. Scroll or expand the Transitions:Transition to This Slide gallery **A** (bottom).

3. Click a transition thumbnail.

   A preview of the transition is shown on the slide. Repeat until you find the transition you want to use.

4. Click the Transitions:Transition to This Slide:Effect Options icon.

   Select an effect option from the menu **B**.

5. *Optional:* To apply the transition to all slides in the presentation, click the Transitions:Apply to:All Slides icon **C**.

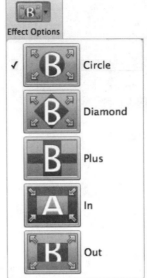

B Available effect options depend on the transition.

C Click this icon to apply the selected transition to all slides.

Scroll gallery
Expand gallery

A The thumbnails in the Transition to This Slide gallery give a rough idea of each transition's effect.

D None is the first transition in the gallery.

Animation

Transition

E In Slide Sorter view, a slide with a transition displays this icon.

Selected transition

F Available in Slide Sorter and Normal views, you can play the transition for one or more selected slides by clicking the Play icon.

Adding Navigation Buttons

Presentations can include clickable navigation buttons. On a slide master, add Next and Previous buttons chosen from the Home:Insert:Shape:Action Buttons submenu. For assistance, search for "Insert an action button to change slides" in PowerPoint's online Help.

TIP You can go directly to the Transitions tab by choosing Slide Show > Transitions.

TIP To apply the same transition to multiple slides, Command-click or Shift-click the slides and select the transition.

TIP A slide can have only one transition. Any new transition that you select replaces the current transition, if any. To remove the transition from selected slides, select the None transition from the Transition to This Slide gallery **D**.

TIP If you create a presentation from a template, slides may already have transitions.

TIP In Slide Sorter view, you can view a slide's transition by clicking the transition icon beneath the slide **E** or selecting the slide and clicking the Transitions:Review:Play icon **F**. You can also set transitions and effect options in this view.

TIP To determine which transition, if any, has been applied to the currently selected slide, check the Transition to This Slide gallery. The thumbnail for the transition (or None) will be surrounded by a gold frame **F**. This procedure can be used in Slide Sorter or Normal view.

TIP Supported transition types change from one version of PowerPoint to the next. For instance, PowerPoint 2001 and v.X supported QuickTime transitions, but they were not supported in PowerPoint 2004. If you open an earlier presentation in PowerPoint 2011, be sure to check the transitions to ensure that they still work or that undesired ones haven't been substituted.

TIP Similarly, to ensure that the current presentation will play properly in another version of PowerPoint, open the Toolbox and run a Compatibility Report, as described in Chapter 2.

Within-Slide Animation

Motion within a slide is known as *animation*. An animation can be applied to objects or text, as well as applied selectively or to all material on a slide. You can apply multiple animations to an object, if desired.

To add animation to a slide:

1. In Normal view, select a slide to which you want to add animation.

2. Select the text box or object on the slide that you want to animate.

   You can also apply an animation to multiple selected objects, if you wish.

3. Click the Animations tab on the Ribbon.

4. Open the Toolbox by clicking its icon on the Standard toolbar or by choosing View > Custom Animation. Select the Custom Animation tab.

   The Toolbox is helpful for fine-tuning animations and managing multiple ones.

5. Select the Animations tab on the Ribbon.

6. Choose an effect from the Entrance Effects, Emphasis Effects, Exit Effects, or the Motion:Paths gallery.

   The effect is numbered on the slide (representing the order in which it will play) and added to the Animation order list **A**.

7. Choose options for the selected effect from the Animations:Animation Options group **B** or the Effect Options section of the Custom Animation tab **C**.

8. If desired, repeat steps 6 and 7 to animate other objects or to add additional effects to an object.

9. To view all the animations applied to objects on the slide, click the Animations:Preview:Play icon **D**.

Numbered animation

Animation order list

A Every animation applied to the current slide is listed in the Animation order list.

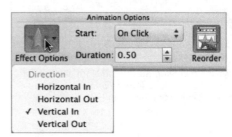

B You can customize effects by selecting options from the Animation Options group...

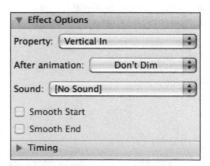

C ...or from the Effect Options area. (To reveal available Effect Options, select the animation in the Animation order list.)

D Click the Play icon to play all animations on the current slide.

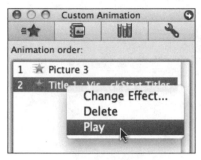

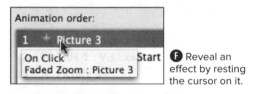

E You can play a single animation by right-clicking it and choosing Play.

F Reveal an effect by resting the cursor on it.

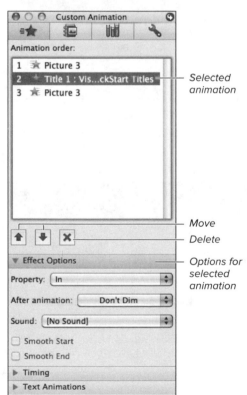

— *Selected animation*

— *Move*

— *Delete*

— *Options for selected animation*

G You can modify effects, change their order, or delete them.

TIP You can go directly to the Animations tab by choosing Slide Show > Animations.

TIP Entrance effects play when you transition to the slide; exit effects play as you transition to the next slide.

TIP In Normal view, you can play a single animation by right-clicking the animation in the Animation order list and choosing Play from the contextual menu that appears **E**.

TIP To determine the nature of an effect in the Animation order list, rest the cursor on it. A ScreenTip appears that describes the effect **F**.

TIP Effects play in the order listed in the Animation order list. To change the order, select an effect and click the Move up or Move down icon **G**. You can also simply drag an effect to a new position in the list.

TIP To remove an unwanted effect, select it in the Animation order list and click the Delete icon **G**. You can also remove an animation by selecting its number on the slide and pressing Delete.

TIP In Slide Sorter view, a slide that contains an animation has a star icon beneath it (see **E** in "Adding Transitions" earlier in this chapter). To preview the applied effect(s), click the icon.

CAUTION Because PowerPoint supplies so many different animation effects, there may be a temptation to overuse them. Multiple animations, sound effects, music, and movie clips can distract from a presentation's message and give it a circuslike effect. A little goes a long way. When applying these features to your slides, think carefully whether you want to elicit shouts of "Bring on the dancing bear!"

Adding Audio

To enliven a presentation, you can add audio, music, or movies to selected slides. For instructions on inserting and working with movies, see Chapter 3.

To insert a sound file:

1. In Normal view, select the slide on which you'd like a sound file to play.

2. Do one of the following:

   ▸ To insert a song or audio clip from iTunes, choose Home : Insert : Media > Audio Browser or Insert > Audio > Audio Browser. The Media Browser opens with the Audio tab selected 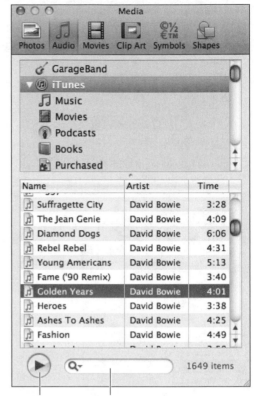. Drag a song or clip onto the slide.

   ▸ To insert an audio file from disk, choose Home : Insert : Media > Audio from File or Insert > Audio > Audio from File. The Choose dialog box appears. Select a sound file and click Insert.

   A speaker icon is added to the slide **B**.

3. Choose a start option from the Format Audio : Audio Options : Start menu:

   ▸ **Automatically.** The audio will begin playing as soon as the slide appears.

   ▸ **On Click.** The audio will play only when/if you click the play control beneath the speaker icon **B**.

   ▸ **Play Across Slides.** The audio will start automatically and continue playing beyond the current slide. (With any other option, the audio halts when you exit the slide.)

   The sound is added to the Animation order list for the slide (see **G** in "Within-Slide Animation" earlier in this chapter). To specify when the sound will play in relation to any animations, move it up or down in the list.

Play button   Search box

A The Media Browser simplifies the process of moving music and podcasts from iTunes into your presentations.

Play

B The speaker icon represents an audio file. Use the controls beneath it to control playback.

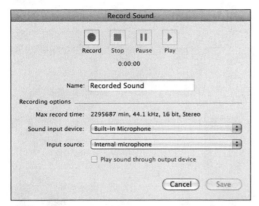

C Create and listen to your audio recording in the Record Sound dialog box.

The Power of QuickTime

In addition to traditional movie file types, such as QuickTime and MPEG-4, you can use the Insert > Movie > Movie from File command to insert any file type supported by QuickTime. For instance, you can insert a multi-page PDF file and flip through its pages using the movie controller. For more information about working with movies, see Chapter 3.

4. *Optional*: Choose commands from the Format Audio : Audio Options : Playback Options menu. All checked commands will be executed.

- ▸ **Hide Icon During Show.** You should choose this option only if you chose Automatically or Play Across Slides in step 3. If you chose When Clicked, you'll be unable to start the audio because you won't be able to see the speaker icon and its play control.

- ▸ **Loop Until Stopped.** This option causes the audio to repeat until you stop it or leave the slide.

- ▸ **Rewind After Playing.** Choose this option to reset the audio back to its beginning.

To record audio commentary:

1. In Normal view, select the slide that will include the recorded audio.

2. Choose Home : Insert : Media > Record Audio or Insert > Audio > Record Audio.

   The Record Sound dialog box appears **C**.

3. Ensure that the choices for Sound input device and Input source are correct, click Record, and speak into your internal or connected microphone.

4. When you're done recording, click Stop.

5. Click Play to listen to the recording, and do one of the following:

   - ▸ If the recording is unsatisfactory, repeat step 3. The new recording will replace the previous one.

   - ▸ If you're satisfied with the recording, enter a name for the recording, and click Save. The dialog box closes and a tiny speaker icon appears on the slide **B**. Set playback options as described in step 3 of "To insert a sound file" on the prior page.

Creating Handouts and Speaker Notes

Within PowerPoint, you can prepare *handouts* (slide printouts to give to the audience) and speaker notes to assist you during the presentation.

To create handouts:

1. Choose View > Master > Handout Master.

   The Handout Master view and its contextual tab appear **A**.

2. Click a Handout Master:Slides Per Page icon **B** to set the number of slides per page that you want to display.

3. Choose a page orientation from the Handout Master:Page Setup: Orientation menu.

4. *Optional:* Edit the header or footer text.

5. Click the Close or Close Master button.

6. Choose File > Print.

   The Print dialog box appears **C**.

7. From the Printer drop-down list, select a printer on which to print the handouts.

8. From the Print What drop-down menu, choose Handouts (*x* slides per page). Review the other settings.

9. Examine the handout pages in the Quick Preview box. The preview reflects the current print settings.

10. Do one of the following:

    ▸ Click the Print button to print the handouts on the designated printer.

    ▸ Click the PDF button and choose Save as PDF to create an Adobe Acrobat file that you can view in Apple's Preview or Adobe Reader.

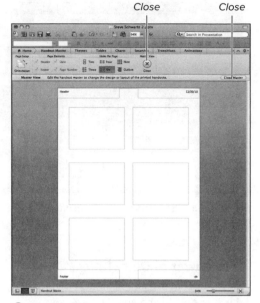

Close   *Close*

A Handout Master view.

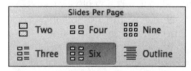

B Set the number of slides per page.

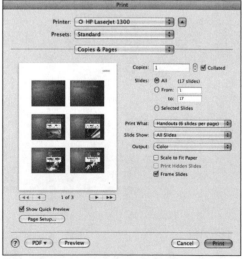

C Set handout print options in the Print dialog box.

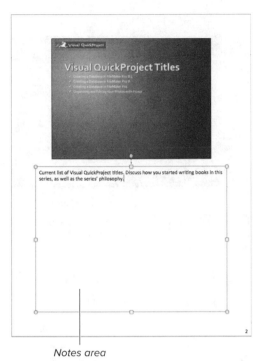

Notes area

D It's convenient to create the speaker notes in Notes Page view.

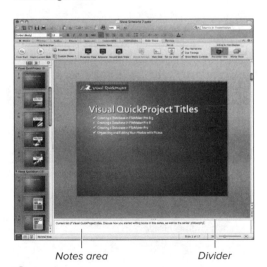

Notes area   *Divider*

E Notes can also be entered in Normal view, but with greater difficulty because they tend to scroll off the screen.

To create speaker notes:

Do any of the following:

- Choose View > Notes Page. Click in the notes text box to type speaker notes for a given slide **D**. Use the vertical scroll bar to switch from slide to slide.

- Switch to Normal view and enter notes in the text window under each slide **E**.

TIP The notes won't be visible to the audience during the presentation.

TIP If you're working in Normal view and need to enter copious notes for a slide, you can enlarge the notes area by dragging the divider between the slide and notes area **E**.

TIP To print each slide along with its associated notes, choose Notes from the Print What drop-down menu in the Print dialog box **C**. Be sure to check the settings for Copies, Collated, and Slides.

Rehearsing the Presentation

It's always a good idea to rehearse a presentation, especially if there's a time limit. When you finish assembling the presentation, you can rehearse it and time how long each slide needs to remain onscreen.

To rehearse a presentation:

1. Click the Slide Show:Presenter Tools: Rehearse icon or choose Slide Show > Rehearse.

   The first slide appears Ⓐ.

2. Perform the presentation exactly as you would in front of the audience.

3. Click the mouse, click the right arrow icon, press the spacebar, or press the right-arrow key to advance from one action to the next within a slide and to move from slide to slide.

   At the end of the slide show, a dialog box appears, showing the presentation's total time Ⓑ.

4. Click Yes or No to indicate whether you want to record the time for each slide (for later use in playing the slide show on automatic).

   If you click Yes, you're switched to Slide Sorter view so you can review the slide times.

> **TIP** You can immediately stop a rehearsal or slide show by pressing Esc or by clicking the Exit Show icon at the top of the screen Ⓐ.

> **TIP** You record slide show narration in a manner similar to running a rehearsal. Click the Slide Show:Presenter Tools:Record Slide Show icon or choose Slide Show > Record Narration.

Control icons

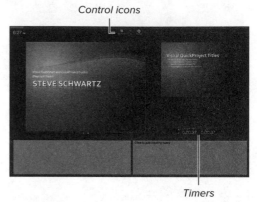

Timers

Ⓐ When rehearsing, a timer shows the time spent on the current slide and the running total for the presentation.

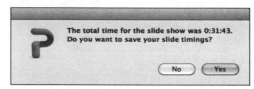

Ⓑ Choose whether to record slide timings (to use when presenting the slide show).

Using an Apple Remote

When presented on a Mac, a PowerPoint 2008 or 2011 presentation can optionally be controlled with an Apple Remote—enabling you to step through animations and slides, as well as change the volume.

After pairing a remote with the playback computer (preventing your show from being hijacked by someone else's Apple Remote), you can press buttons to step through the presentation. For more information, see "Use an Apple Remote to move through your slide show" in PowerPoint's online Help.

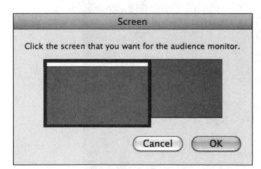

Set Up Show

Show type
- ⦿ Presented by a speaker (full screen)
- ○ Browsed by an individual (window)
- ○ Browsed at a kiosk (full screen)

Show options
- ☐ Loop continuously until 'Esc'
- ☐ Show without narration
- ☐ Show without animation

Annotation pen color: [▮▮▮ ◆]

Slides
- ⦿ All
- ○ From: [ ] To: [ ]
- ○ Custom show: [◆]

Advance slides
- ⦿ Manually
- ○ Using timings, if present

(Screen...)   (Cancel)   (OK)

A Set play options for the slide show in the Set Up Show dialog box.

Screen

Click the screen that you want for the audience monitor.

(Cancel)   (OK)

B When presenting a full-screen show with two monitors, click the Screen button **A** to select the audience's monitor.

Running a Slide Show

You can view your show at any time to get an idea of how it will look to the audience. Before finalizing it, however, consider the available play options. For example, you can manually control when slides change or allow the show to run automatically.

To set options for a slide show:

1. Click the Slide Show: Set Up: Set Up Show icon or choose Slide Show > Set Up Show.

   The Set Up Show dialog box appears **A**.

2. Specify the show type **B**, playback options, the slides to be used, and the method used to advance slides.

   You can advance each slide manually by clicking the mouse, clicking an Apple Remote, or pressing keys. Or you can show each slide for a specific amount of time (using the rehearsal timings).

3. Click check boxes in the Slide Show: Set Up group to set other options and to hide (omit) selected slides.

4. Click OK.

To view a slide show:

Do one of the following:

- To start from the beginning, choose Slide Show > Play from Start, choose View > Slide Show, or click the Slide Show: Play Slide Show: From Start icon.

- To start from a particular slide, switch to Normal or Slide Sorter view, and select the slide. Choose Slide Show > Play from Current Slide, click the Slide Show icon at the bottom of the window, or click the Slide Show: Play Slide Show: From Current Slide icon.

  Press Esc to end the show.

Using Presenter View

If you have a dual-monitor system, you can use Presenter view to assist with the presentation. The presentation appears on the audience's monitor, while tools appear on only your monitor. If you've used the Slide Show > Rehearse command (covered earlier in this chapter), you're already familiar with working in Presenter view.

To use Presenter view:

1. *Optional:* In the Displays System Preferences, enable your Mac to address two monitors by clearing the Mirror Displays check box on the Arrangement tab.

2. Switch to Presenter view **A** by choosing Slide Show > Presenter View, choosing View > Presenter View, clicking the Slide Show : Presenter Tools : Presenter View icon, or pressing Shift as you click the Slide Show icon in the bottom-left corner of the document window.

3. Use normal slide show navigation techniques to move from one slide to the next. You can also:

   ▸ Click an arrow icon to move forward or backward one animation or one slide.

   ▸ Move the cursor to the bottom of the window to reveal thumbnails of all slides in the presentation. Click a thumbnail to move directly to that slide.

4. To end the show, click the Exit Show icon, or press Esc, Command-. (period), or – (minus).

TIP Click the Tips icon at the top of the screen to view keyboard shortcuts for working in Presenter view.

TIP To time a manual show, use the Play and Reset buttons on the stopwatch. Record slide times in the notes.

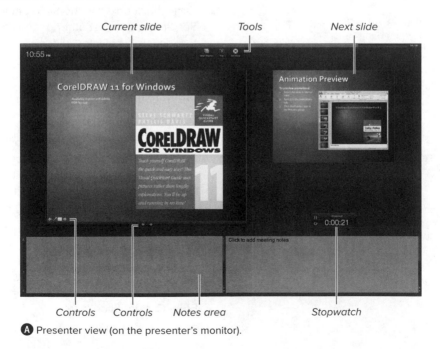

Current slide *Tools* *Next slide*

Controls *Controls* *Notes area* *Stopwatch*

A Presenter view (on the presenter's monitor).

View Full Screen

 The audience can view the broadcast in a browser. New slides and animations appear based on individual slide timings or the presenter's clicks.

Broadcasting a Presentation

In PowerPoint 2010 and 2011, you can broadcast a presentation over the Internet that invited audience members can view with a browser . PowerPoint provides two methods for broadcasting a presentation:

- To broadcast over a network, the company must use SharePoint Services 4.

- To broadcast over the Internet using the PowerPoint Broadcast Service, you must have a Windows Live or Hotmail account.

Note the following limitations:

- The PowerPoint presentation file must be smaller than 20 MB.

- Audience members must use Internet Explorer, Mozilla Firefox, or Apple's Safari browser.

- Although many animations will play correctly, all between-slide transitions will be shown as a Fade.

- Audio (sound effects, music, or narration) and movies won't be transmitted.

In this section, you'll learn to perform a Web broadcast. For information on broadcasting via SharePoint, contact your network administrator.

To broadcast a slide show using the PowerPoint Broadcast Service:

1. Open the PowerPoint presentation that you intend to broadcast.

2. In the Set Up Show dialog box and on the Slide Show tab of the Ribbon, set show options as instructed in steps 2–3 of "To set options for a slide show" earlier in this chapter.

continues on next page

3. Click the Slide Show:Play Slide Show: Broadcast Show icon.

   The Broadcast Slide Show dialog box appears 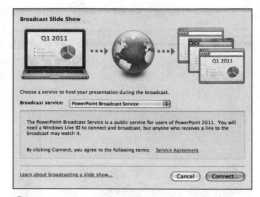.

4. Click the Connect button.

5. If a Windows Live Sign In dialog box appears **C**, enter your Windows Live or Hotmail address and password, and click Sign In to continue.

   Office connects to the PowerPoint Broadcast Service and prepares the show for broadcast. A link to the Web presentation appears **D**.

6. Do any of the following:

   ▸ **Send in E-mail.** Click Send in E-mail to generate an email message containing the link. Address the message, edit the message text as desired, and click Send.

   ▸ **Copy Link.** Click Copy Link to copy the URL to the Clipboard for pasting into an email or instant message. Instruct the recipient to paste the URL into the browser's address box. (If it's received as link text, they can simply click it.)

7. When audience members have the presentation URL opened in their browser, click Play Slide Show.

   The slide show begins **A**.

8. When the presentation is finished, click the End Broadcast button and confirm.

TIP When contacting the audience prior to beginning a broadcast, you may want to ask them to confirm they're ready by clicking Reply in response to your email announcement.

TIP Audience members can view the presentation in full-screen mode by clicking the button at the top of their browser window **A**.

B The Broadcast Slide Show dialog box.

C Enter your Windows Live or Hotmail account information and click Sign In.

D Communicate the show's URL to the audience.

Ⓐ Name the file and select a location in which to save the generated movie.

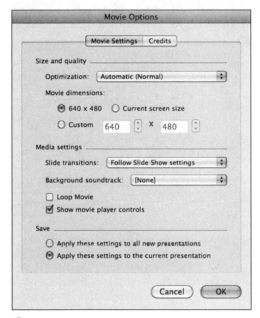

Ⓑ Review and set movie options.

Saving a Presentation as a Movie

Another way to make a presentation easily transportable is to save it as a PowerPoint (QuickTime) movie. The movie can be viewed in any QuickTime-compatible player program, such as Apple's QuickTime Player.

To save a presentation as a movie:

1. Choose File > Save as Movie.

   A Save As dialog box appears **Ⓐ**.

2. Enter a filename for the movie in the Save As text box.

3. Select a location in which to save the movie.

4. To view or change the default movie settings, click the Movie Options button.

   The Movie Options dialog box appears **Ⓑ**.

5. On the Movie Settings tab, set the movie size, quality, and playback options. You can also select a sound track, if desired.

6. On the Credits tab, record details about the presentation's creators.

7. When you've finished, click OK.

8. In the Save As dialog box **Ⓐ**, click the Save button to create the movie.

TIP Not all PowerPoint features are supported in movies. Animations are ignored and transitions may play differently, for example.

TIP Only certain file formats can be used for the sound track. When selecting a sound track, files with unsupported formats will be *grayed out* (unselectable).

Saving a Presentation to iPhoto

As of PowerPoint 2008, you can save a presentation as a series of iPhoto still images and transfer the resulting output to a video iPod for playback. To use the following step list, you must have iPhoto 6.0 or later.

To save a presentation to iPhoto:

1. Open the presentation that you want to transfer to iPhoto.

2. *Optional:* If you only want to include certain slides, switch to Slide Sorter view and select the slides.

3. Choose File > Share > Send to iPhoto.

   The Send to iPhoto dialog box appears **A**.

4. Name the new album in which the slide pictures will be stored, and choose a file format from the Format drop-down menu.

5. Click a Slides radio button to indicate whether you want to include all slides from the presentation or only those that are currently selected.

6. Click Send to iPhoto.

   Each slide is converted to a graphic and stored in the new album **B**.

7. Sync your iPod as you normally do. If iTunes isn't set to automatically sync All photos and albums, add the new album to the sync list on the Photos tab.

A Name the new iPhoto album, set output options, and click Send to iPhoto.

B The selected slides are transferred as images into the new iPhoto album.

TIP If you have a version of iPhoto older than 6.0, you can transfer your slides by choosing File > Save as Pictures. After converting the slides to image files, create a new album in iPhoto and import the files by dragging them into the album.

Introducing Outlook

In Office 2011, Outlook replaces Entourage as the mail/personal organizer application. However, if you're a long-time Entourage user, fear not. Outlook shares many of Entourage's components and capabilities while providing greater compatibility with Outlook for Windows and better Exchange support. Some Entourage features that are not found in Outlook include the Project Center, item linking, and newsgroup support.

Users new to Office may think of Outlook as an email application. But while mail handling is certainly Outlook's main function, it does much more than that. You can add personal and business contacts to Contacts, schedule appointments and meetings in the Calendar, record to-do and follow-up items in Tasks, and store important tidbits of information in Notes.

In this chapter, you'll learn about many of the tools and techniques that are used throughout Outlook. The remaining chapters in Part V are dedicated to the specific Outlook components (called *views*).

The Outlook Interface

Outlook has five components (or views). Although there are differences between views, the most important interface elements **A** (bottom) are present in all views.

View switcher. Click a view's button to switch to that view. Although you can also change views by choosing a View > Go To command, most users rely on the buttons.

Toolbar. The toolbar **B** displays icons for critical commands and is available in all views. The commands are Send & Receive All, Undo, Redo, Print (current item), launch My Day, and open Help.

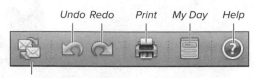

Undo Redo   Print   My Day   Help

Send & Receive All

B This toolbar is displayed at the top of each view. Component windows, such as those for new mail messages or tasks, have a different toolbar.

Navigation pane   Toolbar   Message list   Filters   Reading pane   Ribbon   Search box

View switcher   Status bar

A Elements of the Outlook interface (Mail view shown).

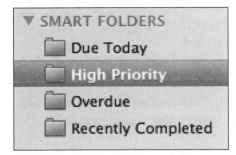

C In non-Mail views, only items that have been assigned the checked categories are displayed.

D Outlook Smart Folders serve the same function as Smart Folders in the Finder. Search criteria are set for each Smart Folder. Clicking the folder icon displays only items that satisfy the folder's criteria.

Ribbon. New in Office 2011, the Ribbon is Office's first step away from the more traditional menu-driven interface. Although you can still use menus whenever you like, most commands are also available on the Ribbon. Each view and Outlook window has its own Ribbon.

Commands within a Ribbon are divided into tabs. Within each tab, procedures are organized into groups according to similarity of function. Unlike other Office applications, Outlook's groups aren't named and are indicated only by vertical dividing lines.

To use the Ribbon, you select a tab and—within the tab—click the icon or choose the command that you want to execute.

Navigation pane. In Mail view, the navigation pane contains the folder list, displaying folders for each email account, as well as subfolders in which account mail is organized, such as Inbox and Sent Items. To view messages, the first step is to select a folder. In other views, the navigation pane presents categories that enable you to selectively display select item classes **C**.

At the bottom of the each folder list is a special folder that contains custom views called Smart Folders **D**. Select an item in this list to see only material that matches certain criteria, such as High Priority Mail, Updated Contacts, or Due Today.

Message list. In Mail view, the message list displays message headers for the mail folder selected in the folder list. You can set a new sort order for any folder's message list by clicking the Arrange By text above the list.

Reading pane. After selecting a message header in the message list, you can read it in the reading pane. If you'd like a larger reading window, you can double-click the header to open it in its own window.

Filters. Available on the Home tab in Mail and Tasks views, you can choose options from the Filters drop-down menu **E** to quickly filter the list to show only items that match the chosen criteria.

Search box. More powerful than filtering, you can type a text string into the Search box and then specify the folders to be searched. Using the Spotlight search engine, matches are returned as you type.

Outlook also supports advanced searches in which you can supply multiple criteria. For more information about displaying only certain items, see "Filtering and Searching" later in this chapter.

Status bar. Outlook status, progress, and error messages are displayed in the status bar **F**. Messages indicate when you're working offline, an IMAP folder is being updated, or there was an error attempting to send or retrieve mail from an account's mailbox, for instance.

TIP The progress of POP3 account send and receive operations isn't shown in the status bar. However, you can see them in the Progress window **G** (choose Window > Progress).

E Choose this option in Tasks view to see only tasks that are due today.

F Status messages (mainly related to email) are shown in the status bar.

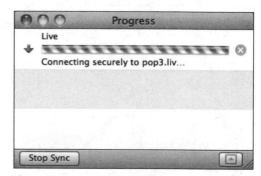

G You can watch the progress of a send/receive for any account in the Progress window.

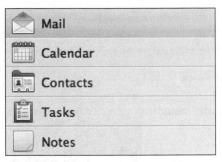

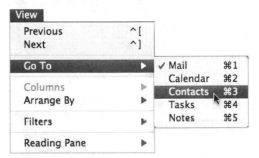

A The most common way to change views is to click a button in the view switcher.

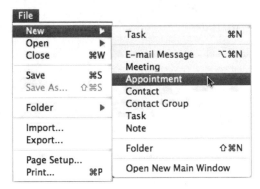

B If you prefer, you can choose a View > Go To command or press its keyboard shortcut.

C You can create a new item of any type without switching views.

Navigating Outlook

As mentioned in the previous section, Outlook has five components called views. To examine, open, or change items in a view, you begin by switching to the view.

To switch to a different view:

Do one of the following:

- Click a button in the view switcher **A**.
- Choose a command from the View > Go To submenu **B**.
- Press the view's keyboard shortcut **B** (Command-1 through Command-5).

TIP If all you want to do is create a new item, it isn't necessary to switch to the appropriate view. You can choose a command from the File > New submenu **C** or the Home:New menu.

Outlook and the Toolbox

Although used less frequently and containing fewer tabs than in Word, PowerPoint, or Excel, the Toolbox **A** is also available in Outlook. You can use it to accomplish the following tasks:

- **Scrapbook.** Paste stored material into email messages and notes, and store copied Outlook material for pasting into future items (such as email) or into other Office documents.

- **Reference Tools.** Improve your writing by looking up definitions and synonyms, translating terms and phrases, and performing Web searches. Enter a term or phrase in the search box, press Return, and then expand the panes that you want to consult, such as Dictionary or Translation.

To open the Toolbox:

Choose a tab from the Tools > Toolbox submenu. The following occurs:

- If the Toolbox is closed, it opens and displays the chosen tab.

- If the Toolbox is open and another tab is active, the chosen tab is displayed.

- If the Toolbox is open and you chose the current tab, the Toolbox closes.

> **TIP** These Toolbox tabs, as well as those available only in Word, PowerPoint, or Excel, are discussed throughout the book.

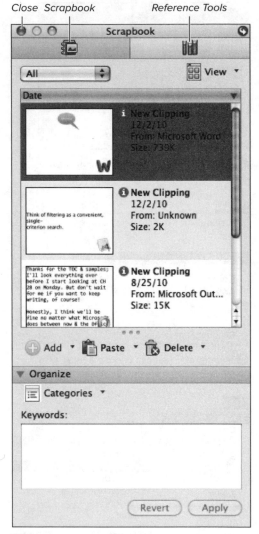

A In Outlook, the Toolbox provides access to the Scrapbook and Reference Tools.

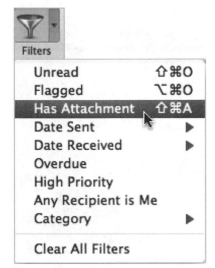

A Mail view filters allow you to quickly display important classes of messages.

B Only messages with attachments (denoted by a paper-clip icon) are shown.

C The state of these check boxes determines whether flagged, overdue, or completed tasks are shown or hidden. They work in conjunction with any filters you've applied.

Filtering and Searching

To simplify the process of finding an email message, event, task, or other Outlook item, you can search or filter in a variety of ways. The usefulness of the techniques described in this section is greater in views in which you've amassed a lot of items, such as Mail, Contacts, or Calendar view.

Filtering mail or tasks

Think of filtering as a criterion-based search—as contrasted with the more familiar keyword-based search. After applying a filter, only items that match the criterion are shown; all others are hidden. In Mail and Tasks views, the filter control is found on the Home tab.

To filter a list:

1. Switch to Mail or Tasks.

2. If filtering email, select an account folder in the folder list.

3. Select a filter type from the Filter icon's drop-down menu **A** (also see **E** in "The Outlook Interface").

   The message list or tasks list shows only items that match the criterion **B**.

4. *Optional:* To further restrict the results, choose additional criteria. The effect of adding criteria is cumulative.

5. When you're finished, you can restore the list by choosing Home : Filters : Clear All Filters or clicking the Filters icon **A**.

TIP To remove the effect of an individual filter, choose its command again from the Filters drop-down menu.

TIP In Tasks view, three critical filters can be controlled via check box settings **C**.

To filter a list by category:

1. Do one of the following:

   ▸ **Mail view.** In the navigation pane, select the account folder you wish to filter. Choose one or more categories to display from the Home : Filters : Category submenu **A**.

   ▸ **Any other view.** In the navigation pane, check only the boxes of the categories that you want to display **D**.

   TIP To quickly clear or select *all* check boxes, click the main check box.

   Only items or Calendar events that have been assigned at least one of the chosen categories are displayed.

2. To restore the full item list or Calendar, do one of the following:

   ▸ **Mail view.** Choose Home : Filters : Clear All Filters or click the Filters icon **A**.

   ▸ **Any other view.** Click the main check box in the navigation pane (Calendar, Address Book, Tasks, or Notes) to enable all categories **D**.

TIP If you use categories extensively, you can view all uncategorized items by clicking only the No Category check box **D** (any view other than Mail) or by choosing None from the Home : Filters : Category submenu (Mail).

TIP You can specify which categories to list in the navigation pane. Choose Outlook > Preferences and click the Categories icon in the Outlook Preferences dialog box. Only the checked categories **E** will appear in the navigation pane. You can also use this Preferences dialog box to rename categories, as well as add or delete categories (by clicking the + and – icons, respectively).

Main check box

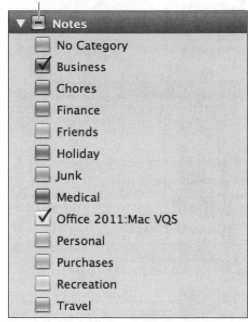

D Only items that have been assigned the Business and/or the Office 2011:Mac VQS category will be visible in the Notes list.

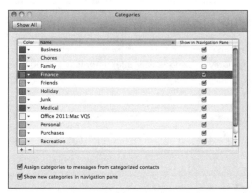

E The Categories section of Outlook Preferences.

Search string   *Clear*

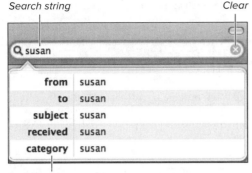

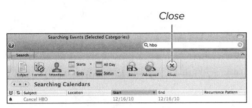

Search fields

F Outlook searches for matches as you type. To restrict the search to a specific field, select it in the drop-down list.

Close

G Outlook displays all matches. For more detail, you can double-click an item to open it in its own window.

Folder   Subfolders   All Mail   All Items

H To change the scope of the search, click an icon in this group on the Search contextual tab.

Performing a basic Find

You perform a basic search by typing a string in the Search box at the top of the Outlook window. By default, all relevant fields are searched, but—if you're quick— you can limit the search to a specific field.

To perform a basic Find:

1. Click in the Search box or choose Edit > Find > Outlook Items.

The Search box is selected, as well as the Search contextual tab.

2. If the Search box contains text from the most recent search, delete it or click the Clear button (X).

3. Type or paste search text into the box. To restrict the search to a particular Item field, click the field in the list that appears **F**.

As you type, Outlook finds and displays all matching items **G**.

4. When you've done examining matches, click the Clear button **F** or the Close icon **G** on the Search contextual tab.

The Search area is cleared and the item list is restored.

> **TIP** Be creative when typing search strings. The text doesn't have to be found at the beginning of items, and you don't have to enter a complete word.

> **TIP** You can search for a category by typing its name or color, such as Medical or red.

> **TIP** By default, every search assumes that you want to restrict the search to the current folder selected in the navigation pane. To change the scope of the search, click a different icon **H**. The icons vary slightly, depending on the active view.

Performing an Advanced Find

A basic Find considers every element and field when identifying matches. If you want to set specific or multiple criteria, build a query using the Advanced Find command.

To perform an Advanced Find:

1. In the folder list (Mail only), select the account folder or subfolder to search.

2. Do either of the following:

   ▶ Choose Edit > Find > Advanced Find. The Search contextual tab appears and is selected **I**. The initial search field is added to the query.

   ▶ Click in the search box. The Search contextual tab appears and is selected **I**. Click a criterion icon to add the first search field to the query.

   TIP If the desired criterion isn't on the Search tab, select any criterion. You can edit any criterion as needed.

3. Specify the first criterion by selecting options from drop-down menus and, if required, typing in a text box **J**.

4. *Optional:* To add another criterion, click the plus (+) icon **J**. Repeat as needed.

   An item must satisfy all criteria to be considered a match. As you add criteria, the match list is continuously updated.

5. When you've finished examining the matches, click the Close icon **I** to restore the item list.

   TIP To remove a criterion, click the minus (–) icon to its right **J**.

   TIP To change the scope, click an icon **H**.

   TIP You can switch from Find to Advanced Find by clicking any criterion icon on the Search contextual tab.

Search contextual tab   *Close*

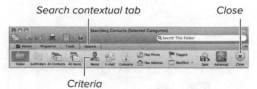

Criteria

I When building an Advanced Find query, criteria can be selected by clicking icons on the Search tab. Available criteria differ for each Outlook view.

Add

Remove

J Create each criterion by choosing options from the drop-down menus and/or typing.

Close Find Next   Search string

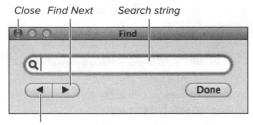

Find Previous

K Use the Find dialog box to search for matching text within an item.

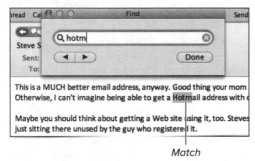

Match

L Outlook searches the item as you type the search string. The first matching instance (if any) is automatically highlighted.

Searching within an item

You can also search within the text portion of any Outlook item. Although handy for searching within lengthy email messages, it can also be useful within notes, the text or comment section of Calendar and Tasks items, and the Notes tab of Contacts records.

To search within an item:

1. Do one of the following:

    ▸ If searching within an email message, select the item in the message list or open it in its own window.

    ▸ If searching within another type of Outlook item, its notes area must be visible. Open the item in its own window or display the notes area in the reading pane.

2. Choose Edit > Find > Find (Command-F).

    The Find dialog box appears **K**.

3. Type a search string.

    Outlook scans the item as you type. If the string is found, the first instance is highlighted **L**.

4. To locate additional instances of the search string, click the Find Next button.

    When the bottom of the item is reached, the search wraps around to the start.

5. To dismiss the Find dialog box, click its red close button or click Done.

Performing a Spotlight search

You can also use Mac OS X's Spotlight to find Outlook items. You can perform Spotlight searches from the Desktop and within file dialog boxes to locate email, events, appointments, tasks, contact records, and other Outlook items. OS X indexes every file stored on connected drives and makes their filenames and contents eligible for Spotlight searches.

To perform a Spotlight search:

1. Type the search string in any Spotlight search box.

   Spotlight lists matches as you type **Ⓜ**.

2. Do one of the following:

   ▸ If you see the Outlook item, double-click it to open it in Outlook.

   ▸ Click Show All to display all matches in a new window **Ⓝ**. Double-click any item to open it.

TIP You can perform a Spotlight search even when Outlook isn't running. If you double-click an Outlook item in Spotlight, Outlook will automatically launch to display the item.

Show All Search box Spotlight icon

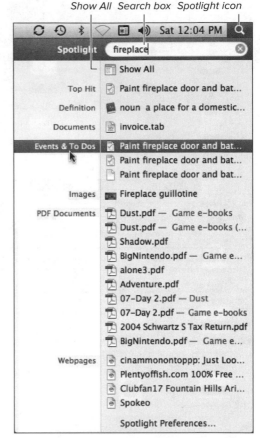

Ⓜ You can perform a Spotlight search by clicking the Spotlight icon in the corner of the menu bar.

Ⓝ When you click Show All **Ⓜ**, a new Finder window opens and displays all matches.

Email

Since electronic mail (*email*) first became available, it has been the centerpiece of most people's Internet use. Outlook is the Office 2011 application that handles your email needs. Using Outlook, you can exchange messages with anyone who has an email address, attach files to messages, and organize incoming and outgoing mail.

In addition to email, Outlook can manage your contacts (Chapter 22), schedule (Chapter 23), to-do list (Chapter 24), and notes (Chapter 25).

Although the general information in this chapter applies to every account type, see your network administrator or Outlook Help for additional instructions on setting up and using a Microsoft Exchange account.

In This Chapter

Setting up an Account

In order to use email, you need an account with an Internet service provider (ISP). The literature you received with your account generally tells whether they support *POP* (Post Office Protocol) or *IMAP* (Internet Message Access Protocol) for email. (Many Web-based services, such as Hotmail and Gmail, also provide POP or IMAP support, enabling you to manage the accounts with Outlook.) The final account type is *Exchange* (Microsoft Exchange Server), used by many corporations.

Your first step in setting up Outlook as an email client is to import information from your current email accounts or create a new Outlook account for each one. If your old accounts weren't imported from Entourage when you first ran Outlook or you've just created a new email account, follow the steps below to add the account.

To add a POP or IMAP account:

1. Choose Tools > Accounts.

   The Accounts dialog box appears.

2. To add the account, click the plus (+) icon beneath the left pane and choose E-mail from the drop-down menu .

   A panel appears 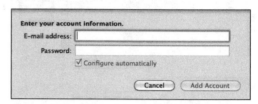.

3. Enter your full email address in the form

   username@domain

   such as **bob723@msn.com**.

4. Tab into the Password field.

   One of the following occurs:

   ▸ If Outlook recognizes the domain (such as AOL, Hotmail, Windows Live, MSN, Yahoo, or Gmail, for example), the pane remains unchanged. Enter the account password and click Add Account.

A Choose E-mail to add the account.

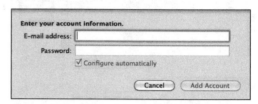

B Common accounts can often be added by entering only the email address and password.

Adding an Exchange Account

If you have an an Exchange account with your company or institution, configuring the account in Outlook is similar to adding a POP or IMAP account:

1. Click the plus (+) icon beneath the left pane and choose Exchange from the drop-down menu **A**.

2. Enter your email address and password in the boxes provided.

3. Enter your user name in the form

   domain\account ID

4. Ensure that Configure automatically is checked, and click Add Account.

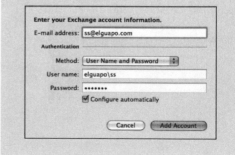

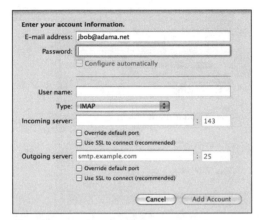

C If Outlook doesn't recognize the account's domain, you'll have to configure it manually.

Menu icon

D Select an account in the left pane, and click the menu icon to set it as your default email account.

About Account Synchronization

With certain types of accounts, Outlook maintains a constant synchronization (or *sync*) between the data stored in Outlook and the data on your service provider's servers.

- **Exchange accounts.** Email messages, calendar events, contacts, tasks, and notes are kept in sync.

- **IMAP accounts.** Only email is kept in sync. Other Outlook data that you create is stored only on your Mac.

- **POP accounts.** No synchronization occurs. Once delivered to your Mac, POP email is automatically deleted from the mail server (unless you specify in the account's settings that copies are to remain on the server).

▶ If Outlook *doesn't* recognize the domain, the window expands **C**. Enter the account password and other requested information. Click Add Account.

The account is added as a new account.

TIP *User name* is either the full email address or the part that precedes the @ symbol.

5. Select the new account in the left pane, review the account information, and make any necessary changes:

- ▶ In the Account description box, enter a descriptive name for the account. This is how it will be identified to you in the navigation pane and menus.

- ▶ In the Full name box, enter your name or how you want you want to be identified to recipients of your messages.

- ▶ Verify/enter the incoming and outgoing mail servers. You can get this information from your ISP, company, or institution.

6. *Optional:* Review advanced account settings by clicking the Advanced button.

7. Close the Accounts window by clicking its red close button.

TIP If you have multiple accounts, make one the default (primary) account. Select the account name in the Accounts dialog box and choose Set as Default from the menu icon beneath the left pane **D**. When you create a new email message, it's assumed that you want to send it using the default account.

TIP To review or change an account's settings, select its name in the Accounts window.

TIP To delete an account (one that no longer exists or which you no longer want to track in Outlook), select its name in the Accounts window and click the minus (–) icon beneath the left pane **A**.

Creating and Sending Mail

One of the most basic functions of email is that of creating and sending messages.

To create and send an email message:

1. Do one of the following:

   ▸ From the Mail section of Outlook, click the Home:E-mail icon, choose Home:New > E-mail Message **Ⓐ**, choose File > New > E-mail Message, or press Command-N.

   ▸ From any Outlook section, choose Home:New > E-mail Message **Ⓐ**, choose File > New > E-mail Message, or press Option-Command-N.

   A new message window appears **Ⓑ**, addressed from your default account.

2. *Optional:* Select a different account from the From drop-down list.

3. In the To box, specify the email address to which you want to send the message by doing one of the following:

   ▸ Type or paste an email address.

   ▸ If the individual is in your Contacts or you've recently received mail from her or him, begin typing the name or email address. As you type, Outlook lists matching names and addresses from which you can select **Ⓒ**.

4. *Optional:* Enter additional To addresses by repeating step 3.

5. *Optional:* You can also include recipients in the Cc (carbon copy) or Bcc (blind carbon copy) boxes. Click in the appropriate box and follow steps 3–4.

6. Enter a Subject to identify the message.

Ⓐ Choose E-mail Message from the New icon's menu.

Address pane   Standard toolbar   Ribbon

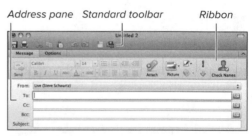

Ⓑ The top of the message window contains the Standard toolbar, Ribbon, and the address pane.

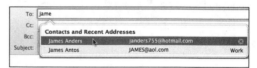

Ⓒ As you type, Outlook displays a list of possible matches. If you don't see the correct name or address, continue typing.

Creating Messages Offline

If you create and try to send a message while working offline, it will be placed in your Outbox. The next time you connect to the Internet, the message will be sent.

Send

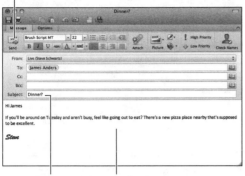

Subject   Message body

D To finish the process, enter the message text.

E If you close a new message without sending or saving it, you can optionally save it as a draft.

F Click this icon to toggle between an HTML and a plain text message.

Using the Address Book Icon

When addressing a message, you can click the Address Book icon to the right of the To, Cc, or Bcc box to search for an address in Contacts.

In the Contacts Search window, enter part of the recipient's name or another detail that might be in the Contacts record. Matches are identified as you type. Click the To, Cc, or Bcc button at the bottom of the match to add the person as a recipient.

7. Move the text insertion mark into the message box by clicking in the box or by pressing Tab. Type the message **D**.

8. Do one of the following:

   ▸ **Send Now.** To send the message immediately, click the Message:Send icon or press Command-Enter.

   ▸ **Save as Draft.** If you want to edit the message before sending it or delay its sending, close the message. Click Save as Draft in the dialog box that appears **E**. The message will be stored in the Drafts folder until you open, edit, and send it.

   Sent messages are automatically stored in the account's Sent Items folder.

TIP Entries in the Cc box represent secondary recipients—people whom you want to receive a copy of the message. Bcc people are "invisible" recipients—that is, no To or Cc recipient will know that a Bcc recipient also received the message. (If the Bcc box isn't displayed, click the Options:Bcc icon.)

TIP Another way to save the current message as a draft is to choose File > Save (Command-S) and then close the message window.

TIP Messages can be composed and sent as plain text (single font, no formatting) or formatted text. To create a formatted message, click the Options:Format icon and ensure that HTML is displayed **F**. To set a default format for new messages, click the Composing icon in Outlook Preferences. The state of the Compose messages in HTML by default check box determines whether plain text or HTML messages will automatically be created.

TIP Depending on the checked commands in the Edit > Spelling and Grammar submenu, Outlook may automatically mark potential spelling errors as you type and also check for grammatical errors. For instructions, see "Checking Spelling," later in this chapter.

Sending Attachments

In addition to sending text messages, you can optionally attach files to any message. The files can be any type, such as pictures, word processing documents, worksheets, or even programs. When sent with email, these files are known as *attachments*.

To attach a file to a message:

1. Click the Message:Attach icon, choose Draft > Attachments > Add, or press Command-E.

   A file panel drops down .

2. Select a file (or Command-click to select multiple files) from a folder, and then click Choose.

   The file(s) are added as attachments 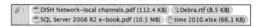.

3. If desired, repeat steps 1–2 to add other attachments from the same or a different folder.

4. Send the message by clicking Send.

TIP You can add attachments at any point during the message-creation process.

TIP To remove an attachment, select it in the Attachments list and press Delete. You can also right-click any attachment and choose Remove or Remove All from the contextual menu that appears.

TIP Image files in most formats can be inserted directly into a message using drag and drop. Simply drag the image's file icon onto the message body 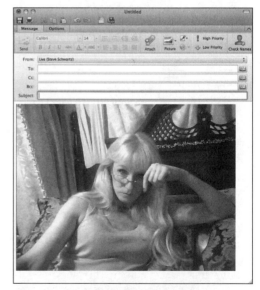. A plus (+) cursor appears when it's over the message body.

TIP If you drag a non-image file into a message window (such as a Word document or PDF file), the material is automatically added as a file attachment.

A Navigate to the correct folder and select one or more files to attach to the message.

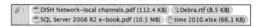

B When you add an attachment, an Attachments box appears at the bottom of the address pane.

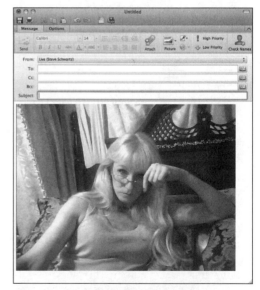

C If you want a recipient to immediately see an image file, you can insert it directly into the message body rather than adding it as an attachment.

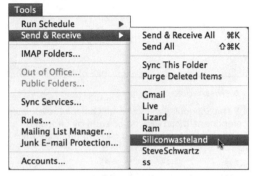

(A) The Send/Receive icon can be found in the Ribbon and on the Standard toolbar (shown here).

(B) You can also perform a general or selective Send/Receive by choosing a command from the Tools menu (shown) or the Home : Send/Receive icon's menu.

The Progress Window

The Progress window (Window > Progress or Command-7) shows the progress of each account send/receive. When closed, send/receive progress—for IMAP and Exchange accounts only—is shown in the status bar.

Send/Receive Errors

Occasionally, errors occur while attempting to send or receive mail. Outlook notifies you of such problems by displaying a yellow alert triangle in the status bar.

To determine the nature of the error(s), click the alert icon or the Tools : Errors icon. Review each error in the Errors window, and click the Delete icon or press Delete to dismiss each one. Close the Errors window when you're finished.

Incoming Email

You can check for new email manually or automatically. To check automatically, you need to define one or more schedules. A *schedule* specifies the circumstances under which Outlook will check for new mail, accounts that will be checked, and when the checks will occur. In this section, you'll learn how to manually check for new mail and on an automatic, repeating schedule.

To check for new email manually:

Do any of the following:

- Click the Home : Send/Receive icon or the icon on the Standard toolbar **(A)** to perform a send and receive for all email accounts that you've associated with the Send & Receive All schedule.

- Click the down arrow beside the Home : Send/Receive icon. Choose Send & Receive All or the name of a specific account (to perform a send/receive only for that account).

- Choose Tools > Send & Receive > Send & Receive All (Command-K) to perform a send/receive for all email accounts that you've associated with the Send & Receive All schedule or choose the name of a specific email account to check **(B)**.

TIP Send & Receive All is a built-in schedule that is provided to help you check for new mail in your primary accounts.

TIP It isn't necessary to add Exchange or IMAP accounts to schedules or to perform manual Send/Receives for them. As long as you're connected to the Exchange or IMAP server, these accounts are automatically updated once every minute.

To automatically check for new mail on a repeating schedule:

1. Choose Tools : Schedules > Edit Schedules or Tools > Run Schedule > Edit Schedules.

   The Schedules preferences appear **C**.

2. Click the plus (+) icon to create a new schedule.

   The Edit Schedule dialog box appears **D**.

3. Name the schedule in the Name box.

4. Choose Repeating Schedule from the drop-down menu in the When section, and specify a time interval and unit **E**.

5. If you want this schedule to run only when you're connected to the Internet, click the Only if connected check box.

6. Choose Receive Mail and an account from the menus in the Action section **E**.

7. If you have additional email accounts you'd like to check on the same schedule, click Add Action and set this action to Receive Mail, as you did for the email account specified in step 6.

8. In the Dial-up options section, select Stay connected—unless you want to immediately disconnect after each receive.

9. Be sure that Enabled is checked, and click OK.

   The Schedules dialog box reappears and includes the new schedule. Whenever Outlook is running, it will check for and receive messages from the specified accounts at the designated interval. (Note that you can still perform manual send/receives.)

TIP To edit a schedule, double-click its name in the Schedules dialog box. To remove a schedule, select it and click the minus (−) icon.

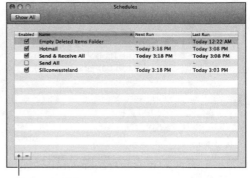

New schedule

C The Schedules window is an Outlook Preferences component. It can also be opened by choosing Outlook > Preferences and clicking the Schedules icon.

When schedule will run   Schedule name

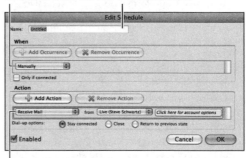

Actions to be performed

D Create and edit schedules in the Edit Schedule dialog box.

Interval   Time unit

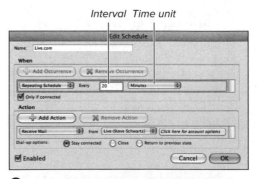

E When creating a repeating schedule, you must choose an interval and unit.

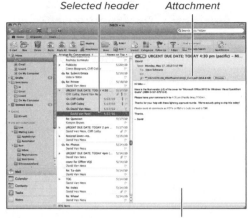

Selected header   Attachment

Reading pane

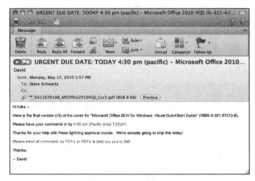

F Select a header in the message list to read the message in the reading pane.

G You can also view a message in its own window.

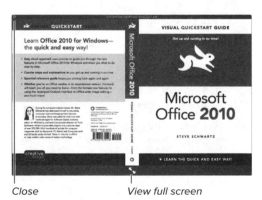

Close   View full screen

H You can view certain types of attachments, such as this PDF, by clicking the Preview button.

To read a message:

1. In Mail, select an email account folder in the navigation pane.

2. Do either of the following:
   - To view the message in the reading pane **F**, select a message header in the message list.
   - Open the message in its own window by double-clicking its header **G**.

3. Use the vertical scroll bar or press the spacebar to scroll a lengthy message.

TIP The reading pane can be placed below or to the right of the message list. Choose a position from the View > Reading Pane submenu.

To manage received attachments:

1. When you view or open a message with attachments (indicated by a paper clip icon), it displays an Attachments list **G**.

2. *Optional:* To manage a single attachment, select it in the Attachments list.

3. Do either of the following:
   - Choose a command from Message > Attachments submenu to preview, save, or delete the attachment. Or right-click any attachment and choose a command from the contextual menu.
   - Double-click an attachment to open it in its native program, such as Preview.

TIP You can also save an attachment by dragging its file icon from the message onto the Desktop.

TIP Unlike Entourage, Outlook only displays image files that have been inserted into the message body—not attachments. If you have Snow Leopard, you can preview image and certain other attachments by clicking the Preview All button. To preview a single attachment, select it and click the Preview button **H**.

Replying to Email

There are several ways to reply to received email. This section explains the options.

To reply to a message:

1. Select the header in the message list or open the message in its own window.

2. Click the Home:Reply (or Message: Reply) icon, choose Message > Reply, or press Command-R.

   A message window opens, addressed to the author. The Subject is the original one preceded by **Re:** (for reply) **Ⓐ**.

3. Type your reply text, and click the Message:Send icon to send the message.

> **TIP** By default, the entire original message is quoted when a reply is generated. However, it's polite to quote only relevant parts. You can delete any unnecessary text from the original message.

> **TIP** Another option is to select the text that you want to quote and then issue the Reply command. Only the selected text will be quoted in the reply.

> **TIP** To specify default behaviors to use when replying to messages, choose Outlook > Preferences and click the Composing category **Ⓑ**.

Subject: | Re: awake yet?

Ⓐ This is a reply to a message with the Subject *awake yet?* Because Outlook and other email clients track conversations based on the Subject, it's best not to modify the Subject when replying.

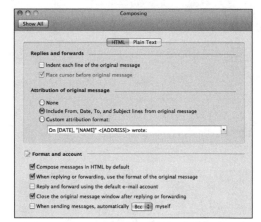

Ⓑ Specify formatting defaults for replies and forwarded messages in Composing Preferences. Note that they're set separately for HTML and Plain Text messages by clicking the tabs.

Three Reply Commands

There are actually three Reply commands. Although you'll usually use Reply, there are occasions in which you should use the other Reply commands:

- **Reply.** Use when replying only to the person who sent the message to you.

- **Reply to All.** Reply to the message author, as well as to all others listed in the To and Cc lines.

- **Reply to Sender.** When replying to a message from a mailing list, this command allows you to address the reply to the message author rather than to all list subscribers.

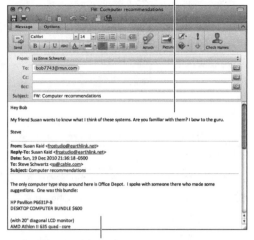

Added text

Forwarded text

Ⓐ This is an example of a forwarded message.

📎 : 🗐 Last chance 2 for 1 FileMaker Pro offer.eml (21.2 KB)

Ⓑ You can also forward a message as an attachment rather than as quoted text.

The Missing Redirect and Resend Commands

The purpose of a Redirect command is to forward received email to someone else who you feel should have been the recipient—your supervisor or a different department head, for example. When redirecting email, you can't alter or add to the message, the email appears to have come from the original sender, and any replies go to that sender.

Similarly, the Resend command is useful when a recipient reports that he or she didn't receive a message or you want to send a previously sent message to additional people.

Although Entourage supported Redirect and Resend, Outlook 2011 currently does not. Your best bet is to simply forward the message to the appropriate people.

Forwarding Messages

If you receive mail that you want to send to others, you can *forward* it. When you forward mail, you can add your own comments, the recipients see a message that came from you, and replies will go to you.

To forward email:

1. With the message selected in the message list or open in its own window, click the Home:Forward icon, choose Message > Forward, or press Command-J.

2. Enter the addresses to which you want to forward the message.

3. By default, the Subject is the original subject preceded by **FW:** (such as, FW: Today's Joke). You can edit the Subject, if you like.

4. *Optional:* Add an introductory note to the message body, edit the forwarded text, and/or add attachments.

5. Click the Message:Send icon to forward the message to the recipients **Ⓐ**.

TIP Because a forwarded message is in essence the beginning of a new conversation, you can freely edit the Subject, if you like.

TIP You can forward email to yourself. For instance, if you receive an important message in a secondary email account (such as Hotmail, Gmail, or Yahoo! Mail), you can forward it to your ISP account. If you ever need to refer to the message again, you won't have to guess the account in which it's stored.

TIP You can also forward a message as an attachment. Select the header in the message list and choose Message > Forward Special > As Attachment. A new message window appears. Instead of quoting the original text, it's included as an attached file **Ⓑ**.

Checking Spelling

Because Office's spelling checker is available to all Office applications, even the poorest spellers can avoid embarrassing misspellings and typos in their messages. Spell-checking options are enabled in the bottom of the Edit > Spelling and Grammar submenu Ⓐ. The options are:

- **Check Spelling While Typing.** As you type, Outlook marks each suspect word with a dotted red underline.

- **Check Grammar With Spelling.** Grammatical errors are marked as you type with a green dashed underline or flagged during routine spelling checks.

- **Correct Spelling Automatically.** Using AutoCorrect, common misspellings are automatically fixed as you type.

To set or change these options, create a new message and choose commands from the Spelling and Grammar submenu.

To fix an "as you type" error:

You can correct an "as you type" error Ⓑ by doing one of the following:

- **Ignore.** If you're sure that the word is spelled correctly, you can ignore it.

- **Edit.** If you know the correct spelling, edit the word. If the revised word is in Office's spelling dictionaries, the wavy red underline will disappear.

- **Spell check.** Right-click the word to display spelling options Ⓒ. Choose a suggested replacement (if one is listed), choose Ignore Spelling to instruct the spelling checker to ignore all instances of the word in this message, or choose Learn Spelling to accept the spelling and add it to your custom dictionary.

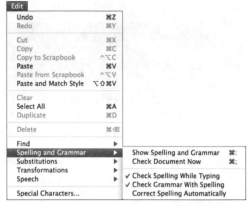

Ⓐ The Edit > Spelling and Grammar submenu.

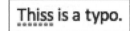

Ⓑ Suspect words are marked in this manner.

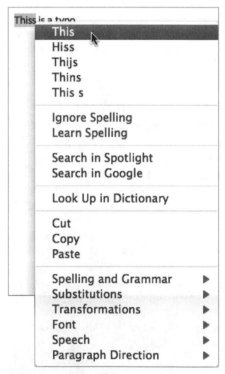

Ⓒ You can correct misspellings by right-clicking the word and choosing an option from the contextual menu.

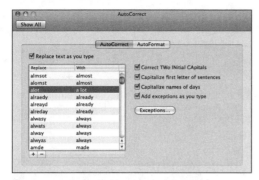

D The AutoCorrect list contains words that are commonly misspelled or incorrectly typed.

Suspect word   Options: Spelling icon

E Performing a manual spelling check.

The Dictionary and Thesaurus

Office includes a dictionary and thesaurus among its tools. If you want to improve your writing by ensuring that you're using the correct word or by substituting a different word or phrase for the current one, you can use these tools. To open the Toolbox and consult the dictionary or thesaurus, click the Options: Reference icon. To look up a word or phrase in Mac OS X's built-in Dictionary application, right-click the word and choose Look Up in Dictionary.

To manage AutoCorrect settings:

1. Choose Outlook > Preferences, and click the Personal Settings: AutoCorrect icon **D**.

2. In the AutoCorrect window, remove check marks from options you don't require.

3. To add a word to the AutoCorrect list, click the plus (**+**) icon, and type the incorrect word and its proper spelling in the blank entry provided.

4. Close the AutoCorrect window.

To perform a routine spelling check:

1. Initiate a spelling check by clicking the Options: Spelling icon in the message window or choosing Edit > Spelling and Grammar > Show Spelling and Grammar.

   The Spelling and Grammar dialog box appears. If a suspect word is found, the word is shown in the dialog box and selected in the message **E**.

2. Do one of the following:

   ▸ If the correct spelling is shown in the Suggestions list, select it and click Change.

   ▸ Correct the spelling by editing the word in the top box and clicking Change.

   ▸ Click Ignore to skip the word, leaving its spelling unchanged.

   ▸ If the word is spelled correctly, click Learn to add it to Office's custom dictionary so it will be ignored in future spelling checks.

   The next suspected mistake (if any) is displayed in the box and highlighted in the document.

3. Repeat step 2 for each additional error.

4. When you've dealt with the final error, close the dialog box.

Organizing the Mail

When you start receiving a significant amount of email, you'll want to organize it. Outlook provides several tools for this purpose:

- You can organize mail in folders that you've created. You can create subfolders of any existing account folder in the navigation pane or additional folders at the same level as an existing folder.

- You can categorize messages, and then sort or filter the message list based on assigned categories. (Filtering is covered in Chapter 20.)

- After reading messages, you can delete those that aren't important.

- You can define rules that take specific actions when messages matching your criteria are received.

To create a new subfolder or folder:

Do either of the following:

- To create a subfolder of a selected account folder, choose Home : New > Folder, choose File > New > Folder, or press Shift-Command-N.

- To create a folder at the same level as a selected account folder, press Shift-Option-Command-N.

  Rename the Untitled Folder .

TIP Many folder-related commands can be performed by right-clicking the folder in the navigation pane and choosing from the contextual menu that appears.

A In this example, I've created a subfolder of my Live folder. Rename the new folder by typing over the placeholder text.

Using Identities

If several people use Office on your Mac, you can create multiple identities so you can share Office while keeping your email and Office documents separate from theirs. You can also use identities to distinguish home and business email.

You create new identities and switch among them by running the Microsoft Database Utility in the Microsoft Office 2011 : Office folder. To switch identities, you must first close Outlook. (The Microsoft Database Utility can also used to rebuild the Outlook database, when necessary.)

To Protect Your Privacy...

Occasionally, an incoming message will display a yellow bar near the top, informing you: "To protect your privacy, some pictures in this message were not downloaded." The images referred to were not embedded in the message; they are links to images on a Web site (generally, the sender's site).

Because spammers can use such links to determine if your email address is a real one, Outlook automatically blocks the download of linked images. However, if you trust the site, you can click the Download pictures button to complete the message and display the missing images.

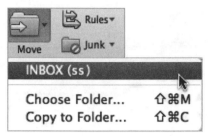

B You can choose a recently used folder as the destination from the Home:Move menu.

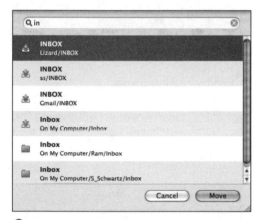

C Type the first few characters of the destination folder's name, select the folder, and click Move.

Manually Marking Messages as Unread or Read

Having read a message, Outlook marks it as read by removing the boldface from its Subject. If the message is important and you don't want to hunt for it later, you can manually change its status to unread by clicking the Home:Unread icon.

Similarly, you can mark unimportant messages as read without reading them by clicking the Home:Read icon. To simultaneously mark all messages in a folder as read, click the Organize:All Read icon.

To move email to another folder:

1. In the navigation pane, select the account folder that contains the message(s) you want to move.

2. Select the message(s) to be moved.

   To select multiple messages, Command-click each one.

3. Do one of the following:

   ▸ Choose a recent folder from the Message > Move submenu or the Home:Move menu **B**.

   ▸ To select the destination from all possible account folders, choose Home:Move > Choose Folder **B** or Message > Move > Choose Folder, right-click a message header and choose Move > Choose Folder, or press Shift-Command-M. In the panel that appears **C**, type the first character or two of the destination folder's name, select the folder, and click Move.

TIP To copy a message rather than move it, choose the Copy to Folder command **B**.

TIP You can also use drag and drop to move or copy messages between folders. When dragged between folders of the same account, the messages are moved. When dragged between folders of different accounts, the messages are copied.

TIP To delete a user-created folder, right-click the folder and choose Delete, select the folder and click the Home:Delete icon, or select the folder and choose Edit > Delete.

To assign categories to messages:

1. Select one or more messages to which you want to assign the same category.

2. Do one of the following:

   ▸ Choose a category from the Home : Categorize menu 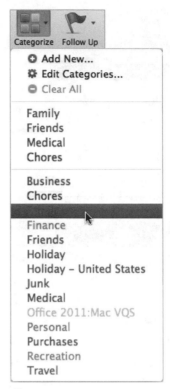 or the Message > Categorize submenu.

   ▸ Right-click a message header. In the contextual menu that appears, choose a category from the Categorize submenu.

3. Repeat step 2 to assign additional categories to the selected message(s).

TIP You can assign categories to messages selected in a message list or to a message that's open in its own window.

TIP To remove all categories assigned to a message, select Clear All **D**. To clear individual categories from the message, select those categories again.

TIP If you assign a category to a record in Contacts, future email from or to the contact will automatically be assigned that category. To disable this automatic message categorization, open Categories preferences and remove the check mark from **Assign categories to messages from categorized contacts**.

D The Home : Categorize menu,

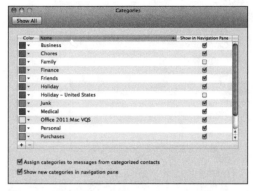

E The Categories preferences window.

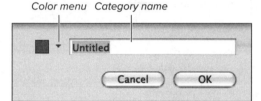

F Name the new category, choose a color, and click OK.

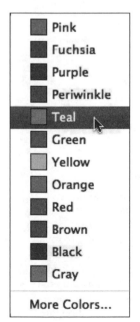

G The color menu.

To modify the category list:

1. Do either of the following:
   - ▸ Choose Edit Categories from the Home:Categorize menu **D** or the Message > Categorize submenu.
   - ▸ Choose Outlook > Preferences, and click the Personal Settings:Categories icon.

   The Categories preferences window appears **E**.

2. To create a new category, click the plus (+) icon beneath the list. An Untitled category appears **F**.

3. Name the category, choose a color by clicking the color icon beside its name **G**, and click OK.

4. To rename an existing category, click its name. Doing so allows the name to be edited.

5. To change a category's color, choose a color from the Color drop-down menu beside its name **G**. Choose More Colors to assign a custom color.

6. To delete a selected category, click the minus (–) icon beneath the list, and confirm the deletion in the dialog box that appears.

7. When you're done making changes, close the Categories window.

CAUTION Try not to duplicate category colors. Although you aren't prohibited from using a color twice, it will make it more difficult for you to quickly distinguish items based on color.

To sort the messages in a folder:

1. Select an account folder in the navigation pane.

2. Do one of the following:

   ▸ If the reading pane is to the right of the message list, click the Arrange By heading above the message list and choose the data on which you want to sort 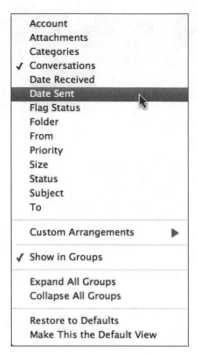.

   To toggle between an ascending and descending sort, click the text to the right of Arrange By, such as Newest on Top.

TIP You can also choose the sort field from the Organize:Arrange By or the View > Arrange By menu.

   ▸ If the reading pane is below the message list or hidden **I**, click a column heading to sort by that column. (The current sort column's heading is blue.)

   To toggle between an ascending and descending sort, click the heading again. You can rearrange columns by dragging headers, as well as choose different columns from the View > Columns submenu.

TIP Every folder can have a different sort field.

TIP You can change the position of the reading pane by choosing a command from the Organize:Reading Pane menu or the View > Reading Pane submenu.

TIP Outlook can also group email messages based on the sort field or date. For instance, if you sort on From with grouping enabled, all messages from a person are listed together in an easy-to-distinguish group. To enable groups for a folder, ensure that Show in Groups is checked in the Arrange By menu **H**.

H The Arrange By menu.

Sort column

I When the reading pane is below the message list or hidden, sort by clicking a column heading.

About Conversations

The default Arrange By order in Office 2011 is Conversations. The messages are sorted by Subject and grouped by date, enabling you to review all messages—both sent and received—on a given topic. Click a triangle icon in the message list to expand a conversation. To see all messages in the conversation, select the conversation itself rather than a particular message.

Account types   Defined rules

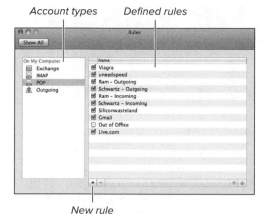

New rule

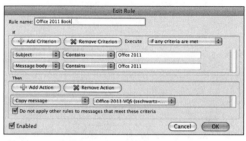

J Define and manage email rules in the Rules component of Preferences.

K Name the message rule, specify criteria, and set actions. This rule scans each message's Subject and body for the text **Office 2011**. If found, the message is copied into the designated folder.

Applying Rules to Existing Messages

Although rules are automatically applied to new messages, you can also apply a rule to existing messages. In the navigation pane, select an account folder of the correct type. Choose Message > Rules, followed by the rule that you want to run.

To delete unwanted messages:

Select the message(s) in the message list, and do one of the following:

- Press Delete or Command-Delete.
- Click the Home:Delete icon.
- Choose Edit > Delete.
- Drag the message header(s) onto the Deleted Items folder.

  Deleted messages are stored in the Deleted items folder until it is emptied.

TIP To delete all messages in the current folder, click the Organize:Delete All icon.

To create rules for processing email:

1. Choose Tools > Rules or click the E-mail: Rules icon in Preferences.

   The Rules window appears **J**.

2. Select an email account type to which you want the rule to apply, and click the plus (+) icon to define a new rule.

   The Edit Rule dialog box appears.

3. Name the rule, specify the criteria that will trigger the rule, and specify the actions that will be taken **K**.

4. Ensure that Enabled is checked. (Only enabled rules will be processed.)

5. Click OK.

   The Rules window reappears, and the new rule is added to the list.

6. Close the Rules window.

TIP Click icons at the bottom of the Rules window to delete a selected rule or move it up or down in the processing order. (Rules are processed sequentially from top to bottom.)

TIP You can temporarily disable a rule by clearing its Enabled check box.

Managing Mailing Lists

Internet mailing lists allow people with a common interest to connect. They provide subscribers with an email-based forum for conducting discussions, asking questions, and sharing experiences. When you're a member of a list, you receive copies of all messages sent to the list. And when you post a message, everyone who subscribes to the list will receive a copy of your message. You can use the Mailing List Manager to handle your list subscriptions.

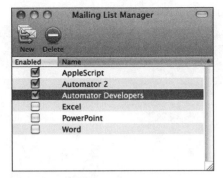

Ⓐ In the Mailing List Manager, you can add new mailing list subscriptions, edit existing ones, and delete others.

To manage a mailing list subscription:

1. Select a received message from the list and choose Tools > Mailing List Manager.

   The Mailing List Manager appears Ⓐ.

2. Click the New toolbar icon.

   The Edit Mailing List Rule dialog box appears Ⓑ.

3. Name the mailing list, type or paste the list address (if it isn't already filled in), and specify where messages to and from the list should be stored.

4. *Optional:* Review options on the Advanced tab and make any desired changes, such as automatically marking all new messages as read.

5. Click OK.

   The new mailing list is recorded in the Mailing List Manager.

> **TIP** To change settings for a list, double-click its name in the Mailing List Manager.

> **TIP** A busy mailing list can flood your Inbox with dozens of individual messages per day. If the list allows it, subscribe in digest mode to request that each day's messages be combined into one message.

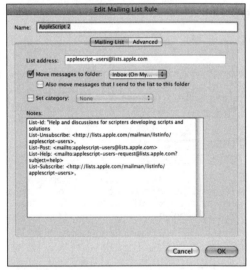

Ⓑ Specify the list address and actions to be taken on list messages.

Keeping List Messages Organized

To make it easier to find list messages, you can create a separate folder for each list to which you subscribe. For example, you could create a Mailing Lists folder and—within it—a subfolder for each list. Then in each list's rule, specify that all messages to and from the list should be moved into its list subfolder.

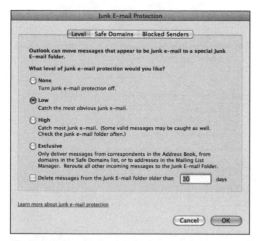

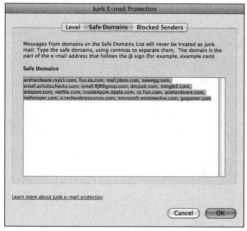

Handling Junk Mail

Anyone with an email account will eventually receive junk mail (*spam*). If you use your regular email address to register on Web sites or send email to corporations, newsgroups, or mailing lists, the volume of incoming junk mail is liable to increase. Use the Junk E-mail Protection feature to filter out much of this time-wasting mail.

To filter out suspected junk mail:

1. Choose Home : Junk > Junk E-mail Protection or Tools > Junk E-mail Protection.

2. On the Level tab of the Junk E-mail Protection dialog box **A**, select a protection level.

   When received, suspected junk mail is automatically assigned the Junk category and is moved into the Junk E-mail folder.

3. To instruct Outlook to automatically delete junk mail after a period of time, click the Delete messages from the Junk E-mail folder older than *x* days check box and enter a number in the box.

4. *Optional:* On the Safe Domains tab **B**, list the *domains* (the part of an email address after the @ sign) whose mail should never be classified as junk. Separate entries with commas.

   On the Blocked Senders tab, enter the list of domains and email addresses that should always be treated as junk.

5. Click OK to save the new settings.

A On the Level tab, specify a filtering level to use to identify incoming junk mail.

B On the Safe Domains tab, enter a comma-delimited list of trusted domains. This will prevent their messages from being classified as junk.

Manually Classifying Messages

To classify a message as junk, select or open it and choose Home : Junk > Mark as Junk. Or choose Block Sender to add the address to the Blocked Senders list.

If a message is incorrectly classified as junk, select it in the Junk E-mail folder, and choose Home : Junk > Mark as Not Junk.

TIP You can specify other actions for junk mail by creating message rules.

TIP To prevent Outlook from classifying mail from certain individuals as junk, create records for them in Contacts (see Chapter 22).

Email Security

Outlook 2011 offers two types of security for your messages. First, you can digitally sign messages, assuring recipients that they actually came from you. Second, messages can be encrypted, allowing only recipients with the software key to decode and read them. While most users won't bother with either of these features, corporate and government employees are likely to find them useful or required.

Before you can employ either feature, you must obtain a digital ID from an authorized issuer, such as VeriSign (**www.verisign.com**). The digital ID can be used for encryption and digital signing.

To enable encryption or a digital signature for an email account:

1. Choose Tools > Accounts.

2. In the The Accounts dialog box, double-click the account for which you want to enable encryption or a digital signature.

   The Edit Account dialog box appears.

3. Click the Advanced button, and click the Security tab in the pane that appears 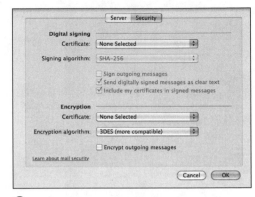.

4. To select a certificate for digital signing, open the top Certificate drop-down list.

5. To select a certificate for encryption, open the bottom Certificate drop-down list.

6. Set encryption and digital signing options by clicking check boxes and making selections from the drop-down lists.

7. Click OK to close the pane, and then close the Accounts dialog box.

> **TIP** To manually secure an outgoing message, choose Options : Security > Digitally Sign Message or Encrypt Message.

Ⓐ Record your digital ID and set encryption and digital signature options.

A Specify the Outlook data to export.

B Name the export file and select a location in which to save it.

Backing up Email and Other Outlook Data

Using the Export procedure, you can back up all or selected Outlook components. If necessary, the exported data can later be imported into the same copy of Outlook, a different copy (when copying messages to your laptop, for example), or into any other email program that supports the Mac Data File (.olm) format.

To create an Outlook backup:

1. Choose File > Export.

   The first screen of the Export wizard appears **A**.

2. Select Outlook for Mac Data File (.olm) and Items of the following types.

3. Click check boxes of the data that you want to export, and click the right-arrow icon.

4. In the Delete After Exporting screen, select No, do not delete items and click the right-arrow icon to continue.

5. In the Save dialog box that appears **B**, name the backup .olm file, select a location on disk, and click Save.

To import an Outlook backup:

1. Choose File > Import.

   The Begin Import screen of the Import wizard appears.

2. Select Outlook Data File (.pst or .olm), and click the right-arrow icon to continue.

3. On the Choose a File Type screen, choose Outlook for Mac Data File (.olm), and click the right-arrow icon to continue.

4. In the Import dialog box that appears, select the .olm file and click Import.

   The imported items appear in the navigation pane under My Computer.

Printing Messages

As is the case with other Outlook components, printing messages is accomplished via a nonstandard Print dialog box. The Quick Preview box reflects the selected print options and settings.

To print a message:

1. Switch to Mail view.

2. Select the header of the message you want to print or open the message in its own window. You can print multiple messages by Command-clicking their headers in the message list.

3. *Optional:* To change the orientation or scaling of the printout, choose File > Page Setup. Make changes in the Page Setup dialog box and click OK.

4. Choose File > Print, click the Print icon on the Standard toolbar, or press Command-P.

   The Print dialog box appears **A**.

5. Select a printer to use from the Printer drop-down list.

6. Indicate the number of copies to print, whether copies should be collated, and whether to print all pages or a range.

7. Set options by clicking check boxes in the Message and Page options sections.

8. Do one of the following:

   ▸ Click Print to generate the printout.

   ▸ To create a PDF, choose a command from the PDF drop-down menu.

TIP **Outlook can't restrict printing to selected text; only entire messages can be printed. To print part of a message, copy and paste the text into a new message or a Word document.**

Quick Preview   Selected printer

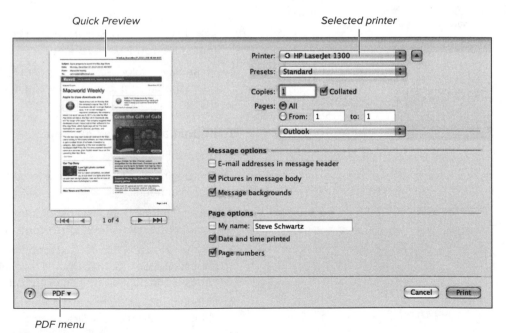

PDF menu

A The Print dialog box.

22

Contacts

Contacts view is the repository of your contact data for people, companies, and organizations. In addition to the standard information normally stored in an address book (such as name, home/work addresses, phone numbers, and email addresses), a contact record can hold a birth date, photo, anniversary, spouse name, children's names, and notes. You can even have custom fields. As explained in Chapter 9, you can use Contacts data in Word to perform merges, create labels, and print envelopes.

Office 2011 supports multiple users (called *identities*). In addition to having separate email, each user who shares a copy of Office:Mac has a separate Contacts database. To learn how to switch from one user to another, see the tip at the end of "Emailing Office Documents" in Chapter 28.

In addition to the Contacts data stored on your Mac, Exchange users can create additional address books that are kept on the server. Those address books can be shared with or delegated to other users.

In This Chapter

Adding Contacts

If you're currently using another program to manage your address data, Outlook can import address information from two popular programs and from exported text files. (Note that if Entourage 2008 is installed, your existing data will be imported on Outlook's first run.)

You can also add contact records manually or create them from received email.

Importing an address book

There's nothing more painful than having to re-create an address book simply because you've changed programs or upgraded to a new version. Happily, Outlook can import contact data from many programs. If your existing data wasn't automatically imported into Office 2011, follow these steps.

To import an existing address book:

1. Click the Tools:Import icon or choose File > Import.

   The Import wizard appears, displaying the Begin Import screen **Ⓐ**.

2. Select one of these options:

   ▸ **Outlook Data File (.pst or .olm).** Choose this option when importing data from Outlook for Windows (.pst) or Outlook for Mac from another computer or a backup file (.olm),

   ▸ **Entourage information from an archive or earlier version.** If you didn't import from a version of Entourage during Office 2011 installation, you can do so now. This option is also useful if you've created an Entourage archive on another computer that you want to import into Outlook.

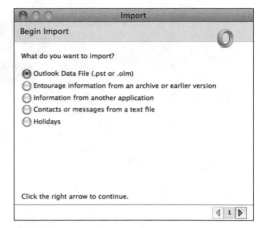

Ⓐ In the Import wizard's first screen, select an import option and then click the right-arrow icon.

Importing Data from Office 2010

For those of you switching from Office 2010 for Windows to Office 2011, follow these steps to export your contact data:

1. In the Backstage of Outlook 2010, click Options.

2. Select the Advanced category in the Outlook Options dialog box.

3. In the Export section, click the Export button.

4. In the Import and Export Wizard, select Export to a file, and click Next.

5. Select Outlook Data File (.pst) and click Next.

6. Select your Contacts folder and click Next.

7. Name the export file, select Do not export duplicate items, and click Finish to create the data file.

You can use this procedure to export any folder from Outlook 2010, such as the Inbox of a POP3 email account.

B When you import data from some sources, you can specify the types of data to import. For other sources, the data types are predetermined.

General Importing Assistance

In addition to importing contact data, the procedure on these pages can be used to import all compatible data into Outlook. Here are some helpful tips:

- If possible, choose an option in step 2 that's designed to import the data in your program's native format.

- If the Import wizard doesn't list your program, check the program's export and Save As options. If it can create a tab-delimited, comma-delimited, or MBOX file, Outlook can import the data using the Information from another application or the Contacts or messages from a text file option **A**.

- If the program can't export or save its data in a supported format, search the Web for a utility to convert the data to an acceptable format.

- The safest time to perform an import is soon after Outlook's first launch. Determine what data is missing and then decide whether you need to perform an import.

▸ **Information from another application.** Select this option to import data from Apple Mail or Qualcomm Eudora (version 5.0 or later).

▸ **Contacts or messages from a text file.** For any other email, utility, or database application in which you've stored contact records, select this option if you're able to export the data as a tab- or comma-delimited text file or as an MBOX file.

▸ **Holidays.** This option adds national and Christian holidays to the Calendar.

Click the right-arrow icon to continue.

3. Depending on the option chosen in step 2, you will be asked to select a program from which to import, select a data file to import, and/or specify the types of data to import **B**.

4. Follow the directions in the remaining screens.

TIP If you're asked which items you want to import **D**, be sure that Contacts is checked—this is the address data. Depending on the import method you select, you may also be able to import other Outlook-compatible data, such as Calendar events and email.

CAUTION Be very careful not to import the same data twice. Eliminating the hundreds or thousands of duplicate contact records, email messages, or Calendar events that can result is a major chore. (If you do end up with duplicates, one tactic is to simply remove Office 2011 and then reinstall.)

TIP Outlook data can also be exported in formats that other programs can read. Click the Tools:Export icon and follow the instructions to create a tab-delimited text file or a file in Mac Data File(.olm) format.

Creating contact records from email messages

You can extract email addresses from received messages and use them as the basis for new contact records.

To create a contact record from a received message:

1. Do one of the following:

   ▸ Select the message header in the message list and choose Message > Sender > Add to Contacts.

   ▸ Right-click the message header in the message list and choose Sender > Add to Contacts **C**.

   ▸ Select the message header in the message list. At the top of the reading pane, move the cursor over the sender name. Click the Open Outlook contact icon in the pop-up balloon that appears **D**.

   TIP You can use this technique to add contacts for other recipients—not just the sender.

   A new contact record for the selected entity appears. If there's already a contact record for this email address, the existing record opens.

2. Fill in as much contact information for the person, company, or organization as you like **E**, clicking in or tabbing from field to field.

3. Do one of the following:

   ▸ **No edits or cancel.** Click the red close button (X).

   ▸ **New or edited.** Save by clicking Contact : Save & Close, clicking the Save toolbar icon, choosing File > Save, or pressing Command-S. If you just close a new or edited record, you'll be prompted to save.

C You can right-click or Control-click a message header and choose Sender > Add to Contacts.

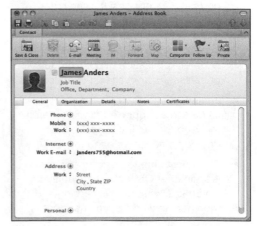

D Click the Open Outlook contact icon.

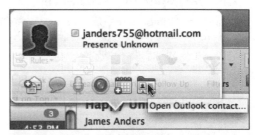

E Enter available contact data, and click the Save & Close icon.

F In Contacts view, you can click the Contact icon to create a new record.

G Regardless of the current view, you can create a contact record by clicking the New icon and choosing Contact.

Manually creating new records

You can also create contact records from scratch by manually entering the data.

To create a new contact record:

1. Do one of the following:

   ▸ If Contacts is the current view, click the Home:Contact icon **F** or press Command-N.

   ▸ Regardless of the current Outlook view, you can choose File > New > Contact or click the Home:New toolbar icon and choose Contact **G**.

   A new contact window appears **E**. The First Name field is selected, and all fields are blank.

2. Enter information for the contact on the General tab **E**, clicking in or tabbing from field to field.

   TIP Elements with a plus (+) symbol (Internet, Address, and Personal) can be used to store data for multiple fields. For instance, the Internet item can record several email addresses, Web sites, and an instant-messaging ID.

3. Save the new record by clicking Contact: Save & Close, clicking the Save toolbar icon, choosing File > Save, or pressing Command-S.

   If you simply close a new contact record, you'll be prompted to save.

Adding a Photo to a Contact Record

Although unessential, adding a photo to a contact record helps identify the person and, frankly, makes the record friendlier and more attractive.

To add or edit a record's photo:

1. In the reading pane or with the record open in its own window, double-click the photo placeholder.

   A selection pane appears **A**.

2. To pick a photo, do one of the following:

   ▶ Check the Recent Pictures drop-down gallery to see if the image is shown there. If so, click its thumbnail.

   ▶ To use a photo that's stored on disk, click the Choose button. Locate the image file in the Open dialog box, select it, and click Open.

   ▶ If your Mac has a built-in or attached video camera, you can take a photo by clicking the camera icon.

   The photo appears in the pane.

3. Select the area of the photo that you want to display by dragging the image and, if necessary, dragging the slider to change the magnification.

4. Click the Set button to accept the selected area of the image.

   The photo is added to the contact record **B**.

> **TIP** To choose a photo from iPhoto, select Media:Photos in the Open dialog box sidebar.

Recent Pictures gallery

From disk   Web cam   Special effects

A You can add a photo to any contact record.

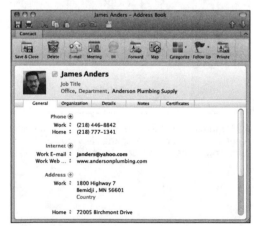

B The photo is added to the record.

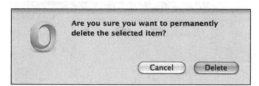

A Contacts view and an open contact record both have a Delete icon on the main tab.

Are you sure you want to permanently delete the selected item?

Cancel   Delete

B Confirm the deletion by clicking Delete.

Editing Contact Records

To edit a contact record, you can select it in the contacts list and make changes in the reading pane. Edits made in this manner are saved automatically.

On the other hand, if you make changes in an open contact record window, you must manually save by clicking the Contact:Save & Close icon, clicking the Save toolbar icon, choosing File > Save, or pressing Command-S.

Deleting Contacts

There are several ways to permanently remove records from your Contacts.

To delete contacts:

1. Switch to Contacts view by clicking the Contacts button in the view switcher, choosing View > Go To > Contacts, or pressing Command-3.

2. In the contacts list, select one or more records to delete.

   You can Shift-click to select contiguous records or Command-click to select noncontiguous records.

3. Click the Home:Delete icon **A**, choose Edit > Delete, press Delete, or press Command-Delete.

   A confirmation dialog box appears **B**.

4. Do one of the following:

   ▸ To delete the selected contact(s), click the Delete button.

   ▸ If you've changed your mind, click the Cancel button.

> **TIP** If a contact record is open in its own window, you can delete it by clicking the Contact: Delete icon, choosing Edit > Delete, or pressing Command-Delete.

> **TIP** You can also right-click selected records and choose Delete from the contextual menu.

> **CAUTION** Deleting a contact record is immediate and permanent. Deleted records are not moved to the Deleted Items folder, and no Undo command is available.

Exchanging Contact Information

You may occasionally receive electronic business cards (vCards) as attachments to email. You can recognize them by their .vcf filename extension. Outlook can read and create new contact records from vCards. You can also email contact records to others as vCard attachments.

To add a received vCard to Contacts:

1. Select the message header in the message list. The attached vCard should be visible in the reading pane **Ⓐ**.

2. *Optional:* If you're running Snow Leopard or a later version of Mac OS X, you can click the Preview button to view the vCard **Ⓑ**.

3. Double-click the vCard attachment.

   A new contact record containing the vCard data opens.

4. Make any necessary changes to the contact data and click the Contact:Save & Close icon.

   The vCard is added to your contacts list as a new record.

Sent: Tuesday, December 7, 2010 1:29 PM
To: Steve Schwartz
📎: 📄 James Anders.vcf (5.3 KB) (Preview)

vCard attachment

Ⓐ In the reading pane, the header shows that a vCard (.vcf) file is attached to this message.

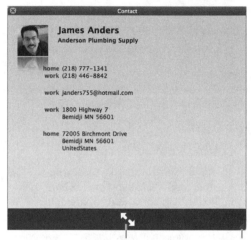

View full screen   Drag to resize

Ⓑ Snow Leopard allows you to preview a vCard before opening or saving it. You can optionally resize the window or display it full screen.

Who Are You?

You can identify one contact record as being you. Select it in the contacts list, and choose Contact > This Contact Is Me. After doing so, you can quickly find and make changes to your record by clicking the Organize:Me icon.

Subject:	FW: M Anderson
📎 :	🗐 M Anderson.vcf (0.3 KB)

C The selected contact record is added as a vCard attachment to a new message.

Viewing the Contacts List

The default Contacts view display has the scrolling contacts list in the center pane and the reading pane on the right. However, you can choose a different display from the View > Reading Pane or Organize:Reading Pane submenu. You can also click the Home:Details or Home:List icon. If you repeatedly click either icon, you'll cycle through the three display options.

When the reading pane is below or hidden, you can specify which fields to show and their order:

- Choose fields from the View > Columns submenu. Checked fields are displayed.

- To rearrange the fields, drag a field's header left or right to a new position.

Like the message list in Mail view, you can set a sort order for the contacts list. Choose a sort field from the View > Arrange By or Organize:Arrange By submenu, or click the Arrange By heading above the contacts list and choose a sort field. To switch from an ascending to a descending sort (or vice versa), click the second heading above the contacts list.

To email a vCard:

1. Switch to Contacts view.

2. In the contacts list, select the record you want to send as a vCard.

   You can select your own record or any other record in your contacts list.

3. Do either of the following:

   ▸ Choose Contact > Forward as vCard (Command-J).

   ▸ Right-click the record and choose Forward as vCard from the contextual menu that appears.

   A new email message opens that contains the contact information as a vCard file attachment **C**.

4. Specify recipients and write the message body.

   The Subject is already filled in for you, in the form FW: *contact name*. You can change it, if you like. You can also enclose other attachments.

5. To send the message, click the Message: Send icon.

TIP To send multiple contact records as vCards, select all the desired records from the contact list before choosing the Forward as vCard command. (Command-click to select multiple records.)

TIP You can also attach a contact record as a vCard by dragging the record from the contacts list into an open email message.

Addressing Mail from Contacts View

In Chapter 21, you learned the most common methods of addressing email. You can also address email from Contacts view, generating new email messages to selected contacts.

To address mail from Contacts view:

1. Switch to Contacts view.

2. In the contacts list, select the person or people to whom you want to send mail. (Command-click to select multiple recipients.)

3. Do one of the following:

   ▸ Click the Home:E-mail icon **A** or choose Contact > New E-mail Message To.

   ▸ Right-click any selected contact record and choose New E-mail to Contact from the contextual menu **B**.

   A new message window opens and is addressed to the selected recipient(s).

TIP To rearrange contacts in the To, Cc, and Bcc sections of the address pane, drag the contacts to where you want them.

TIP You can also address messages by dragging contact records from the contacts list into the To, Cc, or Bcc area of the message's address pane.

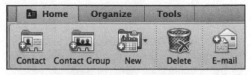

A Click the E-mail icon on the Home tab to address a new message to the selected recipients.

B The quickest way to address email to a contact is to right-click the record in the contacts list and choose this command.

Group name Add member

Member roster

A Specify the group's membership in the Group window.

B Many group members can be added by selecting names from a drop-down list.

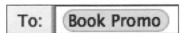

C Addressing a message to the group name is the equivalent of listing its members as recipients.

Creating Contact Groups

If you regularly send email to the same set of people, you can define a contact group for them. New messages can then be sent to the group name rather than to the individual email addresses.

To create a contact group:

1. Choose Home:New > Contact Group or File > New > Contact Group.

   An Untitled Group window appears **A**.

2. Enter a name for the group in the top box.

3. To add a member to the group, click the Add icon or double-click in the member list box.

4. Begin typing the person's name or email address. A drop-down list of matching contacts appears **B**, drawn from Contacts records and people with whom you've recently exchanged email.

5. Do one of the following:

   ▶ Select a listed person or company.

   ▶ To add a person or company who isn't in Contacts, type the complete email address.

6. To add more members to the group, repeat Steps 3–5. To remove a selected member, click the Remove icon.

7. *Optional:* To prevent the display of the group members' email addresses, click Use Bcc to hide member information.

8. Click the Group:Save & Close icon.

   The group is added as a new contact record. To address mail to the group, enter the group name in the To, Cc, or Bcc box of the message's address pane **C**.

Printing the Contacts List

Using the Print command, you can print one record, selected records, or all records (in phone list or address book format).

To print contact records:

1. Switch to Contacts view.

2. *Optional:* To print only certain records, select the records in the contacts list.

   Select a single record, or you can Command-click or Shift-click to select multiple records.

3. Choose File > Print (Command-P).

   The Print dialog box appears **A**.

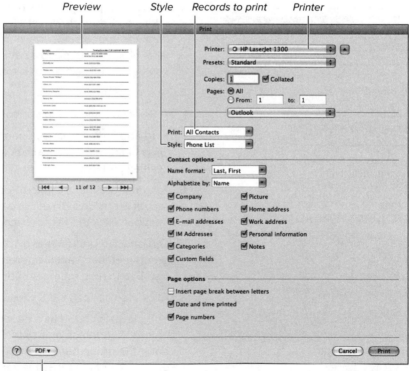

Preview · Style · Records to print · Printer

PDF options

A Set options in the Print dialog box and then click the Print button.

B To create a PDF rather than a printout, choose a command from the PDF drop-down menu.

4. Select a printer to use from the Printer drop-down list.

5. From the Print drop-down menu, choose what you want to print: Selected Contacts, All Contacts, or Flagged Contacts.

6. Choose a print format (Address Book or Phone List) from the Style menu.

7. Choose a method of displaying contact names from the Name format menu.

8. Specify the number of copies to print, whether copies should be collated (when printing multiple copies), and whether to print all pages or a range.

9. Click check boxes to specify the information to print for each record and set page options.

10. Click Print to generate the printout.

TIP You can use these same print procedures when a contact record is open in its own window.

TIP To get an idea of what the printout will look like, examine the preview area. It changes as you select different print options. Click the arrow buttons beneath the preview to review other pages, if any.

CAUTION Changing the style or selecting All Contacts can make Outlook "go out to lunch" as it reformats the output and generates a new preview. This is especially true if you have a contacts list that numbers in the hundreds or thousands of records.

TIP As with other Mac OS X programs, you can create a PDF (Portable Document Format) file from a contacts printout. To save the printout as a PDF file, click the PDF button **B** and choose Save as PDF. Or choose Open PDF in Preview to create a temporary file that will open in the default viewer (Preview or Adobe Reader).

Synchronizing Contacts with an iPod, iPhone, or iPad

Using Sync Services (a central database on your Mac for sharing data among applications and hardware), you can synchronize your Outlook Contacts with those in the Apple Address Book. After synchronization has been enabled (a one-time procedure), you can use iTunes to maintain a sync between your Outlook Contacts and data in the Contacts application on your iPod, iPhone, or iPad.

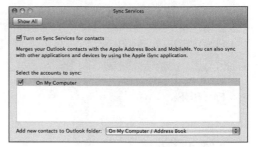

A Enable Sync Services for contacts and specify the Outlook accounts you wish to sync.

B This confirmation dialog box appears. Click OK.

To enable Sync Services for Outlook:

1. Do either of the following:

> ▸ Click the Tools : Sync Services icon.

> ▸ Choose Outlook > Preferences. In the Outlook Preferences dialog box, click the Other : Sync Services icon.

2. In the Sync Services dialog box **A**, click Turn on Sync Services for contacts. This enables Outlook data to be synchronized with Address Book and MobileMe.

3. Click the check boxes of the Outlook accounts you want to sync.

The On My Computer account includes all Outlook contacts that aren't synchronized with an Exchange account.

4. Close the dialog box by click the red close button.

A confirmation dialog box appears **B**.

5. Click OK to dismiss the dialog box.

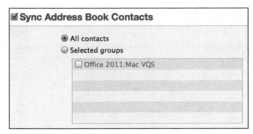

Sync Address Book Contacts

- All contacts
- Selected groups
  - Office 2011:Mac VQS

C Enable Contacts synchronization.

Advanced

Replace information on this iPod
- Contacts
- Calendars
- Mail Accounts
- Bookmarks
- Notes

D Click the Contacts check box to perform a single sync that replaces the Contacts data on your device with your Outlook Contacts data.

To synchronize Outlook data with an iPod, iPhone, or iPad:

1. Connect your iPod, iPhone, or iPad to your Mac.

   iTunes launches, and a synchronization is performed.

2. Select your device in the Devices list in the left pane and click the Info or Contacts tab at the top of the window. (The tab name depends on the device.)

3. Click the Sync Address Book Contacts check box **C** and specify the contacts to sync, such as All contacts.

4. Click Apply.

   A new synchronization is performed. In future sessions, these syncs will continue until you change options in iTunes or disable Outlook support in Sync Services.

TIP In the Advanced section **D**, you can perform a one-time synchronization to replace the Contacts data on your iPod, iPad, or iPhone with data from your Mac.

23

Calendar

Outlook provides a calendar that you can use to record upcoming appointments and events, whether they occur only once or many times. You can schedule reminders for events, send and receive meeting invitations, and view your calendar in a variety of formats.

Upcoming events can also be viewed in My Day, a utility introduced in Office 2008 (see Chapter 26). And if you have an Exchange Server account or simply prefer to manage certain kinds of events separately (work versus home, for example), you can create additional calendars.

Viewing the Calendar

You can display the Calendar in day, work week, week, or month view; or as a sequential event list. You can also specify the date or range of dates to display.

To change the Calendar view:

1. Switch to Calendar view **A** by clicking its button in the navigation pane, choosing View > Go To > Calendar, or pressing Command-2.

   At the top of the navigation pane is a mini calendar. To the right is the current view, showing events and appointments for the day, work week, week, or month.

2. To change the view, do one of the following:

   ▸ Click the Home : Day, Work, Week, or Month icon.

   ▸ Choose the same command from the View menu.

   The current date range is displayed in the new view. The active view is indicated by a darkened Ribbon icon.

   TIP To display a list of events and appointments for the current view, choose View > List or click the Organize : List icon. To return to a normal view, repeat the command.

   TIP In some cases, you may not be able to read the full text of an event by just glancing at the calendar. However, if you rest the cursor on the event for a few seconds, the full text will be displayed.

Mini calendar   View Date   View icons   Appointment   All-day Event

Categories

Calendar button

Adjust display

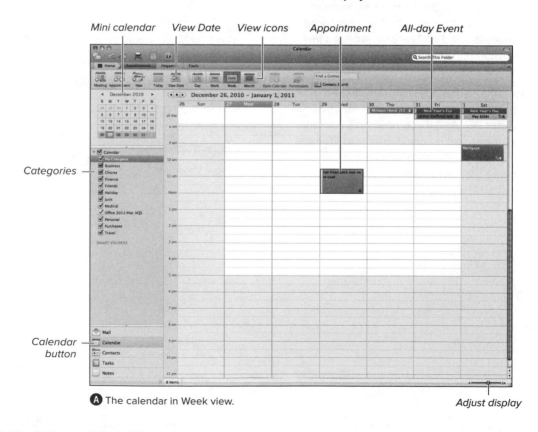

A The calendar in Week view.

Previous Next

December 2010

Today

B Click an arrow icon to move back or forward one unit. Click the center icon to view the range that includes today's date.

February 2011

S M T W T F S

		1	2	3	4	5
6	7	8	9	10	11	12
13	14	15	16	17	18	19
20	21	22	23	24	25	26
27	28					

Today

C Select a date to display from the drop-down calendar.

About Appointments and Events

You'll note that when recording a new Calendar item, the menu or Ribbon command is always referred to as an appointment. Yet Outlook Help speaks of Calendar items as events.

The distinction is that those items with a designated time range are *appointments*, while activities that take all day or can occur at any time during the specified day are *events*. In addition, events appear at the top of each day's items and appointments are shown in their specified time slots **A**.

To view a specific date or range:

To select a date to view, do any of the following:

- Click the left and right arrows above the calendar view **B** to scroll until the desired date is visible.

- Click the left and right arrows above the mini calendar to scroll until the date you want is visible. Click the date or drag-select a date range.

- To jump to a specific date, click the Home: View Date icon **A** or press Shift-Command-T. In the calendar that appears **C**, click the desired date.

- To display today's date, click the Home: Today icon, choose View > Go to Today, press Command-T, or click the Home: View Date Icon **A** and click the Today button **C**.

The selected date or range is displayed in the current view.

TIP To restrict the calendar to showing a particular date range, you can drag-select from one day to several weeks in the mini calendar. Unlike other date-selection techniques, this method changes the view to match the selected range as closely as possible.

TIP You can drag the right edge of the navigation pane to display a pair of mini calendars, if you like.

Adding Events and Appointments

As you might expect, there are multiple ways to record new Calendar items.

To create a standard Calendar item:

1. Do one of the following:

   ▶ On the Calendar, double-click the time slot or date to which you want to add the item.

   ▶ When viewing the Calendar, click the Home:Appointment icon or press Command-N.

   ▶ When viewing any part of Outlook, choose Home:New > Appointment or File > New > Appointment.

   An Untitled Appointment window appears **A**,

   TIP In Month view, if you first select the date, the item will default to that date.

2. Enter a title for the item in the Subject box and, optionally, the Location.

3. If the item has specific start and/or end times, remove the check mark from the All day event check box. Enter start and end times, or set the start time and specify the duration.

4. Verify or edit the item date or date range.

   You can click the calendar icon to the right of each date field to select the date from a pop-up calendar.

5. If the event will occur more than once, choose a schedule from the Appointment:Recurrence drop-down menu. To specify an unlisted schedule, choose Custom, enter the details in the panel that appears **B**, and click OK.

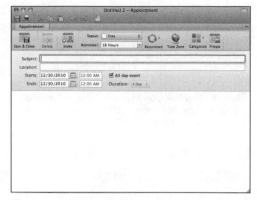

A Enter the item information in the Untitled Appointment window.

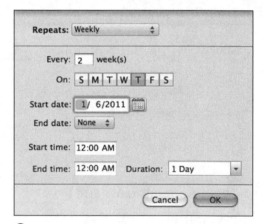

B If this is a recurring event, you can specify a custom recurrence pattern and end date.

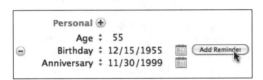

C Optionally, you can be reminded ahead of time about an upcoming event or appointment.

D Click the Add Reminder button beside a date to create a Calendar event for the item.

6. *Optional:* To be reminded of the event prior to its occurrence, choose the number of minutes, hours, days, or weeks before the event that you want to be reminded from the Reminder drop-down menu **A**.

   At the designated time, an alarm will be triggered in Office Reminders **C**. For information about working with Office Reminders, see "Responding to Reminders," later in this chapter, as well as "Managing Reminders" in Chapter 24.

7. *Optional:* Choose one or more categories to associate with the item from the Appointment:Categorize menu.

8. Save the event by clicking the Appointment:Save & Close icon, choosing File > Save, or pressing Command-S.

   The item is added to the calendar. An appointment is shown in its designated time slot; an event is shown at the top of that day's Calendar items.

To create a Calendar event from a date on a contact record:

1. Switch to Contacts view by clicking its navigation pane button, choosing View > Go To > Contacts, or pressing Command-3.

2. Open the contact record in its own window or view it in the reading pane.

3. In the Personal section, move the cursor over the date field (such as Birthday or Anniversary) that you want to add to the Calendar.

   An Add Reminder button appears beside the field **D**.

4. Click the button to create a recurring annual event series for the date.

Modifying Events and Appointments

You can edit any aspect of a saved Calendar item, such as its date, time, or location.

To edit a Calendar item using the Ribbon:

1. Switch to a view that displays the item.

2. Choose new options from the Appointment or Appointment Series contextual tab that appears **A**.

   To edit the entire series for a recurring item, click the Edit Series icon.

3. Click the Close icon.

To edit a Calendar item in its own window:

1. Switch to a view that displays the item.

2. Open the item for editing by double-clicking it or by selecting the item and choosing File > Open > Current Item (Command-O).

   TIP If the item is part of a recurring series, you can edit the current instance or the entire series. To edit the series, click the Appointment:Edit Series icon or the Go to Series button **C**.

3. In the item window, make the necessary changes.

4. Save the edited event or series by clicking the Appointment:Save & Close icon, choosing File > Save, or pressing Command-S. Close the window, if it's still open.

A When a Calendar item is selected, an Appointment (top) or Appointment Series (bottom) contextual tab appears, enabling you to make basic changes to the item without opening it.

Editing Shortcuts

Some edits are simpler to perform without the Ribbon:

- If you only need to edit an item's Subject, select the item in any view and then click it a second time to edit the Subject text.

- You can change the scheduled date or time of an item by dragging it to a new location on the calendar. You can also change an all-day event to a time-based appointment (or vice versa) by dragging it out of or into the all-day area **B**. (This can be done in any view except Month.)

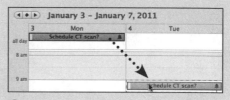

B Changing an all-day event to a scheduled appointment by dragging it to a time slot.

C When you open a series item in its own window, this bar appears above the notes area. You can edit just this instance of the series or click the button at the far-right end to edit the entire series.

Delete icon

 With an appointment or event selected in the calendar, you can always delete it by clicking an icon on the Appointment or Appointment Series contextual tab.

Deleting Events and Appointments

You can delete items that have passed or that you no longer wish to track.

To delete a Calendar item:

1. In Calendar view, switch to a date view that displays the event you want to delete, and select the event.

   The Appointment or Appointment Series contextual tab is selected (see **A** in "Modifying Events and Appointments", earlier in this chapter).

2. Do one of the following:

   ▸ Click the Delete icon **A**.

   ▸ Choose Edit > Delete.

   ▸ Press Delete or Command-Delete.

   The item is immediately deleted.

CAUTION Be careful when deleting events and appointments. There's no Undo command to restore a mistakenly deleted item.

TIP If a Calendar item is open in its own window, you can delete it by clicking the Appointment:Delete icon, choosing Edit > Delete, or pressing Command-Delete.

TIP To delete an entire series (rather than only the selected item within the series), click the Appointment Series:Edit Series icon and then issue the Delete command.

Responding to Reminders

When one or more item reminders are due (or have passed without being handled), they appear in Office Reminders—even if Office isn't running. You can handle reminders in several ways.

To respond to a reminder:

1. In the Office Reminders window **Ⓐ**, select the reminder or reminders that you want to handle.

   You can Shift-click or Command-click to select multiple reminders.

2. Do one of the following:

   ▸ **Dismiss.** To acknowledge a selected reminder and discontinue further notices, click Dismiss. The selected reminder is removed from the Office Reminders window.

   ▸ **Dismiss All.** To simultaneously dismiss all listed reminders, hold down the mouse button as you click Dismiss and choose Dismiss All from the drop-down menu that appears.

   ▸ **Snooze.** To request that the reminder be presented again at a later time or date, hold down the mouse button as you click Snooze and choose a time period from the drop-down menu **Ⓑ**. To snooze a reminder for the default time, click Snooze.

   ▸ **Open the item.** To edit an event or appointment, double-click its reminder.

   ▸ **Do nothing.** If a reminder's time passes without it being handled, the scheduled day changes to Overdue.

3. To handle other displayed reminders, repeat steps 1 and 2.

Ⓐ The Office Reminders window.

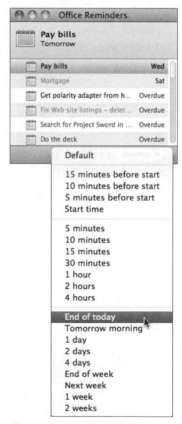

Ⓑ You can snooze an item for the default time or a chosen period.

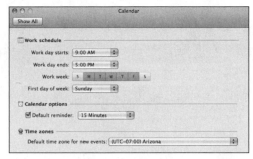

C In the Calendar preferences window, you can specify a new default reminder period, set your time zone, and set options for Work Week view.

TIP Dismissing a reminder doesn't delete its event or appointment from the Calendar. Follow the instructions in the previous section.

TIP You can choose additional commands from the Office Reminder menus or by right-clicking an item.

TIP If you don't like the default reminder of 15 minutes prior to an event or appointment, you can set a new default in Outlook Preferences by clicking the Calendar icon **C**.

TIP If you merely want to get the Office Reminders window out of your way, it isn't necessary to close the window or quit. You can click its minimize (yellow) button to minimize it to the Dock.

Working with Multiple Calendars

Although a single calendar will suffice for most users, you can create additional calendars, if you like. You might want to keep a separate calendar on your home computer for work-related items, for example. (Exchange users will automatically see an Exchange calendar in their navigation pane, in addition to the default Outlook calendar.) To create another calendar, follow these steps:

1. In the navigation pane, select the main calendar.

2. Click the Organize:New Calendar icon.

   A new calendar labeled Untitled Folder appears.

3. Name the new calendar **D**.

When viewing or adding items, click calendar check boxes to specify which calendar's items will be displayed. When only one calendar is checked, only its items are shown; when two are checked, items from both are shown. If you decide to remove one of your user-created calendars, right-click its name in the navigation pane and choose Delete.

D This navigation pane includes a user-created Work calendar.

Creating Meetings

You can use Outlook to email invitations to *meetings* (multiperson events) and reply to invitations that you receive from others. You can create a meeting from scratch, or create an appointment and issue invitations to it when it's convenient for you.

To invite others to an event:

1. Switch to Calendar view.

2. Do one of the following:

   ▸ To create a meeting from scratch, click the Home:Meeting icon. Enter a Subject for the meeting in the Untitled Meeting window that appears **A**.

   ▸ To convert an existing event or appointment to a meeting, select the item on the calendar and click the Appointment:Invite icon. A Meeting window opens, containing all details originally recorded for the event or appointment.

3. *Optional:* If you have multiple email accounts, click the From drop-down list to select the account from which you want to send invitations.

4. In the To box, specify the people whom you want to invite to the meeting.

5. Enter a Location for the meeting.

6. Specify the date, time, and duration of the meeting as you would in any other appointment or all-day event. You can specify the organizer's time zone by clicking the Meeting:Time Zone icon **B**.

7. If this meeting will recur on a regular basis (such as a weekly staff meeting), click the Meeting:Recurrence icon and specify a recurrence interval (see **B** in "Adding Events and Appointments" earlier in this chapter).

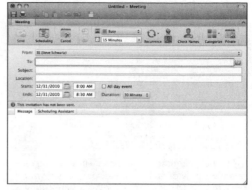

A The Meeting window will be blank or contain basic details, depending on whether it was created from scratch or based on an existing Calendar item.

Time Zone icon

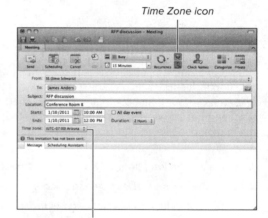

Time Zone

B If some attendees are from out of state or the country, you can specify the organizer's time zone.

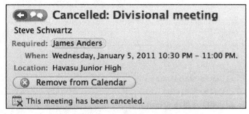

C If participants have Exchange accounts, you can check their schedules to see if they're free during the proposed time period.

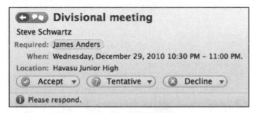

D Invitees running Outlook 2011 will see the meeting information and these buttons at the top of their invitation email.

F When a meeting is canceled, invitees receive this email. If they use Outlook 2011, they can remove the event from their calendar by clicking the button.

8. *Exchange users only:* Click the Meeting:Scheduling icon or the Scheduling Assistant tab above the message area to check everyone's schedule **C**.

9. *Optional:* You can attach files to the invitation by choosing Meeting > Attachments > Add.

10. *Optional:* Enter notes for the participants in the Message text box.

11. Click the Meeting:Send icon to email the invitation to the designated people.

    Recipients receive a message to which, if they are using Outlook, they can respond by clicking the Accept, Tentative, or Decline icon **D**. Outlook then relays the response to the meeting's organizer. (Recipients who don't have Outlook or a compatible email client can reply with a normal email message.)

TIP If you're working in a view other than Calendar, you can create a new meeting by choosing Home:New > Meeting.

TIP If you're the meeting organizer, you can check responses by opening the event and clicking the Scheduling Assistant tab **C**.

TIP Invitation recipients can change their minds at any time by reopening the invitation and clicking a different response icon **D**.

TIP To cancel an invitation you've already sent, open the event, click the Meeting:Cancel icon, and then click the Meeting:Send Cancellation icon. Participants will receive a cancellation email message **E**.

Adding and Removing Holidays

The default Outlook calendar doesn't include holidays. If you like, you can import religious and/or country-specific holidays, adding them as new all-day events. You can also decide later to remove all or some of these holidays.

To add holidays to the Calendar:

1. Choose File > Import.

   The Import wizard appears **Ⓐ**.

2. Click the Holidays radio button.

3. Click the right-arrow icon to continue.

4. After Outlook finishes building the list of country and religious holiday sets, make your selections by entering check marks **Ⓑ**.

5. Click the right-arrow icon to continue.

   The chosen holidays are imported into the calendar and assigned the Holiday category.

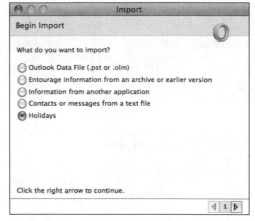

Ⓐ Select Holidays on the first screen of the Import wizard.

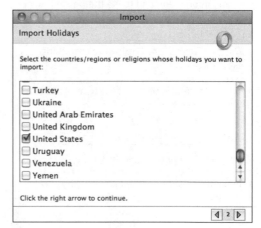

Ⓑ Click the check boxes of the countries and religions whose holidays you want to import.

Search criterion

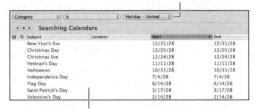

Partial results

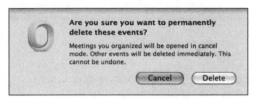 Search for Holidays or a specific Holiday category.

Are you sure you want to permanently delete these events?

Meetings you organized will be opened in cancel mode. Other events will be deleted immediately. This cannot be undone.

[Cancel] [Delete]

D Confirm the deletion(s) in the drop-down panel that appears.

To remove holidays from the Calendar:

1. Switch to Calendar view.

2. Choose Edit > Find > Advanced Find.

   A Searching Calendars area appears at the top of the Outlook window.

3. Choose Category Is, followed by Holiday or a specific holiday set **C**.

   The list of holidays appears.

4. Select the holidays to delete.

   Each holiday is listed multiple times, representing the different years for which it was added to the calendar.

TIP If you want to delete all found holidays, select one of them and choose Edit > Select All (Command-A).

TIP To delete just one or a few holidays, you may find it helpful to sort the search results. Click the Subject heading to group all holidays of the same type (all Easter Day holidays, for instance).

5. Click the Appointment : Delete icon, choose Edit > Delete, or press Delete or Command-Delete.

6. Click Delete in the confirmation panel that appears **D**.

7. To return to the normal Calendar window, click the Search : Close icon.

TIP You can remove individual holidays (marked in red on the calendar) by selecting and then deleting them as you would any other event.

TIP If clicking the Close icon doesn't restore the normal calendar view, click the Search : Advanced icon and then click Close.

Printing a Calendar

Printing a calendar is accomplished via a nonstandard Print dialog box 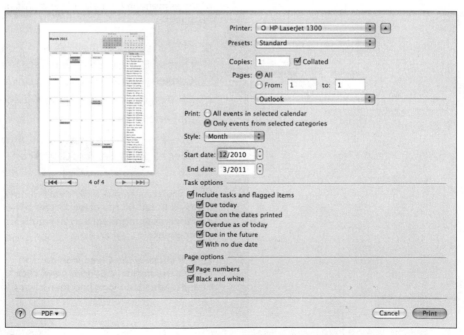. The Quick Preview box reflects current print options.

To print a calendar:

1. Switch to Calendar view.

2. *Optional:* To change the orientation or scaling of the printout, choose File > Page Setup. Make changes in the Page Setup dialog box and click OK.

TIP **Consider using Landscape mode to print the calendar, especially for a format like Month.**

3. To display the Print dialog box Ⓐ, click the Print icon on the Standard toolbar, choose File > Print, or press Command-P.

4. Select a printer to use from the Printer drop-down list.

5. Specify the events to include by clicking a Print radio button.

6. Chose a calendar format from the Style drop-down menu: Day, Work Week, Week, or Month.

7. Specify the date range to include.

8. Review settings in the Task and Page options sections.

9. Indicate the number of copies to print, whether copies should be collated (when printing multiple copies), and whether to print all pages or a page range.

10. Click Print to generate the printout.

TIP **To generate a PDF file rather than a printout (so you can email your schedule to a colleague or friend, for example), choose an option from the PDF button menu.**

Ⓐ Set options in the Print dialog box to print a calendar or to generate a PDF file.

Tasks

You use the Tasks component to track tasks and follow-up items. A *task* is an event or process (such as washing the car, painting the porch, or writing a budget proposal) that you need to complete by a certain date or at some unspecified future time.

Like Calendar events, some tasks are repeating. For example, a rent or mortgage payment could be scheduled at regular intervals. And if you flag an email message, contact record, or Office document for follow-up, a new task is automatically created. You can mark tasks as completed and be reminded when they're due. Although some tasks have specific due dates, tasks are *not* listed on the Calendar.

As explained in Chapter 26, you can use My Day to keep apprised of current and upcoming tasks. And tasks with an associated alarm can be viewed in Office Reminders.

Creating Tasks

As needed, you can create new tasks and add them to the Tasks list.

To create a new task:

1. Do either of the following:

    ▸ To create a new task in the Tasks component, click the Home:Task icon.

    ▸ To create a new task in any Outlook component, choose Home:New > Task or File > New > Task. (If you're in Tasks view, you can also create a new task by pressing Command-N.)

    A new task window opens **A**.

2. Enter a title for the task in the top box.

3. *Optional:* For a time-sensitive task, click the Due and/or Start date text **B**.

    For a task without a start and/or due date, leave the dates set to No date.

4. *Optional:* To set an alarm for the task, click the Reminder text and select a date and time at which you want the reminder to appear **C**.

    At the designated time, the reminder will appear in Office Reminders **D**. See "Managing Reminders" later in this chapter for instructions on using Office Reminders.

5. *Optional:* Assign a priority to the task by clicking the Task:High Priority or Low Priority icon **A**.

6. *Optional:* Associate one or more categories with the task by choosing them from the Task:Categorize menu **A**.

    Working with and applying categories to Outlook items is discussed in "Organizing the Mail" in Chapter 21.

7. *Optional:* Enter task notes or details in the bottom part of the task window **A**.

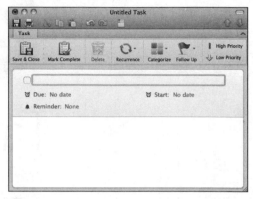

A Enter a title and set options for the new task.

B You can select a Due or Start date from a pop-up calendar.

Clear

C If desired, click the Reminder text to add an alarm for the item. Choose a date from the pop-up calendar and edit the time.

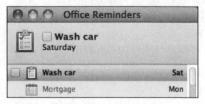

D At the specified time, an alarm for the task will appear in Office Reminders.

E Choose common schedules from the Recurrence menu. If no option is appropriate, choose Custom.

F Specify more complex schedules in this pane. Choose a base repetition from the Repeats menu and then set the specifics using the other controls.

8. If this is a *recurring task* (one that repeats at regular intervals), do one of the following:

▸ Choose a recurrence schedule from the Task:Recurrence menu **E**.

▸ To set a schedule other than the ones listed, choose Custom from the Task:Recurrence menu. In the recurrence pane **F**, specify a recurrence pattern, select a Start date, and set an End date criterion. Click OK.

9. To save the task, click the Task:Save & Close icon **A**, choose File > Save, or press Command-S. If the task window is still open, close it by clicking the red close (X) button.

The task is inserted into the Tasks list in the current sort order **G**.

TIP If a task doesn't have a specific due date and doesn't recur, it's often sufficient to enter just the task's title. Everything else (such as assigning a priority, reminder, or categories) is optional and can be entered when convenient.

TIP You can create a task from an email message by selecting its message header, opening the Scripts menu, and choosing Create Task from Message.

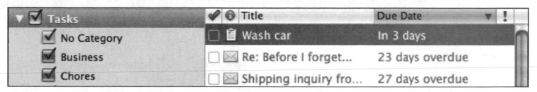

G The new task appears in the Tasks list. You can change the sort order by clicking a heading.

Flagging Items for Follow-Up

By setting a follow-up flag for an email message, contact record, or Office document, you automatically create a new task for the item.

To flag an email message or contact record for follow-up:

1. Select an email message or contact record in its list, or open the item in its own window.

2. Do one of the following:
   - Choose a command from the Follow Up icon's menu 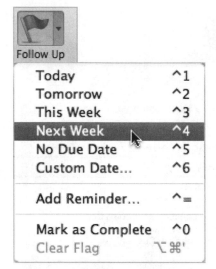.
   - To flag a message for follow up but without specifying details, click the item's flag icon in the message list until a flag appears **B**.

   The item is flagged for follow-up and added as a new task.

To flag an Office document for follow-up:

1. Open the Word, Excel, or PowerPoint document that you want to flag.

2. Choose Tools > Flag for Follow Up.

   The Flag for Follow Up dialog box appears **C**.

3. Edit the proposed reminder date and time, and click OK.

   A new task named Flagged Document: *filename* is created. At the scheduled time, Office Reminders will notify you of the task. You can open the document by double-clicking its listing in Office Reminders.

A Click the Follow Up icon on the Home tab of Outlook's main window or in an open message or contact window.

Follow-up flag

| Introducing Microsoft Office for ... | 10/26/10 |
| Apple | 🚩 |

B You can manually set the follow-up flag for any mail message or contact record by simply clicking the grayed-out flag icon. The follow-up date/time is set to today.

Flag for Follow Up

Flag for Follow Up lets you create a reminder that will alert you to follow up on this document at the date and time you specify.

☑ Remind me on 10/27/2010 at 4:45 PM

Cancel   OK

C Specify a reminder date/time and click OK.

Tasks vs. Appointments

The distinction between Outlook tasks and appointments is up to you. Because a task can occur at a specific time and also have an alarm that appears in Office Reminders, such items can be recorded as tasks or appointments.

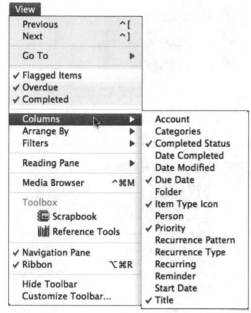

View

Previous   ^[
Next   ^]

Go To   ▶

✓ Flagged Items
✓ Overdue
✓ Completed

Columns   ▶
Arrange By   ▶
Filters   ▶

Reading Pane   ▶

Media Browser   ^⌘M

Toolbox
    Scrapbook
    Reference Tools

✓ Navigation Pane
✓ Ribbon   ⌥⌘R

Hide Toolbar
Customize Toolbar...

Account
Categories
✓ Completed Status
Date Completed
Date Modified
✓ Due Date
Folder
✓ Item Type Icon
Person
✓ Priority
Recurrence Pattern
Recurrence Type
Recurring
Reminder
Start Date
✓ Title

B Checked fields appear as column headings.

Viewing the Tasks List

When viewing the Tasks list, you can sort the tasks, choose column headings that you find useful, and filter the list of visible items to make it more manageable.

To view the Tasks list:

1. Click Tasks button at the bottom of the navigation pane, choose View > Go To > Tasks, or press Command-4.

   The Tasks list appears **A** (page bottom).

2. To sort the list, click any column heading. To reverse the sort order, click the same column heading again.

   The sort column's heading is blue.

3. *Optional:* To change the column headings in the Tasks list, choose fields from the View > Columns submenu **B**.

4. *Optional:* To change the column order, click and drag any column heading left or right to a new position.

> **TIP** To restore the column headings and their original order, choose View > Arrange By > Restore to Defaults.

Current sort column

✓ ⓘ	Title	Due Date ▲	!
☐ ✉	RE: old Happy Diamonds watch	No Due Date	
☐ ✉	Re: Catalog writeups	No Due Date	
☐ 📋	Paint fireplace door and bathroom window	No Due Date	
☑ ✉	FW: FTP site for— Microsoft Office 201...		
☐ 📋	Possible FTP folder structure for Office ...	No Due Date	

A The Tasks list (showing the default column headings).

To search or filter the Tasks list:

Do any of the following:

- Restrict list entries by clicking check boxes on the Home or Organize tab **C**. Only checked items are displayed.

- Choose one or more criteria from the Home:Filters menu. To restore the list after choosing filters, choose the same filters again or choose Clear All Filters.

- Select a Smart Folder in the navigation pane, such as Due Today or Overdue.

- Only tasks associated with checked categories in the navigation pane are shown. To restrict the Tasks list to items that have been assigned one or more specific categories, ensure that only those categories are checked.

- Click in the search box or choose Edit > Find > Outlook Items. The Search contextual tab appears **D** (page bottom). Do any of the following:

  ▸ Type a text string in the search box **E**. As you type, Outlook filters the list to show only items that contain the typed characters. You can refine the search results by clicking an option in the drop-down list.

  ▸ Create an advanced query by clicking the Search:Advanced icon **D** or individual Search icons, such as Overdue or Important. Specify criteria by typing or choosing options from the drop-down menus **F**. The Tasks list is filtered to show only the items that meet all specified criteria.

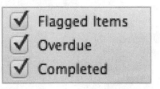

C These types of tasks can be shown or hidden, depending on the state of their check boxes.

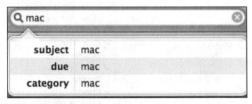

E To perform a basic search, type a search string in this box. You can restrict the search to a specific task component (such as subject) by clicking the component name in the drop-down list.

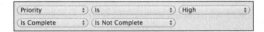

F In this advanced query, only items that are high priority and incomplete are displayed in the Tasks list. Click the Search:Close icon to restore the list.

Scope   *Search criteria*   *End search*

D The Search contextual tab has controls for filtering the Tasks list and building complex queries.

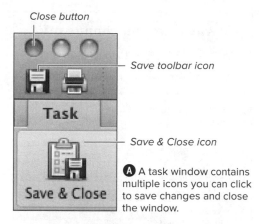

Close button

Save toolbar icon

Task

Save & Close icon

Save & Close

A A task window contains multiple icons you can click to save changes and close the window.

Plague of Automatic Categories

Have you noticed that some new tasks seem to be automatically associated with a category? Although this happens with greater frequency with Calendar events, it can also affect new tasks, notes, and contacts. There are two reasons for this troublesome behavior:

- Outlook remembers the last folder and item you selected in each component (Calendar, Tasks, Mail, and so on) and automatically selects them the next time you use the component.

- The navigation pane for Tasks, Notes, Calendar, and Contacts contains a list of all categories. If one of those categories is highlighted when you create a new item, the category is assigned to the new item.

Thus, to avoid associating categories—or the wrong category—with a new task, event, note, or contact, you must ensure that either the No Category option or the folder name (such as Tasks) is selected when you create a new item.

Editing Tasks

You can change any aspect of an existing task or follow-up item.

To edit a task or flagged for follow-up item:

1. Open the item for editing by doing one of the following:

    ▸ Double-click the item in the Tasks list, My Day, or Office Reminders.

    ▸ Select the item in the Task list and choose File > Open > Current Item (Command-O).

    ▸ Right-click the item in My Day and choose Open in Outlook from the contextual menu.

    If the selected item is a task, its task window opens. If the item is one flagged for follow up (email, contact record, or Office document), the original item opens.

2. Make any desired changes (as described In "To change a task's attributes," later in this section).

3. Save the edited task by doing one of the following:

    ▸ Click the Task:Save & Close icon **A**.

    ▸ Click the Save toolbar icon.

    ▸ Choose File > Save (Command-S).

4. If the task window is open, close it by clicking the window's close button.

To change a task's attributes:

Do any of the following:

- To change a task's title, select the task in the Tasks list and edit the title in the reading pane **B**. If you've opened the task for editing, you can change the title in the task window.

  A follow-up item's title is taken from its email subject, contact name, or document title. It can't be changed in Tasks.

- To change an item's completion status, click its check box in the Tasks list **B**, Office Reminders, or My Day **C**, or click the Task:Mark Complete icon in an open item's window.

  A completed task's title is displayed in strikethrough text in the reading pane **D** or the task is hidden, depending on the state of the Completed check box on the Home or Organize tab (see **C** in "Viewing the Tasks List" earlier in this chapter).

- To alter an item's due date, start date, or reminder, make changes in the reading pane or in an open item's window.

- To change a recurrence schedule, open the item window and choose a new option from the Task:Recurrence menu.

- To set or change categories associated with an item, choose from the Categorize icon's menu **E**. To remove a category, choose its name from the menu. To remove all categories, choose Clear All.

- You can change the priority or follow-up date by choosing Ribbon commands above the Tasks list or in the item window.

TIP When you want to make several changes to a task, it may be more convenient to open the task than to edit it in the Tasks list.

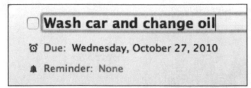

B You can edit the title of a selected task in the reading pane.

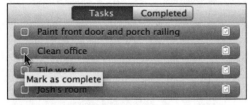

C You can mark an item as complete by clicking the check box that precedes the title (My Day shown here).

D Completed items are displayed in the reading pane in strikethrough type and have a check mark in their status check box.

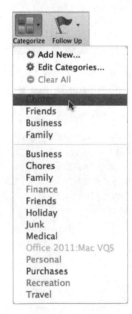

E Choose a category from the Categorize menu. Recently used categories are listed in the top section.

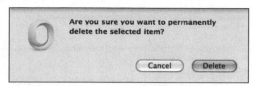

A You must confirm task and follow-up item deletions.

Deleting Tasks

When you've completed or are no longer interested in tracking a task or follow-up item, you can remove it from the Tasks list.

To delete a task:

1. Select one or more items in the Tasks list.

   To select multiple items, Command-click for noncontiguous items or Shift-click for contiguous items.

2. Click the Home:Delete icon, choose Edit > Delete, press Delete, or press Command-Delete.

   A confirmation dialog box appears **A**.

3. Click Delete to delete the task(s) and/or follow-up item(s).

   The deleted items are removed from the Tasks list.

> **TIP** With a task open in its own window, you can delete the task by clicking the Task:Delete icon, choosing Edit > Delete Task, or pressing Command-Delete.

> **CAUTION** You cannot undo a task deletion.

> **CAUTION** Deleting a follow-up item from the Tasks list deletes the actual message or contact record—not just its instance in the list. To remove a selected follow-up item from the Tasks list (rather than delete it), choose Home:Follow Up > Clear Flag.

Managing Reminders

Task reminders aren't the same as Calendar event reminders. Rather than specifying how far in advance you want to be reminded, you set a specific time at which the task reminder will appear.

Office 2011 presents reminders for tasks, follow-up items, and Calendar events using a separate program called Office Reminders. This enables reminders to appear any time your Mac is on, regardless of whether an Office application is running.

To respond to a reminder:

1. When the Office Reminders dialog box appears Ⓐ, select the item to which you want to respond. (Tasks are preceded by a status check box.)

2. Do one of the following:
   ▶ If you've performed the task, click the status check box. Doing so dismisses the reminder and marks the task or follow-up item as complete in the Tasks list.
   ▶ To dismiss the reminder so it doesn't reappear, click the Dismiss button.
   ▶ If this is a recurring task, you can dismiss this and all future occurrences of the reminder by holding down the Dismiss button and choosing Dismiss All from the drop-down menu.
   ▶ To delay the reminder for the default snooze interval (when it will reappear), click the Snooze button.
   ▶ If you want to be reminded later (from 5 minutes to 2 weeks from now), hold down the Snooze button and choose a delay interval Ⓑ.

Ⓐ When a task or Calendar event reminder is due, an Office Reminders notification occurs.

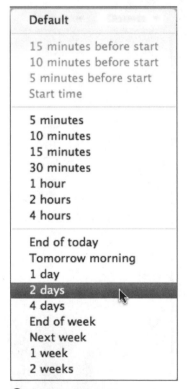

Ⓑ Click the Snooze button to be reminded again in 5 minutes or choose a delay interval from the Snooze menu.

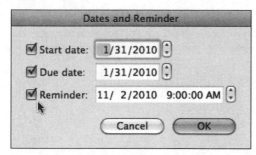

Dates and Reminder

☑ Start date: 1/31/2010
☑ Due date: 1/31/2010
☑ Reminder: 11/ 2/2010 9:00:00 AM

Cancel OK

C Clear the Reminder check box to remove the reminder from a task or follow-up item. (Use this dialog box to add or change a reminder, too.)

TIP Office Reminders remains open until you've responded to each reminder or until you close or quit it.

TIP If you want to open a task or follow-up item, you can double-click it in Office Reminders.

TIP Tasks are not listed as events on the Calendar. This is why it's important to carefully decide which items should be tasks and which ones should be recorded as Calendar events.

TIP In addition to dismissing a task or follow-up item in Office Reminders, you can remove a task or follow-up item's reminder. Open the item in Outlook, choose Add Reminder from the Follow Up icon's menu, clear the Reminder check box in Dates and Reminder dialog box **C**, click OK, and save the changed item.

TIP You can turn Office Reminders off and on by choosing Outlook > Turn Off Office Reminders. They'll remain off until you choose Outlook > Turn On Office Reminders.

TIP Upcoming tasks and follow-up items are also listed in My Day. You can mark items as complete by clicking their My Day check boxes, if you like. See Chapter 26 for information about using My Day.

Printing Tasks

As is the case with other Outlook components, printing tasks are accomplished via
a nonstandard Print dialog box **A**. The
preview area reflects your print settings.

To print tasks:

1. Switch to the Tasks component by
   clicking the Tasks button in the navigation pane.

2. *Optional*: To print only certain items,
   select their titles in the Tasks list. (You
   can Shift-click or Command-click to
   select multiple items.)

3. Choose File > Print, click the Print
   icon in the Standard toolbar, or press
   Command-P.

   The Print dialog box appears **A**.

4. Select a printer to use from the Printer
   drop-down list.

5. From the Print drop-down list, indicate
   what you want to print, such as All Tasks,
   Selected Tasks, or Tasks Due Today.

6. To set the format for the printout, select
   Memo or Table from the Style drop-
   down list.

7. Click check boxes in the Task options
   section to specify task components to
   print **B**. You can set additional options
   in the Page options section.

8. Indicate the number of copies to print,
   whether copies should be collated
   (when printing multiple copies), and
   whether to print all pages or a page
   range.

9. Click Print to generate the printout.

> **TIP** You can also use these Print procedures
> when a task or follow-up item is open in its
> own window.

Preview

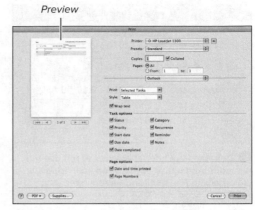

A Select print settings and click Print.

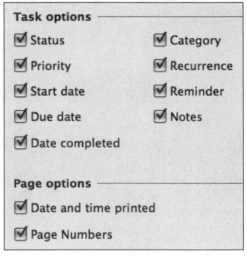

B In these sections of the Print dialog box,
specify the information from each task to print.

25

Notes

The Notes component is designed as a free-form note-taking utility. You can combine text and images in notes, but not audio or movies. You can optionally assign categories to notes. Unlike most simple note-taking applications, Outlook allows you to create formatted text notes. Any note can contain multiple fonts, sizes, styles, colors, and paragraph formatting.

To view or work with your notes, switch to Notes view by clicking the Notes button in the view switcher, choosing View > Go To > Notes, or pressing Command-5.

Note: If you have a Microsoft Exchange account, Outlook notes are synchronized with the account.

In This Chapter

Creating Notes

You can create as many notes as you like. Although most notes are mainly text, they can also include photos and other images.

To create a new note:

1. Depending on the current view, do one of the following:

   ▸ **Notes view.** Click Home:Note, choose Home:New > Note **Ⓐ**, choose File > New > Note, or press Command-N.

   ▸ **Other views.** Choose Home:New > Note **Ⓐ** or choose File > New > Note.

   A blank note window appears **Ⓑ**.

2. Enter a title for the note.

3. Fill in the body by typing, pasting, or dragging and dropping text.

4. *Optional:* To format selected text, choose character and paragraph formatting commands from the Format menu.

   Alternatively, you can right-click the note body and choose Font > Show Fonts. Select character formatting options in the Fonts window **Ⓒ**.

5. *Optional:* To add an image, set the text insertion mark where the image will be placed, and do one of the following:

   ▸ Paste a copied image by choosing Edit > Paste (Command-V).

   ▸ Drag the image's file icon into the note window.

   ▸ To add an image from iPhoto or Photo Booth, choose View > Media Browser. Drag the image from the Media Browser into the note window.

6. To save the note, choose File > Save (Command-S). Close the note window by clicking its close icon (Command-W).

Ⓐ To create a note when working in other Outlook views, choose this Ribbon command.

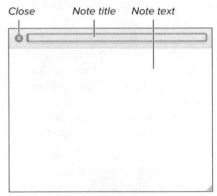

Ⓑ In the new note window, enter a title, type the note text, and close the window.

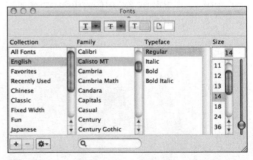

Ⓒ When you need to apply multiple fonts, sizes, colors, and the like to the current note, the Fonts window is more convenient to use than the menus.

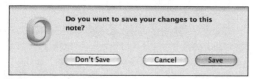

D Click Save to save the current note, Cancel if you want to continue editing, or Don't Save to discard the changes.

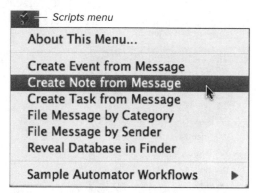

— Scripts menu

E Special Outlook commands (AppleScripts) can be found in the Scripts menu.

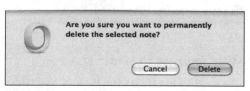

F Click Delete to permanently delete the note.

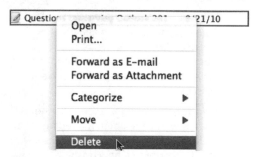

G You can right-click a note title in the note list to apply other commands, such as deleting the note or assigning it to a category.

TIP If you close a note window that contains changes without first saving it, a dialog box appears that offers the option to save **D**.

TIP To save an email message for future reference, you can create a note from it. Select the message's header in the message list, open the Scripts menu, and choose Create Note from Message **E**. After creating the note, you can edit its text, if you like.

TIP You can keep track of important Web addresses (URLs) by dragging them from Safari into a note. You can drag a link from the Address box or from anywhere in the body of a page. If the link can be added to the note, a plus (+) cursor appears when you drag it over the note. Web page images can often be dragged into notes, too.

To delete a note:

1. Switch to Notes view and select the note in the note list.

2. Click Home:Delete, choose Edit > Delete, or press Command-Delete or Delete.

3. In the dialog box that appears **F**, confirm the deletion by clicking Delete.

TIP You can also delete a note that you've opened for reading. Any of the deletion methods described above can be used, except pressing Delete.

TIP Another way to delete a note is to right-click its title in the note list and choose Delete from the contextual menu **G**.

TIP To simultaneously delete multiple notes, hold down Command to select the additional notes from the note list, and perform the deletion as you would for an individual note. You can also hold down Shift to select multiple contiguous notes.

CAUTION Note deletions can't be reversed. There is no Undo Delete command.

Reading Notes

You can read notes, sort the note list, and filter the list to show only notes that have been assigned certain categories.

To view notes:

1. Switch to Notes view by clicking Notes in the navigation pane.

2. Do one of the following:

   ▸ To view a note in the reading pane, select its title in the note list.

   ▸ To open the note in its own window, double-click its title in the note list. Or you can select it in the note list and choose File > Open > Current Item (Command-O).

3. Click the column name to sort notes by title or by date. To reverse the sort order, click the column name again.

   The sort column is indicated by a blue heading and the sort direction by the triangle's direction in the heading **A**.

4. *Optional:* In the navigation pane, expand the Notes check box and ensure that only categories you wish to display are checked **B**.

> **TIP** When a note is open in its own window, you can view other notes by choosing View > Next (Control-]) or View > Previous (Control-[).

> **TIP** If a note is longer than its window or the reading pane, you can use the Page Up and Page Down keys to navigate.

Sort column   Sort indicator

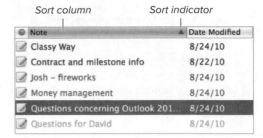

A Click a column heading to sort by that column.

B Show notes that have been assigned any checked category.

Customizing the Note List

As you use the Notes component, you can customize it to better suit your needs and the way you work. Do any of the following:

- **Remove unwanted headings or add others.** Choose column headings to display from the View > Columns submenu. Checked ones will appear above the note list. Choose a currently checked heading to remove it.

- **Rearrange headings.** To change the order in which the column headings are displayed, you can drag any heading left or right to a new position.

- **Widen/narrow the panes.** You can drag the divider between the note list and reading pane to change each pane's width.

Search string   Clear

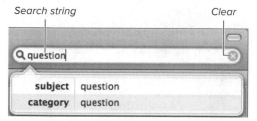

Ⓐ Enter search text in this box. Outlook checks for matches as you type.

Search contextual tab   Close

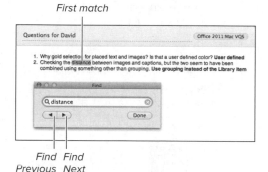

Ⓑ Whenever you perform a search, the Search contextual tab appears on the Ribbon. To dismiss the tab, click the Close icon when you're done.

First match

Questions for David   Office 2011 Mac VQS

1. Why gold selection for placed text and images? Is that a user defined color? **User defined**
2. Checking the distance between images and captions, but the two seem to have been combined using something other than grouping. **Use grouping instead of the Library item**

Find

🔍 distance

◀ ▶   Done

Find   Find
Previous Next

Ⓒ Use the Find dialog box to search within a note.

Creating Smart Folders for Notes

Another way to filter the note list is to create a Smart Folder. Whenever you select a Smart Folder in the navigation pane, only notes that match the folder's criteria are shown in the note list.

To create a new Smart Folder, perform an Advanced Search that specifies the desired criteria, click the Search:Save icon, and name the folder in the Smart Folder list. (You can delete a Smart Folder by right-clicking it and choosing Delete from the contextual menu that appears.)

Searching for and within Notes

You can use Outlook's search feature to quickly find a particular note or all notes that match your criteria. A search can be based on a text string found anywhere within a note (basic) or on one or more field-specific criteria (advanced). And when reading a lengthy note, you can search for text within the note.

To perform a basic search:

1. In Notes view, enter a search string in the search box **Ⓐ**.

   As you type, Outlook displays matching notes in the note list. A match can be based on any part of a note, such as its title, text, category, or date.

2. *Optional:* To improve result specificity, continue typing. For example, **micro** or **microsoft** may provide more accurate matches than **mic**.

3. To restore the note list, click the search box's clear (X) icon or Search:Close **Ⓑ**.

To search for text within a note:

1. Select the note in the note list to display it in the reading pane or double-click its title to open it in its own window.

2. Choose Edit > Find > Find (Command-F).

   The Find dialog box appears.

3. Type the search string.

   The first instance of the text (if there is one) is highlighted in the note **Ⓒ**.

4. *Optional:* To search for additional instances, click the Find Next icon.

5. When you're done searching, click the Done button.

To perform an advanced search:

1. To begin an advanced search, do either of the following:

   ▸ Choose Edit > Find > Advanced Find (Shift-Command-F).

   ▸ Click in the search box at the top of the Outlook window, and then click Search : Advanced, Search : Subject, or Search : Modified (see **B** in "Searching for and within Notes" earlier in this chapter).

   The first search criterion appears **D**.

2. Complete the first criterion by choosing options from the drop-down menus and/or typing. Outlook displays the initial matches in the note list.

   Note that if the criterion type is incorrect, you can easily replace it with another from the drop-down menu.

3. To add another criterion, click the plus (+) icon at the right end of the last added criterion **D**. Repeat as needed for additional criteria.

   In an advanced search, specifying multiple criteria results in an AND search—that is, a note must meet *all* criteria in order to be considered a match.

4. To end the search and restore the note list, click Search : Close.

TIP You can remove a criterion by clicking its minus (–) symbol icon **D**.

Notes and Categories

You may have noticed that assigning categories to a new note is more difficult than doing so after you've created and saved the initial note. Unlike other item windows, a note window has no Ribbon. Similarly, if you right-click the window, no Category or Categorize command appears. To apply categories to notes, you must do one of the following:

- While creating the note, choose a category from the Note > Categorize submenu.

- Immediately before creating the note, highlight the desired category in the navigation pane **E**. To avoid assigning a category to the new note, you must ensure that Notes or No Category is highlighted.

- Assign categories after the note is created by selecting the note in the note list and then choosing a category from the Note > Categorize submenu or from Home : Categorize.

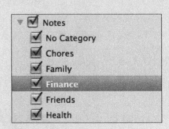

E In this example, the Finance category will be assigned to the new note.

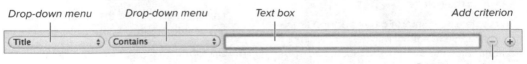

Drop-down menu   *Drop-down menu*   *Text box*   *Add criterion*

Remove criterion

D Set each criterion by choosing components from drop-down menus and typing in text boxes.

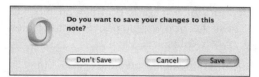

A Click Save to save the changes, Cancel to continue editing, or Don't Save to close the note and discard the changes.

B Click anywhere in the note title to set the text insertion mark and then make the desired edits.

A Note on Note Formatting

The note window's lack of a Ribbon may make it more convenient for you to first create a note, save it, and then apply any necessary formatting in the reading pane. Character- and paragraph-formatting commands can be chosen from the Home tab, the Format menu, or the contextual Fonts menu.

Inserting Hyperlinks

Notes can optionally contain clickable hyperlinks that open your browser to a specific Web page or create a blank, preaddressed email message. To add a hyperlink to a note, do the following:

1. Type or select the text in the note that will serve as the link, such as **KSU home page** or **Send mail**.

2. With the link text selected, choose Format > Hyperlink.

3. In the Link dialog box, type the link and click OK. For instance, to create an email link, enter `mailto:`, followed by the address.

To remove a hyperlink, select the link text within the note and choose Format > Remove Hyperlink.

Editing Notes

You can easily change any aspect of a note—its text, formatting, assigned categories, or even its title. A selected note can be edited in the reading pane or by opening the note in its own window.

To edit a note:

1. Switch to Notes view, and do one of the following:
   - ▸ To edit in the reading pane, select the note title in the note list.
   - ▸ Open the note by double-clicking its title or by selecting the note title and choosing File > Open > Current Item (Command-O).

2. Make any desired changes.

   Edits made in the reading pane are saved automatically. On the other hand, if you opened the note, you must elect to save the changes. Choose File > Save, press Command-S, or close the note window and confirm that you want to save **A**.

To change a note's title:

1. Open the note or select its title in the note list.

2. Click the note's title in the reading pane or the open note.

   The title is ready for editing **B**.

3. Edit the title.

   Edits made in the reading pane are saved automatically. On the other hand, if you opened the note, you must elect to save the changes. Choose File > Save, press Command-S, or close the note window and confirm that you want to save **A**.

Printing Notes

You can print selected notes or all notes. Printing can be initiated from an open note window or directly from the note list.

To print notes:

1. In Notes view, do one of the following:

   ► To print a single note, open the note or select its title in the note list.

   ► To print several notes, Command-click each title in the note list.

   ► To print all notes, select or open any note.

2. *Optional:* Choose File > Page Setup to review or change paper size, orientation, and scaling settings.

3. Choose File > Print, click the Print toolbar icon, or press Command-P.

   The Print dialog box appears **A**.

4. Select a printer to use from the Printer drop-down list.

5. From the Print drop-down menu, indicate whether you want to print Selected Notes or All Notes.

   When multiple notes are printed, they appear in a continuous list, separated by horizontal rules.

6. Indicate the number of copies to print, whether copies should be collated (when printing multiple copies), and whether to print all pages or a range.

7. Set Note options and Page options by clicking check boxes.

8. Turn on your printer and click Print.

TIP The Print dialog box includes a print preview that reflects current print settings. Click the arrow buttons beneath the preview to review other pages, if any.

TIP As with other Mac OS X applications, you can create a PDF (Portable Document Format) file from a notes printout. Click the PDF button and choose Save as PDF, or choose Open PDF in Preview to create a temporary PDF file that will open in Preview.

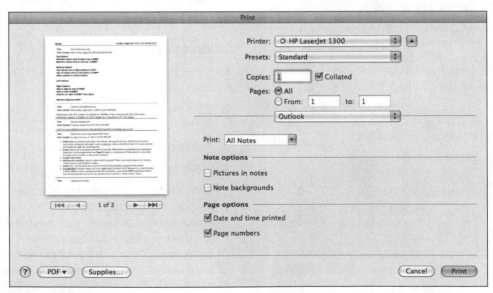

A The Print dialog box.

26

My Day

Introduced in Office 2008, My Day is a separate application that displays upcoming appointments, events, and tasks—even when Outlook and other Office applications aren't running. Unlike Office Reminders, My Day shows every Outlook event and task—not just those for which you've set reminders. You can use My Day as a convenient way to check on upcoming appointments, determine when there's free time in your schedule, and remind yourself of tasks you need to perform.

Note that if you aren't an Outlook user, you won't have much use for My Day. It draws its material from and interacts with the appointments, events, and tasks you've defined and stored in Outlook.

In This Chapter

Launching My Day

You can launch My Day automatically or manually, depending on whether you want it running all the time or only at certain times.

To launch My Day manually:

Do one of the following:

- At the top of the main Outlook window, click the Open My Day toolbar icon **A**.

- In Outlook, choose Window > My Day or press Command-9.

- In Applications, choose Microsoft Office 2011:Office:My Day.

- If you've enabled the My Day preference to Show My Day in menu bar (see the next section), click the My Day menu bar icon **B**. The icon works as a toggle, alternately showing and hiding My Day.

To launch My Day automatically:

1. Launch My Day by performing one of the procedures described in the previous task.

2. Click the Preferences icon at the bottom of the My Day window **C**.

   The Preferences window appears **D**.

3. If the General tab isn't automatically selected, click its icon now.

4. Check Open My Day when computer starts, and close the dialog box.

   In future computing sessions, My Day will automatically launch at startup.

TIP If you also set Show My Day in Dock **D**, My Day menus will appear whenever My Day is running. Otherwise, they'll be unavailable.

Open My Day

A Click the Open My Day icon to launch My Day.

My Day

B When Show My Day in menu bar is enabled, you can click this icon to open or close the application.

C Open Preferences by clicking this icon at the bottom of the window.

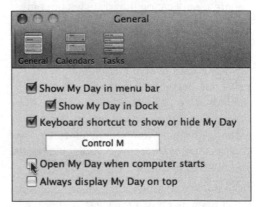

D Click this Preferences option to instruct My Day to launch automatically whenever you turn on your Macintosh.

Quitting My Day

It isn't necessary to quit My Day before shutting down. But if you want to do so, choose My Day > Quit My Day, right-click My Day's Dock icon and choose Quit from the contextual menu, or select the My Day window and press Command-Q. To restart My Day after quitting, use any of the techniques described on this page.

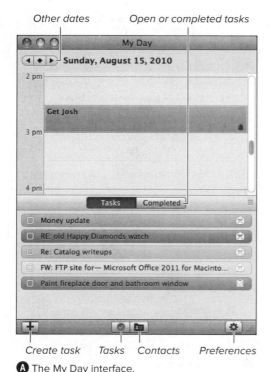

Other dates   Open or completed tasks

Create task   Tasks   Contacts   Preferences

A The My Day interface.

B If you need a phone number or email address, you can search for Outlook contacts in My Day.

Navigating My Day

Following are the important elements of the My Day interface **A**, what they do, and how to use them:

Date. The date you're viewing is shown at the top of the window. If you click it, a calendar appears; select another date to view. Click the calendar's Today button to return to today.

TIP You can also go back or forward a day by pressing **Command-left** arrow or **Command-right** arrow, respectively.

Other dates. Click these icons to view the events, appointments, and tasks for other dates. Click an arrow icon to go back (left) or forward (right) one day. Click the center (bullet) icon to view today's information.

Calendar events and appointments. A day's *events* (all-day, unscheduled items) appear at the top of the window. *Appointments* (scheduled items) are shown in their time slots and can be viewed using the vertical scroll bar. Double-click an event or appointment to open it in Outlook.

Tasks and to-do items. To show or hide the task list, click the Tasks button. To mark a task as complete (removing it from the list), click its check box. You can view active tasks or completed ones by clicking the appropriate button.

Create task. To create a new Outlook task, click this icon.

Contacts. Click the Contacts icon to search for someone in your Outlook Contacts **B**.

Preferences. Click this icon, choose My Day > Preferences, or press Command-, (comma) to review or change My Day preferences (see **D** in "To launch My Day automatically" on the previous page).

Creating and Managing Tasks

One difference between My Day and Office Reminders is that the former allows you to view and manage Outlook tasks.

To work with tasks:

Do any of the following:

- To show or hide the task list **A**, click the Tasks icon at the bottom of the My Day window.

- To switch between viewing active and completed tasks, click the Tasks or Completed tab **A**.

- To mark a task as complete in the task list, click the check box to the left of the task's title. The task is automatically removed from the list.

  Similarly, you can make any task active again by clearing its check box in the Completed list.

- To create a new Outlook task, click the Create task icon **A**. In the window that appears **B**, enter a task title and set other options, if desired. Click Save to add it to the task list; click Cancel if you change your mind.

- To set preferences for working with tasks in My Day, click the Preferences icon **A**. In the Preferences dialog box **C**, click the Tasks icon, make any desired changes, and close the dialog box.

TIP You can right-click a task and choose commands from a contextual menu to perform other functions, such as deleting the task, assigning categories to the task, or specifying a follow-up date.

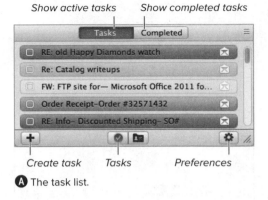

Show active tasks   *Show completed tasks*

Create task   *Tasks*   *Preferences*

A The task list.

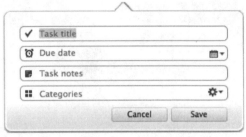

B To create a new task, type its title and click Save. The other settings are optional.

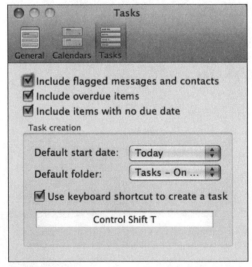

C Set Tasks preferences and close the dialog box.

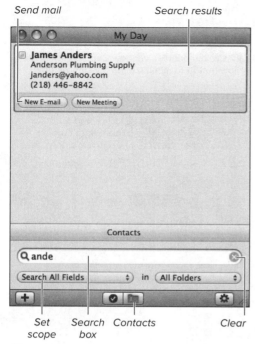

Send mail   Search results

My Day

☐ **James Anders**
Anderson Plumbing Supply
janders@yahoo.com
(218) 446-8842

(New E-mail) (New Meeting)

Contacts

🔍 ande

(Search All Fields ‡) in (All Folders ‡)

Set   Search   Contacts   Clear
scope   box

A Performing a Contacts search.

Finding Contacts

If you routinely leave My Day running, you'll find its Contacts search capability to be a life saver. Rather than launching Outlook, waiting for it to load, selecting the Contacts component, and then performing the search, you can make short work of the same chore within My Day.

To search for a contact:

1. Click the Contacts icon at the bottom of the My Day window.

   A search pane slides up from the bottom of the window **A**.

2. *Optional:* Set the search's scope by choosing options from the two drop-down menus.

3. Type a search string in the search box.

   As you type, My Day displays the matches, if any. You can continue typing to further restrict the match list.

4. *Optional:* Select the desired contact. To address mail or schedule a meeting with the person, click the appropriate button.

5. When you're done viewing contacts, click the Contacts icon again to close the search pane.

> **TIP** To perform a new search, click the Clear icon (X) at the right end of the search box or delete the search string.

> **TIP** My Day doesn't search all fields. You can't search for a company, city, or state, for example. Also, some other searches (such as looking for a phone number) produce results only when the search string appears at the beginning of the field. If you restrict most searches to names, however, you'll be happy with the results.

Changing the Display

Like other applications, My Day provides several ways for you to change the way it is displayed.

To change how My Day is displayed:

Do any of the following:

- **Hide/show.** To hide My Day, choose My Day > Hide My Day (Command-H). A better approach, however, is to press the keyboard shortcut shown in the General tab of the Preferences dialog box (see **D** in "Launching My Day" earlier in this chapter). Press the shortcut again to reveal My Day.

- **Minimize/restore.** To minimize My Day to the Dock, click the yellow minimize button **A** at the top of the window or press Command-M. To restore My Day, click its Dock icon.

- **Keep on top.** My Day can be made to float atop other windows, remaining visible at all times. Open Preferences, click the General tab, and ensure that Always display My Day on top is checked (see **D** in "Launching My Day" earlier in this chapter).

- **Change the window size.** Click the bottom-right corner of the window **B** and drag to resize My Day.

- **Resize the task list.** To change the height of the task list (and the number of tasks you can see without scrolling), drag the resize icon up or down **C**.

Minimize

A As with most Mac windows, you can click the yellow button to minimize the My Day window.

Resize

B Click and drag the bottom-right corner to resize the window.

Resize

C Change the height of the task list by clicking here and dragging up or down.

Combining Office Data

Separately, each Office 2011 application is impressive. But when combined, they form a powerful system for sharing information.

One simple way of combining information from different Office applications is by copying, embedding, or linking. You can copy a table of numeric data from Excel into a Word document to add some relevant numbers to a memo, for example. Or to ensure that later changes to the Excel data automatically flow to the table in the Word document, you can link the data between the documents.

In addition to explaining copying, linking, and embedding, this chapter provides several specific examples of ways to share data among Office applications.

In This Chapter

Copying, Linking, and Embedding

Office lets you easily share information among its applications. The three main methods are to copy, embed, or link information from one application to another.

The simplest method is to copy and paste or drag and drop material between programs. For example, you can copy a range in Excel and paste it into a Word document. Or you can simply drag the range into Word. The data becomes part of the Word document as an editable table. Similarly, after switching to Slide Sorter View in PowerPoint, you can drag a copy of a slide into a Word document. Data added via the copy and paste or drag and drop method becomes a part of—and is saved with—the destination document. This means you can move the document to another machine or email it to someone secure in the knowledge that the copied or dropped data will be intact.

If you want to maintain a link between the original data or object and the new document, you can use embedding or linking. The difference between the two procedures lies in where the data is stored. Embedded data becomes part of the destination document, making it transportable. Linked data, on the other hand, is stored only in the original document and is referenced by the destination document. Thus, linking is an excellent choice for working with files on a network or when combining data from several members in a workgroup project.

Adding Office Material to Email

In Outlook, HTML email messages can include Word tables, Excel charts and cell ranges, SmartArt layouts, WordArt, and other objects:

1. Create a new message, and ensure that Draft > HTML Format is checked.
2. Select an Excel chart or data range, Word table, SmartArt layout, WordArt, or other object.
3. Choose Edit > Copy (Command-C).
4. Set the text insertion mark in the email message body.
5. Choose Edit > Paste (Command-V).

Note that you can also add material to HTML messages using drag and drop.

	A	B	C	D	E
1	Student	Sex	Test Score	Weight	Result
2	Marci	F	12	0.2	2.40
3	Joni	F	14	0.2	2.80
4	Jason	M	19	0.2	3.80
5	Jeremy	M	8	0.2	1.60
6	Stan	M	18	0.2	3.60
7	Chris	M	20	0.2	4.00
8	Kendra	F	6	0.2	1.20
9	Michelle	F	19	0.2	3.80
10	Sammy	M	15	0.2	3.00
11	Average		14.56		2.91

A To duplicate this section of an Excel worksheet in a Word document, start by selecting the data range to be copied—in this case, A1:E11.

Pasted material

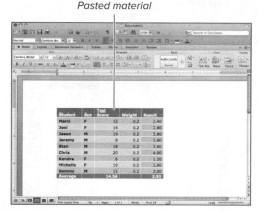

B When pasted into a Word document, the Excel range becomes a Word table.

Using copy and paste

Copy and paste (and cut and paste) are the simplest, most familiar methods of duplicating data between two documents—even if the documents are from different applications. Pasted material maintains no link with the original data or its document.

To copy and paste between documents:

1. In the first document, select the material that you want to copy, such as a text block, cell range, slide, or one or more objects **A**.

2. Choose Edit > Copy, click the Copy icon on the Standard toolbar, or press Command-C.

   The material is copied to the Clipboard, a temporary area in memory that stores the most recent item you've copied or cut.

3. Switch to or open the target document.

   Note that the document must be capable of accepting the type of data you're about to paste. Office 2011 applications can accept most types of material created in other Office applications.

4. In the destination document, specify the location in which you'll paste by setting the text insertion mark, selecting a cell, or making a slide active, for instance.

5. Choose Edit > Paste, click the Paste icon on the Standard toolbar, or press Command-V.

   The material is pasted from the Clipboard **B**.

> **TIP** Every Office 2011 application also has an Edit > Paste Special command. If you need to control the format when pasting certain material, be sure to check the options provided by this command.

Using drag and drop

Other than copy and paste (or cut and paste), the easiest way to move something from one application to another is to use drag and drop. The drag and drop process is the same whether it's between applications or within a single application. Arrange the document windows of the two applications so you can see them both. Then drag selected text or an object from one window to its destination in the other application's document window. **Table 27.1** lists some items that you can drag and drop between applications.

To drag and drop an object:

1. Arrange the applications' document windows so you can see both the source object and its intended destination **C**.

2. Select the object or text, such as a worksheet range.

3. Drag the border of the object or text to its destination in the other window.

4. Release the mouse button.

   The object or text appears in the destination document **D**. You are free to modify the dragged object or text in the destination document.

> **TIP** When you drag and drop an item, it becomes part of the destination document. The item will not reflect changes made to the original material unless you establish a link. See "Linking objects," later in this section.

> **TIP** If you hold down Option-Command as you drag material between applications, a contextual menu allows you to either copy or move the object. (Note that moving deletes the original object.)

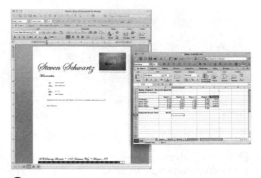

C Using drag and drop, you can copy a cell range from an Excel worksheet into a Word document, for example.

D Release the mouse button when the Excel object is correctly positioned in the Word document.

TABLE 27.1 Common Objects to Drag and Drop

Source Application	Object
Word	Selected text or table cells
Excel	A cell, range, graphic, or table
PowerPoint	A slide from Slide Sorter view

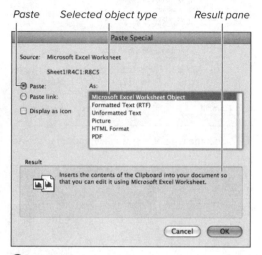

▲	A	B	C	D	E	F
1	Sales Report: Second Quarter					
2	(Amounts in millions)					
3						
4		Region 1	Region 2	Region 3	Region 4	Average
5	Envelopes	0.75	0.4	1.1	0.27	0.63
6	Paper Clips	0.11	0.17	0.18	0.15	0.1525
7	Blank CDs	1.15	2.03	1.58	0.99	1.4375
8	Blank DVDs	2.78	3.04	1.96	4.17	2.9875
9	Total	4.79	5.64	4.82	5.58	

E Select and copy the material that you want to embed, such as this Excel worksheet range.

Paste   Selected object type   Result pane

In the Paste Special dialog box:

Paste Special

Source: Microsoft Excel Worksheet

Sheet1!R4C1:R8C5

- ⦿ Paste: As:
- ○ Paste link: Microsoft Excel Worksheet Object
- ☐ Display as icon   Formatted Text (RTF)
  Unformatted Text
  Picture
  HTML Format
  PDF

Result

Inserts the contents of the Clipboard into your document so that you can edit it using Microsoft Excel Worksheet.

Cancel   OK

F In the Paste Special dialog box, select the appropriate object type from the As list. The Result pane shows the type of object that will be inserted.

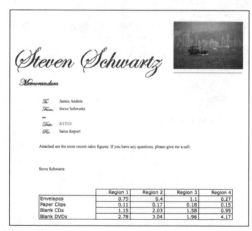

G The embedded object appears in the Word document.

Embedding objects

An *embedded object* is material that is copied in its source application and pasted into the target application as a Microsoft Object. The advantage to embedding material rather than linking it (see the next section) is that the material resides entirely in the destination document. As a result, you can safely move the document to other computers.

Unlike a linked object (which is updated whenever the source data changes), an embedded object changes only when you edit it from within the target document. This ensures that the object will change only when—or if—you want it to change.

This section explains how to embed an existing object in a target application, as well as how to create an embedded object from scratch.

To embed an existing object:

1. Select the object or text in its source application **E**.

2. Choose Edit > Copy, click the Copy icon on the Standard toolbar, or press Command-C.

3. Switch to the target application and click to set the destination for the object.

    The embedded object will appear at the text insertion mark.

4. In the target application, choose Edit > Paste Special.

    The Paste Special dialog box appears **F**.

5. Select the item labeled as an object (such as Microsoft Excel Worksheet Object, for example). Ensure that the Paste radio button is selected, and click OK.

    The embedded object appears in the target document **G**.

To create an embedded object:

1. In the target document, click to set the destination for the object.

   The embedded object will appear at the text insertion mark.

2. Choose Insert > Object.

   The Object dialog box appears 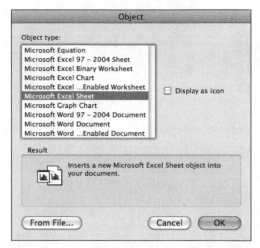.

3. Select the object type, and click OK.

   The appropriate Office application opens and a new document appears.

4. Create the object 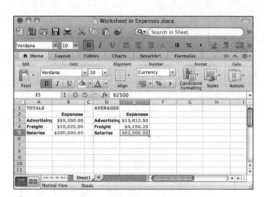.

5. *Optional:* Save the object document by choosing File > Save Copy As.

6. Close the object document.

   The object appears in the document at the text insertion mark. (You may need to alter the text wrap setting or fill color in order for the object to display properly.)

To edit an embedded object:

1. Do either of the following:

   ▸ Double-click the object 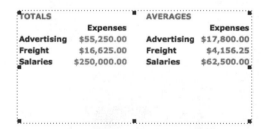, such as a sheet embedded in a Word document.

   ▸ Select the object and choose Edit > *object type* > Edit.

   The source application launches, and the object appears. As you modify the object, the changes automatically appear in the embedded object, too.

2. When you're finished editing, close the document window.

   It isn't necessary to save changes when editing an object. Any changes you make to the object are automatically conveyed to the document in which the object is embedded.

H Select the type of object that you want to create.

I Create the new object. If sample data is presented, replace it with your own data.

J Double-click the embedded object (such as this Excel sheet) to open it for editing.

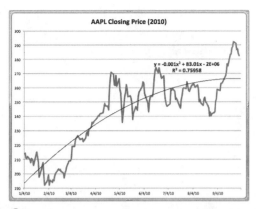

K Select and copy the object or material to which you want to link, such as this Excel chart.

Paste link   Selected object

L Click the Paste link radio button, select the specific object type, and click OK.

Linking objects

When you link rather than embed an object, the object remains in the original application's document. A copy of the object—linked to the original—is displayed in the second application's document. Think of the copy as representing the linked object. It is merely a reference to the original. Any changes that are made to the original object also appear in the linked copy.

You create linked objects using the Copy and Paste Special commands. The object is updated whenever you reopen the destination file, ensuring that the object is always current. Linking is ideal for any object whose data regularly changes or is being edited. In addition to (or instead of) updating a link automatically, you can update it manually.

To link an object:

1. Select the object in the source document that you wish to link **K**.

2. Choose Edit > Copy, click the Copy icon on the Standard toolbar, or press Command-C.

3. Open the destination document, and click where you want the linked object to appear.

4. Choose Edit > Paste Special.

   The Paste Special dialog box appears **L**.

5. Click the Paste link radio button, select the object to link, and click OK.

   The linked object appears in the destination document.

TIP Double-click the linked object in the destination document to edit the original object.

TIP When you open a document containing links that automatically update, the links are checked for any necessary updates.

To manually update a link:

1. Choose Edit > Links.

   The Links dialog box appears 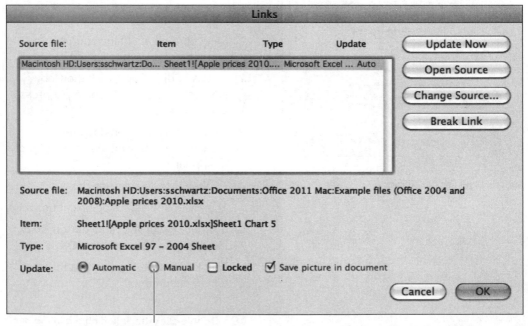.

2. Select the link in the list box and click Update Now.

   The linked object is updated.

3. Click OK to close the Links dialog box.

TIP The linked object will appear in the target document at its original size. You can resize it as necessary.

TIP To set the link so that it updates only when you click Update Now, select **Manual** as the Update option.

TIP To change a linked object into an embedded object, select the link and click the **Break Link** button.

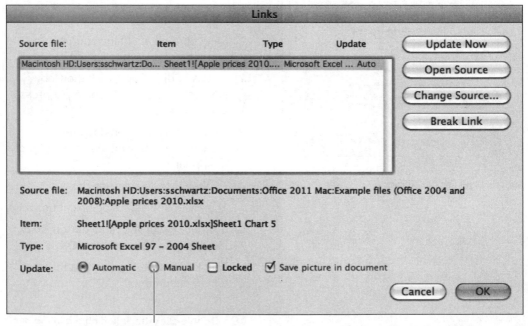

Manual updates

M In the Links dialog box, click Update Now to update the selected link.

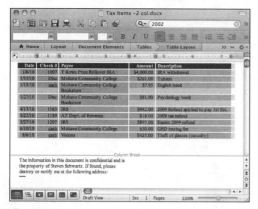

A Select the entire table in the Word document.

Paste Options icon

B Specify the formatting for the pasted material.

C The formatted Word table in the Excel sheet.

Word Table into Excel

Word and Excel work well together, especially when you're creating Word documents that display structured numeric data. The previous sections showed how to copy and link Excel data into Word documents. In this section, you'll learn to do the reverse: copy a Word table into an Excel worksheet. Later in this chapter, you'll see how to copy normal Word text into Excel or PowerPoint.

To copy a Word table into Excel:

1. In Word, click any cell within the table that you want to copy.

2. To select the table **A**, choose Table > Select > Table or drag-select its cells.

3. Choose Edit > Copy, click the Copy icon on the Standard toolbar, or press Command-C.

4. Switch to Excel, and select the cell in which the Word table will begin.

5. Choose Edit > Paste, click the Paste icon on the Standard toolbar, or press Command-V.

   The Word table appears in the worksheet.

6. *Optional:* To make the formatting of the pasted material match that of the target cells, click the Paste Options icon **B** and select Match Destination Formatting.

7. Adjust the column widths as necessary to fully display the contents of each column **C**.

> **TIP** A table copied in this manner is fully editable within Excel. You can also change the formatting, if desired. The pasted data is not linked to the original Word document.

Sharing Outlines: Word and PowerPoint

You can use Word and PowerPoint together, too. This section explains how to move an outline from one application to the other. Note that the procedures are different from those used in Office 2008.

To use a Word outline file in a PowerPoint presentation:

1. Open or create a presentation outline in Word **Ⓐ**. Each Heading 1 paragraph will become the title of a new slide. Heading 2 paragraphs will become first-level text.

2. Choose File > Save As.

3. In the Save As panel, name the file, specify a location for it, choose Rich Text Format (.rtf) from the Format drop-down menu, and click Save.

4. Create a PowerPoint presentation or open an existing one to which you want to add the Word outline. (Note that no link is maintained between the presentation and the Word outline.)

5. In PowerPoint's navigation pane, select the slide after which the outline will be inserted.

6. Choose Home : New Slide > Insert Slides from Outline.

   The Choose a File dialog box appears.

7. Select the Word outline, and click Insert.

   The new slides are added to the presentation **Ⓑ**.

> **TIP** Starting a presentation in Word isn't outlandish. Most people find writing and editing easier to do in Word than in PowerPoint.

Ⓐ Open the Word outline. In this example, the outline is part of the table of contents for a book.

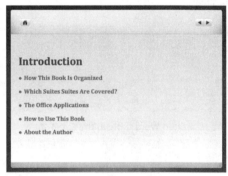

Ⓑ The outline is incorporated into new slides. Reformat the text and backgrounds as needed.

Tweaking the Word Outline

If the first line of your Word outline is its title, this will result in only one slide—because only the title is a Heading 1 paragraph. To prepare such an outline for PowerPoint, select all the outline text after the first line, click the Home : Outline Tools : Promote icon to raise every point by one level, and then delete the title line.

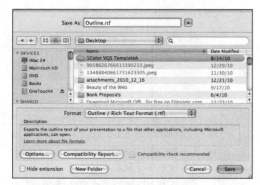

C Save the presentation in Word outline format.

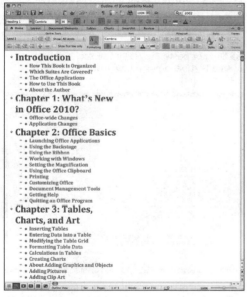

D This is the PowerPoint outline opened in Word.

To copy a PowerPoint presentation outline into a Word document:

1. In PowerPoint, choose File > Save As.

   A Save As panel drops-down **C**.

2. Name the file, select a location for it, choose Outline/Rich Text Format (.rtf) from the Format drop-down menu, and click Save.

3. Open the new outline file in Word.

4. Switch to Outline View by choosing View > Outline or by clicking the Outline View icon in the bottom-left corner of the document window.

5. Reformat the text as desired **D**.

Word Text into Excel or PowerPoint

You can transfer text from Word into Excel or PowerPoint using copy and paste or drag and drop.

To copy text from Word:

1. Arrange the Word document window so you can also see the PowerPoint or Excel document window.

2. In Word, select the text to be copied.

3. Do one of the following:

   ▸ Choose Edit > Copy (Command-C). Paste the text into an Excel cell or a PowerPoint slide by choosing Edit > Paste (Command-V).

   ▸ Drag the text to the starting cell of the destination range in Excel or onto a PowerPoint slide (Ⓐ and Ⓑ).

TIP Text formatting, such as font, size, and style, is also copied and will appear in the Excel worksheet. In PowerPoint, however, the formatting of the destination placeholder text and the amount of pasted text determine the initial font size.

TIP In Excel, pasted Word text frequently overflows the cells. If necessary, you can expand the column width or enable text wrapping for the affected cells.

TIP Excel mimics the paragraph formatting of copied Word text. A tab within a paragraph is treated as an instruction to place the text in the next cell; a return is treated as an instruction to move down to the next row.

TIP You can also paste Word text as a floating object. In Excel or PowerPoint, choose Edit > Paste Special and select Microsoft Word Document Object as the format. The result is an embedded text object that you can continue to edit in Word.

Destination cell (A1)

	A	B	C
1	Lesson Outline:		
2	What Is a Database?		
3	1. Introducing FileMaker Pro		
4	2. Working with Databases		
5	3. Creating a Simple Database		
6	4. Customizing a Database – Part 1 (Ac		
7	5. Customizing a Database – Part 2 (Cr		
8	6. Sorting and Searching		
9	7. Reports: Previewing and Printing		
10	8. Going Relational		
11	9. Automating with ScriptMaker		
12	10. Using FileMaker Pro in a Workgroup		
13	11. Publishing a Database on the Web		

Ⓐ Drag or paste the text into Excel. Each line of pasted text becomes a new row.

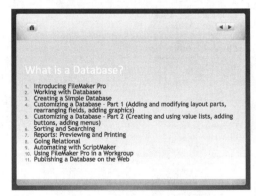

Ⓑ You can also drag or paste text into a text placeholder on a PowerPoint slide.

28

Office 2011 and the Internet

In addition to using Outlook to handle your email, Office has features that let you tap into the power of the Internet. This chapter shows how to add Internet links (called *hyperlinks*) to your documents so you can direct readers to the Web to see a graphic, hear audio, or read additional information on a topic. For example, a Word letter about your summer vacation could contain a link to a site where you've posted digital photos.

You'll also learn to perform these Internet-related activities:

- Without leaving Word, PowerPoint, or Excel, send the current document in email.

- Save an Office document in HTML format so you can publish it on the Web. Because the resulting files can be viewed in any browser, you can also give or email them to people who don't use Office.

- Download additional clip art images.

- Check for Office software updates.

- Visit Mactopia, the Macintosh section of Microsoft's Web site.

- Search the Web for reference material.

In This Chapter

Working with Hyperlinks

Including hyperlinks in an Office document is a handy way to enhance content. Clicking a hyperlink can launch a browser to display a particular Web page, open a file on your hard disk, or address new email.

To create a Web hyperlink in a Word, Excel, or PowerPoint document:

1. Position the text insertion mark where you want to insert the hyperlink, or select existing text or an object that you want to serve as the link.

2. Choose Insert > Hyperlink (Command-K).

   The Insert Hyperlink dialog box appears.

3. If it isn't selected, click the Web Page tab.

4. Type or paste the Web address in the Link to text box **A** or select a recently linked-to address from the drop-down list.

5. *Optional:* To specify different text in the Display box, edit as desired.

6. *Optional:* Click the ScreenTip button to specify the text that will appear when the cursor rests over a hyperlink **B**.

7. *Optional:* To link to a specific spot on the Web page (called a *bookmark* or *anchor*), click the Locate button. In the dialog box that appears, select an anchor and click OK. Note that the Web page designer must have already created the anchor. You can't arbitrarily select a link spot.

8. Click OK to create the hyperlink.

Link address   Select a recently used address

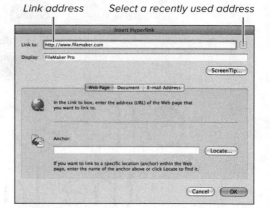

A You can create a clickable link in the current document that will open a Web page, open a document on disk, or create an email message.

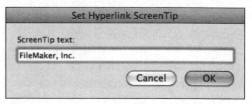

B This ScreenTip will automatically appear when someone rests the cursor over the hyperlink.

Document tab

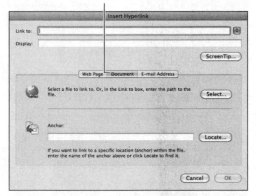

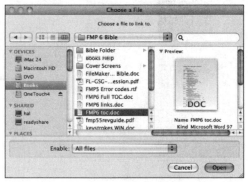

C To create a link to a file on your hard disk, click the Document tab.

D Select the document file to which you want to link (Mac OS X 10.6.5/Snow Leopard shown).

E This is an example of a ScreenTip.

To create a document hyperlink in a Word, Excel, or PowerPoint document:

1. Do one of the following:

   ▸ Position the text insertion mark where you want to insert the text link.

   ▸ Select existing text or an object that you want to designate as the link.

2. Choose Insert > Hyperlink (Command-K).

   The Insert Hyperlink dialog box appears.

3. On the Document tab **C**, click Select.

   The Choose a File dialog box appears **D**.

4. Select a file and click Open.

   To restrict listed files to one type, select a file type from the Enable drop-down list.

5. *Optional:* To specify different text in the Display text box, edit as desired.

6. *Optional:* Click ScreenTip to customize the pop-up text that will appear when the cursor rests over a hyperlink **E**.

7. *Optional:* To link to a bookmarked spot in the document, click the Locate button, and in the dialog box that appears, select a bookmark and click OK.

8. Click OK to create the hyperlink.

   When the link is clicked, the document will open in an appropriate program (if one is installed on the computer).

To create an email hyperlink in a Word, Excel, or PowerPoint document:

1. Do one of the following:

   ▸ Position the text insertion mark where you want to insert the text link.

   ▸ Select the text or object that you want to designate as the link.

2. Choose Insert > Hyperlink (Command-K).

   The Insert Hyperlink dialog box appears.

3. Click the E-mail Address tab **F**.

4. Do one of the following:

   ▸ Type or paste the recipient's email address in the To text box.

   ▸ Select an address from the Recent Addresses drop-down list.

   ▸ To look up an address in your default email program, click Launch E-mail Application.

5. *Optional:* Enter a subject for the message in the Subject text box.

6. *Optional:* To specify different text in the Display box, edit as desired.

7. *Optional:* Click ScreenTip to customize the pop-up text that appears when the cursor rests over a hyperlink **E**.

8. When the settings are satisfactory **G**, click OK.

   When the link is clicked, an email message is generated in the user's default email program. It will be addressed to the designated recipient, use the specified Subject (if any), and be ready for the message text to be entered.

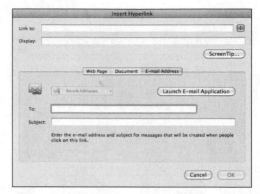

F On the E-mail Address tab, enter the recipient's email address and the message's Subject.

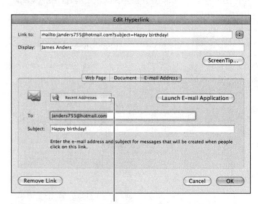

Recent Addresses

G When an email hyperlink is clicked, a message with the specified Subject will be sent to the designated recipient.

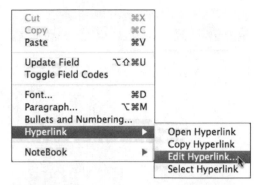

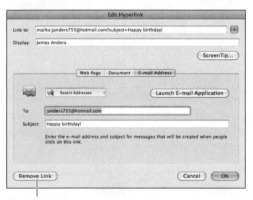

H To modify a link in Word or PowerPoint, right-click the link and choose Hyperlink > Edit Hyperlink. In Excel, choose Edit Hyperlink.

Remove Link

I In the Edit Hyperlink dialog box, you can modify or remove an existing link.

To add a hyperlink to an Outlook email message:

Type or paste the complete link address into the message. The following examples illustrate the proper syntax:

- **http://www.msn.com** (Web address)
- **ftp://ftp.microsoft.com** (FTP site)
- **mailto:roadrunner@cox.net** (email address)

Whether the link will be clickable depends on the recipient's mail program.

To modify a hyperlink in a Word, Excel, or PowerPoint document:

1. Do one of the following:

   ▸ Right-click the hyperlink text or object to reveal the contextual menu. In Word or PowerPoint **H**, choose Hyperlink > Edit Hyperlink. In Excel, choose Edit Hyperlink.

   ▸ Select all or part of the hyperlink and choose Insert > Hyperlink.

   The Edit Hyperlink dialog box appears **I**.

2. Make the changes and click OK.

To remove a hyperlink:

1. Do one of the following:

   ▸ Right-click the hyperlink text or object to reveal the contextual menu. In Word or PowerPoint **H**, choose Hyperlink > Edit Hyperlink. In Excel, choose Edit Hyperlink.

   ▸ Select all or part of the hyperlink and choose Insert > Hyperlink.

   The Edit Hyperlink dialog box appears **I**.

2. Click the Remove Link button.

   The link text or object remains but will no longer function as a clickable link.

TIP When clicked, a Web or email hyperlink automatically launches the user's default Web browser or email program.

TIP A document hyperlink can be made to any document on your hard disk—not just Office documents. When clicked, the appropriate application will launch and open the specified document.

TIP When giving someone an Office file with document links to other files, be certain to also give them the linked-to documents.

TIP You can create a clickable table of contents in any Word document. First, assign a bookmark to every major heading. Then create a document hyperlink from each table of contents entry to the matching bookmark.

TIP You can also create a hyperlink by typing it directly into a document or by copying it from another source (such as the address box of your Web browser, a link on a Web page, or the body of an email message) and then pasting it into the document.

TIP For typed hyperlinks to be recognized in Word, you must set AutoCorrect to transform eligible text into links. Choose Tools > AutoCorrect and click the AutoFormat As You Type tab. Ensure that Internet and network paths with hyperlinks **J** is checked, and click OK.

TIP For a Web page hyperlink to work when clicked, the computer must have an Internet connection.

TIP Deleting hyperlink text or a hyperlinked object simultaneously removes the link.

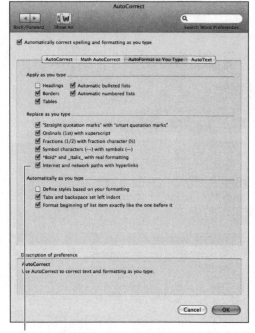

Internet options

J Word ignores typed hyperlinks unless this option is enabled.

Microsoft Messenger

Included with Office 2011 and available as a free download from Mactopia.com, Microsoft Messenger 8 is a messaging utility that allows you to conduct computer-to-computer chats with text, audio, and/or video. You must have a Windows Live ID (Live.com, Hotmail.com, or MSN.com) to use Messenger. In addition to chatting, you can use Messenger to exchange files with other users and send messages to mobile devices.

Emailing Office Documents

You can email any open Office document without leaving Office. Using the Share command in Word, PowerPoint, or Excel, you can send any open document as an email attachment. In Word or Excel, you can elect to translate the document into a formatted HTML message. This option is especially useful when the recipient doesn't have Office.

To email an Office document:

1. Choose File > Share > E-mail (as Attachment) or E-mail (as HTML).

   Your default mail program launches and creates a new message with the document attached or converted to an HTML message .

2. Specify recipients and the Subject, write the message text (if sending the document as an attachment), and send the message.

TIP When converting a document to HTML, carefully examine the generated message before sending it. Many Office documents are poorly suited for HTML conversion. If the results aren't true to the original document, you can use the File > Print command to create a PDF file that can be sent as an email attachment. (PDF files can be opened and viewed in Preview or Adobe Reader.) See "Printing Word Documents" in Chapter 4 for an example of creating a PDF file from an Office document.

TIP PowerPoint does not support the File > Share > E-mail (as HTML) command; Word and Excel do.

A If a recipient doesn't have Word or Excel, you can send a document formatted as HTML.

Other Internet/Network Utilities

Unless you're in a corporate environment, it's unlikely that you'll ever use or explore the two other utilities in Office 2011, but just in case...

- **Communicator.** Requiring Microsoft Office Communications Server 2007 R2, Communicator allows for real-time collaboration between corporate users. Within Word, PowerPoint, and Outlook, Communicator shows the presence status of others and offers multiple ways to connect with them.

- **Remote Desktop Connection.** With this utility installed on your Mac and the necessary permissions secured, you can connect to and take control of one or multiple Windows PCs. Primarily used as a troubleshooting tool, Remote Desktop Connection can also be used to provide software demos and instruction.

Other Internet Capabilities

Office 2011 has other Internet capabilities that you may wish to explore. Here are some of the most useful ones:

- You can create Web pages from Word or Excel documents using the File > Save as Web Page command, enabling you to publish the pages on the Web or a company network. If you have friends or coworkers who don't use Office, they can view the resulting documents in any browser.

  Use the File > Web Page Preview command to quickly see how the current Word or Excel document will look if saved as a Web page.

- You can download clip art images from Office Online. In Excel, choose Insert > Clip Art > Clip Art Gallery. In Word or PowerPoint, choose Home : Insert : Picture > Clip Art Gallery. Then click the Online button in the Clip Gallery window **Ⓐ**.

- On the Reference Tools tab of the Toolbox **Ⓑ**, you can search the Web for information about a topic. If the Toolbox is visible, click the Reference Tools tab. Otherwise, choose View > Toolbox > Reference Tools or click the Toolbox icon on the Standard toolbar. Select the Reference Tools tab, enter a search string, and press Return.

- The Help menu offers the following Internet-related commands:

  - Choose Help > Check for Updates to launch Microsoft AutoUpdate.

  - Choose Help > Visit the Product Web Site or Get Started with *application* to view the Mactopia site in your browser.

Launch browser

Ⓐ You can download additional clip art images from Microsoft's site.

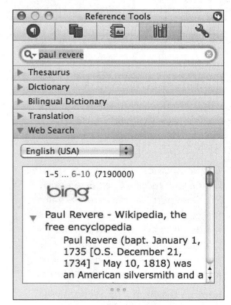

Ⓑ Enter a search string on the Reference Tools tab and review the results.

Office Web Apps

In January 2010, Microsoft launched Windows Live SkyDrive, providing 25 GB of free online storage to anyone with a Windows Live account. Later in 2010, the new Office Web Apps were rolled out. Unlike Office, the Office Web Apps aren't programs installed on your computer. They reside on Microsoft servers. Using them is an example of cloud computing.

Using SkyDrive storage and the Office Web Apps individually or together, users can now do the following with a browser and Office 2010 (Windows) or 2011 (Mac):

- Use SkyDrive to store backup copies of Office and non-Office documents.

- Create and make edits to Word, Excel, PowerPoint, or OneNote documents using Internet Explorer, Safari, or Mozilla Firefox—even without an installed copy of Office on the computer.

- Save and open files on SkyDrive from within Office (treating SkyDrive as just another hard drive).

- Share selected Office files on SkyDrive with others and allow collaborative, simultaneous editing.

In This Chapter

Creating an Account

SkyDrive is the repository for the Office files you'll be creating, editing, and sharing with the Office Web Apps. Each time you use SkyDrive, you must log in to Windows Live. If you haven't registered, you can gain access by creating a free Hotmail or Windows Live account.

To create a Windows Live or Hotmail account:

1. In any browser, go to **www.hotmail.com** or **www.live.com**.

2. Click the Sign up button **A**.

3. On the Create your Windows Live ID or Create your Hotmail account screen, choose live.com or hotmail.com as the account type and enter your desired user name in the box **B**.

   If the user name is already in use **C**, try a different name, try a variation, or select one of the Available IDs suggestions.

4. Enter an account password and the other information requested.

5. Click I accept to complete the registration.

> **TIP** If the user name you want isn't available, try combining it with some numbers.

> **TIP** Because Hotmail is many years older than Windows Live, most simple words and combinations are already taken as user names. You may find, however, that an unavailable name in Hotmail can be yours in Windows Live.

> **TIP** A Windows Live or Hotmail account has advantages in addition to SkyDrive access. For instance, you can send and receive email from the account using a browser or an email client such as Outlook, use Messenger for instant messaging, and create photo albums.

A A Sign Up button appears on both the Hotmail and Windows Live home pages.

B Choose a service (Live or Hotmail) and enter a user name. If you don't immediately receive a response, click the Check availability button.

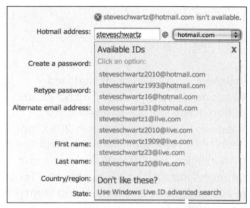

C If the user name is already taken, similar alternatives are proposed. Select one or try again by entering a different name.

Microsoft Moving Targets

SkyDrive and the Office Web Apps are true moving targets. Because SkyDrive and the Office Web Apps are Web-based, Microsoft is free to enhance their capabilities (as it did when it added chart support to Excel), as well as reorganize and change menus and procedures. The material in this chapter represents the state of SkyDrive and the Office Web Apps as of January 2011.

Choose SkyDrive from the Windows Live menu.

Working with SkyDrive

You can use SkyDrive as a external drive for storing backups of important files, or you can view and edit the Office documents you've uploaded to it with Office 2011, 2010, or the Office Web Apps. Regardless of how you intend to use SkyDrive, you'll need to familiarize yourself with its folder- and file-management procedures. You can access SkyDrive from your browser or the Microsoft Document Connection application.

To access SkyDrive using a browser:

1. In Safari, Firefox, or Internet Explorer, log into your Windows Live, Hotmail, or MSN account.

2. Choose SkyDrive from the Windows Live menu at the top of the page **A**.

   The SkyDrive page appears **B**. By default, each account has four folders: My Documents and Favorites (private), Shared Favorites (accessible to others by invitation only), and Public (accessible to anyone). In addition, you can create other folders as needed.

Folders   Menus and commands   Used space   Log out

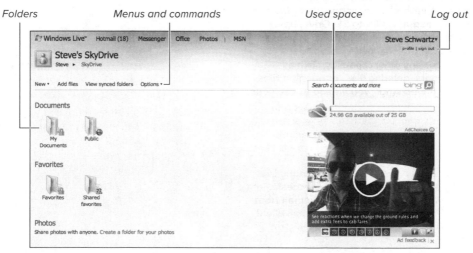

B The SkyDrive interface as viewed in Safari.

To access SkyDrive using Microsoft Document Connection:

1. Click the Microsoft Document Connection icon in the Dock or choose it from the Applications: Microsoft Office 2011 folder.

2. In the Document Connection window, choose Add Location > Sign In to SkyDrive.

3. In the panel that appears **C**, enter your Live, Hotmail, or MSN email address and password.

4. *Optional:* To enable automatic sign-ins for future sessions (jumping directly to step 6), click the check box to Save password in my Mac OS keychain.

5. Click Connect.

   A list of your SkyDrive folders appears **D**.

6. Double-click a folder to view its contents.

7. When you're finished using the application, choose Document Connection > Quit Document Connection.

TIP Compared with accessing SkyDrive with a browser, Microsoft Document Connector offers only a limited set of capabilities. You can use it to upload new files to SkyDrive, open them in the appropriate Office 2011 application, and save the changed versions back to SkyDrive. For any other capability, such as creating folders, deleting files, or opening files in the Office Web Apps, you'll need to use your browser.

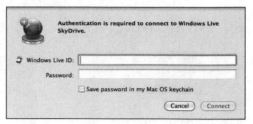

C To connect to your SkyDrive, you must enter your Windows Live user name and password.

Current folder   Toolbar

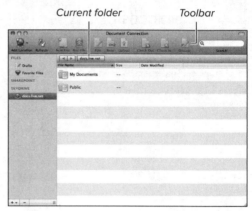

D After you sign in to your Windows Live account, you can work with SkyDrive files as though they're on your computer—although you'll need an active Internet connection.

E Name the new folder.

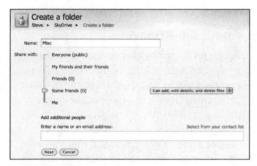

F Indicate who can access the files and what privileges (viewing or editing) they have.

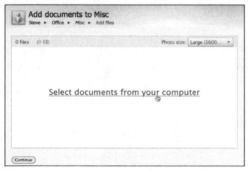

G To upload initial files to the new folder, click the text link in the center of the list box.

Folder management

SkyDrive folders can be created and managed to organize your files any way you like. You can create a folder at the same level as the main folders (My Documents, Favorites, and so on) or within one of those folders. Note that subfolder permissions always match those of the parent folder.

To create a main folder:

1. Log in to SkyDrive with your browser.

2. Choose New > Folder.

   The Create a folder page appears **E**.

3. Enter a name for the new folder.

4. If the folder's contents will be private (Just me), click Next, and go to step 7.

5. To set sharing privileges for the folder, click Change **E**.

6. On the screen that appears **F**, set sharing options and then click Next.

7. *Optional:* On the The Add documents to New folder page **G**, upload files to the folder, if you want; then click Continue.

   You can upload files immediately or at any time it's convenient.

To create a subfolder:

1. From the main level of SkyDrive, open the parent folder with the desired sharing and privileges, and continue opening folders within it as necessary.

   Any new folder created as a subfolder takes on the sharing and privileges of the parent folder.

2. Choose New > Folder.

   The Create a new folder page appears **H**.

3. Name the folder and click Create folder.

   Add files to the folder when it's convenient, as described later in this section.

To navigate among the folders:

Do any of the following:

- To open a folder, go to the SkyDrive main page by clicking a SkyDrive link (when available) or choosing Windows Live > SkyDrive **A**. Then click the icon of the main folder you want to open. If the destination folder is a subfolder of the current folder, continue clicking folder icons until the desired folder is open.

- To go up in the folder hierarchy, click a folder link at the top of the page. You can also choose Windows Live > SkyDrive or click a SkyDrive link to return to the root and drill down from there.

H Creating a folder within the current folder requires only that you name the folder.

About Zip Archives

An *archive* is a file that contains one or more files and/or folders that have been compressed to reduce their total size. A zip archive uses a compression algorithm popularized by WinZip (**www.winzip.com**), now part of Corel Corporation. Current versions of the Windows and Macintosh operating systems can extract the contents of a Zip archive (such as the folder archives described in "To modify a folder" on the next page), restoring them as files and folders.

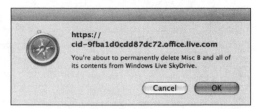

I Confirm the folder deletion by clicking OK.

J Edit or replace the folder name and click Save.

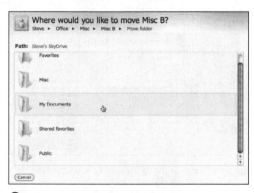

K Select the destination parent folder.

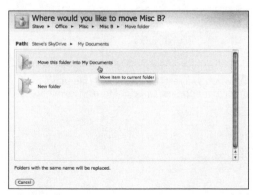

L Complete the move by confirming your choice in **K** or electing to move the folder's files into a new folder.

To modify a folder:

1. Open the folder that you want to modify.

2. Do one of the following:

   ▸ Click Download as .zip file to download the folder's files as a Zip archive. The files are compressed and downloaded to your default location, such as the Desktop or Downloads folder.

   ▸ Choose Share > Edit permissions to modify the folder's access privileges. Available only for root folders, choose this command to change the sharing status and permissions for the current folder and any subfolders. Set options as shown in **G** and click Save.

   ▸ Click Delete to delete the folder and its contents. Confirm the deletion by clicking OK **I**.

   ▸ Choose More > Rename to change the folder's name. The Rename *folder name* page appears **J**. Enter a name in the New name box and click Save.

   ▸ Choose More > Properties to add a folder description.

   ▸ Choose More > Move to move a subfolder to a different parent folder. Select a new parent folder from the list that appears **K**. To complete the move **L**, click Move this folder into *destination folder* or click New folder to move the folders files into a new folder within the parent folder.

File management

File-management actions that you can perform on SkyDrive are similar to those available for your computer's hard drive. In addition to uploading files to SkyDrive, you can click links to perform other common actions on a selected file.

To add files to a folder:

1. In Microsoft Document Connection, open the SkyDrive folder into which you want to add a file or files **M**.

2. Click the Add File toolbar icon.

   The Upload New Files dialog box appears **N**.

3. Navigate to the drive and folder that contains the files you wish to upload, select one or more files (Command-click to select multiple files), and click Upload.

4. To upload additional files from other folders, repeat steps 1–3.

> **TIP** To upload files using your browser, open the destination SkyDrive folder and click the Add files link.

To download a file to your hard drive:

1. Using your browser, open the SkyDrive folder that contains the file you want to download.

2. Hover the cursor over the filename and choose More > Download from the menu bar that appears **O**.

   The file downloads to your default location, such as the Downloads folder or the Desktop.

M Open the SkyDrive folder into which you want to add files.

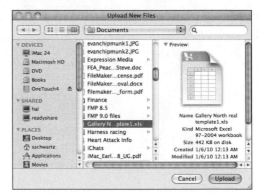

N Select one or more files and click Upload.

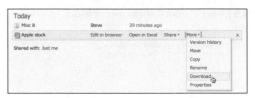

O When you rest the cursor on a filename, a menu bar appears. Choose More > Download.

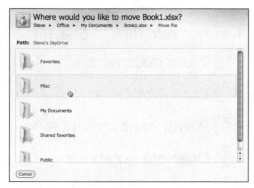

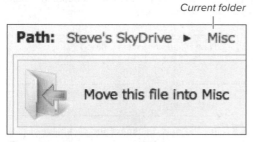

Current folder

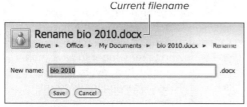

Current filename

P Click to open folders until you've opened the destination folder.

Q When you're within the destination folder, click the Move (or Copy) option to complete the process.

R Type the new filename and click Save.

To delete a file:

1. Using your browser, open the folder that contains the file you want to delete.

2. Hover the cursor over the filename and click the delete (X) icon in the menu bar that appears **O**.

3. Click OK in the confirmation dialog box.

> **TIP** You can also delete a file by choosing More > Properties and then More > Delete.

To move or copy a file to another folder:

1. Using your browser, open the folder that contains the file you want to move or copy.

2. Hover the cursor over the filename and choose More > Properties from the menu bar that appears **O**.

   The file's page appears.

3. Choose More > Move or More > Copy.

   The Where would you like to move (copy) *filename*? page appears **P**. The root folders of your SkyDrive are displayed.

4. Click the folder or parent of the folder in which you want to move/copy the file.

5. Continue opening folders until the destination folder is shown.

6. Click Move (Copy) this file into *folder name* **Q**.

To rename a file:

1. Open the folder that contains the file you want to rename.

2. Hover the cursor over the filename and choose More > Rename from the menu bar that appears **O**.

3. Enter a new filename in the New name box **R** and click Save.

About the Office Web Apps

Think of the Office Web Apps as light browser-based versions of Word, Excel, PowerPoint, and OneNote. That is, although the Web Apps are real applications and are useful for light work, they lack the power, speed, and flexibility of their Office counterparts. Here are some useful facts about the Office Web Apps:

- You can access the Office Web Apps with Internet Explorer, Safari, or Firefox.

- Your computer is not required to have an installed version of Microsoft Office. On the other hand, if Office is installed, you can switch from the Web Apps to Office when editing needs demand it.

- The Office Web Apps have no Save command because changes are automatically saved as you work.

Within Windows Live, you connect to the Web Apps through SkyDrive by opening an existing Office document or creating a new one.

To create a new Office document:

1. Log into SkyDrive and open the folder in which you want to create the new file.

2. From the New menu, choose the type of Office document you'd like to create **Ⓐ**.

3. On the page that appears **Ⓑ**, name the new file and click Save.

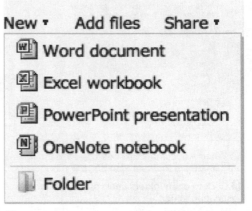

Ⓐ The New menu lists the Office documents that you can create.

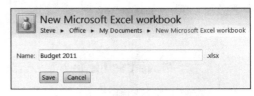

Ⓑ Name the new document and click Save.

Saving in the Office Web Apps

When working on a file opened for editing in an Office Web App, all edits are saved automatically. While this relieves you of having to remember to save manually, it also means that every change is saved. To avoid saving inadvertent changes, there are two options:

- Save a backup copy of the document at the start of each editing session. You can choose File > Save As or File > Download a Copy.

- Repeatedly click the Undo icon to step back through the changes you want to discard. (The Undo and Redo icons are directly above the File tab.)

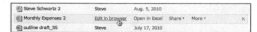

C Hover the cursor over the filename and click Edit in browser.

Edit in Browser

Microsoft
Word Web App Steve Schwartz resume on SkyDrive

File | W Open in Word | Edit in Browser | Share | Find | 100% ▾

E When a document has been opened for viewing only, an Edit in Browser icon is in the Ribbon.

To open an existing Office document in an Office Web App:

1. Log into SkyDrive and open the folder that contains the Office document you'd like to view or edit.

2. Do one of the following:

   ▸ To open the file for viewing only, click the filename.

   ▸ To edit the file, hover the cursor over the filename and click Edit in browser in the menu bar that appears **C**.

   The document opens in an Office Web App for viewing or editing **D** (bottom).

   TIP To switch from viewing to editing, click the Edit in Browser icon **E**.

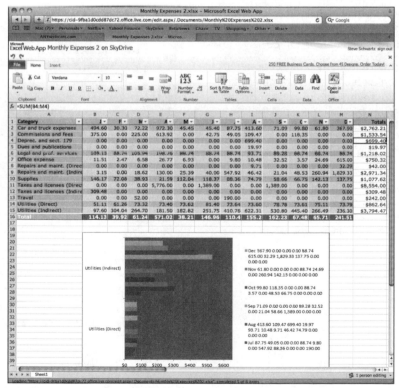

D An Excel workbook opened for editing in the Office Web Apps.

Using the Office Web Apps

You can use the Office Web Apps to view and edit your own documents as well as ones that others have elected to share with you. Regardless of whether you're viewing or editing a document, the Office Web Apps works much like Office:

- Each Web App features the tabbed Ribbon interface introduced in Office 2007 . Within each tab (such as Home and Insert), commands are organized into functional groups.

- ScreenTips appear for Ribbon icons **B**.

- Certain commands present dialog boxes.

- Click the File tab **C** to reveal a menu of file-related commands, such as saving a copy of the document, printing, and opening the document in Office.

- Selecting certain items on the document page (such as a chart, for example) may cause a contextual tab to appear on the Ribbon, as it does in Office 2011.

- There are no contextual menus—that is, right-clicking is not supported.

TIP If you need the full editing power of the installed version of Office on the current computer, choose File > Open in *application* **C** or click Home:Office:Open in *application*.

A Excel's Insert tab has commands for inserting tables, charts, and hyperlinks.

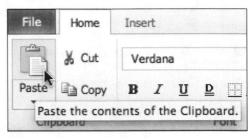

B ScreenTips help identify the purpose of Ribbon icons.

C Each app's File tab has commands similar to those in Office 2010's Backstage.

Open in Word

Office

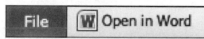

File **W** Open in Word

Ⓐ When editing in a Web App, click this icon to open the current document in Office.

Ⓑ When viewing a document in a Web App, click the Open icon to open the document in Office.

Office Documents and SkyDrive

After you upload an Office document to SkyDrive, you can view and edit it with the Office Web Apps. And if you have Office 2010 or 2011 installed on your computer, you can access Office documents on SkyDrive in these additional ways:

- While viewing or editing with the Office Web Apps, you can launch Office to perform more advance editing on the current document.

- While working in Office, you can save the current document to SkyDrive.

- Documents that have been saved to or uploaded to SkyDrive can be opened from within Office.

To launch Office from a Web App:

1. In Office Web Apps, open the SkyDrive Office document for viewing or editing.

2. Do either of the following:

   ▸ Click the Open in *Office application* icon. When editing a document, the icon can be found in the Home : Office group **Ⓐ**. When viewing a document, the icon is beside the File tab **Ⓑ**.

   ▸ Choose File > Open in *Office application* (see **Ⓒ** in "Using the Office Web Apps," earlier in this chapter).

To save a document to SkyDrive from Office 2011 (first save):

1. Select File > Share > Save to SkyDrive.

   A Save As panel appears **C**.

2. *Optional:* Edit the filename.

3. Expand the root folders as necessary and select the destination folder.

4. Click the Save button.

   The file is uploaded to SkyDrive in the designated folder.

To open an Office document stored on SkyDrive:

Do one of the following to open a document that you previously saved or uploaded to SkyDrive:

- In Microsoft Document Connection, select the SkyDrive file and click the Edit icon.

- If you previously saved the document to SkyDrive, you may find it in the Office 2011 application's File > Open Recent documents list. A SkyDrive file will display a URL beside its filename **D**.

To save a document to SkyDrive from Office 2011 (subsequent saves):

1. Open the document by loading it from SkyDrive.

2. After editing the document, you can save the changed version to SkyDrive by clicking the Save icon on the Standard toolbar, choosing File > Save, or pressing Command-S.

TIP You can go directly to your SkyDrive by entering www.skydrive.com in the browser's address box.

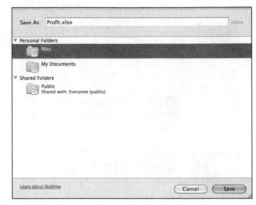

C Select a destination folder on SkyDrive and click Save.

D A SkyDrive document in the Open Recent list will show that it's located on the Web (**https://**).

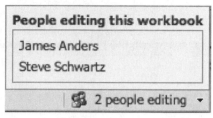

People editing this workbook

James Anders

Steve Schwartz

🔐 2 people editing ▾

A When multiple people are simultaneously editing a shared document, you can see it in your browser's status bar.

Send a link

James ▸ Office ▸ Stocks ▸ Send a link

To   steve@hotmail.com   ×

☑ Require recipients to sign in with Windows Live ID
By not requiring recipients to sign in, anyone who receives this link will be able to view these files.

Send   Cancel

B To help designated users access your shared files, you can email a link to them.

Sharing and Coediting Office Documents

A sharing status is set for every SkyDrive root folder and its subfolders. The specified access privileges apply to every file in the folder(s), as well as to other files that you later save in or upload to the folder(s).

An Office document in a shared folder can be accessed individually or simultaneously by Office and Office Web App users **A**. As one person makes a change, it's instantly seen by the other users.

TIP When you set or change sharing permissions for a SkyDrive folder, an email notification can be sent to the folder sharers **B**. The message will contain a View folder link to access documents in the shared folder(s). To speed future access to the SkyDrive, they can save the link as a browser favorite or bookmark.

Index

artwork, 43, 54, 122. *See also* clip art; graphics

attachments, 352, 355, 445

audio (in PowerPoint presentations), 324–325

audio clips, 52

Audio Notes tab (Word), 153

Auditing commands (Excel), 237–238

author bio, xvi

Authoring options (Excel), 180, 285

AutoComplete list (Excel), 182, 228, 244

AutoCorrect feature
    Outlook, 359
    Word, 86, 87, 444

AutoFill options (Excel), 183

Auto Fill Options button (Excel), 236

AutoFit menu (Word), 134, 136

AutoFormat As You Type feature (Word), 444

automatic page breaks (Word), 104

Automator workflows, 40, 178

AutoRecover feature, 16

AutoShapes, 222–223

AutoSum feature
    Excel, 232
    Word, 138

AutoText feature (Word), 84–85, 102

AutoUpdate feature, 41, 446

axes
    in Excel charts, 254, 262
    in PowerPoint charts, 311

B

background
    in Excel printouts, 203
    for PowerPoint slides, 298–301
    removing, from images, 67
    setting document, 106

backups
    Outlook, 369
    storing online, 447

bar code option (Word), 171

Bar option (Word), 117

Blank icon (Word), 105

Blank Sheet command (Excel), 194

blinking insertion mark, 26, 76

Blocked Senders tab (Outlook), 367

borders, 64, 121–122, 143, 216

Borders and Shading dialog box (Word), 121–122, 143

Borders gallery (Excel), 216

Break Link icon (Word), 162

breaks
    column, 107
    page, 104
    section, 105–106

Brightness control, 44, 61

Broadcast Service (PowerPoint), 331–332

browser, accessing SkyDrive using, 449

browser-based document creation, 447, 456–457

bulleted lists (Word), 118–120

Business edition, Microsoft Office for Mac, 6

C

calculated columns (Excel), 242, 249

calculations
    in Excel databases, 270
    in Excel tables, 242, 249, 250
    in Excel worksheets, 227–240
    in Word tables, 138

Calendar (Outlook), 387–400
    adding appointments to, 390–391
    adding events to, 390–391
    adding holidays to, 398–399
    creating meetings in, 396–397
    deleting items in, 393
    editing items in, 392
    printing calendars in, 400
    purpose of, 387
    responding to reminders in, 394–395
    restricting date range in, 389
    setting preferences for, 395
    viewing, 388–389
    working with multiple calendars in, 395

captions, 46

cascading windows (Excel), 195

case options (Word), 111

categories
    for Outlook contacts, 362
    for Outlook email messages, 362–363
    for Outlook notes, 418
    for Outlook tasks, 407, 408, 424

clippings
   defined, 21
   filtering, 23
   inserting in documents, 22
   organizing, 23
cloud computing, 447
color saturation, 62
color scales (Excel), 220
color schemes (PowerPoint), 302
color tone, 62
column breaks (Word), 107
column charts (Excel), 256
columns. *See also* cells; tables
   in Excel tables, 245, 248
   in Excel worksheets, 181, 227, 231–232
   in Word tables, 139, 141
Columns dialog box (Word), 107
command conventions, xiv–xv
comments (Excel), 187
Communications Server, Microsoft Office, 445
Communicator utility, 445
Compare Changes window (PowerPoint), 318
Compare Documents command (Word), 93
Compatibility options (Excel), 180
Compatibility Report (PowerPoint), 321
compatibility reports, document, 24
Compress command, 68
compression algorithms, 452
conditional formatting (Excel), 220
Consolidate dialog box (Excel), 198–200
consolidation formula (Excel), 199–200
constants (Excel), 229, 233
contact groups (Outlook), 381
contacts (Outlook), 371–385
   adding photos to, 376
   addressing mail to, 380
   assigning categories to, 362
   creating
      from email messages, 374
      manually, 375
      from vCards, 378–379
   defining groups of, 381
   deleting, 377
   editing, 377
   flagging for follow-up, 404
   importing, 372–373

contacts (Outlook) *(continued)*
   printing, 382–383
   searching, 423, 425
   sorting, 379
   synchronizing with other devices, 384–385
   viewing, 379
Contacts Search window (Outlook), 351
Contacts view (Outlook)
   addressing mail from, 380
   purpose of, 371
content pages (Word), 156, 157
contextual menus, xv, 19, 248, 458
Contrast control, 61
Conversations option (Outlook), 364
Convert Table to Text command (Word), 144
Convert Text to Table dialog box (Word), 144
Convert to Range tool (Excel), 243
copy and paste, 46, 428–429, 430, 433, 438
Cover gallery (Word), 164
cover pages (Word), 166
Create Theme Colors dialog box (PowerPoint), 302
cropping photos, 65–66
Currency formatting (Excel), 215
currency symbols (Media Browser), 226
customization options, 34–37
Customize Bulleted list dialog box, 120
Customize Keyboard dialog box, 36
Customize Numbered list dialog box, 120
Customize Toolbars and Menus dialog box, 35–36
Custom Views. *See* Smart Folders
cut and paste, 429, 430

D

data (Excel). *See also* databases
   entering, 182, 244, 264, 267
   protecting, 281–284
   publishing on Web, 276–277
   validating, 237
data arrays (Excel), 265
data bars (Excel), 220
databases (Excel), 264–273
   converting to tables, 266
   creating, 266

Go To Special dialog box (Excel), 252
gradients (in PowerPoint slides), 300
grammar checker
  Outlook, 351, 358
  Word, 88–89
graphics, 43–59. *See also* images
  aligning, 56
  as clickable links, 44
  editing, 44
  inserting
    from disk, 45
    by dragging and dropping, 44, 430
    from iPhoto, 45–46
  layering, 57
  moving, 54
  in PowerPoint presentations, 295–296, 305
  reordering with dynamic ordering, 58
  resizing, 54
  rotating, 55
  setting text wrap for, 59
graphs, 253, 305. *See also* charts
grayscale images, 62
gridlines
  in Excel charts, 254, 262
  in Excel printouts, 203
  in PowerPoint charts, 309
  in Word tables, 132
Group command (Word), 163
guides (Word), 154, 158–159
gutter margins (Word), 101

H

Handout Master view (PowerPoint), 326
handouts (PowerPoint), 326
Hand Tool (Word), 163
hanging indents (Word), 114, 115
headers
  Excel, 202
  Word, 101–102
headings
  in Excel printouts, 203
  in Excel worksheets, 179, 181, 209, 212
  in Outlook Notes list, 416
  in Outlook Tasks list, 405
  in Word documents, 31, 73, 75, 104, 123, 444

headings *(continued)*
  in Word outlines, 146, 436
  in Word tables, 140
Help system, 40–41, 446
Hide extension check box, 13
Highlight Cells Rules (Excel), 221
Highlight Changes dialog box (Excel), 279
high-low-close charts, 314
holidays (in Outlook Calendar), 398–399
Home edition, Microsoft Office for Mac, 6
horizontal windows (in Excel), 195
Hotmail, 348, 357, 448
.htm files, 277
HTML format, 428, 439, 445
http:// hyperlinks, 443
Hyperlink command, 440, 441, 442
hyperlinks, 439–444
  adding to email messages, 443
  creating in Office documents, 440–442
  modifying in Office documents, 443
  in notes, 419
  between objects, 433–434
  removing from Office documents, 443, 444
  syntax for, 443
  between text boxes, 161–162

I

I-beam cursor, 26
icon sets (Excel), 220
identities, 5, 360, 371
image-editing programs, 60
image-editing tools, 4, 44, 60–70
image links, 44, 46
images
  adding to notes, 414
  cropping, 65–66
  editing, 44, 60–70
  inserting in email messages, 352, 355
  inserting in Office documents, 45–48, 293–294
  resizing, 46, 54
  sources of, 47, 48
IMAP accounts (Outlook), 348–349, 353
iMovie, 51–52, 293
Import Cell Styles dialog box (Excel), 219

links, 44, 46, 161–162. *See also* hyperlinks
Links dialog box, 434
list management features (Excel), 241
lists
    Excel, 241
    Outlook, 341–342, 366
    Word, 118–120
Lock Aspect Ratio check box, 55
locked cells (in Excel worksheets), 282

M

Mac Data File format, 373
Macintosh Sync Services, 384
Mac OS X
    Clipboard, 21
    Dictionary application, 359
    foreign language support, 38
    outliners, 147
    Spotlight search, 346
Mactopia, 439, 444, 446
magic wand, 13
magnification percentages
    Excel, 32, 180
    PowerPoint, 32
    Word, 32, 74
mail application. *See* Outlook
Mailing List Manager (Outlook), 366
mail-merge feature (Word), 172–174
mailto: hyperlinks, 443
Make Alias command, 8
margin guides (Word), 158
margin settings
    Excel, 202, 203
    Word, 100, 101
Mark as Junk option (Outlook), 367
masking, 67
master pages (Word), 154, 156, 157
Master view (PowerPoint), 289
Media Browser
    inserting audio clips from, 52
    inserting clip art from, 47, 224
    inserting movies from, 51–52
    inserting shapes/lines from, 49
    opening/closing, 25
    purpose of, 4, 25

Meeting window (Outlook), 396
menu bar
    in Excel, 17, 72, 178
    mini version of, 35
    purpose of, 17
    in Word, 72
menu commands, xiv, 17
menus, 17, 19, 35–36
Merge Cells command (Word), 140
merged documents (Word), 172–174
message categories (Outlook), 362–363
message list (Outlook), 337
message rules (Outlook), 365
Messenger, Microsoft, 444
Microsoft
    AutoUpdate feature, 41, 446
    Clip Gallery application, 48, 224, 298
    Database Utility, 360
    Document Connection application, 4, 450
    Excel (*See* Excel)
    Exchange accounts (*See* Exchange
        accounts)
    Exchange Server, 348
    Help system, 40–41, 446
    instant-messaging utility, 444
    Internet Explorer, 447, 449
    Mactopia site, 439, 444, 446
    Messenger, 444
    Objects, 431
    Office (*See* Office)
    Office Communications Server, 445
    Outlook (*See* Outlook)
    PowerPoint (*See* PowerPoint)
    Word (*See* Word)
Mirror margins check box (Word), 101
misspelled words. *See* spelling checker
MobileMe, 384
Modify Style dialog box (Word), 125
Move Chart command (Excel), 255
Movie from File command (PowerPoint), 325
Movie Options dialog box (PowerPoint), 333
movies
    aligning, 56
    avoiding overuse of, 323
    inserting in documents, 25, 51–52, 152, 293
    moving to new location, 52

W